Postwar Productivity Trends
in the United States,
1948-1969

NATIONAL BUREAU OF ECONOMIC RESEARCH
NUMBER 98, GENERAL SERIES

Postwar Productivity Trends in the United States, 1948-1969

by

JOHN W. KENDRICK
The George Washington University

ASSISTED by MAUDE R. PECH

 **DISCARDED**

NATIONAL BUREAU OF ECONOMIC RESEARCH
NEW YORK
1973

Distributed by Columbia University Press
New York and London

Copyright © 1973 by the National Bureau of Economic Research
All Rights Reserved
Library of Congress card no. 72-188341
ISBN: 0-87014-240-2
Printed in the United States of America

RELATION OF THE DIRECTORS
TO THE WORK AND PUBLICATIONS
OF THE NATIONAL BUREAU OF ECONOMIC RESEARCH

1. The object of the National Bureau of Economic Research is to ascertain and to present to the public important economic facts and their interpretation in a scientific and impartial manner. The Board of Directors is charged with the responsibility of ensuring that the work of the National Bureau is carried on in strict conformity with this object.

2. The President of the National Bureau shall submit to the Board of Directors, or to its Executive Committee, for their formal adoption all specific proposals for research to be instituted.

3. No research report shall be published until the President shall have submitted to each member of the Board the manuscript proposed for publication, and such information as will, in his opinion and in the opinion of the author, serve to determine the suitability of the report for publication in accordance with the principles of the National Bureau. Each manuscript shall contain a summary drawing attention to the nature and treatment of the problem studied, the character of the data and their utilization in the report, and the main conclusions reached.

4. For each manuscript so submitted, a special committee of the Board shall be appointed by majority agreement of the President and Vice Presidents (or by the Executive Committee in case of inability to decide on the part of the President and Vice Presidents), consisting of three directors selected as nearly as may be one from each general division of the Board. The names of the special manuscript committee shall be stated to each Director when the manuscript is submitted to him. It shall be the duty of each member of the special manuscript committee to read the manuscript. If each member of the manuscript committee signifies his approval within thirty days of the transmittal of the manuscript, the report may be published. If at the end of that period any member of the manuscript committee withholds his approval, the President shall then notify each member of the Board, requesting approval or disapproval of publication, and thirty days additional shall be granted for this purpose. The manuscript shall then not be published unless at least a majority of the entire Board who shall have voted on the proposal within the time fixed for the receipt of votes shall have approved.

5. No manuscript may be published, though approved by each member of the special manuscript committee, until forty-five days have elapsed from the transmittal of the report in manuscript form. The interval is allowed for the receipt of any memorandum of dissent or reservation, together with a brief statement of his reasons, that any member may wish to express; and such memorandum of dissent or reservation shall be published with the manuscript if he so desires. Publication does not, however, imply that each member of the Board has read the manuscript, or that either members of the Board in general or the special committee have passed on its validity in every detail.

6. Publications of the National Bureau issued for informational purposes concerning the work of the Bureau and its staff, or issued to inform the public of activities of Bureau staff, and volumes issued as a result of various conferences involving the National Bureau shall contain a specific disclaimer noting that such publication has not passed through the normal review procedures required in this resolution. The Executive Committee of the Board is charged with review of all such publications from time to time to ensure that they do not take on the character of formal research reports of the National Bureau, requiring formal Board approval.

7. Unless otherwise determined by the Board or exempted by the terms of paragraph 6, a copy of this resolution shall be printed in each National Bureau publication.

(Resolution adopted October 25, 1926 and revised February 6, 1933,
February 24, 1941, and April 20, 1968)

CONTENTS

TABLES

* * *

For Tables A-1 through A-80, see listing on pp. ix-xi

CHARTS

ACKNOWLEDGMENTS

It was Solomon Fabricant who, while Director of Research, invited me in 1965 to prepare a sequel to my earlier volume, *Productivity Trends in the United States*. Wide use had been made of the output, input, and productivity estimates contained in that monograph, and Fabricant felt the estimates and analysis should be updated and revised as necessary, with special attention paid to the post-World War II period.

I was encouraged to accept this assignment by the fact that Maude R. Pech was once again available to give me major assistance in preparing the estimates. By the time of her retirement in early 1969, Mrs. Pech had completed the extensive computations required to revise and extend the estimates contained in the earlier work, and I had written up the appendix notes on sources and methods. I am happy once again to recognize Mrs. Pech's contribution on the title page of the volume.

During the subsequent year and one-quarter I concentrated on analyzing the economy and industry productivity movements and relationships with associated variables, and on writing up the findings. In the statistical analysis, I was aided by my research assistants at The George Washington University: Yvonne Lethem, Ralph R. Young, and Hiwhoa Moon. At the National Bureau, Elizabeth Simpson Wehle helped in the final stages of manuscript preparation, Irving Forman did the chart work, and Hedy D. Jellinek edited the manuscript.

I was pleased to be able to draw on the analysis of cyclical productivity movements done by Anthony Cluff for a doctoral dissertation prepared under my direction at The George Washington University for a section of Chapter 4; and on estimates of output per man-hour and related variables for 395 manufacturing industries, 1954-63, based on Census Bureau production indexes and related data, prepared by Henry Linsert for a thesis under my direction, which I used in a section of Chapter 5. I was assisted in the estimates of productivity in the transport sector by Ramon Knauerhase and Raymond Sheppach of the University of Connecticut.

Helpful comments on the preliminary draft of the manuscript were made by the members of the staff reading committee: Solomon Fabricant, Lawrence Miller, and Ishaq Nadiri. Robert Lipsey, Vice President-Research of the National Bureau, within whose province the project fell, was particularly helpful in his comments and suggestions during the latter phases of the study. I am also indebted to the NBER Board of Directors' reading committee, whose members were Otto Eckstein, Nathaniel Goldfinger, and David L. Grove.

This study has been financed from grants to the National Bureau by the Alfred P. Sloan Foundation and the Alex C. Walker Educational and Charitable Foundation for studies of productivity, employment, and price levels. We are most grateful for this support.

Our work on this volume has been made easier by the publication since 1962 of estimates by the Office of Business Economics[1] of real product originating in major industry groups of the economy. But government statistical agencies do not yet publish estimates of real capital stocks and inputs, man-hours worked, and partial and total factor productivity for the corresponding industry groupings—although now the Bureau of Labor Statistics does publish annual and quarterly real product-per-man-hour estimates for the private economy by three major sectors.

If complete industry estimates of inputs and productivity, as well as of real product, are eventually published on a regular basis by the federal statistical agencies, the need for yet another sequel to *Productivity Trends* will be obviated. We are glad to work ourselves out of specific jobs, in the best tradition of the National Bureau, by performing developmental work in economic statistics and encouraging governmental agencies to take over and maintain new series which have been proved feasible and useful. Since there is more than enough pioneering work in the realm of economic statistics and analysis remaining to be done, unemployment is but a remote worry for the economic researchers at NBER, and for the profession at large.

John W. Kendrick

[1] Under a reorganization effective January 1, 1972, the OBE has been redesignated the Bureau of Economic Analysis in a new Social and Economic Statistics Administration. However, for the sake of continuity, it is referred to as OBE throughout this volume.

Postwar Productivity Trends
in the United States,
1948-1969

1

INTRODUCTION AND PREVIEW

The present volume is intended primarily to update the estimates and analyses contained in my earlier *Productivity Trends in the United States*.[1] As stated in the opening sentence of that volume: "The story of productivity, the ratio of output to input, is at heart the record of man's efforts to raise himself from poverty." After a discussion of concepts and methods of measurement, we traced the productivity story for the U.S. economy and its major industry divisions for the period 1889 to 1957. The impacts of productivity change on economic aggregates and structure were quantified and causal factors discussed.

The current study focuses on postwar productivity trends, by industry groupings, for the period 1948-66, with preliminary aggregate estimates through 1969. The earlier estimates for aggregates have been revised for the period since 1929, and the industry estimates have been revised beginning with 1948.

With additional data for another decade or so, it has become possible to discern more clearly the trends and relationships that have emerged since 1948, when the post-World War II readjustment period was largely completed. We are now in a better position to see to what extent the postwar trends represent a continuation of earlier trends or a break with the past, and to analyze the relationships between productivity change and other variables in the postwar period and compare them with the relationships in earlier periods. At least as important as our findings on these matters are the new output, input, and productivity estimates in the appendix, for use by other economists in their analyses.

---

[1] John W. Kendrick, assisted by Maude R. Pech, *Productivity Trends in the United States*, Princeton, Princeton University Press for the National Bureau of Economic Research, 1961. Hereinafter, that volume will be referred to as *Productivity Trends*.

The Continuing Significance
of Productivity Advance

At the time of publication of the earlier volume in 1961, economic growth was a widely accepted national goal. There was considerable concern in the United States over the slowdown in the growth rates of real gross national product and productivity that appeared in the latter 1950s. In the presidential election campaign of 1960, both major parties pledged an accelerated rate of economic growth, "to get America moving again," as John Kennedy put it.

During the following decade the intellectual climate changed appreciably. No longer is economic growth accepted uncritically as a national goal. Increasing emphasis is being placed on the costs of growth, in the forms of pollution and other environmental deterioration and the social disorganization attributed by some in part to technological advance and other dynamic economic changes. Some commentators would even slow down or level off the growth of real income per capita.

It is our view that the more critical attitude toward economic growth reduces neither the importance of productivity change nor the desirability of understanding more about it. With regard to the need to counteract the deterioration of the physical and social environment, the most acceptable approach would seem to be to divert more resources toward this objective. A continued strong rate of growth in output and productivity will be necessary to make possible substantial improvements in the quality of the environment while continuing to increase real product per capita. Actually, diversion of resources from the production of final goods to the intermediate outlays required to combat pollution and other environmental deterioration will somewhat reduce the measured rate of advance in productivity and real product per capita, since real gross national product estimates fail to reflect most changes in the quality of life.

With regard to the issue of the "desirable" economic growth rate, it must be pointed out that, in a democratic society with a predominantly free economy, the realized rate of economic growth depends on the saving propensities of individuals as individuals and as owners of businesses, on the expected rates of return on investment, and on public policies reflecting the composite aspirations of citizens. It is my judgment that the overwhelming majority of Americans desires continued substantial increases in real product and income per head, and will take the appropriate individual and collective economic action to secure this result. But even if basic values and aspirations gradually change in the decades ahead in such a way as to retard the rate of economic growth, this would neither reduce the significance of productivity change nor the importance of understanding more about its causes and economic impacts.

Whatever the economic growth rate that emerges as a result of the interplay of the forces mentioned above, productivity advances would make possible the attainment of rising real product with a progressive saving in labor, capital, and natural resources compared to the quantities required with a static technology. In particular, increases in total factor productivity and further substitution of capital for labor would continue to make possible the progressive reduction of the workweek and the workyear, which has clearly been an objective of the labor force along with rising planes of living.

In fact, it is the very cost savings associated with productivity advance that induce the expenditures designed to enhance the productive efficiency of the tangible human and nonhuman factors of production. In Chapter 4 we emphasize that, whereas there are also other forces behind productivity advance, it results to a major degree from "intangible investments" in research and development, education, training, health, and mobility, all of which raise the quality of the factors in which the resulting intangible capital is embodied. So long as the community generates net saving, some of it will flow into productivity-increasing outlays, as well as into tangible capital outlays—ideally, to the point where the prospective rates of return on the various types of investment are equalized (after allowance for differential degrees of risk, nonpecuniary returns to human investment, and so on).

Consequently, whatever the rate of economic growth, productivity advance will remain one of its important components and contribute to the chief goals it serves—rising planes of living, increased leisure, adequate national security, and provision for future growth. Further, as rates of advancing productivity differ in the various industries, this will be an important element in the changing industrial structure of the economy. The estimates described in this volume are intended to enhance our understanding of these matters.

The Basic Conceptual Framework

The same basic concepts of productivity and similar estimating methodology are employed in this volume as in *Productivity Trends*. This is desirable to provide continuity with the long historical series presented there. More fundamentally, we believe that our approach is still a useful one, despite the subsequent development by others of alternative conceptual schemes. Here we shall review briefly the basic concepts and methodology, particularly for the benefit of those who may wish to skip the detailed discussion in Chapter 2, in order to proceed directly to the substantive discussions beginning in Chapter 3.

Our index numbers of "total factor productivity" are based on ratios of net output (real product) to weighted averages of the human (labor) and nonhuman (capital) tangible factor inputs. The weights represent the shares of factor income accruing to each of the two major factor classes in successive base periods. Labor input is measured in terms of man-hours worked. Capital input is assumed to move proportionately to the real stocks of tangible capital assets.[2] The inputs are estimated without allowance for changes in their "quality" or marginal physical productivity, so that changes in the ratios of output to input may be interpreted as reflecting all the diverse forces that affect the quality, or "productive efficiency," of the factors. In addition to total factor productivity, we present the more conventional measures relating output to man-hours and to capital individually. Movements of these "partial productivity" ratios reflect substitutions between factors as well as changes in productive efficiency.

Rather extensive use has been made by other economists of our earlier estimates. The divergence in the growth of output relative to the growth of the combined tangible factor inputs has challengingly been called a "measure of our ignorance" by Abramovitz,[3] and Domar[4] has termed it more simply "the residual." The movements of total factor productivity have served as a point of departure for a number of studies of economic growth involving attempts to explain away the residual.

Some of the investigations have sought to narrow the residual, or differences between rates of change in output and the tangible factor inputs, by expanding the inputs to include various qualitative elements that have improved the productive efficiency or intensity of use of the human and nonhuman factors of production. Thus, Denison adjusted labor input (man-hours) so as to reflect the effects of increasing educational attainments of the work force and the assumed increase in man-hour output occasioned by

---

[2] The asymmetry in the treatment of labor and capital inputs has been criticized by Stanley H. Ruttenberg in his "Director's Comment," *Productivity Trends*, pp. 224-27. The author's rationale was presented in that volume on pp. 31-32, and is elaborated below, pp. 25-27. Nathaniel Goldfinger, member of the Directors' reading committee for the present volume, has also expressed continuing reservations concerning the author's total factor productivity concept.

[3] Moses Abramovitz, "Resource and Output Trends in the United States since 1870," *American Economic Review*, May 1956, p. 11.

[4] Evsey D. Domar, "On the Measurement of Technological Change," *The Economic Journal*, December 1961, p. 709.

declines in the average number of hours worked, per week and per year. He then attempted to quantify the contributions of the other variables which he believes explain the increase in total factor productivity, with his final residual representing "advances in knowledge."[5]

More recently, Griliches and Jorgenson not only adjusted labor input for the factors selected by Denison but also adjusted capital inputs for qualitative improvements and for changes in rates of capacity utilization, and corrected for several other alleged "errors" in the measurements of outputs and inputs.[6] By these means they have reduced the increase in total factor productivity almost to the vanishing point.[7] Indeed, they even question the usefulness of the concept of technological advance or economic growth.

These and other studies which have sought theoretically and statistically to explain the growth of output over and above the growth of tangible inputs have helped to reduce our ignorance concerning this important subject. But I remain convinced that measures of tangible factor inputs, unadjusted for quality changes, and the associated total and partial productivity measures remain a useful point of departure for analysis of growth and change in economic aggregates and structure. In the last analysis, it is not crucial whether we count certain variables as inputs or as part of the statistical explanation of the productivity residual—so long as we correctly sort out and identify the significant forces at work.

For example, some analysts still prefer to use output-per-man-hour measures, in which case productivity changes must be explained in terms of changes in real tangible stocks and associated input per man-hour, as well as in terms of all the other forces that produce changes in total tangible factor productivity.[8] At the other extreme, I have attempted, in another study, to estimate the total real capital stocks and inputs that result from all invest-

---

[5] Edward F. Denison, *The Sources of Economic Growth in the United States and the Alternatives Before Us*, Supplementary Paper 13, New York, Committee for Economic Development, 1962.

[6] Dale W. Jorgenson and Zvi Griliches, "The Explanation of Productivity Change," *The Review of Economic Studies*, July 1967, reprinted with correction in *Survey of Current Business*, May 1969, Part II. See also the work of Robert J. Gordon in which he attempts to improve estimates of fixed capital outlays and stocks, in *Fiftieth Annual Report*, National Bureau of Economic Research, September 1970, pp. 29-30.

[7] In a later article, Jorgenson (with L. R. Christensen) revised his earlier estimates, and concluded: "... We estimate that changes in total factor productivity are substantial for 1929-1967 and for both the subperiods we have considered. The conclusion of Jorgenson and Griliches that productivity growth is negligible must be revised accordingly." L. R. Christensen and D. W. Jorgenson, "U.S. Real Product and Real Factor Input, 1929-1967," Discussion Paper 109, Harvard Institute of Economic Research, February 1970.

[8] See "Director's Comment," *Productivity Trends*, pp. 224-27.

ments, intangible as well as tangible, designed to increase income- and output-producing capacity. In this case, movements in the ratio of output to total input reflect only the variables not associated with investments, such as changes in scale, allocative efficiency, and other variables enumerated in the concluding section of Chapter 4. In between, the scope of the input estimates may be more or less comprehensive, producing different measures of the productivity residual.

In the present study, however, we continue to use estimates of output, tangible inputs, and productivity employing basically the same concepts, sources, and methods used in the earlier *Productivity Trends* volume. Those investigators who found my conceptual framework useful will welcome the extension of the former series on a comparable basis. Those who wish to adjust or modify the productivity series or their components to accord with alternative frames of reference can do so, since all the component output and inputs series are shown, permitting reshuffling to taste.

Plan and Preview of the Study

The first section of the present chapter introduced the study and stated its objectives. This section will help guide the reader through the organization of the rest of the volume and highlight some of the findings of Chapters 3 through 6, which comprise the descriptive and analytical materials.

Review of Concepts and Methodology (Chapter 2)

Since the interpretation of movements in productivity and its relationship to other variables depends on the concepts of productivity and its component variables and on methods and sources of estimation, the next chapter is devoted to these matters. Stress is placed on our concept and estimation of total factor productivity, within the framework of the national economic accounts, as the ratio of real product to the associated real factor costs. The relationship of movements of total factor productivity to those of the "scalar" in statistical production functions and to the "residual," or difference between rates of change in output and in a weighted mean of the associated inputs, is reviewed briefly, with references to the growing literature on the subject. The concepts and measures employed for the constituent series of output, or real product, labor input, and capital input, and the weighting schemes used to obtain the aggregates of each are discussed in relation to some of the alternatives that have been developed. Summaries of the underlying sources and methods are brief, since they are treated in some detail in the statistical appendix, which also contains the basic tables.

National Productivity Trends (Chapter 3)

In Chapter 3 we are concerned with the rates of change during the postwar period of productivity in several variant forms in the economy as a whole (or major segments thereof). We examine most closely the trend rates of growth in total factor productivity in the private domestic economy, which is free of the artificial assumptions involved in estimates of real product and productivity in the general government and foreign sectors. This examination leads to the conclusion that there has been no significant acceleration in the trend rate of growth in total factor productivity since World War II, at 2.3 per cent a year, compared with the earlier epoch beginning around the time of World War I, when the rate of advance had picked up markedly. (See Chart 3-1.) The rates of advance in real product per man-hour and per unit of "labor input" (weighted man-hours), however, have shown further acceleration since World War II, due to a much faster rate of increase in capital per unit of labor input than prevailed during the interwar period.

We also examine variations in rates of change in the productivity ratios between cycles, and from year to year. While the variations are considerable, it is significant that they are markedly smaller than in earlier epochs. This is due chiefly to the steadier pace of economic growth generally since World War II. The lesser variability may also be interpreted as reflecting a broader and more persistent rate of technological advance.

National Productivity and Economic Growth (Chapter 4)

In Chapter 4 we first quantify the contribution of productivity to economic growth, as measured by the trend rate of increase in net national product. Ever since World War I, gains in total factor productivity have accounted for more than half of aggregate economic growth. The period since 1948 has been no exception. The trend rates for total factor productivity and economic growth have been estimated to be 2.3 and 4.1 per cent a year, respectively. From 1948 to 1966, gains in total factor productivity accounted for almost all the increase in planes of living, as measured by real NNP per capita, which rose at an average rate of 2.4 per cent a year. Total input per capita rose only fractionally, as substantial increases in capital input relative to population did little more than offset a persistent decline in labor input per capita.

Of interest from the viewpoint of the functional distribution of income in the private domestic business economy is the fact that real average hourly labor compensation rose at an average annual rate of 3.3 per cent between 1948 and 1966. This growth rate exceeds that of output per unit of labor input by 0.2 percentage points, a difference that can be deemed a measure of the proportionate rate of increase in labor's share of factor income originating in the business economy—from 69.7 in 1948 to 72.5 in 1966. This represents a continuation of the 1929-48 drift. It is associated with a historical elasticity of substitution between capital and labor input of around 0.66, reflecting the relationship between the relative rates of growth of the factor inputs and the relative rates of change in their real prices. Measured in this way, elasticity is also influenced by the nature of the innovation and possibly other factors.

Chapter 4 is concluded by some observations concerning the causes of productivity advance. It is my hypothesis that the chief proximate determinant of the rate of growth in total factor productivity is the rate of growth in the real stocks of intangible capital embodied in the tangible factors. These intangible investments enhanced the "quality," or productive efficiency, of the factors. Reference is made to a current study by the author in which estimates are made of the total real stocks of capital, which show a significant increase in intangibles relative to tangibles. Other possible causes of productivity change are discussed, including changes in economic efficiency, scale, the inherent quality of resources, and rates of capacity utilization.

Industry Patterns of Productivity Change (Chapter 5)

In looking at changes in productivity of more than thirty industry groups, we find that the degree of dispersion is considerable for the post-1948 period, but no greater than in earlier periods of comparable length. No group for which estimates were constructed showed declines in total factor productivity, while some showed increases of up to 8 per cent a year, on the average. Dispersion was somewhat greater in subperiods measured between cycle peaks; some groups showed productivity declines in one of the four subperiods covered, while a few other groups showed increases of over 10 per cent. There was also considerable variability in industry productivity movements over subperiods and from year to year, but as in the case of the private economy as a whole, variability was considerably less after 1948 than before.

Chapter 5 also presents rates of change in the partial productivity ratios by industry, as well as summary measures of their dispersion and variability. Since capital per unit of labor input rose in almost all industry groups, the rates of increase in labor productivity generally exceed those in total factor productivity, while rates of increase in the output-capital ratio are lower. Industry dispersion in rates of change in the partial productivity ratios are much the same as pre-1948, with the dispersion in the capital-output ratio higher than that in labor productivity. Variability in the output-capital ratio is still much higher than that in labor productivity, reflecting the greater difficulty in adjusting fixed capital to output over the short run than adjusting man-hours employed. As would be expected, variability and dispersion in rates of change are greater the wider the degree of industry detail studied.

While of some interest in their own right, industry differentials in productivity advance are of particular value as a means of analyzing economic impacts and causal factors on a cross-sectional basis. This is the objective of the sixth and final chapter.

Interrelationships Among Rates of Change in Productivity, Output, and Associated Variables (Chapter 6)

As was discovered for earlier periods, there is a significant positive correlation for the period 1948-66 between rates of change in productivity and in output for the manufacturing groups, and for the broader set of thirty-two two-digit industry groups (which do not include agriculture, construction, finance, and services). Additional regression analyses indicate that this relationship may be explained by the fact that relative changes in productivity are negatively correlated with relative changes in output prices by industry (since there is no significant degree of correlation with input prices), and that relative industry changes in prices and in output are likewise negatively correlated, indicating that the effects of price elasticities of demand are not outweighed by other factors. The relationship between relative industry changes in output and in productivity is somewhat closer than is explained by the price factor, suggesting that the relationship is reciprocal, and that relative scale economies in the faster-growing industries augment other forces producing above-average productivity advance in these industries. Similar results were reported by Fuchs for seventeen industries in the trade and service sector.[9]

Our results also confirm Fuchs's findings that changes in productivity and in output are not positively correlated for the one-digit industry groups, including extractive industries and the service sectors, for reasons which we

[9] See Victor R. Fuchs, *The Service Economy*, New York, National Bureau of Economic Research, 1969, Chapters 3 and 4.

adduce. As a result, employment in the service sector, which had below-average productivity advances, showed large increases, while the opposite was true of the extractive sector. In the two-digit industry sectors, however, relative changes in productivity and in employment were not negatively correlated in 1948-66, and in earlier periods there was a mildly significant positive correlation.

For the twenty-one two-digit manufacturing groups, we assembled estimates of a number of possible causal variables. A matrix of simple correlation coefficients is presented. Due to a high degree of multicollinearity among the variables as well as incomplete specification of all the significant variables, it is felt that the results of multiple regression analysis are questionable. Cross-sectional industry analyses are also complicated by the fact that the productivity advance of any given industry is affected by variables at work in the industries from which purchases are made, as well as by forces promoting technological advance from within the industry. Additional work is needed to estimate more comprehensively all the chief factors, direct and indirect, affecting productivity in the various industry groupings and thereby the industrial structure of the economy.

2

REVIEW OF CONCEPTS AND METHODOLOGY

The term "productivity" is generally used to denote a relationship between output and the associated inputs used in the production process. In this study we are not concerned with the marginal and average productivity concepts used in static equilibrium theory. We are concerned, rather, with the relationship between outputs and inputs, in real terms, over time in a dynamic economy. The basic objective of productivity estimates is to obtain at least rough measures of the impact on production of the investments and other variables that advance knowledge, improve technology and organization, and otherwise enhance the productive efficiency of the factors of production.

The meaning of productivity measures depends on the definitions accorded to output and input, the methodology by which the concepts are statistically implemented, including the weighting patterns used to combine unlike units of outputs and inputs, and the manner in which outputs are related to inputs. We shall consider each of these matters in turn, starting with the notion of the production function, which is the organizing principle behind measurement of the productivity relationship.

Productivity Ratios and the Production Function

The general notion of the production function may be expressed as follows:

$$O = f(I_1, I_2 \ldots I_n)(T). \tag{1}$$

"O" designates the potential or actual physical volume of output. Output may be defined in various ways; the important thing is that, given the output definition, the associated inputs (I) on the right-hand side be defined and measured consistently. In this study we generally take inputs to represent the real potential or actual services of the basic factors of production. Measures of factor service input are consistent with measures of net output, or "value added."

The factor inputs may be defined broadly or narrowly. Broadly, they may include the services of tangible as well as intangible resources—i.e., the stock of productive knowledge incorporated in the labor force and in nonhuman instruments of production, or "disembodied" as in the organization of production. Or, they may be taken to include only the tangible factor inputs unadjusted for changes in knowledge and other factors affecting efficiency. It is the latter approach which is used in this study. The tangible inputs themselves may be measured in terms of various types of labor and non-human capital services, or they may be collapsed into the two broad factor classes of labor (L) and capital (K) (which includes land as well as man-made capital goods). Since we have used the convenient two-factor approach, the production function can be narrowed to:

$$O = f(L, K)(T). \qquad (2)$$

The variable "T," sometimes loosely called "technology," really embraces all the forces that influence output in addition to changes in the physical volume of the tangible factor inputs. It is less misleading to refer to T as the "productive efficiency" of the tangible factors, or "total (tangible) factor productivity." Since the intangible capital stock accumulated through invest-ments in research and development, engineering, education and training, and so on is the chief element behind productive efficiency, one would expect T to show much less change if intangible capital inputs were also included along with tangible inputs. But there would still be variations for reasons discussed subsequently.

If one develops time series for O, L, and K, one can measure changes in T either from statistical production functions, using the usual regression tech-niques, or by computing ratios of output to inputs. Since the latter is the approach generally used in *Productivity Trends* and the present study, we shall compare the two methods.

It is appropriate to start with the widely known Cobb-Douglas function, which is expressed in the following equation:

$$O_t = A_t L_t^b K_t^{1-b} \quad . \qquad (3)$$

The symbols are as before, except that A_t, rather than T, is the level of productive efficiency in year t; and b and $1-b$ are the elasticities of output with respect to labor and real capital services, respectively. Under pure competition, neutral technological change, constant returns to scale, and certain other conditions, b and $1-b$, as applied to index numbers of the inputs, indicate the labor and property proportions of factor costs or income. Since the function is defined for the given state of knowledge, if it is to be fitted to logarithmic time series for O, L, and K under conditions of changing technology, provision must be made for estimating the rate of shift in the scalar A as well as the exponent b. One method, noted by Fabricant, is to substitute for A_t the expression $(1 + r)^t$. With t measured in years, the coefficient r measures the average annual (trend) rate of shift in the scalar A as a result of changes in technology and other factors affecting productive efficiency.[1] Presumably, the value for r is the same one would obtain with the slope of a trend line fitted to the index numbers of productivity computed as the ratio of output to a weighted geometric mean of the inputs, using as weights the exponents obtained from the statistical production function.

$$\frac{O_t}{L_t^b \, K_t^{1-b}} \qquad (4)$$

One trouble with the approach just described is that it yields only the trend rate of productivity advance. An advantage of productivity ratios noted in my earlier study is that they " ... provide greater flexibility for the analysis of movements and of relationships with other variables."[2]

Yet, as Nelson points out,[3] the period-to-period rates of change in the scalar, or productivity, may be obtained as the difference between rates of change in ouput and in the rates of change in labor and tangible capital inputs, each weighted by its share of income as derived from the statistical production function or directly from national income estimates. That is, when one differentiates the production function shown in equation (3), the result is:

$$\Delta A/A = \Delta O/O - b(\Delta L/L) - (1 - b)(\Delta K/K). \qquad (5)$$

Here again, the residual rate of change is presumably the same as would be obtained by directly computing the rate of change in the consistent productivity ratio. Also, we could obtain a productivity time series by successively

[1] This form of the function is presented by Solomon Fabricant in his article "Productivity" in the *International Encyclopedia of the Social Sciences*.

[2] *Productivity Trends*, p. 8. For a recent review of the literature on productivity and production functions, see M. Ishaq Nadiri, "Some Approaches to the Theory and Measurement of Total Factor Productivity," *Journal of Economic Literature*, December 1970.

[3] R. R. Nelson, "Aggregate Production Functions," *The American Economic Review*, September 1964, p. 578.

linking the annual rates of change in the residual to a given base period taken as 100.

The point is that productivity estimates derived from output-input ratios are essentially interchangeable with those derived from statistical production functions, if the component variables and the underlying shape of the relationship are consistently specified. Actually, our total factor productivity ratio is specified somewhat differently from that implied in the Cobb-Douglas production function, as noted by Fabricant (see footnote 1 above). It may be written as follows:

$$\frac{O}{b^* L + (1-b)^* K} . \tag{6}$$

In other words, our total tangible factor input is a weighted arithmetic average of labor and capital inputs. The asterisks indicate that the weights are derived not from a statistical production function but as the estimated shares of factor income; further, the weights are changed periodically and the total input indexes linked together for successive subperiods. We shall now discuss the implications of these differences from the Cobb-Douglas approach.

In the first place, by changing factor input weights occasionally, we avoid the assumption underlying the Cobb-Douglas production function of linear homogeneity with unit elasticity of substitution between the factors. Various statistical studies suggest that in the United States the elasticity of substitution is significantly below 1.0. (See Chapter 4.) Further, the national income estimates for the United States indicate that factor shares have changed over time. For the private domestic economy, the labor share has increased from 67.3 per cent in 1929 to 74.7 per cent in 1957—although this might reflect biased technological change as well as an elasticity of substitution of less than unity coupled with an increase in the quantity of capital per unit of labor input. In any case, we felt it was more realistic to posit a production function that was consistent with changing factor shares of income. It seemed adequate to change weights (for outputs as well as inputs) approximately every decade or so, since the structure of production and production relationships changes slowly, so that average proportions of outputs and inputs may be expected to alter significantly only over intermediate time periods.

Second, we did not obtain the weights for labor and capital in the successive subperiods by fitting statistical production functions to the data. Instead, we relied on the national income estimates of the U.S. Department

of Commerce, with a few adjustments. In particular, we had to partition the
net income of proprietors between the labor and capital components, as
described in the appendix. And in the case of the nonbusiness sectors, we had to
impute a net rental value to the capital goods in order to obtain a capital
weight.

Actually, the exponents of statistical production functions have sometimes
come quite close to the shares revealed by national income estimates. But
because of the considerable instability of the coefficients in successive time
periods and the variations in coefficients obtained from different types of
functions, we have felt that national income estimates provide a better guide
to relative shares. Besides, they are more readily accessible.

Finally, the fact that our total input index is a weighted arithmetic mean
of the labor and capital input indexes, rather than a weighted geometric
mean, implies a logarithmic linear relationship within successive subperiods.
Our procedure is the simpler one usually employed in productivity ratios, and
is consistent with the weighting procedure implicit in the real product
indexes. It is true that it does not allow for the tendency toward diminishing
marginal productivity of individual factors, given neutral technological
change. But the difference in results of the alternative weighting procedures is
small over the subperiods within which fixed weights are used in this study,
given the historical differentials in the growth rates of labor and capital. For
example, with average annual growth rates of output, labor, and capital taken
at 3.5, 1.5, and 3.0 per cent, respectively, the total productivity index using a
weighted geometric mean of the inputs (0.8 labor and 0.2 capital) would
grow at an average annual rate of 1.70 per cent over successive decades. The
growth rate of the productivity index based on inputs combined with arithmetic weights would average 1.68 per cent over one decade, and 1.66 per cent
over two decades. Thus, the difference in results of the alternative weighting
procedures would not generally show up over the subperiods when the
productivity growth rates are rounded to tenths of percentage points.

Concepts and Methodology Underlying the
Output and Input Indexes

The definitions and statistical content given to output and input can make
much more difference in productivity movements than variations in the form
of the underlying output-input relationship. In this section we discuss in some
detail the operational concepts of output and of labor and capital inputs used

in this study, contrasting them with alternative concepts suggested in the literature, or concepts which are considered possible. We summarize only briefly the sources of the estimates or of the data underlying our own estimates, since these are fully described in the appendix. Alternative time series are available which yield somewhat different results. Generally speaking, differences in the movement of most reasonable alternative series are not great. More important is the fact that the various estimates are subject to margins of error and possible biases that are not generally quantifiable. As pointed out in *Productivity Trends,* the output, input, and productivity indexes are not "precision tools," but they do indicate general orders of magnitudes of change, given the theoretical and conceptual framework within which they have been constructed and in terms of which they must be interpreted. A not unimportant test of their general reliability is provided by the reasonableness of the results obtained from statistical analyses based on productivity estimates and related series.

Output

Levels. There are three main levels at which aggregate output may be measured. The first is total gross output, which includes all goods and services produced without deductions for intermediate products consumed in the production process, or for capital consumption. In this case, the corresponding inputs include not only the gross factor inputs but also real intermediate product inputs. As far as gross product originating in the economy is concerned (or major sectors such as the business economy), inclusion of intermediate inputs obviously involves double counting, since such inputs have already been included in the final products and the factor services required to produce them are likewise included in total factor input. It is the final products included in national product that are the objective of production. These are the goods that satisfy current consumer wants or that add to stocks of productive capacity for satisfying future wants, to use the definition of Kuznets and many earlier national income theorists.[4]

Thus, at the economy-wide level, we are interested in the efficiency with which the basic factor resources are converted into the goods men want, so the appropriate productivity measure relates real (final) product to total factor input. We shall consider shortly the other choice as to whether real

---

[4] In addition to goods, men also desire maintenance of the social fabric, so the value of all government services (at cost), including national security, is included, not just direct services to consumers and public investment. See the discussion in Appendix A of *Productivity Trends,* pp. 231-39.

product and factor input should be gross or net of real capital consumption.

At the industry (or enterprise) level, the choice is not quite so clear-cut. For production analysis it may be useful in some cases to use total gross output estimates and relate them to factor inputs, plus intermediate inputs purchased outside the industry (or enterprise). The reason is that in production decisions management has to weigh alternative combinations of all inputs in the light of their relative prices so that the least-cost combination may be selected. On the other hand, from a macroeconomic viewpoint, there are persuasive arguments for using real product estimates (i.e., real value added, in which real intermediate costs are deducted from the real value of total gross output). The real industry product estimates in relation to real factor costs alone indicate changes in the efficiency with which the basic factors resident in the industry are used to add value to the intermediate products purchased from other industries. More important, the real industry product estimates are additive to real national product, and productivity in the economy as a whole represents, in effect, a weighted average of productivity in the component industries. For these reasons, our preferred industry measure is real product in relation to total factor input. In the cases of two-digit industries, we have had to use total output measures, but these have been used as proxies for real product and are also related to real factor cost alone for consistency with the sector and one-digit industry measures.

The other major choice must be made between the use of real gross product or real net product, and thus also between real gross or net capital stock on the input side. Here, again, the choice appears clear-cut from the standpoint of economic welfare: the production of capital goods required to offset capital consumption is not desired for its own sake, but is necessary to maintain capital intact. The consensus of national income specialists, likewise, is that NNP rather than GNP is the preferred measure from a welfare standpoint.[5] Because of the difficulties of measuring real capital consumption allowances as distinct from book depreciation, however, real GNP is frequently used as a proxy for real NNP, and we use it as such in our measures. Based on our estimates of real NNP for the private domestic economy and the business economy as a whole (shown in Table A-2), the ratios of real net to

5 See, for example, Edward F. Denison, *Why Growth Rates Differ*, Washington, The Brookings Institution, 1967, pp. 14-15. As Denison puts it: "Insofar as a large output is a proper goal of society and objective of policy, it is net product that measures the degree of success in achieving this goal. Gross product is larger by the value of capital consumption. There is no more reason to wish to maximize capital consumption—the quantity of capital goods used up in production—than there is to maximize the quantity of any other intermediate product used up in production, such as, say, the metal used in making television sets."

gross product varied remarkably little over the entire period 1948-66. For both sectors, the ratios were 0.915 both in 1948 and in 1966. The nonfarm industry product estimates (for which we rely on OBE) are all gross, so we cannot analyze net-gross ratios on an industry basis. Indeed, were real net product data available by industry as well as for the business economy as a whole, we would have used it throughout. But the overall comparison suggests that trends are not significantly affected by use of real gross product estimates in lieu of the theoretically preferable net measures.

Griliches and Jorgenson attempt to rationalize use of real gross product and real gross capital input as preferable to the net measures: "Exclusion of depreciation on capital introduces an entirely arbitrary distinction between labor input and capital input, since the corresponding exclusion of depreciation of the stock of labor services is not carried out."[6]

Most national income specialists believe, however, that, from a welfare viewpoint, the personal consumption outlays required to offset depreciation of human capital (and to maintain it) should be included in NNP.[7] Denison argues as follows: "I am not aware of a definable labor counterpart to capital depreciation as a component of GNP that there is no advantage in increasing because it is not wanted—feeding, clothing, and housing children surely do not fall into this category—but if there be such, the appropriate remedy would be to change the measures of output and labor earnings."

A formal symmetry between labor and capital can be quite misleading, since man is the end as well as a means of production. On the other hand, from the viewpoint of productive capacity, the notion of human capital consumption has meaning, since over the long run it must be offset in order to maintain total capital intact. Unfortunately, little work has been done on estimating human capital and capital consumption. In view of the lack of estimates in this area, there is some merit in the suggestion of Griliches and Jorgenson that by including depreciation in the weight for capital input the relative weight of labor is reduced, as would be the case if both factor returns were measured net of depreciation. Further, since real gross product measures are used in estimating productivity, it would be of some interest to use real gross capital and total inputs with corresponding gross weights for capital as well as labor. This would make it possible to see the difference in movement between the gross productivity measure and our basic total factor produc-

[6] Dale W. Jorgenson and Zvi Griliches, "The Explanation of Productivity Change," *The Review of Economic Studies*, July 1967, p. 256.

[7] Edward F. Denison, "Some Major Issues in Productivity Analysis: An Examination of Estimates by Jorgenson and Griliches," *Survey of Current Business*, May 1969, Part II, p. 2.

tivity measure, in which capital input is measured net of depreciation and weighted accordingly.

The variant indexes of gross capital input, gross capital productivity, and total gross productivity are presented in the appendix tables. In general, the effect is to produce a somewhat smaller rate of increase in the gross productivity measure than in the standard measure, not because gross capital input rises more than net but because of the greater weight accorded to the capital measures, which generally rise significantly more than labor input.

Aggregation. In order to combine units of the many diverse types of output, market price weights are used to obtain the real product aggregates. For production and productivity analysis a case can be made for using unit factor cost weights. But as a practical matter the differences in movement of real product using the alternative weighting patterns are probably small, and the work of eliminating the differential effects of unit indirect business taxes less subsidies on market prices would be enormous.

Since relative market prices change gradually, the price weights in successive periods were changed in line with the procedures described in *Productivity Trends.* We have used average prices in the boundary years of the following subperiods: 1919-29; 1929-37; 1937-48; and 1948-53. For the final period beginning 1953, we have used 1958 weights in line with current government practice in order to keep the estimates open-ended. This is consistent with our weighting system for inputs. Although there is no unique solution to the "index number problem," it seems appropriate to weight outputs and inputs on the basis of their relative prices in successive subperiods of sufficient length for allowing changes in the structure of production to become perceptible.

In reweighting the estimates for periods prior to 1953, we employed the breakdown of real product by industry, rather than by type-of-product groupings as in *Productivity Trends.* The earlier weight bases tend to produce larger apparent increases in real product than do later bases. This is due to the negative correlation between relative changes in prices and in quantities. But the differences are not large. Since the effects of alternative weight bases on aggregate inputs are in the same direction, the effects on the productivity ratios are even smaller than the effects on output and input separately.

Scope of the Economy, Sector, and Industry Product Estimates. Like any other statistical construct, the national product is what it is defined to be. The United States, and most other countries, largely confine the estimates to legal market transactions. Such transactions are usually clearly economic, involving a quid pro quo, and the market provides an objective means for valuing the goods and factor services. Further, data are generally available for at least a sample of the transactions.

Nevertheless, most countries also include imputed values for certain important nonmarket activities that also seem clearly economic (in that they are undertaken primarily for the sake of the resulting product rather than for the sake of the activity itself, as in social and recreational activities). Imputations in the United States are confined to selected activities for which there are significant market counterparts to provide a means of valuation. Official imputations—of which the major ones are for the rental value of owner-occupied houses, food produced and consumed on farms, and payments in kind—comprised a relatively small share of GNP: about 8.6 per cent in 1929, 5 per cent in 1948, and 7.2 per cent in 1966.

Obviously, imputations could be expanded much further to include, for major examples, the value of unpaid household labor, schoolwork, volunteer labor, and, on the capital side, imputed rental values of nonbusiness capital goods. In another study for the National Bureau, my associates and I developed estimates of imputed valuations for the above items and several others which together add more than 50 per cent to the GNP in 1966.[8] We have not included these estimates in the present study, however, with the exception of rental values of nonbusiness capital stocks.

The chief reason for not expanding product imputations in a productivity study is that the values are imputed from the cost side. That is, the inputs into nonmarket economic activities are estimated and values assigned on the basis of their opportunity costs. This is basically what is currently done by the Commerce Department in estimating current-dollar product originating in the nonbusiness sectors, although the Department largely confines itself to the labor inputs, neglecting the contribution of the stocks of nonbusiness capital, except for owner-occupied residences. Estimates are not made of the volume of nonmarket outputs and their unit and total values. So only half of the information needed for productivity comparisons is available. Therefore we have not expanded the scope of present official GNP estimates, except as noted.

The exception relates to our inclusion of the gross rental values of the stocks of tangible capital used in the general government sector and in private nonprofit institutions. Already, OBE counts the compensation of employees as product originating in these sectors (and households). But since a major aspect of our study involves estimating capital as well as labor inputs, we have

[8] See *Forty-seventh Annual Report*, National Bureau of Economic Research, June 1967, pp. 9-15.

done so for governments and private nonprofit institutions in order to maintain symmetry with the private business sector. Since returns to capital comprise part of private domestic business product, we have likewise imputed the rental value of the capital inputs in the aforementioned nonbusiness sectors. With product originating in the household sectors confined to paid employees, we have not included the imputed rental value of household durables and inventories, since these are predominantly used by unpaid family labor, the value of which we do not add in this study.

By convention, the Commerce Department deflates product originating in the nonbusiness sectors largely by corresponding input price indexes, so that real product parallels the movement of input without adjustment for productivity change. Likewise, our real rental values of tangible capital parallel the movements of the real capital stocks. Thus, it is clear that productivity analysis is best confined to the private domestic business economy, for which there are relatively independent real product estimates. For analysis of long-run trends, however, we have used the private domestic economy, since adequate input and real product estimates for households and nonprofit institutions are not separately available prior to 1929. We also refer briefly in the next chapter to productivity trends in the economy as a whole, since such estimates are useful for certain purposes so long as one recognizes the downward bias imparted by the conventions used in the nonbusiness sectors.

In addition to varying delimitations of the scope of national product, there are also alternative concepts with regard to the definition of the final products to be included, as opposed to intermediate products considered to be incorporated in the final products. Some items charged off to current expense by business and likewise considered intermediate by OBE might be classified as final—small tools, research and development, welfare services to employees, and entertainment or education provided to the public as part of advertising expense. Some personal outlays might be adjudged intermediate, such as commuting expenses, or personal business expenditures. Even if one considers national security outlays to be final services (as we do on the grounds that national security is a goal of society just like want satisfaction), it is possible to argue that some government services are designed to promote private business and should be viewed as an offset to indirect business taxes. In *Productivity Trends*, in addition to the official GNP estimates, we also presented variant output and productivity estimates based on the work of Simon Kuznets, which excluded a portion of government purchases as being intermediate. The Kuznets estimates, including national security, actually showed much the same movements as the Commerce estimates, due to the relatively small volume of government cost services (which were estimated quite roughly). Since the Kuznets series has not been continued, we do not extend the variant based on his estimates.

Thus, we rely largely on the official national product estimates by sector, but we have pointed out the alternative concepts and definitions that would result in somewhat different movements in the aggregates and probably also in the productivity ratios. All in all, at this stage of our knowledge, it would not be advisable to expand imputations or redefine final product for purposes of productivity analysis. In the area of growth analysis, with particular reference to inputs or real costs, further experimentation can add to our knowledge, judging from preliminary results of the National Bureau's current studies in the national economic accounts referred to above.

Turning to the scope of our industry estimates, from 1948 forward these follow the definitions of the 1957 Standard Industrial Classification (SIC). This is in line with the recent economic censuses and with the 1965 revisions of the OBE national income and product accounts.[9]

We use the OBE estimates of income and product originating by industry for the major SIC one-digit industry groupings and the broad subgroup aggregates which OBE also publishes. Actually, OBE obtained its real industry product estimates on the basis of the difference between real value of total output and real intermediate costs—the so-called "double deflation" method—for only about 50 per cent of the business economy. For most of the other industries, base-period gross product was extrapolated by physical output series, or by the deflated value of total output, on the assumption that net-gross ratios did not change significantly. In the remaining industries, current-dollar gross product was deflated directly by output price indexes or, in a few cases, by input price indexes, which may result in a downward bias in the resulting real product series, as noted in the next section.

For the two-digit industries, we have used production indexes that, in the case of manufacturing and mining, have been "benchmarked" on the periodic economic censuses. The OBE does not regularly publish real product estimates at the two-digit level. Those that have been published on an occasional basis reveal some erratic movements, which may be expected from the double-deflation approach when the underlying data are imperfect. So even if the real product estimates for two-digit industries were regularly available, there would be some advantage in using gross production indexes due to their greater stability. The trends of aggregates based on the two types of measures

---

[9] *The National Income and Product Accounts of the United States, 1929-1965,* Statistical Tables, a supplement to *The Survey of Current Business,* U.S. Department of Commerce, 1966.

are compared in the appendix (pp. 194-95). The aggregates based on gross production indexes have a slightly higher trend in the postwar period. This should be kept in mind if one compares, in Part III of the appendix, productivity in two-digit industries with industry-group or industry-sector aggregates that are based on real product estimates.

Output Units. It would be ideal for the economic statistician if output units of various types were standardized and unchanging through time. Further, if he had complete physical volume data and unit values in the base period, or value data and corresponding price indexes for deflation, he would have no problem in obtaining weighted production aggregates.

In the real world, however, the ceaseless changes that frequently benefit consumers create problems for the statistician. Certain goods are custom-built and services adapted to individual requirements, the quality of many goods and services may improve—or at least change—with time, and new products may appear while old ones disappear. Further, quantity as well as value and price data may leave much to be desired, particularly in the finance and services industries.

These problems were discussed in some detail in the text and appendixes of *Productivity Trends*. In brief, our conclusion is that real product estimates tend to understate somewhat the growth of output and productivity.

With regard to nonstandard products, the use of cost indexes (including wage rates) as deflators of value estimates imparts a downward bias insofar as productivity has increased in a particular industry. The areas involved are mainly parts of construction, shipbuilding, aircraft manufacturing, machine building, and some of the services areas—although, when households and nonprofit institutions are excluded, price indexes are available to deflate most of the remaining private service outlays. Some offset to the upward bias of cost deflators is provided by the fact that price indexes for the standardized portion of the output of some industries are also used to deflate the value of the custom-built portion, as in the case of machinery. It seems likely that productivity increases less in custom work than in standardized production, lending a downward bias to the price indexes.

New products that appear after a base period are usually assigned the same ratio to the average price of like goods as they had in the first year of significant commercial production. This convention would have little effect on real product other than some understatement of the increase in the small amounts produced prior to the beginning of full commercial production, when price data collection would begin. This assumes that the relative price of new products typically declines during the developmental phase.

Much more important than the new product phenomenon is the improvement in quality of existing products. Indeed, it is sometimes hard to draw a dividing line between improved versions of old products and new products. One must also distinguish between the improvement of given product lines and a relative shift of purchases toward higher-quality, higher-price lines. The latter phenomenon is reflected in increases in real product obtained by price deflation, since the price data underlying the indexes relate to homogeneous items with given specifications.

Two chief methods are used to deal with quality changes in the price indexes used for deflation. According to one method, the price agency attempts to divide the price change associated with a new model between that which represents an increase in unit real costs and that which is the "pure" price change. In this way, deflated product reflects improvements in products that are associated with unit real cost differentials. To the extent that quality improvements exceed real cost changes, the real product estimates have a downward bias.

This may be offset to some extent by the other way in which model and quality changes are handled. The new price may be directly linked to the old, so that the entire price increase of a new model shows up as an increase in real product. In an inflationary era, as that under study in the present volume, this method may tend to overstate quality improvements, or at least understate it less than the first method.

Not all model changes represent quality improvements, of course, particularly those which are largely stylistic. And some goods and services have undoubtedly deteriorated over time. But the consensus of observers is that, on balance, quality has increased more than the changes in unit real costs of improved products. Thus, real product and productivity measures probably tend to have some downward bias on this score, which, insofar as the bias differs among products, affects industry comparisons. Unfortunately, however, we cannot quantify the extent of the quality bias, which is even difficult to define in measurable terms due to the highly subjective element involved.

Tangible Factor Inputs

The general discussion in this and the following two sections on labor and nonlabor inputs is confined to the basic factors of production. The concepts and measurement of intermediate inputs have already been treated in the preceding section on output, since intermediate product inputs of one industry are simultaneously the outputs of other industries.

Definition of Factor Stocks and Inputs. Factor services or "inputs," as we view them, represent the time available for use in production of the stocks of the tangible labor and nonlabor factors of production weighted by the base-period value products per unit of the available factor time. The nonlabor factor comprises man-made capital goods—structures, equipment, and inventories—and "land," which comprises all natural resources stocks. We do not distinguish between land and man-made capital goods, since they are alike in all important economic respects. When we refer to "capital" generally, or "property," we mean the total of the nonhuman factor. We shall refer to the human factor as "labor," for short.

It is useful to distinguish between the human and nonhuman tangible factor categories (labor and capital), despite their basic similarities as agents of production, because of even more important dissimilarities. Property is owned, and can be sold as well as leased, whereas human beings are free agents and only their services can be sold. The source of labor compensation is work, whereas the source of property income is prior savings. The division of national income between labor and nonlabor compensation is basic to studies of income distribution by function and size, reflecting the inevitably man-centered focus of the social sciences. Accordingly, we measure factor stocks and inputs in terms of this fundamental dichotomy.

In our definition of factor inputs, we referred to the time available for use in production of the factor stocks. As discussed in *Productivity Trends*, this points up a basic asymmetry between labor and capital. Productive human capital is obviously not coterminous with the population. Substantial portions of the population—the very young, the very old, and the infirm—are unable to work. Of those able to work, a certain proportion become members of the labor force. Of the total labor force, at any time there is some portion of voluntary or involuntary unemployment. We would count as productive human capital only the employed labor force, and, to obtain the time rate of use, count the man-hours "at work" during the periods for which output is measured—years, in this study.

While at the workplace, men may be more or less fully and efficiently utilized, at any given level of technology. As matters of both principle and expediency, we do not try to adjust man-hours at work for the degree or intensity of utilization. We count only the man-hours at work; changes in the utilization factor would show up as changes in the productivity ratio.

It is useful, however, to construct measures relating to labor utilization rates which may help explain changes in productivity. The ratio of employment (or unemployment) to labor force is one such variable, since employees, particularly nonproduction workers, are often not utilized as fully while at work in periods of decelerated growth or contraction as they are in periods of expansion. Deviations from trend of average hours worked would tend to measure the same phenomenon. As a trend factor, however, the decline in average hours worked per week and per year has been considered by some to enhance the efficiency of man-hours worked up to some point. Denison has tried to allow for this effect in his measures of labor input.[10] Apart from the fact that such estimates are speculative, we prefer to let the effects of changing average hours worked show up in the productivity ratios, and use average hours series as a possible explanatory variable. A preferable variable would be a direct measure of the average hourly intensity or relative efficiency with which people work, at successive levels of technology. Although "work measurement" attempts to get at this factor for selected individuals and groups at the establishment level, it would be impossible to obtain aggregate measures for entire industries or the business economy as a whole.

In contrast to the human population, the entire living population of capital goods (those that have not been discarded, including items in active "standby" status) is available for productive use at all times, and involves a per annum cost, regardless of degree of use. The purpose of capital assets is for use in production of current output and income. The degree of capital utilization reflects the degree of efficiency of enterprises and the social economy generally. Hence, in converting capital stocks into inputs, we do not adjust capital for changes in rates of capacity utilization, and thus these are reflected in changes in the productivity ratios.[11]

Efforts to measure the percentage utilization of the productive capacity of real capital stocks are to be welcomed as adding to our information on explanatory variables. Unfortunately, no reliable long-run measures of this variable are available either for the business economy or for most of its industrial divisions. Griliches and Jorgenson, for example, attempted to devise such a measure for purposes of converting a real capital input series to a utilization basis, as opposed to the availability basis employed in this study. Their measure showed a significant increase over the period, reducing their magnitude for total factor productivity by an average of 0.6 per cent a year.[12] But as Denison has argued, the statistical basis of their measure is

---

[10] Edward F. Denison, *The Sources of Economic Growth in the United States and the Alternatives Before Us*, Supplementary Paper 13, New York, Committee for Economic Development, 1962, pp. 265-66.

[11] In *Productivity Trends* (pp. 76-77) a variant productivity measure is presented for the private economy from a "social cost" viewpoint, in which all available labor is counted as input, so that changes in rates of utilization of labor show up in the productivity ratio. Productivity trends are not affected, however. Lack of data prevents this approach from being implemented on an industry basis.

[12] D. W. Jorgenson and Z. Griliches, "The Explanation of Productivity Change," 1967, reprinted with corrections in *The Survey of Current Business*, May 1969, Part II. Jorgenson has subsequently reduced the scope and magnitude of his capacity utilization

very tenuous, and it is extremely doubtful that there has been nearly as large a secular increase in the rate of utilization of capacity in the entire private domestic economy as their measure shows.[13]

Thus, to our theoretical argument for not adjusting real capital stock and input for changing rates of utilization is added the pragmatic consideration that adequate measures are not yet available. Such a measure would be very useful as one of the several variables discussed later which may help to explain the movements of total factor productivity as we measure it. Those investigators who wish to use it for adjusting capital input should be careful to provide it as a separate component of the input measure, so that its influence may be isolated. It should be noted that the unadjusted capital series generally rise significantly in relation to labor inputs in recession years.

Finally, there is the question of using real gross or net stocks of capital as the appropriate base from which to estimate depreciable capital inputs. In principle, this issue is distinct from the matter of weights—it will be recalled that our basic capital input series incorporate net capital compensation weights, with a variant measure using gross weights that include capital consumption allowances. In the latter measure, we use real gross stocks. That is, the full value of the depreciable capital units at base-period prices are carried until they are discarded from stock. From a productivity standpoint, this implies that their output-producing capacity is maintained over their lifetime. But even with adequate maintenance and repair, it is probable that output-producing capacity of depreciable units does decline somewhat as these age—due to physical deterioration, increased downtime for repair, and creeping obsolescence which may result in shifts of the assets to less productive uses. Under these circumstances, an increase in the average age of depreciable assets would tend to be associated with decreases in productivity, other things being equal, and vice versa. This suggests that a time series on the average age of depreciable assets would be a useful explanatory variable in causal analysis. (See Chapter 4.)

In our basic capital and associated productivity measures, we used real net

---

adjustment; see L. R. Christensen and Dale W. Jorgenson, "U.S. Real Product and Real Factor Input, 1929-1967," Discussion Paper No. 109, Harvard Institute of Economic Research, February 1970.

13 "This list of possible reasons for changes in average machine hours may not be exhaustive. But it suffices to make clear that, unless the reasons for changes in capital utilization are known and their effects can be isolated and quantified, data on capital utilization cannot be integrated into a classification of growth sources of the type Jorgenson and Griliches and I use. It is possible that the entire change indicated by the Jorgenson-Griliches series is already reflected in capital and labor input or counterbalanced by higher maintenance costs, and is not a component of the Jorgenson-Griliches output per unit of input series prior to their utilization adjustment, or of my series." Denison, *Survey of Current Business*, May 1969, Part II, p. 21.

stocks of depreciable units, with consistent net capital compensation weights. Available evidence suggests that a declining balance method of estimating depreciation is appropriate when it is desired to approximate the decline in value of durable goods as they age.[14] But it is not plausible that the output-producing capacity (as distinct from the present value of the future net income stream) declines more in early years than in later years. Accordingly, we have used real net stock estimates for the private economy and the component industries based on straight-line depreciation, as in *Productivity Trends.*

In effect, this means that we have employed a type of "vintage weighting" of depreciable assets. That is, fixed capital goods of different ages are treated as separate goods, with progressively declining price weights for successive age categories. Thus, an increase in the average age of the stock would be reflected in a decline in the ratio of real net stocks to gross stocks, reflecting the probable decline in output-producing capacity, other things being equal.

Actually, even though use of straight-line depreciation means a smaller proportionate decline in net stock in early years and a larger proportionate decline in later years, it probably tends to overstate the overall decline in output-producing capacity of depreciable assets as they age. Goldsmith has suggested that an average of real gross and net stocks is more appropriate for productivity analysis than either separately, and Denison uses a weighted average of real gross and net stocks in his empirical work. We do not make use of such a variant, but since we present both real net and gross capital stock estimates, the reader is enabled to experiment with combinations if he wishes. Actually, the overall net-gross ratios generally have not changed greatly during the period under study. In the private domestic economy as a whole, real net capital stocks and input rose about 3½ per cent more than the real gross capital measure between 1948 and 1966 (see Tables A-19 and A-19a).

Finally, we must stress that the real capital stock and input estimates have not been adjusted for changes in the quality of individual new capital goods as models change. The price deflators result in increases only when the unit real cost of new models increase as compared with the models being supplanted. The productive efficiency of newer models in terms of output-producing capacity may increase considerably more, of course. But as Denison pointed out long ago, to adjust capital outlays, stocks, and inputs for changing productive efficiency would lead to essentially uninteresting results in analy-

[14] See George Terborgh, *Realistic Depreciation Policy*, Chicago, Machinery and Allied Products Institute, 1954.

sis of production and productivity.[15] Measures of the advance in productive knowledge, as embodied in human and nonhuman capital and as reflected in organization of production, would be of great interest, however, as a major force helping to explain productivity advance as we measure it. We refer to preliminary results of experimental measures of this type in Chapter 4.

The real reproducible capital stock estimates for the private domestic business economy, by farm and nonfarm components, are from the Office of Business Economics. Our preferred variant for the depreciable asset component was based on Treasury Bulletin "F" service lives less 15 per cent, the Winfrey S-3 retirement curve, and "constant cost 2," which adjusts the nonfarm construction cost deflator for upward bias; the net stock estimates are those calculated under straight-line depreciation. The trends of these estimates are compared with trends in other variants of the gross and net stock in the appendix (Table A-ii). Since the depreciable stock estimates are obtained by OBE via the perpetual inventory method and their own real gross investment series, they are consistent with the real product estimates. The real private inventory estimates, farm and nonfarm, are also derived from OBE estimates by cumulating the real net changes forward and back from the real inventory stock estimates for the base period. The land estimates are based largely on the estimates and methodology developed by Raymond Goldsmith, as cited in the appendix (p. 159). Despite Goldsmith's ingenuity, due to poverty of basic data, the land series are probably the weakest portion of the capital stock estimates.

The real nonfarm depreciable capital estimates by industry are drawn largely from the work of Daniel Creamer and Michael Gort (see pp. 200-208). Although based on different sources and methods from the aggregate estimates prepared by OBE, they appear to reconcile quite closely (see Table A-xii in the appendix).

Factor Inputs. To obtain factor inputs at constant prices, the hours that tangible stocks are available for use in the various industries are in effect multiplied by base-period average hourly compensation. In the case of labor, man-hours worked by industry are weighted by base-period average hourly labor compensation. Persons engaged in production (comprising all classes of employees, plus proprietors, self-employed, and unpaid family workers) are multiplied by average hours worked per year, by industry. The labor compensation weights include not only wages and salaries but all supplements, as

15 Edward F. Denison, "Theoretical Aspects of Quality Change, Capital Consumption, and Net Capital Formation," *Problems of Capital Formation*, Studies in Income and Wealth, Volume Nineteen, Princeton University Press for NBER, 1957.

estimated by OBE, plus imputed compensation for hours worked by proprietors and unpaid family workers. Industry factor weights are not intended as a means of adjusting for quality, but only as a means of making the business economy measures an internal weighted mean of the component industry measures. As such the labor input estimates reflect interindustry shifts.[16] The weighted man-hour aggregate could alternatively be obtained by deflating labor compensation by a composite variable-man-hour-weighted average hourly compensation index.

The real capital stock estimates are weighted directly by the base-period percentage rates of return in the component sectors. The estimates of capital compensation (interest, net rents and royalties, and profits) are on a before-tax basis, as is labor compensation, and are likewise obtained from the OBE national income accounts. Profits include not only corporate profits but the nonlabor portion of net proprietors' income, estimated as described in the appendix. For our basic capital input measure, capital compensation after capital consumption allowances is related to the real net capital stock. For purposes of weighting real gross capital input to obtain the gross input and productivity variants, gross capital compensation, including depreciation and other capital consumption allowances, is used to obtain the gross rate of return in the base period.

The real capital input estimates so obtained are equivalent to those that might be computed by deflating gross and net capital compensation by indexes of gross and net rental rates. Such price deflators represent a composite of the replacement prices of the underlying capital assets and the net or gross rates of return on the net or gross capital stocks.[17] These rental rates may be construed as an average hourly rental charge for machines or other types of real capital; but since we maintain that, in contrast to labor stocks, capital is in principle available for use throughout the period, we may as well conceive of them as monthly, quarterly, or annual rental rates.

It has been suggested that the asset price indexes should be adjusted for the element that reflects expected capital gains over and above the expected net income stream from use of the assets in production. Since our depreciable asset price indexes represent replacement costs rather than actual market prices, this would not appear to be an appropriate adjustment, even if

---

[16] See p. 157. Interoccupational shifts are not reflected. For a discussion of the latter, see R. L. Raimon and V. Stoikov, "The Quality of the Labor Force," *Industrial and Labor Relations Review*, April 1967, p. 3

[17] See John W. Kendrick and Ryuzo Sato, "Factor Prices, Productivity, and Economic Growth," *American Economic Review*, December 1963, p. 977.

feasible.[18] The asset most likely to be significantly affected by a speculative element in pricing is land. But the estimates used for land values, as described in the appendix, are generally regarded as conservative, and in the present unsatisfactory state of knowledge concerning asset prices, particularly land values, it is not at all certain that the relative prices and price movements reflect a speculative element.

Within the several broad sectors for which separate capital weights are applied, it is assumed that the net rates of return on the various types of assets are the same, so that, in effect, net earnings are assumed to be allocated among them in proportion to base-period net asset values in our basic measures. Griliches and Jorgenson would have used gross capital compensation (rental) weights, and thus would have weighted depreciable assets more heavily than nondepreciable ones. But since our basic measures attempt to relate net output to real factor cost exclusive of nonhuman capital consumption, their procedure would not be appropriate.[19]

When gross capital weights are employed, one might weight the depreciable and nondepreciable assets separately, adding the capital consumption rate to the net capital compensation rates only in the case of the former types of assets. Capital movements would be affected to the extent that capital composition changed. It is uncertain in practice how much difference such an internal weighting scheme would make—it might be significant in agriculture, for example. But since the gross capital and productivity estimates have a subsidiary place in this study, we have not undertaken the lengthy procedure involved in weighting by type of asset within the several sectors.

Total Factor Productivity: Characteristics and Meaning

Total factor productivity may be viewed as the relationship between real product and real tangible factor cost. So expressed, the measures flow directly from the national income and product accounts, in the aggregate and by sector and industry.[20]

18 See Denison, *Survey of Current Business,* May 1969, Part II, pp. 8-9.

19 With regard to this point and some earlier ones, the following statement by Denison (ibid., p. 13) is pertinent: "Jorgenson and Griliches criticize John W. Kendrick for not using service prices as his weights. They are wrong. Kendrick analyzed growth of net product and appropriately used net earnings weights. To include depreciation in the weights in an analysis of the growth of net product, as Jorgenson and Griliches insist he should do, would be a plain error that would lead to overstatement of the contribution of capital to growth. That the other aspect of their service prices—their capital gains and tax adjustment—would have improved his estimates is just not credible on the basis of my preceding discussion."

20 For a discussion of the usefulness of the economic accounts as a framework for productivity measurement and analysis, see my Introduction to *Output, Input, and*

The use of the national income and product accounts as the framework for our output, input, and productivity estimates contributes greatly to the consistency of the estimates. The Department of Commerce economic accounts are used to provide not only weights for outputs and inputs but also the more aggregative output (real product) estimates and important components of the labor and capital input estimates. The scope of the sector and industry output and input estimates is the same; and since income and product are estimated within an accounting framework, the magnitudes of the two sets of estimates are broadly consistent. That is, although the current dollar estimates of income and product are drawn from largely independent sources, the aggregates of each reconcile within relatively small net margins of error, as indicated by the statistical discrepancies. This is true not only with respect to the aggregates but also for the sum of the industry income and product estimates, which represents an alternative statistical approach to obtaining business economy aggregates. Here, again, the statistical discrepancies are not large, indicating broad consistency between the aggregate and industry estimates. Within the industry groupings, too, income and product reconcile closely.

If, as is customary, GNP or NNP estimates at market prices are deflated by market price indexes, the resulting real product estimates may be reduced by the base-period ratio of indirect business taxes less subsidies to gross or net product in order to approximate real product at factor cost, which lends the desirable attribute of equality with real factor cost, gross or net, in the base period. Factor cost or income, after division into the labor and property components, may be deflated by composite price indexes for the labor and capital inputs, as discussed above. To reiterate, the same result is obtained in this study by extrapolating base-period labor and property compensation through the measures of real labor and capital input.

The application of base-period factor compensation weights to factor input units, unadjusted for changes in quality or efficiency, results in productivity ratios with the following general meaning. Real product in the given year indicates what the factor cost requirements would have been assuming the base-period conditions of productive efficiency, compared with what they actually were (given-year real factor cost), reflecting the effects of technological change and other variables affecting productive efficiency. Or, to state the same notion differently, the productivity ratio indicates the relation of real

Productivity Measurement, Studies in Income and Wealth, Vol. 25, Princeton University Press for NBER, 1961. This approach has subsequently been stressed by Z. Griliches and D. Jorgenson, although their suggested deflation procedure differs from mine.

product in the given year to the real product that would have been produced (real factor cost) if the productive efficiency of the factors had been the same in the given year as in the base year.

It may be helpful to look at some of the characteristics of the total factor productivity measures as background for the quantitative analysis of subsequent chapters. Our basic measure of productivity is the index number of the ratio of real product to real factor cost (see Table 2-1, column 3). The index

TABLE 2-1

Private Domestic Business Economy:
Changes in Real Product, Factor Cost, and Productivity, 1958-66

	1958	1966		Average Annual Rates of Change (Per Cent)
	Billions of Dollars	Billions of Dollars	Index, 1958=100	
1. Net product, at factor cost	312.2	519.9	166.5	6.6
2. Implicit product price deflator $(1 \div 3)^b$			110.4	1.2
3. Real product	312.2	471.1^a	150.9	5.3
4. Implicit factor price deflator $(1 \div 5)^b$			138.4	4.2
5. Real factor cost	312.2	375.6^a	120.3	2.3
6. Total factor productivity $(3 \div 5)^b$			125.4	2.9
7. Factor product price ratio $(4 \div 2)^b$			125.4	2.9
8. Productivity increment $(3 - 5)$		95.5^a		

Source: Line 1: U.S. Department of Commerce estimates of national income originating in the private domestic business economy, adjusted as indicated in the appendix (pp. 149-51); line 3: net product (factor income) in 1958 extrapolated to 1966 by the real product estimates underlying Table A-20, less real capital consumption allowances; line 5: Table A-20, index number of total factor input for 1966 (1958=100) applied to base-period factor cost.

^{a} Billions of 1958 dollars.

^{b} This holds for rates of change when 100 is first added to each rate.

number for total factor productivity in 1966 (1958=100) is 125.4, which means an average annual rate of increase of 2.9 per cent (line 6, column 4). This is approximately equal to the difference between the rates of change in real product (5.3 per cent) and in real factor cost (2.3 per cent). Actually, the relationship is multiplicative when 100 is added to each of the percentage rates of change (102.9 × 102.3 = 105.3); but when the rates of change of input and productivity are small, they are additive to the rate of change in real product with ±0.1 per cent.

Note also that since NNP at factor cost and national income are equal in current prices, the total factor productivity ratio must equal the ratio of the factor cost deflator to the product price deflator (column 3: line 4 ÷ line 2 = line 3 ÷ line 5 = line 6 = line 7). Another way of looking at this relation is that factor prices rise by more than product prices to the degree that total factor productivity advances. In fact, this is the means by which the market distributes productivity gains. The relation also indicates that the impact of the rise in factor prices on product prices is mitigated to the degree that productivity advances. None of these statements implies a causal relationship; they all merely verbalize truistic relationships.

A final way in which we may regard productivity advance is as an increment in the given period over and above what real product would have been at base-period efficiency (column 2: line 8 = line 3-5). The increment represents the same per cent increase over base-period real product as is indicated by total factor productivity, of course. But the advantage of calculating a productivity increment in real dollars is that its distribution between the factors of production can be calculated, as was done in *Productivity Trends*. The size of the productivity increment obviously depends on the period chosen as a base for comparing the given period.

3

NATIONAL PRODUCTIVITY TRENDS

This chapter is concerned with productivity trends in the economy as a whole, with particular reference to the post-World War II period 1948 to 1966. For selected measures preliminary extensions of the estimates have been made through 1969. Actually, much of our analysis relates to productivity in the private domestic economy, or the business economy, since adequate output and productivity measures cannot be made yet for general governments, households, nonprofit institutions, and the rest-of-the-world sector. However, with the domestic business sector contributing about 85 per cent of the national product as measured by the U.S. Department of Commerce, business sector productivity is of paramount importance in the national economy as a whole.

National productivity movements are of particular significance. The economy-wide measures are, in effect, weighted averages of productivity in the various component sectors and industries (covered in Chapter 5). They thus provide an overall measure of average changes in productive efficiency, reflecting the net effect of cost-reducing innovations and other forces affecting productivity in all parts of the economy. As such, they afford one approach to the study of the causal factors by time-series analyses that relate aggregate measures of these forces to the overall productivity measures.

The total and partial productivity measures for the economy may also be used effectively in analyzing the macroeconomic impacts of changes in technology and the other forces affecting real unit costs of production. Thus, we can measure the contribution of productivity changes to economic growth and rising planes of living, the relationship between factor prices and product prices, and the stages of price level inflation. Further, the movements of the partial labor and capital productivity ratios, in conjunction with measures of the relative prices of labor and capital, are essential to an analysis of changes in the functional distribution of national income. Finally, while we confine ourselves to an analysis of the U.S. economy here, it should be mentioned that productivity measures are also germane to the comparative study of economic growth among nations.

The Time Frame

Most of the analysis will relate to the period 1948-66, generally in terms of average annual percentage rates of change as computed by the compound-interest formula. Not only is this approach convenient but it permits precise reconciliations between rates of change in productivity and in the output and input components, which is not the case with trend rates computed by fitting time trends to the series by correlation techniques. Also, one can use the compound-interest formula to compute rates of change during subperiods covering complete cycles (measured here from peak to peak) during the period 1948-66, whereas fitted time trends would be inappropriate for the relatively short subperiods.

Yet it is well known that the choice of the first and last years between which the rates of change are computed will affect the result, although the effect will be diminished the more regular the series and the longer the time period. We shall supplement the rates computed under the compound-interest formula with rates obtained by fitting time trends to the logarithms of the series. The trend rates will also be affected by the period chosen, but the influence of the possible deviations from trend of the first and last year's values will be reduced.

Actually, the years 1948 and 1966 were chosen because it was felt that they were broadly comparable. 1948 was a cycle peak and the first full year following World War II without wage and price controls. Although 1966 has not been designated a peak, it was the last year in the long, strong expansion from the trough of 1961 and was followed by a marked retardation of growth, sometimes referred to as the "mini-recession" of 1967. Yet, as we shall see, total factor productivity was a bit below trend in 1948 and above it in 1966. So the rates of increase obtained by the compound-interest formula are slightly higher than the rates obtained from least-squares trend lines.

It may seem that we are unduly concerned with small differences in secular rates of change in productivity that result from a particular choice of methodology, concepts, and time periods. Yet it was not long ago that the secular growth rate in real private product per man-hour, then presumed to be 3.2 per cent per annum, was used by the Council of Economic Advisers as a "guidepost" for noninflationary wage increases. Differences of tenths of a percentage point can be very important, particularly if compounded, when applied to a large base. At the same time, while we present various estimates of rates of change and try to appraise them, we must recognize, in the last analysis, that there is no unique estimate of *the* secular rates of change in an economic time series, though we can frequently obtain a good notion of the order of magnitude of the secular drift. Even the very concept of a secular trend has its limitations, of course, particularly if used as a basis for projection, since the underlying, unmeasured forces are subject to change.

Alternative Segmental Productivity Measures, 1948-66

Rates of change between 1948 and 1966 for three alternative measures of total factor productivity, by major economic segments, are shown in Table 3-1. We concentrate initially on the first column of the table, which relates to our basic productivity measure, in which capital stock is measured net of depreciation and weighted accordingly by various segments of the economy.

The average rate of growth in this basic measure of total factor productivity is 2.0 per cent a year for the total national economy, accounting for about half of overall economic growth. This rate of advance in the total

TABLE 3-1

Major Economic Segments: Alternative Total Factor Productivity Measures, Average Annual Percentage Rates of Change, 1948-66

| | Total Factor Productivity | | |
| | Weighted Inputs | | |
Economic Segment	Net Capital	Gross Capital	Unweighted Inputs[a]
National economy	2.0	1.9	
Adjusted[b]	2.3	2.2	
Private domestic economy	2.5	2.3	2.8
Households and nonprofit institutions	1.0		
Private domestic business economy	2.5	2.3	
Nonfarm	2.4	2.3	

Source: Tables 5-1, A-17, A-19–21, A-17a, A-19a–A-21a, and A-19b.

[a] The aggregate factor input index on which this variant is based does not incorporate industry compensation weights for labor and capital; that is, total man-hours are combined with total real capital, using 1958 shares of factor cost in the private domestic economy as a whole.

[b] In this variant, real government product is obtained by applying a productivity increase of one per cent a year to real factor cost in the public sector.

economy is significantly below that shown for the private domestic economy. The reason for this, as pointed out in Chapter 1, is that OBE estimates real gross product originating in general government (and the small rest-of-the-world sector) without allowance for productivity advance. This downward bias is further accentuated in our estimates by the fact that our real labor input estimates for general government rise a bit more than the OBE real government product estimates, and that we add real capital costs of general governments to both real product and factor input, thereby increasing the relative importance of the public sector.

The treatment of real government product undoubtedly imparts a downward bias to real national product and productivity estimates—there is mounting evidence that productivity does indeed increase in the public sector. A pilot study of productivity in a number of federal government agencies indicated that during the post-World War II period productivity rose but little in three of the agencies, but rose markedly in the other two.[1] Estimates are not available for enough agencies to strike an average, but the implication of significant productivity advance in governments yielded by selected studies is hardly surprising. After all, government agencies have benefited from improved equipment, new management techniques, and other innovations that have raised productivity in the business economy, particularly the services sector. Improved office machines, especially electronic data processing equipment, are a case in point.

Given this evidence and reasoning, we have provided a variant of the national product and productivity estimates for the period 1948-66, in which we impute a productivity-growth factor to obtain an adjusted real product for general governments that raises the growth of overall real national product and productivity.[2] Specifically, we base the adjustment on the trend rate of increase in output per unit of labor input in the services sector, excluding households and nonprofit institutions but including government enterprises, which averaged 1.2 per cent a year during 1948-66 (see Table 5-5 in Chapter 5). We do not have capital and total factor productivity estimates for the services sector; but we assume the same relationship in that sector between growth rates in total factor productivity and labor productivity as in the private domestic economy as a whole. On this basis, the 1.2 per cent is

---

[1] See *Measuring Productivity of Federal Government Organizations*, U.S. Bureau of the Budget, 1965; see also the earlier work by Solomon Fabricant, assisted by Robert E. Lipsey, *The Trend of Government Activity in the United States Since 1900*, National Bureau of Economic Research, 1952.

[2] The need for this type of adjustment was indicated by Victor R. Fuchs, *The Service Economy*, New York, NBER, 1969, pp. 73-74.

reduced to a 1.0 per cent annual adjustment on total factor input. This is cumulated back and forward from the base period (1958) estimate of real factor cost in general government. The difference between adjusted and unadjusted real government product is added to real gross national product as a basis for computing adjusted total factor productivity in the national economy. The adjusted trend rate is 2.3 per cent a year. No adjustment is made for the small item of real product originating in the rest of the world, since this is almost entirely real property compensation, and there has been little net change in "capital productivity" in the postwar period.

The adjusted 2.3 average annual percentage rate is probably a better indication of past and prospective productivity trends in the national economy than the 2.0 per cent national rate. (We use the adjusted estimates for analysis in Chapter 4.) In projections, however, one is generally attempting to approximate changes in the official estimates, in which case the 2.0 per cent rate is more applicable—at least until OBE changes its method.[3] It is even better to project real private product and add on real government product based on the anticipated growth of real factor costs in the public sector.

Table 3-1 distinguishes between the private domestic economy and the business (enterprise) economy, since, as noted earlier, the OBE estimates of real product originating in households and private nonprofit institutions may be subject to a downward bias through time. Actually, the average rates of productivity advance in the private domestic and business sectors during 1948-66 round off alike—2.5 per cent. First, even the OBE real product estimates do imply some increase in productivity in the household and institutions sector—1.0 per cent a year on the average between 1948 and 1966. Second, the sector is small; real product originating there comprised 2.8 per cent of real private product in 1958 and declined to 2.5 per cent in 1966.

In the rest of this chapter we focus on productivity in the private domestic economy, in part because we have a continuous record back to 1889 for historical perspective. The business sector estimates begin in 1929, and we compare the overall productivity estimates for this segment with the industry estimates for the postwar period in Chapters 5 and 6. As a practical matter, however, there is little difference between the productivity estimates for the two sectors.

---

[3] For a suggested modification of the official methodology, see John A. Gorman, "Economic Change as Viewed Through the National Income and Product Accounts: The Implications of an Alternative Deflation Technique," *1969 Proceedings of the Business and Economic Statistics Section,* American Statistical Association, Washington, D.C., 1969, pp. 169-78; and John W. Kendrick, "Discussion," p. 192 of the same volume.

For some purposes, particularly wage analysis, economists are interested in productivity in the nonfarm business sector. As shown in Table 3-1, the rate of productivity advance in this sector averaged 2.4 per cent a year. This rate is slightly smaller than that in the business sector as a whole, reflecting a 3.3 per cent average annual increase in total factor productivity in the farm sector. Further segmentation of the nonfarm business economy by industry divisions and groups is deferred to Chapter 5.

Variant Total Factor Productivity Measures

One variant of total factor productivity referred to earlier is that in which real capital stocks and inputs are measured gross of real capital consumption, and weighted by base-period gross property income for combination with labor input. These variants show average annual growth rates 0.1 or 0.2 percentage points below the net productivity measures for the several segments. (See second column of Table 3-1.) This difference is due to the fact that capital input, which has grown faster than labor input, is accorded a significantly higher relative weight in gross productivity measures. The gross measure is more symmetrical in that the labor weight is also gross of depreciation on human capital. But since that portion of labor compensation promotes welfare whereas intangible capital consumption does not, we consider the net measure to be basic and center most of our analyses around it.

Another variant measure (shown in the third column of Table 3-1) for the private domestic economy is "unweighted productivity." The basic total factor productivity measure incorporates an aggregate of industry labor and capital inputs combined by industry compensation weights. Since there has been a relative shift of both labor and capital inputs towards industries providing higher rates of compensation per unit, weighted input rises by an average of about 0.3 percentage point more per annum than an unweighted input aggregate. Consequently, the unweighted total factor productivity index rises at an average annual rate of 2.8 per cent, compared with 2.5 per cent for the basic measure between 1948 and 1966 in the private domestic economy. We prefer the weighted measure, since in effect it is an internal mean of the component industry productivity measures and hence seems preferable for comparisons with industry measures. The internally weighted productivity index does not reflect the effects of interindustry resource shifts, since the shift effects are absorbed by the input measures. As indicated in the appendix (p. 157), between 1948 and 1966, labor input rose at an average annual rate of 0.4 per cent more than unweighted man-hours, reflecting a relative shift of man-hours to higher-pay industries.

Total and Partial Productivity in the Private Domestic Economy

Now we turn to a more intensive examination of productivity trends in the private domestic economy, looking at the partial productivity ratios as well as total factor productivity. First we examine the compound rates of change between 1948 and 1966 and compare them with growth rates in the earlier periods 1889-1919 and 1919-1948. Then the growth rates for the postwar period based on the compound-interest formula are compared with rates based on fitting trend lines to the logarithms of the time series. (See Table 3-2.) In the case of total factor productivity, we shall later refer to trend lines fitted for segments of the entire period since 1889.

TABLE 3-2

Private Domestic Economy:
Average Annual Percentage Rates of Change
in Output, Inputs, and Productivity Ratios, 1889-1966, by Three Subperiods

	Compound Rates			Trend Rates
	1889 to 1919	1919 to 1948	1948 to 1966	1948 to 1966
Real gross product	3.9	2.8	4.0	3.6
Inputs				
Labor (weighted man-hours)	2.2	0.9	1.0	0.7
Man-hours	1.8	0.6	0.6	0.3
Capital (net)	3.3	1.2	3.5	3.3
Total	2.6	1.0	1.5	1.2
Productivity ratios				
Real product per unit of:				
Labor input	1.6	1.9	3.0	2.9
Man-hours	2.0	2.2	3.4	3.24
Capital	0.5	1.6	0.4	0.3
Total factor input	1.3	1.8	2.5	2.33
Capital-labor input ratio	1.1	0.3	2.5	2.6

Source: Computed from the estimates in Table A-19 and extrapolated from 1929 to 1889 by the series contained in John W. Kendrick, *Productivity Trends in the United States,* Princeton University Press for NBER, 1961, Table A-XXII.

Real gross product, the numerator of the productivity ratios, increased at an average compound rate of 4.0 per cent a year between 1948 and 1966. Total factor input rose at a rate of 1.5 per cent a year—a weighted average of a 1.0 per cent increase in labor input and a 3.5 per cent increase in (net) capital input. Thus, total factor productivity rose by 2.5 per cent a year over the period—a weighted average, in effect, of a 3.0 per cent increase in labor productivity and a 0.4 per cent rise in output per unit of capital input. Real product per man-hour rose at an average annual rate of 3.4 per cent. The 0.4 percentage point difference from output per unit of labor input represents the effect of relative shifts of man-hours from lower-pay to higher-pay industries, which causes labor input (man-hours by industry weighted by base-period average hourly compensation) to rise more than unweighted man-hours.

Looking over the decades before 1948 on Table 3-2, note that real GNP rose at an average annual rate of almost 4 per cent during the years from 1889 to 1919, and advanced at the much lower rate of 2.8 per cent in the 1919-48 period before resuming the 4 per cent trend. But the rates of increase in total factor input dropped even more between the first two periods, so that the growth rate in total factor productivity accelerated from 1.3 per cent a year in the period from 1889 to 1919 to 1.8 per cent during 1919-48, based on the compound-interest formula. From Table 3-2 it would appear that there was a further acceleration during 1948-66. Our subsequent trend analysis indicates, however, that there has been no further acceleration in the growth of total factor productivity since World War I if one abstracts from the effects of the Great Depression.

On the other hand, there has been a progressive acceleration in the rate of increase in output per unit of labor input—from 1.6 to 1.9 and to 3.0 per cent across the three periods shown in the table. The acceleration was reduced between the first two periods by a marked drop in the rate of substitution of capital for labor—from 1.1 to 0.3, as measured by the rate of increase in capital per unit of labor input. But the acceleration between 1919-48 and 1948-66 was accentuated by a pickup in the growth rate of the capital-labor ratio from 0.3 to 2.5 per cent a year, reflecting the high-investment aspect of the economy since World War II. Rates of increase in real product per man-hour showed a similar pattern of acceleration.

Rates of change in output per unit of capital mirror the movements in growth rates of capital. That is, increases of the output-capital ratio in periods before 1919 and after 1948 were around 0.5 per cent a year, reflecting the massive growth of capital. But during 1919-48, the increase averaged 1.6 per cent as the growth rate of capital fell more than that of real product, reflecting lowered investment during the depressed 1930s and World War II.

For the period since 1948, we have also fitted least-squares trend lines to the logs of the output, input, and productivity indexes. For output and all the inputs, the trend rates of increase are somewhat less than the rates computed by the compound-interest formula applied to the first and last years. In other words, the values for output and inputs were below the estimated trend values in 1948 and above them in 1966. But the trend rate for output was farther below the compound rate for output than in the case of inputs, and the trend rates of growth in the productivity ratios were 0.1 or 0.2 less than the compound rates (see Table 3-2). Thus, the trend rate of increase in total factor productivity was 2.33 per cent a year, compared with the 2.5 compound rate. The trend rates for the two partial productivity ratios were 0.1 percentage point less each, while that for real product per man-hour was 3.24 per cent, compared with 3.4 on the compound-interest basis.

Subsequent preliminary estimates for the 1966-69 period suggest that the trend rates may provide a better indication of the secular drift of productivity in the post-World War II period than the 1948-66 compound rates. (See Table 3-3.) That is, an average annual growth rate of 0.9 per cent during 1966-69 in the private domestic economy was less than half the trend rate for 1948-66, and even farther below the compound rate. The mini-recession of 1967, which slowed growth of real product to 2.3 per cent, retarded productivity advance more than proportionately, to 0.8 per cent. The subsequent renewed growth of real product to 5 per cent in 1967-68 produced a respectable increase in total factor productivity of 2.1 per cent. But another significant slowdown in growth of real product in 1968-69 to less than 3 per cent caused a decline in productivity of 0.2 per cent.[4]

Compound rates for the period 1948-69 are thus closer to the trend rates than those for 1948-66 shown in Table 3-2. Also, if one calculated compound rates for the periods of 1946-66, or 1951-66, they would also be 2.3 with respect to total factor productivity—the same as the trend rate—since the values for the initial years 1946 and 1950 were above estimated value, as was true in the terminal year 1966. Rates of change between any pair of years during the period 1916-69 are shown in Table 3-3.

[4] For a discussion of the 1966-70 productivity movements, see John W. Kendrick, "The Productivity Slow-down," *Business Economics*, September 1971. The author has calculated preliminary estimates of rates of change, 1969-72, in total factor productivity and real product per man-hour for industry groups in "U.S. Productivity Trends," *The Conference Board Record*, July 1973.

TABLE 3-3

Private Domestic Economy: Total Factor Productivity,
Average Annual Compound Rates of Growth Between Each Year
and All Succeeding Years, 1916–69

Final Date	Initial Date												
	1916	1917	1918	1919	1920	1921	1922	1923	1924	1925	1926	1927	1928
1917	−5.5												
1918	0.5	6.9											
1919	2.1	6.1	5.4										
1920	1.3	3.6	2.0	−1.2									
1921	2.0	4.0	3.0	1.8	5.0								
1922	1.7	3.2	2.2	1.2	2.5	0.1							
1923	2.3	3.6	3.0	2.4	3.6	3.0	5.9						
1924	2.5	3.7	3.1	2.7	3.7	3.3	4.9	3.9					
1925	2.2	3.2	2.7	2.2	2.9	2.5	3.3	2.0	0.1				
1926	2.2	3.1	2.6	2.2	2.8	2.4	3.0	2.1	1.2	2.3			
1927	2.0	2.8	2.4	2.0	2.5	2.1	2.5	1.6	0.9	1.3	0.4		
1928	1.9	2.6	2.1	1.8	2.2	1.8	2.1	1.3	0.7	0.9	0.2	0.1	
1929	2.0	2.7	2.3	2.0	2.4	2.1	2.4	1.8	1.4	1.7	1.5	2.1	4.2
1930	1.6	2.1	1.7	1.4	1.7	1.3	1.5	0.9	0.4	0.4	−0.0	−0.2	−0.3
1931	1.5	2.0	1.6	1.3	1.6	1.2	1.4	0.8	0.4	0.4	0.1	−0.0	−0.1
1932	1.1	1.6	1.2	0.9	1.1	0.7	0.8	0.2	−0.2	−0.2	−0.7	−0.9	−1.1
1933	1.0	1.4	1.0	0.7	0.9	0.6	0.6	0.1	−0.3	−0.4	−0.7	−0.9	−1.1
1934	1.4	1.8	1.5	1.2	1.4	1.1	1.2	0.8	0.5	0.6	0.4	0.4	0.4
1935	1.6	2.0	1.7	1.5	1.7	1.5	1.6	1.2	1.0	1.1	0.9	1.0	1.1
1936	1.8	2.2	1.9	1.7	1.9	1.7	1.8	1.5	1.3	1.4	1.3	1.4	1.6
1937	1.7	2.1	1.8	1.6	1.8	1.6	1.7	1.4	1.3	1.4	1.3	1.4	1.5
1938	1.7	2.1	1.8	1.6	1.8	1.6	1.7	1.4	1.3	1.4	1.3	1.4	1.5
1939	1.8	2.2	2.0	1.8	2.0	1.8	1.9	1.6	1.5	1.6	1.5	1.6	1.8
1940	1.9	2.2	2.0	1.9	2.0	1.9	2.0	1.7	1.6	1.7	1.7	1.8	1.9
1941	2.0	2.3	2.1	2.0	2.1	2.0	2.1	1.9	1.7	1.9	1.8	1.9	2.1
1942	1.9	2.2	2.0	1.9	2.0	1.9	2.0	1.8	1.7	1.8	1.7	1.8	2.0
1943	1.9	2.2	2.0	1.9	2.0	1.9	2.0	1.8	1.6	1.7	1.7	1.8	1.9
1944	2.0	2.3	2.2	2.0	2.2	2.1	2.2	2.0	1.9	2.0	2.0	2.1	2.2
1945	2.1	2.4	2.3	2.1	2.3	2.2	2.3	2.1	2.0	2.1	2.1	2.2	2.3
1946	1.9	2.2	2.0	1.9	2.0	1.9	2.0	1.8	1.8	1.8	1.8	1.9	2.0
1947	1.8	2.1	1.9	1.8	1.9	1.8	1.9	1.7	1.6	1.7	1.7	1.7	1.8
1948	1.9	2.1	2.0	1.8	2.0	1.8	1.9	1.8	1.7	1.7	1.7	1.8	1.9
1949	1.9	2.1	2.0	1.9	2.0	1.9	1.9	1.8	1.7	1.8	1.8	1.8	1.9
1950	2.0	2.3	2.1	2.0	2.1	2.0	2.1	2.0	1.9	2.0	2.0	2.0	2.1
1951	2.0	2.2	2.1	2.0	2.1	2.0	2.1	1.9	1.9	1.9	1.9	2.0	2.1
1952	1.9	2.2	2.0	1.9	2.0	1.9	2.0	1.9	1.8	1.9	1.8	1.9	2.0
1953	2.0	2.2	2.1	2.0	2.1	2.0	2.0	1.9	1.9	1.9	1.9	2.0	2.0
1954	2.0	2.2	2.1	2.0	2.1	2.0	2.1	1.9	1.9	1.9	1.9	2.0	2.0
1955	2.1	2.3	2.1	2.1	2.1	2.1	2.1	2.0	2.0	2.0	2.0	2.1	2.1
1956	2.0	2.2	2.1	2.0	2.1	2.0	2.1	1.9	1.9	1.9	1.9	2.0	2.0
1957	2.0	2.2	2.1	2.0	2.0	2.0	2.0	1.9	1.9	1.9	1.9	2.0	2.0
1958	2.0	2.2	2.1	2.0	2.1	2.0	2.0	1.9	1.9	1.9	1.9	2.0	2.0
1959	2.0	2.2	2.1	2.0	2.1	2.0	2.1	2.0	1.9	2.0	2.0	2.0	2.1
1960	2.0	2.2	2.1	2.0	2.1	2.0	2.0	1.9	1.9	1.9	1.9	2.0	2.0
1961	2.0	2.2	2.1	2.0	2.1	2.0	2.1	2.0	1.9	2.0	1.9	2.0	2.1
1962	2.1	2.2	2.1	2.1	2.1	2.1	2.1	2.0	2.0	2.0	2.0	2.1	2.1
1963	2.1	2.2	2.1	2.1	2.1	2.1	2.1	2.0	2.0	2.0	2.0	2.1	2.1
1964	2.1	2.3	2.2	2.1	2.2	2.1	2.1	2.1	2.0	2.1	2.1	2.1	2.2
1965	2.1	2.3	2.2	2.1	2.2	2.1	2.2	2.1	2.0	2.1	2.1	2.1	2.2
1966	2.1	2.3	2.2	2.1	2.2	2.1	2.2	2.1	2.0	2.1	2.1	2.1	2.2
1967	2.1	2.2	2.1	2.1	2.1	2.1	2.1	2.0	2.0	2.0	2.0	2.1	2.1
1968	2.1	2.2	2.1	2.1	2.1	2.1	2.1	2.0	2.0	2.1	2.0	2.1	2.1
1969	2.0	2.2	2.1	2.0	2.1	2.1	2.1	2.0	2.0	2.0	2.0	2.0	2.1

(continued)

TABLE 3-3 (continued)

					Initial Date							
1929	1930	1931	1932	1933	1934	1935	1936	1937	1938	1939	1940	1941
−4.6												
−2.1	0.4											
−2.8	−1.9	−4.1										
−2.4	−1.7	−2.7	−1.3									
−0.3	0.8	0.9	3.5	8.5								
0.6	1.7	2.0	4.2	7.0	5.5							
1.2	2.2	2.6	4.3	6.3	5.2	4.9						
1.2	2.0	2.3	3.6	4.9	3.7	2.9	0.8					
1.2	2.0	2.2	3.3	4.2	3.2	2.4	1.2	1.5				
1.6	2.3	2.5	3.5	4.3	3.5	3.0	2.3	3.1	4.7			
1.7	2.4	2.6	3.5	4.2	3.5	3.0	2.6	3.2	4.0	3.3		
1.9	2.5	2.7	3.5	4.1	3.5	3.2	2.9	3.4	4.0	3.6	3.9	
1.8	2.3	2.5	3.2	3.7	3.1	2.8	2.5	2.8	3.1	2.6	2.2	0.5
1.7	2.2	2.4	3.0	3.5	2.9	2.6	2.3	2.5	2.7	2.2	1.8	0.8
2.1	2.5	2.7	3.3	3.7	3.3	3.0	2.8	3.1	3.3	3.1	3.0	2.7
2.2	2.7	2.8	3.4	3.8	3.4	3.2	3.0	3.2	3.5	3.3	3.3	3.1
1.9	2.3	2.4	2.9	3.2	2.8	2.5	2.3	2.5	2.6	2.3	2.1	1.8
1.7	2.1	2.2	2.6	2.9	2.5	2.2	2.0	2.1	2.1	1.8	1.6	1.2
1.7	2.1	2.2	2.6	2.9	2.5	2.3	2.0	2.2	2.2	2.0	1.8	1.5
1.8	2.1	2.2	2.6	2.9	2.5	2.3	2.1	2.2	2.3	2.0	1.9	1.6
2.0	2.4	2.5	2.8	3.1	2.8	2.6	2.4	2.5	2.6	2.4	2.4	2.2
2.0	2.3	2.4	2.7	3.0	2.7	2.5	2.3	2.4	2.5	2.3	2.2	2.1
1.9	2.2	2.3	2.6	2.8	2.5	2.3	2.2	2.3	2.3	2.1	2.1	1.9
2.0	2.2	2.3	2.6	2.8	2.6	2.4	2.3	2.3	2.4	2.2	2.2	2.0
2.0	2.2	2.3	2.6	2.8	2.5	2.4	2.3	2.3	2.4	2.2	2.2	2.0
2.1	2.3	2.4	2.7	2.9	2.6	2.5	2.4	2.5	2.5	2.4	2.3	2.2
2.0	2.2	2.3	2.6	2.8	2.5	2.4	2.2	2.3	2.4	2.2	2.1	2.0
1.9	2.2	2.3	2.5	2.7	2.4	2.3	2.2	2.3	2.3	2.2	2.1	2.0
2.0	2.2	2.3	2.5	2.7	2.4	2.3	2.2	2.3	2.3	2.2	2.1	2.0
2.0	2.2	2.3	2.6	2.7	2.5	2.4	2.2	2.3	2.3	2.2	2.2	2.1
2.0	2.2	2.3	2.5	2.6	2.4	2.3	2.2	2.3	2.3	2.2	2.1	2.0
2.0	2.2	2.3	2.5	2.6	2.4	2.3	2.2	2.3	2.3	2.2	2.1	2.0
2.1	2.3	2.3	2.6	2.7	2.5	2.4	2.3	2.3	2.4	2.3	2.2	2.2
2.1	2.3	2.3	2.6	2.7	2.5	2.4	2.3	2.4	2.4	2.3	2.2	2.2
2.1	2.3	2.4	2.6	2.7	2.5	2.4	2.3	2.4	2.4	2.3	2.3	2.2
2.1	2.3	2.4	2.6	2.7	2.5	2.4	2.3	2.4	2.4	2.3	2.3	2.2
2.1	2.3	2.4	2.6	2.7	2.5	2.4	2.3	2.4	2.4	2.3	2.3	2.2
2.1	2.3	2.3	2.5	2.6	2.4	2.4	2.3	2.3	2.3	2.3	2.2	2.2
2.1	2.3	2.3	2.5	2.6	2.4	2.4	2.3	2.3	2.4	2.3	2.2	2.2
2.0	2.2	2.3	2.4	2.6	2.4	2.3	2.2	2.3	2.3	2.2	2.2	2.1

(continued)

TABLE 3-3 (continued)

Final Date	Initial Date												
	1942	1943	1944	1945	1946	1947	1948	1949	1950	1951	1952	1953	195
1917													
1918													
1919													
1920													
1921													
1922													
1923													
1924													
1925													
1926													
1927													
1928													
1929													
1930													
1931													
1932													
1933													
1934													
1935													
1936													
1937													
1938													
1939													
1940													
1941													
1942													
1943	1.2												
1944	3.8	6.5											
1945	4.0	5.5	4.5										
1946	2.1	2.4	0.4	−3.5									
1947	1.4	1.4	−0.2	−2.5	−1.5								
1948	1.6	1.7	0.6	−0.7	0.7	3.0							
1949	1.8	1.9	1.0	0.1	1.4	2.8	2.6						
1950	2.4	2.6	2.0	1.4	2.7	4.2	4.7	6.9					
1951	2.2	2.4	1.8	1.3	2.3	3.3	3.4	3.8	0.9				
1952	2.0	2.1	1.6	1.2	2.0	2.7	2.6	2.6	0.5	0.2			
1953	2.1	2.2	1.8	1.4	2.2	2.8	2.7	2.8	1.4	1.7	3.3		
1954	2.2	2.2	1.8	1.5	2.2	2.7	2.7	2.7	1.6	1.9	2.8	2.3	
1955	2.3	2.4	2.1	1.8	2.4	2.9	2.9	3.0	2.2	2.6	3.4	3.4	4.
1956	2.1	2.2	1.9	1.6	2.2	2.6	2.5	2.5	1.8	2.0	2.4	2.1	2.
1957	2.1	2.2	1.8	1.6	2.1	2.4	2.4	2.4	1.7	1.9	2.2	1.9	1.
1958	2.1	2.2	1.9	1.7	2.1	2.4	2.4	2.3	1.8	1.9	2.2	2.0	1.
1959	2.2	2.2	2.0	1.8	2.2	2.5	2.5	2.4	2.0	2.1	2.4	2.2	2.
1960	2.1	2.2	1.9	1.7	2.1	2.4	2.3	2.3	1.9	2.0	2.2	2.1	2.
1961	2.1	2.2	1.9	1.8	2.1	2.4	2.3	2.3	1.9	2.0	2.2	2.1	2.
1962	2.2	2.3	2.1	1.9	2.3	2.5	2.5	2.5	2.1	2.2	2.4	2.3	2.
1963	2.3	2.3	2.1	2.0	2.3	2.5	2.5	2.5	2.2	2.3	2.5	2.4	2.
1964	2.3	2.3	2.1	2.0	2.3	2.6	2.5	2.5	2.2	2.3	2.5	2.4	2.
1965	2.3	2.4	2.2	2.0	2.3	2.6	2.6	2.6	2.3	2.4	2.5	2.5	2.
1966	2.3	2.3	2.2	2.0	2.3	2.5	2.5	2.5	2.2	2.3	2.5	2.4	2.
1967	2.2	2.3	2.1	2.0	2.2	2.4	2.4	2.4	2.1	2.2	2.4	2.3	2.
1968	2.2	2.3	2.1	2.0	2.3	2.4	2.4	2.4	2.2	2.2	2.4	2.3	2.
1969	2.2	2.2	2.0	1.9	2.2	2.3	2.3	2.3	2.1	2.1	2.3	2.2	2.

(continued)

TABLE 3-3 (concluded)

						Initial Date							
1955	1956	1957	1958	1959	1960	1961	1962	1963	1964	1965	1966	1967	1968
0.4													
0.5	1.3												
1.1	1.8	2.3											
1.6	2.3	2.8	3.4										
1.5	2.0	2.3	2.2	1.1									
1.7	2.1	2.3	2.3	1.7	2.3								
2.0	2.5	2.7	2.8	2.6	3.3	4.4							
2.1	2.5	2.7	2.7	2.6	3.1	3.5	2.6						
2.2	2.6	2.7	2.8	2.7	3.1	3.3	2.8	3.1					
2.3	2.6	2.7	2.8	2.7	3.0	3.2	2.8	3.0	2.9				
2.2	2.5	2.6	2.7	2.6	2.8	2.9	2.6	2.6	2.4	1.9			
2.1	2.3	2.4	2.5	2.3	2.5	2.5	2.2	2.1	1.8	1.3	0.8		
2.1	2.4	2.4	2.5	2.4	2.5	2.5	2.2	2.2	1.9	1.6	1.5	2.1	
2.0	2.2	2.2	2.2	2.0	2.2	2.1	1.8	1.7	1.5	1.1	0.9	0.9	-0.2

Source: Table A-19 productivity index numbers extrapolated from 1929 to 1916 by series in *Productivity Trends*, Table A-XXII.

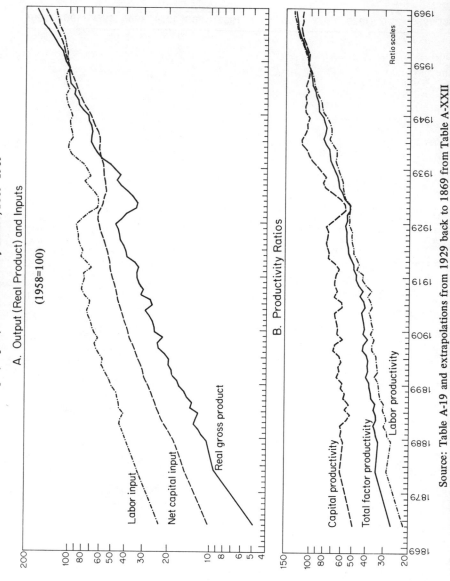

Chart 3-1: A Century of Economic Growth—U.S. Private Domestic Economy: Output, Inputs, and Productivity Ratios, 1869–1969[a]

A. Output (Real Product) and Inputs

(1958=100)

Labor input

Net capital input

Real gross product

B. Productivity Ratios

Capital productivity

Total factor productivity

Labor productivity

Ratio scales

Source: Table A-19 and extrapolations from 1929 back to 1869 from Table A-XXII of *Productivity Trends*

Chart 3-1 contains index numbers of total factor productivity and related series in the private domestic economy for the period 1869-1969 (the pre-1889 period is based on decade averages). Careful inspection of the time series on total factor productivity in panel B yields a number of interesting observations. First, there appears to have been an important change in trend during World War I, as noted in *Productivity Trends.* In that work, we fitted the new and steeper trend line to estimates beginning with 1919. But here we have chosen 1916 as the dividing year. Rates of advance between the peak years 1913 and 1916 are in line with those of the earlier period 1889-1916, while the rate between the peaks of 1916 and 1919 is in line with that of the subsequent period. The average rate of advance for the early period 1889-1916 is 1.0 per cent a year; the comparable rate for the subsequent period 1916-29 accelerates to 2.3 per cent (see Table 3-4).

It is possible to fit a trend line to the annual estimates for the entire half-century 1916-66.[5] But close inspection of the data reveals that the trend was seriously interrupted by the major depression of the early 1930s. The productivity peak of 1929 was not exceeded until 1935. Beginning in 1936, the former trend rate of 1916-29 was resumed, although at a slightly lower level, and it continued without apparent change for the subsequent three decades through 1966. The downward shift of the trend line between 1929 and 1936 is not surprising in view of the severe drop in tangible and intangible investment, entailing a loss of productive capacity and efficiency that could never be fully made up.

The trend rate of advance for the period 1936-66 averaged 2.3 per cent a year—very close to that for the earlier period 1916-29, prior to the interruption of the Great Depression. If the trend line is fitted to the postwar period 1948-66, the slope is also 2.3 per cent, exactly the same as that for the thirty-year period 1936-66, and the coefficient of correlation is also very high—0.993 as compared with 0.994. The same rates of growth are obtained using productivity estimates for the business economy alone.

When estimates for total gross factor productivity are used, the trend rates are 0.24 per cent less, reflecting the use of gross capital inputs and correspondingly higher capital weights. When unweighted factor inputs are used, the trend rates for 1948-66 are about 0.3 per cent greater, since the shift effect shows up in the productivity rather than the input measures.

Whether the trend is fitted to the thirty-year period beginning in 1936 or the eighteen-year period beginning 1948, total factor productivity in 1948 is

[5] The indicated average annual rate of increase is 2.1 per cent for 1916-66.

TABLE 3-4

Private Domestic Economy:
Trend Rates of Growth in Variant Measures
of Total Factor Productivity,
Selected Periods,[a] 1889-1966

	Time Trend Only		Time Trend plus Ratio of Employment to Civilian Labor Force	
	Per Cent Growth Rate	Coefficient of Correlation	Growth Rate	Coefficient of Correlation
Total net factor productivity				
1889-1916	1.03	.935	0.98	.955
1916-1966	2.06	.990	2.02	.996
1916-1929	2.29	.966	2.29	.966
1936-1966	2.33	.994	2.18	.994
1948-1966	2.33	.993	2.36	.993
Total net unweighted factor productivity				
1916-1966	2.2	.969		
1936-1966	2.7	.994		
1948-1966	2.6	.992		
Total gross factor productivity				
1936-1966	2.09	.993		
1948-1966	2.09	.991		

Source: Table A-19, A-19a, and A-19b; extrapolations back to 1889 via Table A-XXII in *Productivity Trends*.

[a] The straight-line time trends were fitted to the logarithms of the productivity measures for the years indicated.

below the trend value. This explains the fact that the average annual rate of productivity advance between 1948 and 1966 is 2.5 per cent, compared with the 2.33 per cent average rate based on the least-squares trend line. We believe that the latter gives the best measure of the long-run trend prevailing during the postwar period. But due to its convenience for comparisons with sub-period rates and with rates for outputs and inputs, we shall use the 2.5 per cent figure as the standard of comparison in subsequent sections.

An alternative method of trend fitting was also tried, with results quite similar to those already cited. In addition to using a time trend, we added a cyclical variable, the ratio of employment to civilian labor force, which would tend to reduce the trend rate of growth. The indicated productivity growth rate for the half-century period 1916-66 was 2.02, compared with 2.06 yielded by use of time trend alone, and the coefficient of (multiple) correlation was higher, 0.996 compared with 0.990, reflecting the fact that productivity had a cyclical element, particularly during the Great Depression. The correlation coefficient differed insignificantly in the periods beginning 1936 and 1948, however.

But the indicated trend rates are somewhat different in the latter periods when multiple correlations are used in place of the simple time trend. For 1936-66 the growth rate obtained by the former approach is 2.18, compared with 2.33 by the latter, and for 1948-66 it is 2.36 as against 2.33. Thus, addition of a cyclical variable suggests a slight acceleration of productivity growth since 1948 compared with the results shown by the simple trend rate. But both approaches yield a lower trend rate for 1948-66 than that obtained by the compound-interest formula.

Variations in Growth Rates

The time path of growth seldom runs smoothly. To abstract from the effects of the business cycle, we have computed average annual percentage rates of change in real product and productivity ratios between annual cycle peaks, as designated by the National Bureau of Economic Research (see Table 3-5). Although 1966 is not officially a peak year, it did precede a marked slowdown of activity in 1967, so we feel it is not inappropriate to use the period 1960-66 for obtaining rates of change for comparison with earlier peak-to-peak changes.

Total factor productivity showed a high rate of growth in the first subperiod 1948-53, a marked slowdown in the subsequent two subperiods between 1953 and 1960, and a resumption of strong advance in 1960-66, followed by a marked retardation in the subperiod 1966-69 (not shown in the table). Output per unit of labor input (and per man-hour) exhibited much the same patterns of change, although the rate of increase in the last of the four subperiods was less than in the first. The pattern of peak-to-peak changes in output per unit of capital input was quite different. There was little change in this ratio from 1948 to 1960, as the real stock of tangible capital was expanded at much the same rate as output. Between 1960 and 1966, however, output went ahead significantly faster than the capital stock, and the ratio rose at an average annual rate of 1.7 per cent. This contributed

TABLE 3-5

Private Domestic Economy:
Average Annual Percentage Rates of Change in Real
Product and the Productivity Ratios, by Cycle Subperiods, 1946-67

A. Peak to Peak

	1948-66	1948-53	1953-57	1957-60	1960-66
Real gross product	4.0	4.6	2.5	2.6	5.2
Total factor productivity	2.5	2.7	1.9	2.2	2.8
Real product per unit of					
Labor input	3.0	3.5	2.6	2.7	3.1
Man-hours (unweighted)	3.4	4.2	2.7	2.6	3.6
Capital input	0.4	0.2	−1.1	0.2	1.7

B. Cycle Average to Cycle Average

	1946-49 to 1961-67	1946-49 to 1949-54	1949-54 to 1954-58	1954-58 to 1958-61	1958-61 to 1961-67
Real gross product	3.8	4.4	3.3	2.6	4.8
Total factor productivity	2.4	2.7	2.2	2.0	2.7
Real product per unit of					
Labor input	3.0	3.4	2.8	2.5	3.0
Capital input	0.3	0.1	−0.5	−0.3	1.6

Source: Tables A-19 and A-19b.

significantly to the resumption of a strong advance in total factor productivity. It should be noted that much of the advance in "capital productivity" was due to increasing utilization of capacity.[6] If capital stock is adjusted for utilization rates, little movement is seen in the output-capital ratio over the entire period 1948-66.

This brings up the interrelationship between subperiod rates of change in output and in productivity, apart from cycle changes. As can be seen in Table 3-5, real product likewise showed a strong rate of advance in 1948-53, retardation in the two following subperiods, and the strongest growth rate of all after 1960—reflecting acceleration in underlying secular demographic forces, as well as increased rates of capacity utilization. We shall discuss the

[6] According to estimates by the Federal Reserve Board, the rate of utilization of manufacturing capacity increased from 81 per cent in 1960 to 90 per cent in 1966. For earlier years, see *Federal Reserve Bulletin,* July 1967.

apparent correlation between rates of change in output and in productivity further when we look at a longer time span.

Another way of measuring subperiod changes, abstracting from the business cycle, is to average the various time series over completed cycles and compute rates of change from cycle average to cycle average. For present purposes, we average the annual observations from trough to trough of each cycle as a basis for calculating intercycle rates of change. The patterns are quite similar to those based on peak-to-peak rates of change. (See part B of Table 3-5.)

Variations in rates of change in output, input, and productivity have been a normal aspect of economic growth. This can be seen clearly in the following tables, which show rates of change from peak to peak since 1890 (Table 3-6) and from cycle average to cycle average since the 1888-91 cycle (Table 3-7). The sometimes wavelike movements in these rates of change have earned them the appellation of "trend cycles," or "long swings." The long swing is being studied intensively by Abramovitz, and we shall make only a few general observations here with particular reference to productivity.[7]

In the first place, it is clear that intercycle growth rates have been steadier since World War II than in earlier periods. (See Chart 3-2.) Both sets of measures for real product and total factor productivity show a significantly lower average deviation from the mean rates of growth in the period since 1948 (or 1946-49) than over the entire period since 1890 (or 1888-91). The average deviation in the postwar period is significantly lower, not only absolutely but also as a per cent of the mean growth rate. (See parts B of Tables 3-6 and 3-7.) In the case of real product, the mean deviation is significantly higher in the middle of the three subperiods delineated— 1918-48 (in Table 3-6), and 1914-19 to 1946-49 (in Table 3-7)—reflecting the effects of major depression and war. In the case of total factor productivity, the average deviation falls progressively over the three periods when rates of change are calculated from peak to peak; it rises in the middle period when calculated on a cycle-average basis, although as a percentage of the mean growth rate it is about the same as in the early period. In general, rates of growth are somewhat more stable between cycle averages than between cycle peaks. On both bases, average deviations from mean growth rates for each partial productivity ratio are also lowest in the last period. There is greater variation throughout in rates of change in the output-capital ratio, reflecting the fixed nature of capital as we measure it.

[7] See Moses Abramovitz, *Evidences of Long Swings in Aggregate Construction Since the Civil War*, Occasional Paper 90, New York, NBER, 1964.

TABLE 3-6

Private Domestic Economy:
Output, Inputs, and Productivity Ratios,
Average Annual Percentage Rates of Change Between Cycle Peaks

A. *Change from Previous to Current Peak*

Cycle Peak Years	Real Product	Factor Inputs			Productivity Ratios		
		Total	Labor	Capital	Total	Labor	Capital
(1890)							
1892	7.0	4.2	3.5	5.8	2.7	3.4	1.1
1895	1.3	1.4	0.3	4.0	-0.1	1.0	-2.6
1899	4.7	3.2	3.2	3.2	1.5	1.4	1.5
1903	4.9	4.0	4.1	3.7	0.9	0.8	1.2
1907	4.8	2.9	2.8	3.4	1.8	2.0	1.4
1910	1.3	1.8	1.4	2.8	-0.5	-0.1	-1.5
1913	4.4	2.5	2.4	2.9	1.8	2.0	1.4
1918	2.5	1.8	1.6	2.5	0.6	0.9	0.0
1920	1.8	-0.2	-1.2	2.3	2.0	3.0	-0.4
1923	5.4	1.8	1.9	1.4	3.6	3.5	3.9
1926	3.9	1.9	1.6	2.7	2.0	2.3	1.1
1929	2.8	1.3	0.8	2.6	1.5	1.9	0.3
1937	-0.4	-1.5	-1.7	-1.0	1.1	1.3	0.6
1944	6.2	3.1	3.7	1.1	3.0	2.4	5.1
1948	1.1	0.6	-0.1	3.1	0.5	1.2	-2.0
1953	4.6	1.8	1.1	4.3	2.7	3.5	0.2
1957	2.5	0.6	-0.1	3.7	1.9	2.6	-1.1
1960	2.6	0.4	-0.1	2.4	2.2	2.7	0.2
1966	5.2	2.3	2.0	3.4	2.8	3.1	1.7

(continued)

TABLE 3-6 (concluded)

B. Averages of Peak-to-Peak Rates of Change,[a] with Mean Deviations, by Three Subperiods

Period	Real Product	Factor Inputs			Productivity Ratios		
		Total	Labor	Capital	Total	Labor	Capital
1890-1966:							
Rate	3.5	1.8	1.4	2.9	1.7	2.0	0.6
Average deviation	1.7	1.0	1.3	0.9	0.8	0.8	1.3
1890-1918:							
Rate	3.9	2.7	2.4	3.5	1.1	1.4	0.3
Average deviation	1.6	0.9	1.0	0.7	0.9	0.8	1.3
1918-1948:							
Rate	3.0	1.0	0.7	1.7	2.0	2.2	1.2
Average deviation	1.9	1.2	1.5	1.1	0.8	0.7	1.9
1948-1966:							
Rate	3.7	1.3	0.7	3.4	2.4	3.0	0.2
Average deviation	1.2	0.8	0.8	0.6	0.4	0.3	0.7

Source: Table A-19; extrapolations back to 1890 via Table A-XXII in *Productivity Trends*.

[a] Unweighted averages of rates of change shown in corresponding periods in part A.

TABLE 3-7

Private Domestic Economy:
Output, Inputs, and Productivity Ratios,
Average Annual Percentage Rates of Change Between Cycle Averages, 1888-1967

A. Change from Previous to Current Cycle Average

Cycle Years	Real Product	Factor Inputs			Productivity Ratios		
		Total	Labor	Capital	Total	Labor	Capital
(1888-91)							
1891-94	4.2	3.0	2.2	5.1	1.2	2.0	-0.9
1894-96	2.0	1.6	0.5	4.2	0.2	1.3	-2.2
1896-1900	5.4	3.2	3.3	3.3	2.1	2.1	2.0
1900-04	5.3	3.9	4.1	3.4	1.4	1.2	1.9
1904-08	4.0	3.0	2.8	3.4	1.0	1.2	0.6
1908-11	3.0	2.4	2.1	3.1	0.6	0.9	-0.2
1911-14	3.3	2.6	2.5	2.9	0.7	0.8	0.5
1914-19	2.6	1.8	1.4	2.5	0.8	1.1	0.0
1919-21	2.8	0.2	-0.7	2.3	2.7	3.6	0.5
1921-24	4.2	1.2	1.1	1.6	2.8	2.9	2.5
1924-27	5.2	2.9	3.1	2.4	2.3	2.1	2.8
1927-32	-0.1	-0.4	-1.3	2.1	0.3	1.2	-2.1
1932-38	-1.4	-2.5	-2.9	-1.3	1.1	1.5	-0.1
1938-46	6.4	3.1	3.9	0.7	3.1	2.4	5.5
1946-49	3.2	1.8	1.6	2.2	1.5	1.6	1.1
1949-54	4.4	1.7	0.9	4.3	2.7	3.4	0.1
1954-58	3.3	1.1	0.4	3.8	2.2	2.8	-0.5
1958-61	2.6	0.6	0.0	2.9	2.0	2.6	-0.3
1961-67	4.8	2.0	1.7	3.1	2.7	3.0	1.6

TABLE 3-7 (concluded)

B. *Averages of Rates of Change Between Cycle Averages,*
with Mean Deviations 1888-91 to 1961-67,
by Three Subperiods

Period	Real Product	Factor Inputs			Productivity Ratios		
		Total	Labor	Capital	Total	Labor	Capital
1888-91 to 1961-67:							
Rate	3.4	1.7	1.4	2.8	1.7	2.0	0.6
Average deviation	1.4	1.1	1.4	0.9	0.8	0.7	1.4
1888-91 to 1914-19:							
Rate	3.7	2.7	2.4	3.5	1.0	1.3	0.2
Average deviation	1.0	0.6	0.8	0.6	0.4	0.4	1.0
1914-19 to 1946-49:							
Rate	2.9	0.9	0.7	1.4	2.0	2.2	1.5
Average deviation	2.1	1.5	2.0	1.0	0.9	0.7	1.8
1946-49 to 1961-67:							
Rate	3.8	1.4	0.8	3.5	2.4	3.0	0.2
Average deviation	0.8	0.5	0.5	0.5	0.3	0.3	0.7

Source: Table A-19; extrapolations back to 1888 via Table A-XXII in *Productivity Trends.*

Chart 3-2: Long Swings in Economic Growth—U.S. Private Domestic Economy:
Average Annual Rates of Change in Real Product, Total Factor
Input, and Productivity Between Cycle Averages, 1881–91 to 1961–67

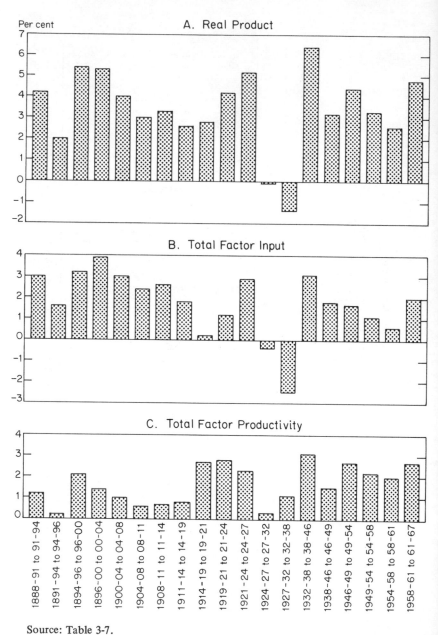

Source: Table 3-7.

The tables indicate a definite correlation between rates of change in real product (X) and in total factor productivity (Y) across cycles. In most (but not all) subperiods, the two variables move in the same direction. Using rates of change from peak to peak, the coefficient of correlation is 0.71, significant at the 0.05 level, and the estimating equation is $Y = 1.2610 + 1.3948\ X$. Using rates of change based on cycle averages, the coefficient of correlation is 0.58, and the estimating equation is $Y = 1.4064 + 1.2082\ X$.

The interaction between rates of change in real product and in productivity reflects a number of forces. To the extent that a larger than average growth in demand from one cycle to another raises utilization of productive capacity closer to an optimum rate, productivity advance would be favorably affected. Apart from the capacity utilization effect, greater increases in demand and output could lead to larger-scale economies than those accompanying smaller output increases. Conversely, greater productivity growth would contribute to larger output increases, assuming sufficient demand and the same rates of increase in real input. Some of the indicated correlations may be spurious, of course, to the extent that there are errors in the output measures. One could get away from the possibly spurious element in the output-productivity relation by narrowing the focus to correlations between rates of change in total factor productivity and rates of capacity utilization. Such correlations may be expected to have lower coefficients than those relating productivity to output, since changes in utilization rates are only one element in the latter relationship.

Variations in Annual Changes

The average deviations of annual percentage changes in productivity from trend rates are much bigger than average deviations of intercycle changes from their means. As shown in Table 3-8, the mean deviation of annual per cent changes in total factor productivity from the average per cent change of 1.8 over the entire period 1889-1966 is 2.7. This compares to an average deviation of 0.8 for intercycle average annual per cent changes from their means (see Table 3-6). The degree of variability in intercycle and annual changes in total factor productivity is quite similar to that in real product relative to its average rates of change.

The large variations in annual changes in real product and productivity reflect primarily the annual changes in demand and capacity utilization. They may also reflect some variations in the underlying forces of technological

TABLE 3-8

Private Domestic Economy:
Output, Inputs, and Productivity Ratios,
Mean Average Annual Percentage Rates of Change, 1889-1966,
by Subperiods and by Business Cycle Phase

Period	Real Product	Factor Inputs			Productivity Ratios		
		Total	Labor	Capital	Total	Labor	Capital
A. All Years							
1889-1966							
Rate	3.7	1.8	1.6	2.6	1.8	2.1	1.1
Average deviation	4.7	3.0	3.8	1.4	2.7	2.5	4.7
1889-1916							
Rate	4.2	2.8	2.6	3.5	1.3	1.5	0.8
Average deviation	5.2	2.3	3.2	0.8	3.3	2.7	5.1
1917-47							
Rate	3.1	0.9	0.9	1.2	2.1	2.2	2.0
Average deviation	5.4	4.2	5.4	1.9	2.9	2.8	5.5
1948-66							
Rate	4.0	1.5	1.0	3.6	2.5	3.0	0.5
Average deviation	2.8	2.0	2.4	0.9	1.2	1.2	2.6

B. Expansions

1889-1966 (54)[a]							
Rate	6.3	3.6	3.9	2.7	2.6	2.3	3.6
Average deviation	3.3	1.8	2.5	1.4	2.5	2.4	3.7
1889-1916 (18)							
Rate	7.4	4.2	4.6	3.3	3.0	2.7	3.9
Average deviation	4.1	1.6	2.2	0.8	2.8	2.7	4.0
1917-47 (20)							
Rate	6.6	3.7	4.6	1.3	2.7	1.9	5.4
Average deviation	3.2	2.5	3.3	1.9	2.7	2.4	3.6
1948-66 (14)							
Rate	5.3	2.7	2.4	3.8	2.5	2.8	1.5
Average deviation	2.1	1.0	1.3	0.9	1.5	1.4	2.3

C. Contractions

1889-1966 (23)							
Rate	−2.5	−2.4	−4.0	2.4	−0.1	1.6	−4.8
Average deviation	3.9	2.9	3.5	1.4	3.0	3.0	3.2
1889-1916 (9)							
Rate	−2.0	0.1	−1.3	3.7	−2.2	−0.8	−5.6
Average deviation	3.9	1.9	2.6	0.8	2.9	2.6	3.6
1917-47 (10)							
Rate	−3.8	−4.6	−6.5	1.1	0.8	2.9	−4.9
Average deviation	4.6	3.4	4.1	1.7	3.2	3.4	3.6
1948-66 (4)							
Rate	−0.3	−2.6	−3.9	2.9	2.3	3.7	−3.1
Average deviation	1.0	1.0	1.3	0.7	0.1	0.4	1.2

Source: Table A-19; extrapolations back to 1889 via Table A-XXII in *Productivity Trends*.
[a] Figures in parentheses indicate the number of per cent changes averaged for period. Two expansions (1916-17 and 1947-48) are included in the period 1889-1966 under A. and B., but not in subperiods.

progress, which are themselves influenced by variations in demand, particularly for investment goods and services. In addition, there are some erratic forces at work that have a different impact from year to year, as well as errors in the estimates, which, in all probability, also exert a significant influence.

When one correlates annual per cent changes in total factor productivity (Y) and in real product (X), the coefficient of correlation is 0.77, and the estimating equation is $Y = 1.2045 + 1.3460\ X$. The fit is better than in the correlation between peak-to-peak rates of change, which is not surprising in view of the greater influence of changes in rates of capacity utilization on year-to-year changes in productivity. It is noteworthy that the regression coefficients are quite similar on both bases. The correlation between annual per cent changes in total factor productivity and in employment is not significant at the 0.05 level.

It is important to observe that average variations in annual productivity changes have become substantially narrower over the period studied. Thus, the average deviation dropped from 3.3 in the period 1889-1916 to 2.9 in 1917-47, and to 1.2 in 1948-66. The decline is much more pronounced when the average deviation is computed as a ratio to the mean per cent change in productivity, since the rate of productivity advance rose over the three periods. The average deviation in real product annual changes did not drop between the first two periods. Over 1948-66, however, it was substantially smaller, although larger relative to the mean per cent change than was true of productivity in the postwar period.

The relatively low variability of annual productivity changes in the period 1948-66 reflects in part the lessened variability in demand and real product. But it also reflects the gradual strengthening in the forces promoting technological advance. In the next chapter we shall see the substantial absolute and relative growth in research and development, as well as education and training, since the 1920s, indicating the growing institutionalization of cost-reducing innovation. Our interpretation is further supported by the fact that the average deviation of annual productivity changes from their mean fell between 1889-1916 and 1917-47 even in the face of an increase in the mean deviation of real product changes relative to their mean.

Annual variability of per cent changes in output per unit of labor input is somewhat less than that in total factor productivity, particularly in relation to mean changes. The variability of annual changes in output per unit of capital input is much larger than that in either one of the other two productivity measures. This reflects the relatively "fixed" nature of capital as we measure it; abstracting from the secular trend in the output-capital ratios, annual changes in the ratio closely parallel changes in output itself.

During the years of business cycle expansion over the 1889-1966 period, percentage changes in total factor productivity averaged 2.6 per cent, but during the years of contraction, the average change was -0.1 per cent. (See parts B and C of Table 3-8.) In the early period 1889-1916, the average change during contractions was -2.2 per cent. During the middle period, 1917-47, the average change was a positive 0.8, and in the postwar period, it was 2.3 per cent, not far below the 2.5 per cent average increase of the expansion years, despite a small average decline in real product in the contractions. In the early period, the average increase during expansions was even sharper, 3.0 per cent, reflecting the rebounds following the declines during contractions.

The mean deviations from average annual per cent changes were slightly higher during contractions than during expansions, with the exception of the last period, 1948-66, when the average deviation from the mean increase during contractions was very small.

The average change in output per unit of labor input in contraction years was 1.6 per cent, compared with 2.3 per cent during expansions. The average changes in labor productivity in the contraction increased successively throughout the three periods.

As would be expected, output per unit of capital input showed large increases during expansions, averaging 3.6 for the seventy-seven-year period, and large decreases during contractions, averaging -4.8 per cent. The increases and decreases were smallest during the final period, 1948-66, reflecting the lessened variability in output itself.

In summary, it is clear that the degree of variability in productivity advance from year to year, as well as from cycle to cycle, has been significantly reduced since World War II. In part, it reflects a strengthening of the forces promoting cost-reducing innovations, and in part, the more stable rate of economic growth.

4

NATIONAL PRODUCTIVITY
AND ECONOMIC GROWTH

Here we focus our attention on the relative contribution of total factor input and productivity to economic growth in the national economy during the period 1948-66. To obtain growth rates, we use the real net national product (NNP), adjusted to allow for a 1 per cent per annum average increase of total factor productivity in general government. But since economic progress cannot occur unless real NNP grows faster than population, we shall also look at the relative contributions of total factor productivity and real total factor input, per capita, to rates of growth in real NNP, per capita.

There is also interest in the relative growth rates of labor and property income—in the changing functional distribution of income. We shall examine this aspect of growth in terms of relative changes in productivity and in real price of the two major classes, as well as more broadly in terms of the historical elasticity of substitution during the period covered. This analysis is confined to the business economy, for which independent measures of property and labor income are available.

In view of its major role in economic growth, perhaps the greatest interest centers on the causal factors behind productivity growth. In the final section, we shall discuss causes, with particular emphasis on the proximate determinants in the form of growth in real intangible capital stock resulting from investments in research and development, education and training, and other activities designed to increase the quality, or productive efficiency, of the tangible factor inputs, human and nonhuman.

The Role of Productivity in
Economic Growth and Progress

Between 1948 and 1966, real NNP (adjusted for government productivity advance, as described in the previous chapter) increased at an average annual rate of 4.1 per cent. Total net factor productivity rose at an average annual rate of 2.3 per cent, while real tangible factor inputs grew at a comparable rate of 1.8 per cent. (See Table 4-1). Thus, we may say that productivity advance accounted for roughly 56 per cent of total economic growth over the period. It will be recalled from *Productivity Trends* that prior to 1919 productivity accounted for well under half the overall growth rate. After 1919 it generally accounted for more than half. We recognize, of course, that productivity as "the residual" reflects various forces that affect the productive efficiency of the tangible factors. But we defer until the last section of the chapter an attempt to probe more deeply into underlying causes.

The relative impact of productivity advance differed considerably in the subperiods. In the first and last subperiods, 1948-53 and 1960-66, when the growth rate of real NNP exceeded 5 per cent, productivity grew only slightly faster than real tangible inputs. During the two middle subperiods, the rate of productivity advance decelerated, but the rate of increase in real factor input fell much more, so that productivity advance accounted for around three-quarters of the aggregate growth rate.

The role of productivity stands out much more prominently when we view it in relation to the rate of economic progress. Real NNP per capita rose at an average annual rate of 2.4 per cent. Real factor input per capita increased by only 0.1 per cent a year, so the 2.3 per cent annual rate of productivity advance accounted for almost all of the economic progress achieved between 1948 and 1966. (See Table 4-1 and Chart 4-1.) The figure 2.4 per cent may seem small, but given the power of compound interest, it means that real NNP per capita doubles every thirty years or so, thanks almost entirely to the forces that promote productivity advance. This is the same rate of progress experienced from 1889 to 1919,[1] but in the earlier period input per capita grew at a 1.0 per cent rate per annum. From 1919 to 1948, productivity advance accelerated, but input per capita fell somewhat, and the annual growth rate of real NNP was retarded to 1.5 per cent. Although the 2.4 per cent growth rate since 1948 is the same as in the period before 1919, the relative importance of productivity advance is much greater.

We recognize that real NNP per capita is scarcely an ideal welfare measure. National product, as currently estimated, excludes various kinds of non-market economic activity, the value of which would add more than 50 per cent to the present aggregates.[2] Also, deductions are not made for certain costs of producing final goods and services that are not included in NNP, or, more importantly, that might be imputed, such as the costs and disutilities

[1] See *Productivity Trends*, Table 8, p. 84.
[2] For rough estimates of the imputed values of major nonmarket economic activities, see the *Forty-seventh Annual Report* of NBER, June 1967, pp. 9-15.

TABLE 4-1

National Economy:
Components of Real Net National Product,
Total and per Capita,
Key Years, 1948-66

	Real NNP (Adjusted) (Col. 2 × Col. 3) (1)	Total Factor Input (2)	Total Net Factor Productivity (Col. 1 ÷ Col. 2) (3)	Population (4)	Total Factor Input per Capita (Col. 2 ÷ Col. 4) (5)	Real Adjusted NNP per Capita (Col. 3 × Col. 5 = Col. 1 ÷ Col. 4) (6)
			A. Index Numbers (1958 = 100)			
1948	72.1	89.2	80.9	83.9	106.4	86.0
1953	92.1	100.4	91.7	91.6	109.6	100.5
1957	101.2	102.9	98.3	98.3	104.6	102.9
1960	109.8	104.9	104.7	103.3	101.5	106.3
1966	148.9	122.1	122.0	112.6	108.5	132.3
		B. Average Annual Percentage Rates of Change				
1948-66	4.1	1.8	2.3	1.7	0.1	2.4
1948-53	5.0	2.4	2.6	1.8	0.6	3.2
1953-57	2.4	0.6	1.8	1.8	-1.2	0.6
1957-60	2.8	0.6	2.1	1.7	-1.0	1.1
1960-66	5.2	2.6	2.6	1.4	1.1	3.7

Note: For the average annual percentage rates of change, the relationships are approximately additive rather than multiplicative as in the case of index numbers.

Source: Col. 1: text; Col. 2: Table A-17; Col. 4: Bureau of the Census.

Chart 4-1: Components of Real Net National Product per Capita, Average Annual Rates
of Change, 1948–66

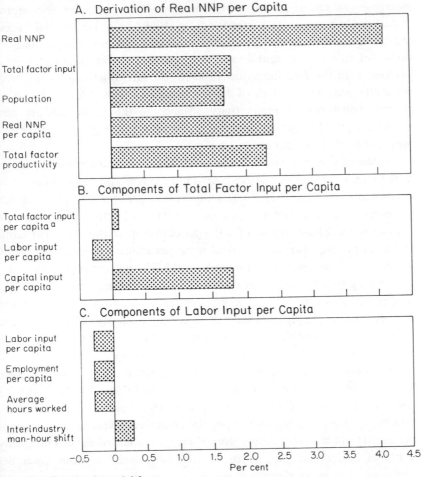

A. Derivation of Real NNP per Capita

B. Components of Total Factor Input per Capita

C. Components of Labor Input per Capita

Source: Tables 4-1 and 4-2.
ª The difference between real NNP per capita and total factor productivity shown in
panel A.

associated with environmental pollution. Even if NNP could be fully and
accurately estimated, it would only furnish the basis for estimates of changes
in *potential* welfare. Nevertheless, if its limitations are borne in mind, real
NNP per capita provides a useful point of departure for assessing the rate of
material progress.[3]

3 See Moses Abramovitz's essay "The Welfare Interpretation of Secular Trends in
National Income and Product" in *The Allocation of Economic Resources*, Stanford
University Press, 1959.

As shown in Table 4-1, the rates and components of change differ significantly over the several subperiods. Real NNP per capita increased at an average annual rate of 3.2 per cent between 1948 and 1953, but decelerated during the subsequent two subperiods to 1960, reflecting not only some deceleration in the rate of productivity advance but, more importantly, a decline of around 1 per cent a year, on the average, in real total factor input per capita. In the final subperiod 1960-66, the rate of advance in real NNP per capita rose to a new high of 3.7 per cent a year. This reflected the return of the annual rate of productivity advance to the almost 2.6 per cent recorded in the first period, and an acceleration in the growth rate of real input per capita to 1.1 per cent a year.

In view of the importance of real input per capita, particularly for swings in the rates of change of real NNP per capita, it is worthwhile to examine its components (see Table 4-2). First of all, the 0.11 per cent average annual rate of increase in total factor input per capita during the period 1948-66 represents a weighted average of a 0.3 per cent drop in labor input per capita and a 1.8 per cent increase in capital input per capita. The decline in factor input in the two middle subperiods, 1953-57 and 1957-60, reflected a decelerating growth rate in real capital and substantial declines in labor input relative to population. The 1.1 per cent rate of growth in the 1960-66 subperiod mirrored a renewed surge in capital input per capita back to around 2 per cent a year and the highest growth rate in labor input per capita of the postwar period—almost 1 per cent a year, on the average.

The rates of change in labor input per capita may be, in turn, broken down into the three components shown in Table 4-2 and Chart 4-1. Thus, the 0.3 per cent annual rate of decline during 1948-66 reflects declines of 0.3 per cent each in the percentage of the population in work status (persons engaged per capita) and in average hours worked per year, counterbalanced in part by a rise of 0.3 per cent a year in the rate of increase in labor input per man-hour. The latter element measures the relative shift of workers and man-hours into high-pay industries, continuing a historical trend. The decline in the proportion of population working was due to a drop in the ratio of labor force to total population as the proportion of unproductive age groups rose during the period covered; the ratio of employment to labor force was the same in 1966 as in 1948. The decline in average hours worked also represents a continuation of a secular trend.

The drop in labor input per capita during the two middle subperiods reflects primarily a decline in the proportion of the population in work status, due largely to an upward creep in the ratio of unemployment to the

TABLE 4-2

National Economy:
Components of Total Factor Input per Capita,
Key Years, 1948-66

	Capital Input per Capita (1)	Labor Input per Capita (Col. 3 × Col. 4 × Col. 5) (2)	Persons Engaged per Capita (3)	Average Hours Worked per Year (4)	Labor Input per Man-Hour (5)
A. Index Numbers (1958 = 100)					
1948	83.0	113.5	110.3	106.3	96.8
1953	92.5	114.2	111.1	102.7	100.1
1957	99.2	106.1	104.3	101.1	100.6
1960	101.8	101.4	99.9	101.1	100.4
1966	114.4	106.9	102.9	100.6	103.3
B. Average Annual Percentage Rates of Change					
1948-66	1.8	-0.3	-0.3	-0.3	0.3
1948-53	2.2	0.1	0.1	-0.7	0.7
1953-57	1.8	-1.9	-1.6	-0.4	0.1
1957-60	0.9	-1.5	-1.5	0.0	-0.1
1960-66	2.0	0.9	0.5	-0.1	0.5

Note: For the average annual percentage rates of change, the relationships are approximately additive rather than multiplicative as in the case of the index numbers.

Source: Tables 4-1, A-6, A-10, A-13, and A-17.

civilian labor force, from 2.9 per cent in 1953 to 4.3 per cent in 1957 and on up to 5.5 per cent in 1960.

The significant rise in labor input per capita in the last subperiod reflects a renewed rise of an average 0.5 per cent a year in persons engaged per capita as unemployment fell back to 3.8 per cent of the civilian labor force in 1966; an increase of 0.5 per cent a year in labor input per man-hour; and a retarded decline in average hours worked of less than 0.1 per cent a year.

Factor Prices, Productivity, and Income Shares

It is a truism that the rate of change in productivity is equal to the rate of change in the ratio of average input prices to average output prices (at factor cost). Thus, between 1948 and 1966 the private domestic business economy showed average annual increases of 3.9 per cent in the average factor price, of 1.4 per cent in the average output price, and of 2.5 per cent in the ratio of the two price series—the same rate of increase as in total factor productivity (see Table 4-3). The rise in factor input prices relative to output prices, which is proportionate to the productivity increase, is the means whereby productivity gains are distributed to the owners of the factors of production. One can regard productivity gain as an increase in the "real price" of a unit of factor input, or as the increase in unit real factor income, since it is the same as factor income per unit deflated by the index of average prices of outputs (at factor cost).

These relationships do not tell us anything about inflationary processes. We cannot know whether factor price increases (less the productivity increase) pushed up product prices or product price increases (plus the productivity increase) pulled up factor prices, nor do we know the extent to which there was an interaction between the two. An analysis of inflation would have to include the study of disaggregated industry estimates, timing relationships, monetary factors, the profit-rate component of the price of capital, institutional factors, and so on. But we do know that the owners of the factors of production, in the aggregate, are unable to raise the real price per unit of combined factor input any faster than total factor productivity advances permit.

If the increase in average factor prices exactly equaled the increase in productivity, there would be no change in the product price index. The product price index would also remain stable if the average price of each factor rose exactly in proportion to the increase in the corresponding partial productivity ratio and the factor shares of national income remained constant. Or, given changes in the product price level, product shares would

TABLE 4-3

Private Domestic Business Economy:
Factor Incomes, Inputs, Prices, and Productivity, 1948-66,
Link Relatives and Rates of Change

	Link Relative, 1966 (1948 = 100)	Average Annual per Cent Rate of Change, 1948-66
Factor income		
Total	259.7	5.44
Labor	269.8	5.67
Property	236.1	4.89
Implicit price deflator	128.1	1.38
Real factor income		
Total	202.7	4.00
Labor	210.6	4.22
Property	184.3	3.46
Percentage shares of income		
Labor	104.0	0.22
Property	90.8	−0.54
Real factor input		
Total	129.6	1.45
Labor	117.4	0.89
Property	186.3	3.52
Factor productivity		
Total	156.6	2.52
Labor	172.9	3.09
Property	108.9	0.47
Factor price		
Total	200.4	3.94
Labor	229.8	4.73
Property	126.7	1.32
Real factor price		
Total	156.4	2.52
Labor	179.4	3.30
Property	98.9	−0.06

Note: Property refers to net capital.

Source: Factor income and percentage shares of income: Table 4-4; implicit price deflator: Department of Commerce; real factor input and factor productivity: Table A-20; real factor income, factor price, and real factor price: by computation.

remain constant if the real price of each factor rose in proportion to the increase in the corresponding partial productivity ratio.

But if the real price of one factor rises more than its productivity ratio (made possible by a drop in the real price of the other factor relative to its productivity ratio), then the share of that factor in national income will increase. This is precisely what happened to labor income in the business economy from 1948 to 1966, on net balance. The real price of labor rose at an average rate of 3.3 per cent a year, representing a 4.7 per cent rate of increase in average hourly compensation deflated by the product price deflator, which rose at a 1.4 per cent annual rate. Average annual labor compensation was obtained by dividing total labor compensation by weighted man-hours, so that the 4.7 per cent rate of increase does not reflect inter-industry man-hour shifts, and thus the real-average-hourly-compensation series is consistent with the real-product-per-unit-of-labor-input series. The 3.3 per cent rise in real average hourly compensation exceeds by a bit more than 0.2 per cent the 3.1 per cent average annual rate of increase in real product per unit of labor input. This 0.2 per cent relative increase may also be called the increase in real unit labor costs, which is the quotient of real average hourly earnings and labor productivity.

As a result of this rise, the labor share of factor income originating in the domestic business economy expanded from 69.7 per cent in 1948 to 72.5 per cent in 1966—another average annual rate of increase of 0.2 per cent (see Table 4-4), and approximately the same rate of advance as that recorded between 1929 (when the labor share was 67.3 per cent) and 1948. It is also

TABLE 4-4

Factor Income Originating in the
Private Domestic Business Economy,
by Type,
Selected Years, 1929-66

	Factor Income (Billions of Dollars)			Per Cent Distribution	
	Total	Labor	Property	Labor	Property
1929	78.8	53.0	25.8	67.3	32.7
1948	200.2	139.6	60.6	69.7	30.3
1953	263.7	194.8	68.9	73.9	26.1
1957	314.3	234.7	79.6	74.7	25.3
1960	351.4	264.8	86.7	75.3	24.7
1966	519.9	376.7	143.1	72.5	27.5

Note: Details may not add to total due to rounding.

Source: Department of Commerce estimates, with an allocation of proprietors' income as described in the appendix.

the same rate I obtained in a previous study for the expansion in the labor share of gross private domestic product (including households and private nonprofit institutions, excluded from the present analysis) between 1919 and 1960.[4] As shown in Table 4-4, however, there was a drop in the labor share between 1960 and 1966, but the increase was subsequently resumed.

The uptrend in the real price of labor and its share in national income was accompanied by an average decline in the real price of capital of 0.06 per cent a year, compared with a 0.47 per cent annual increase in capital productivity. The 0.5 per cent rate of decline in real capital cost annually per unit of output is consistent with the decline in its share of business factor income from 30.3 per cent in 1948 to 27.5 per cent in 1966. (See Tables 4-3 and 4-4.) Note also that the 0.5 per cent rate of decline in unit real capital cost per year, weighted by the 0.25 per cent share of capital, approximately equals the 0.2 per cent rate of increase in unit real labor cost, weighted by its percentage share in the base period.[5]

If the capital deflator shows the same movement as the overall product deflator, then the slight decline in the real price of capital may be interpreted as occurring in the rate of return on capital assets at market prices. We have not disentangled the rate-of-return and capital-asset price components of our capital price measure. But in view of the high rate of return prevailing in 1948 due to postwar capital shortages, it seems unlikely that the 1966 rate of return was higher, despite the significant increase from 1960. Unfortunately, time has not permitted us to pursue this aspect of postwar economic developments more fully.

Another way of explaining statistically the rise in the real price of labor and its income share is to view it as the product of changes in the relative quantities of factor inputs and in the relative prices of the factors. Thus, labor input relative to total factor input dropped by an average annual rate of 0.55, while the price of labor rose by an average 0.80 per cent a year relative to total factor price. The sum of these two rates is 0.25, which is approximately the rate of change in labor's share.

Since the rate of decline in relative labor input was more than offset by

4 See John W. Kendrick and Ryuzo Sato, "Factor Prices, Productivity, and Economic Growth," *American Economic Review*, December 1963. The relationships among the variables discussed in this section are developed mathematically in Appendix A of that article, pp. 985-96.

5 The implications of this relationship for "wage-price guideposts" are discussed in Kendrick and Sato (see footnote 4), p. 979; see also John W. Kendrick, "The Wage-Price-Productivity Issue," *California Management Review*, Spring 1962.

the rate of increase in the relative price of labor, it is apparent that the "historical" elasticity of substitution for the period was less than unity. In interpreting the coefficients presented below, it must be remembered that elasticities of substitution calculated from historical time series do not have the same meaning as the concept used in equilibrium theory. That is, in addition to indicating the relationship between relative changes in the prices and quantities of the factors, the coefficients may also reflect changes in the degree of disequilibrium in a dynamic economy, technological changes that are not neutral with respect to labor and capital requirements per unit of output, and so on. Nevertheless, the coefficients are useful summary measures of the historical relationship between relative changes in prices and quantities (we shall refer to them simply as "coefficients" in order to remind the reader of the several forces that may affect the relationship).

One way of estimating the coefficient of substitution is as the quotient of the two rates given above: 0.55/0.80 = 0.69. An alternative formula involves the difference between the growth rates of capital and labor inputs, divided by the difference between the growth rates of the real prices of labor and capital. Presumably, the small difference between the two estimates is due to rounding of the underlying index numbers and the derived rates of change. The coefficient of substitution estimated here compares to one of 0.58 I estimated for the period 1919-60 in the article cited earlier.[6] It is even closer to an estimate by Kravis of 0.64.[7]

The rates of change in factor shares can be related directly to the coefficient of substitution.[8] Thus, the growth rate of the labor share can be estimated as the difference between the rates of growth in real labor and capital inputs (0.89 − 3.52 = −2.63) times 1 minus the reciprocal of the coefficient of substitution (1 − 1/0.66 = −0.52), weighted by the share of capital in factor income, 0.25. The result is 0.3, which approximates the rate of growth of the labor share (with allowance for rounding errors). In other words, with a coefficient of substitution of less than unity, the factor with a relative decline of input obtains an increasing share of income. Given the relative growth of the factor inputs 1948-66, the coefficient of 0.66 is consistent with the increases in the real price of labor and its share of income as we have estimated them.

It has been argued that these relationships, and the market mechanisms

---

[6] Kendrick and Sato, p. 981.

[7] Irving B. Kravis, "Relative Income Shares in Fact and Theory," *American Economic Review,* December 1959, pp. 917-49.

[8] Kendrick and Sato, Appendix A, equations 14 and 15.

which facilitate them, augur well for the viability of the American economy.[9] That is, there appears to have been no pronounced long-run trend in the rate of return on capital, despite a significant fraction of income saved. Further, the rate of return has generally been adequate to induce a volume of tangible investment consistent with a high level of employment of resources. The rate of investment has provided a significant rate of increase in real capital stock and input per worker and per unit of labor input. As a result of the increasing relative abundance of capital and relative scarcity of labor, real income per unit of labor input has risen even faster than labor productivity. Given a historical coefficient of substitution of less than unity, as we have seen, this means that labor's share of factor income has risen.

Some economists argue that a rising labor share of income has made it easier to sustain adequate levels of aggregate demand. We would stress, rather, the development of built-in stabilizers and more informed macroeconomic stabilization policies as an explanation for the steadier rate of economic growth since World War II. Whatever its sources, the steadier growth of recent decades has been associated with a reduced variability in rates of productivity advance, as documented in Chapter 3.

Causal Factors Behind Productivity Advance

The analysis of the causal factors behind productivity advance is extremely complex. The purpose of this section is not to undertake such an analysis. Rather, my approach to the subject will be sketched briefly, with reference to a related study I am currently conducting for the National Bureau of Economic Research. In that study we present estimates of total investment and capital stocks, and analyze their relationship to economic growth.[10]

It is our basic hypothesis that the chief proximate determinant of productivity advance is the growth of the real stock of intangible capital resulting from investments designed to increase the quality, or productive efficiency, of the tangible human and nonhuman factors of production. In *Productivity Trends* (pp. 104-10), we alluded to outlays for research and development, education and training, and medical care as "hidden investments." They are

9 Ibid.

10 See *Forty-seventh Annual Report*, NBER, pp. 9-15. A preliminary summary of the findings is presented in John W. Kendrick, "The Treatment of Intangible Resources as Capital," *Review of Income and Wealth*, March 1972, and in Kendrick, "Economic Impacts of Scientific and Technological Progress," in Helen Perlman, ed., *The Research Revolution and the Outlook for R&D in the 1970's*, Menlo Park, Calif., Pacific Books, Inc., forthcoming.

indeed investments, in the same sense as tangible capital outlays, to the extent that they increase output- and income-producing capacity in future accounting periods. They are "hidden" in that they are not officially recognized as investments in the income and product accounts. Indeed, some of the intangible investments are not even included in the Commerce Department estimates, particularly those which are charged to current expenses by business, and those which involve imputations, such as the opportunity cost of students.

In the companion study, we have prepared comprehensive estimates of intangible investments, by type and by sector, in current and constant dollars for the period since 1929. Further, we have developed experimental estimates of the stocks of intangible capital, in current and constant dollars, for the same period, also by type and by sector of ownership and of use. Preliminary results indicate that there has been a substantial rise since the 1920s not only in intangible investment as a proportion of GNP but also in real stocks of intangibles in relation to real tangible capital stocks. However, presentation of our finished estimates, description of the sources and methods of estimation, and a summary of the findings will have to await completion of the study now in progress.

We recognize, of course, that there are factors other than the growth of intangible capital stocks which may have an important bearing on productivity changes. In the short run, productivity change appears to have a systematic relationship with the business cycle, as discussed in Chapter 3. Chief among the longer-term factors are: changes in the degree of economic efficiency as reflected in the allocation of resources, including the speed of adjustment to dynamic changes in the economy; the rate of diffusion of innovations; economies of scale, both internal and external, which are progressively affected by technological advance; and the average inherent quality of human and natural resources which reflect changes in the resource mix as well as possible trends within given resource categories. If analysis is confined to the private economy, there is also the additional factor of the changing volume of governmental inputs that affect productivity trends in the private sectors.

More fundamental are the basic values and socioeconomic institutions of society. Whereas these generally change slowly with regard to their net impact on productive efficiency and technological change, differences in values and institutions among regions and nations are presumably an important element in explaining differences in productivity levels and rates of change.

5

INDUSTRY PATTERNS OF
PRODUCTIVITY CHANGE

The degree of dispersion among industries in the rates of change in real product and productivity has been quite similar in the post-1948 period to that prevailing in earlier periods. The variability in subperiod and annual rates of change in industry measures, however, has been less than before 1948, reflecting a steadier rate of economic growth. The degrees of dispersion and variability are greater, of course, the greater the amount of industry detail used in the analysis.

This chapter is essentially descriptive, providing a summary review of the post-1948 record of productivity changes in major industry segments and groups. Total factor productivity and output per unit of tangible capital input measures are available for study of seven segments and thirty-two two-digit industry groups. Real product and labor productivity measures are available for all nine one-digit segments and forty industry groups. In addition, we have supplementary measures of output per man-hour for 395 four-digit manufacturing industries for the 1954-63 period.

While of some interest in their own right, the industry productivity index numbers are of particular value for analyzing changes in industry structure and the causal forces behind productivity advance. The analysis of relationships between productivity changes and associated variables is presented in the following chapter; readers who are in a hurry can skip the verbal description in this chapter and, after looking at the summary tables and charts below, turn to Chapter 6.

Total Factor Productivity

Compound percentage rates of change in total factor productivity over the period 1948-66 differed considerably among the major industry segments.

TABLE 5-1

Private Domestic Business Economy: Total Factor Productivity,
by Industry Segment and Group, Average Annual Percentage Rates of Change

	1948-66	1948-53	1953-57	1957-60	1960-66	Average Deviation
Private domestic business economy	2.5	2.8	1.9	2.3	2.9	0.4
Farming	3.3	3.7	2.5	4.4	3.1	0.5
Mining	4.2	5.1	3.4	3.6	4.2	0.5
Metal	2.4	1.4	1.5	0.9	4.6	1.2
Coal	5.2	3.5	6.9	4.8	5.7	1.1
Oil and gas	3.2	2.7	1.8	2.7	4.9	1.1
Nonmetal	2.6	2.4	3.6	4.5	1.3	1.0
Contract construction	1.5	3.6	2.8	1.1	-1.0	1.8
Manufacturing	2.5	2.9	1.5	2.0	3.2	0.6
Nondurables	2.6	2.5	2.6	2.4	2.8	0.1
Foods	3.0	2.2	4.0	4.0	2.6	0.7
Beverages	2.2	0.1	4.2	1.2	3.1	1.5
Tobacco	1.1	0.9	1.6	0.5	1.2	0.3
Textiles	4.0	3.2	4.7	5.4	3.6	0.7
Apparel	1.9	1.5	3.3	2.8	0.9	0.9
Paper	2.5	1.7	2.4	2.3	3.4	0.6
Printing, publishing	2.7	2.3	4.1	2.8	2.0	0.7
Chemicals	4.9	4.7	4.5	5.8	4.7	0.4
Petroleum refining	3.0	3.5	1.4	4.7	2.8	0.8
Rubber products	3.9	3.6	4.8	3.2	4.0	0.4
Leather products	1.7	1.4	3.7	0.9	0.9	0.9
Durables	2.4	2.9	0.8	1.7	3.4	0.9
Lumber products	3.5	4.2	3.8	3.7	2.5	0.6
Furniture	2.9	2.0	4.9	3.4	2.2	1.0
Stone, clay, glass products	2.4	2.9	2.3	1.3	2.7	0.4
Primary metals	1.6	1.2	1.2	-0.2	3.1	1.0
Fabricated metals	1.9	1.8	1.1	1.5	2.6	0.5

Machinery excluding electric	2.6	3.1	1.3		3.0	2.8	0.6
Electric machinery	3.7	5.0	2.5		2.3	4.2	1.0
Transportation equipment and ordnance	3.2	4.8	1.0		3.3	3.2	1.0
Instruments	2.9	1.3	2.7		6.1	2.8	1.1
Miscellaneous	3.5	1.8	3.7		4.2	4.3	0.9
Transportation	3.4	1.9	3.2		3.4	4.9	1.0
Railroads	5.2	3.2	3.8		5.0	7.9	1.8
Nonrail	2.1	0.1	2.4		2.3	3.5	1.1
Local transit			n.a.				
Intercity bus lines			n.a.				
			n.a.				
Motor freight transportation	0.5	0.9	2.2		2.4	-2.0	1.6
Water transportation	8.0	12.3	5.1		1.6	9.7	3.5
Air transportation			n.a.				
Pipeline transportation							
Communication and public utilities	4.0	4.4	3.2		4.0	4.1	0.3
Communication	3.8	4.4	2.4		4.6	4.0	0.6
Electric, gas, and sanitary service	3.9	4.4	4.0		3.2	3.8	0.3
Electric and gas	4.9	4.8	5.6		4.3	4.7	0.4
Trade	2.5	1.8	2.4		1.8	3.6	0.7
Wholesale	2.5	1.2	2.8		2.7	3.2	0.7
Retail	2.4	2.0	2.0		1.2	3.6	0.8
Finance, insurance, and real estate				n.a.			
Services[a]				n.a.			
Average deviation:							
7 Industry segments	0.8	1.1	0.9		1.2	1.4	
34 Industry groups[b]	1.0	1.4	1.4		1.4	1.4	

Source: Tables A-20, A-22, A-24, A-26–31, A-33, A-35, A-37–58, A-60, A-62, A-67–68, A-70–71, A-73–77. Here and in subsequent productivity summary tables, average deviations across subperiods are weighted by length of period, while average industry deviations are unweighted.

[a] Excludes households and nonprofit institutions, includes government enterprises, here and in subsequent tables.

[b] Includes two-digit industries and one-digit industries that are not subdivided. Excludes nondurables, durables, nonrail, and electric and gas subcategories.

Average rates of increase ranged from a low of 1.5 per cent a year in contract construction (without adjustment for possible deflator bias) to 4.2 per cent in mining (see Table 5-1). We do not have total factor productivity estimates for the finance and service segments due to lack of capital estimates, but the labor productivity estimates suggest that the rate of increase in finance, insurance, and real estate was about the same rate as in construction, and that the rate of gain in the services segment was even lower—probably under 1 per cent a year in terms of total factor productivity. The real product and productivity estimates for the finance and services sectors may be subject to some downward bias, however, as a result of inadequate output price deflators. (See p. 179 in the appendix.)

The manufacturing and trade segments showed the same average annual rate of gain in total factor productivity as the private domestic business economy as a whole—2.5 per cent. Farming, transportation, and communication and public utilities were higher, with better than 3 per cent average annual increases. (See Chart 5-1.) Compared with the trend rates of increase in the earlier decades 1919-48, for which we had estimates covering five segments, manufacturing and transportation had lower rates of advance in the postwar period, while farming, mining, and communication and public utilities exhibited some acceleration. The residual segment as a whole also appears to have accelerated its rate of productivity advance.[1]

As would be expected, the degree of dispersion in rates of productivity advance in the thirty-four industry groups was somewhat greater than in the seven segments. For example, within transportation, average annual rates of increase ranged from 8.0 per cent in air transportation to 0.5 per cent in water transportation. No group registered a productivity drop. (See Chart 5-2.) As shown at the bottom of Table 5-1, the mean deviation of rates of increase in total factor productivity from the average rate in the business economy as a whole was 1.0 for the industry groups, compared with a 0.8 mean deviation for the segments.

Chart 5-3 contains a frequency distribution of rates of change, 1948-66, in total factor productivity and in the partial productivity ratios (discussed below). The distribution looks quite similar to that in earlier periods. For total factor productivity, annual rates are heavily concentrated in the 1 to 4 per cent classes, with a right skew.

Dispersion of rates of productivity change in most of the four subperiods was somewhat larger than for the period 1948-66 as a whole. For example, in

[1] See *Productivity Trends*, Table 34, pp. 136-37, and Table 5-1 above.

Chart 5-1: Private Domestic Business Economy, Industry Segments: Total Factor
Productivity (1948–66)[a] and Output per Unit of Labor Input (1948–69)

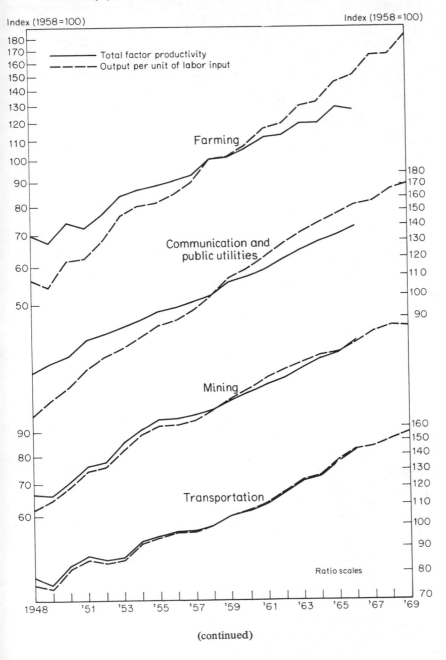

(continued)

Chart 5-1 (concluded)

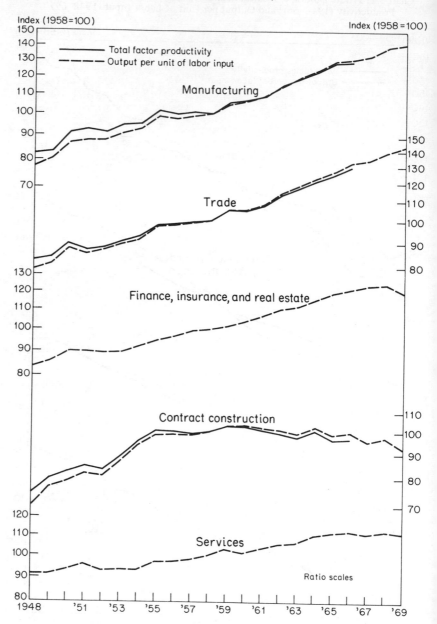

Index (1958=100)

Index (1958=100)

— Total factor productivity
--- Output per unit of labor input

Manufacturing

Trade

Finance, insurance, and real estate

Contract construction

Services

Ratio scales

Source: Tables A-22, A-24, A-30, A-31, A-58, A-70, A-75, A-78, and A-79.
a Not available for finance, insurance, and real estate, and for services.

the first subperiod, 1948-53, average rates of increase ranged from 12.3 in air transportation down to 0.1 in beverage manufacturing. In some subperiods there were small productivity declines. The averages of the subperiod mean deviations from rates of productivity change for the business economy were

Chart 5-2: Private Domestic Business Economy, Thirty-three Industry Groups:[a] Divergence of Total Factor Productivity, 1966 Relative to 1948

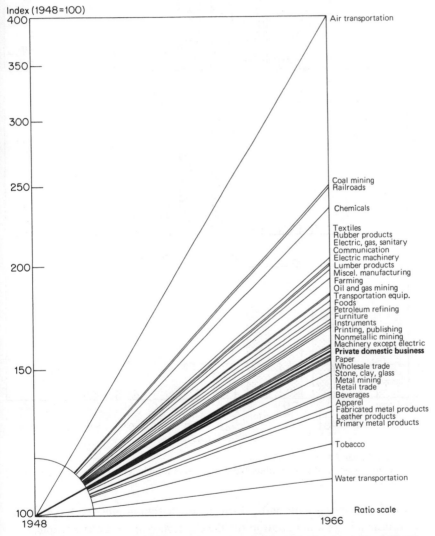

Source: Tables A-20, A-22, A-26–29, A-37–57, A-60, A-67–8, A-71, A-73, A-76–77.
[a] Excludes contract construction; finance, insurance, and real estate; and services.

Chart 5-3: Private Domestic Business Economy, Thirty-four Industry Groups:[a]
Average Annual Rate of Change in Productivity Ratios, 1948–66

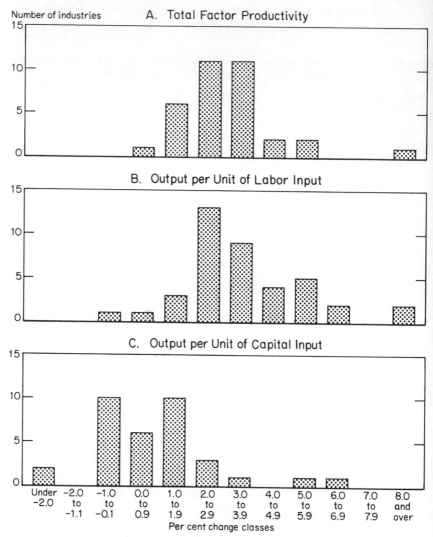

Source: Tables 5-1, 5-5, and 5-6.
[a] See note a on each source table. Note that Panel B includes 40 industry groups (see Table 5-5).

1.2 for the seven segments and 1.4 for the thirty-four groups—each 0.4 above the corresponding mean deviation for the eighteen-year period as a whole.

There was more variability in subperiod rates of change in total factor productivity for most segments and groups than for the business economy as a whole. Even though the subperiod rates are measured between peak years of the business cycles, the rates of capacity utilization probably differed more between the peak years for industry segments and groups than the economy as a whole. This factor, as well as variations in rates of innovation, lies behind the variations in rates of change in total factor productivity—not to mention possible errors in the estimates.

It will be recalled that total factor productivity in the business economy as a whole rose at average rates of close to 3 per cent a year during the first and last subperiods, 1948-53 and 1960-66, and sagged in the two middle subperiods. The same pattern is evident in the total manufacturing segment, particularly in the durable goods subdivision, which experienced a much more pronounced sag in the growth of demand and output than nondurables. The mining segment, dominated by crude petroleum and natural gas, showed a similar pattern, in less pronounced form. The other segments had different patterns. Thus, in farming, the highest rates of increase came in the first and third subperiods, while in trade, the second and fourth subperiods were the strongest. In transportation, the rates of increase gradually accelerated over all four subperiods, while in contract construction the rates steadily decelerated, although deflator bias may be involved in the latter case. In communication and public utilities, only the second subperiod showed some deceleration in rates of productivity advance. (See Table 5-1.)

As measured by the mean deviation of subperiod rates from the rate for the eighteen-year period, the least variability in productivity advance was exhibited by the communication and public utility segment—0.3 per cent. The highest mean deviation was that for the volatile contract construction segment: 1.8 per cent. The mean deviations for the other segments are shown in the last column of Table 5-1.

Patterns of productivity change were even more varied in the industry groups than in the broader segments. The mean deviations of subperiod rates from the total period rates for the given industries averaged 0.94 and 0.77, respectively. In the most volatile group, air transportation, rates of advance swung from better than 12 per cent in 1948-53 down to 1.6 per cent in 1957-60, then back up to almost 10 per cent in 1960-66. A few groups showed productivity drops, but in no more than one of the four subperiods each.

Year-to-year variations in percentage changes in total factor productivity were, of course, much greater than variations in average rates from peak to peak of successive cycles. This reflected not only cyclical influences but also erratic factors, including possible statistical errors in the estimates. Thus, the mean deviation of annual per cent changes in the segments from their period rates averaged 2.4 per cent (see Table 5-2), compared with a 0.8 per cent mean deviation of subperiod rates from period rates. The corresponding mean deviations for the industry groups were 3.0 and 0.9 per cent.

TABLE 5-2

Private Domestic Business Economy:
Mean Deviations of Subperiod and Annual Rates of Change
in Output and Productivity Ratios from Average
Annual Rates of Change, 1948-66, by Industry Segment
(per cent)

Industry Segment	Real Product	Total Factor Productivity	Real Product per Unit of	
			Labor Input	Capital Input
Private domestic business economy				
Period rate	4.0	2.5	3.1	0.5
Mean deviation				
Subperiod	1.1	0.4	0.3	0.9
Annual	3.0	1.2	1.3	2.7
Farming				
Period rate	0.9	3.3	5.6	0.2
Mean deviation				
Subperiod	0.6	0.5	0.7	0.7
Annual	2.9	3.2	3.8	2.8
Mining				
Period rate	2.1	4.2	4.6	2.9
Mean deviation				
Subperiod	1.0	0.5	0.7	2.0
Annual	4.6	2.0	1.7	n.a.
Contract construction				
Period rate	3.1	1.5	2.0	−3.8
Mean deviation				
Subperiod	1.6	1.8	1.8	0.9
Annual	3.5	3.0	2.9	4.3
Manufacturing				
Period rate	4.3	2.5	2.9	0.8
Mean deviation				
Subperiod	2.4	0.6	0.6	1.5
Annual	5.9	2.8	2.0	5.8
Nondurables				
Period rate	3.8	2.6	3.2	0.7

(continued)

TABLE 5-2 (continued)

Industry Segment	Real Product	Total Factor Productivity	Real Product per Unit of	
			Labor Input	Capital Input
Mean deviation				
Subperiod	0.9	0.1	0.2	0.1
Annual	3.6	1.9	1.3	3.6
Durables				
Period rate	4.7	2.4	2.8	0.3
Mean deviation				
Subperiod	3.4	0.9	0.8	1.5
Annual	7.7	3.1	2.6	7.4
Transportation				
Period rate	2.3	3.4	3.7	0.6
Mean deviation				
Subperiod	2.2	1.0	0.9	2.3
Annual	4.6	2.6	2.5	4.6
Railroads				
Period rate	0.6	5.2	5.8	0.6
Mean deviation				
Subperiod	2.8	1.8	1.6	3.0
Annual	6.6	3.8	3.5	6.6
Nonrail				
Period rate	3.7	2.1	2.3	−2.4
Mean deviation				
Subperiod	1.5	1.1	1.0	2.6
Annual	3.6	2.7	2.7	3.8
Communication and public utilities				
Period rate	7.1	4.0	5.8	1.2
Mean deviation				
Subperiod	0.7	0.3	0.9	1.0
Annual	1.2	0.9	1.2	1.8
Communication				
Period rate	7.0	3.8	5.5	0.7
Mean deviation				
Subperiod	0.8	0.6	0.9	0.8
Annual	1.9	1.4	1.9	2.4
Electric, gas, and sanitary services				
Period rate	7.1	3.9	6.1	1.5
Mean deviation				
Subperiod	1.2	0.3	0.9	0.8
Annual	1.6	1.3	1.6	1.7

(continued)

TABLE 5-2 (concluded)

Industry Segment	Real Product	Total Factor Productivity	Real Product per Unit of	
			Labor Input	Capital Input
Trade				
Period rate	4.1	2.5	2.9	0.0
Mean deviation				
Subperiod	0.6	0.7	0.7	0.8
Annual	2.6	2.0	1.8	2.7
Wholesale				
Period rate	4.8	2.5	3.1	-0.3
Mean deviation				
Subperiod	0.8	0.7	0.5	1.5
Annual	2.6	2.2	2.2	2.0
Retail				
Period rate	3.7	2.4	2.7	0.0
Mean deviation				
Subperiod	0.8	0.8	0.8	0.5
Annual	2.6	2.1	2.0	3.1
Finance, insurance, and real estate				
Period rate	5.1	n.a.	2.1	n.a.
Mean deviation				
Subperiod	0.3	n.a.	0.6	n.a.
Annual	1.0	n.a.	1.1	n.a.
Services				
Period rate	3.5	n.a.	1.2	n.a.
Mean deviation				
Subperiod	1.0	n.a.	0.4	n.a.
Annual	1.5	n.a.	1.4	n.a.
ADDENDUM				
Average mean deviation				
Industry segments[a]				
Subperiod	1.2	0.8	0.8	1.3
Annual	3.1	2.4	2.0	3.7
Industry groups[b-]				
Subperiod	1.5	0.9	0.9	2.2
Annual	4.8	3.0	2.6	5.5

Source: Tables 5-1, 5-5, 5-6, 6-1, A-22, A-26–30, A-37–57, A-60, A-64–69, A-71, A-73, A-76–79.

[a] Based on segments (6-9) for which data are available.

[b] Based on groups for which data are available: 40 for real product and real product per unit of labor input, 34 for total factor productivity, and 30 for real product per unit of capital input.

With regard to the cyclical factor in annual variations in total factor productivity, most of the segments showed somewhat smaller percentage increases in the contraction years 1949, 1954, 1958, and 1961 than during the expansion years. Contract construction was the only exception.[2] A number of the industry groups showed absolute declines during contraction years, but most industries merely exhibited retardation in their rate of productivity advance during contractions. (See Table 5-3.)

TABLE 5-3

Private Domestic Business Economy:
Average Annual Rates of Change in Output and Productivity Ratios,
Expansions[a] Versus Contractions, 1948-66, by Industry Segment
(per cent)

| | | | Real Product per Unit of | |
	Real Product	Total Factor Productivity	Labor Input	Capital Input
Private Domestic Business Economy				
Expansion	5.4	2.6	2.9	1.6
Contraction	−0.4	2.4	3.8	−3.2
Farming				
Expansion	1.0	3.5	5.8	0.4
Contraction	0.8	3.2	5.3	0.0
Mining				
Expansion	4.7	4.5	4.2	n.a.
Contraction	−5.5	3.1	5.8	n.a.
Contract construction				
Expansion	3.9	1.0	1.4	−3.0
Contraction	0.6	3.5	4.4	−5.8
Manufacturing				
Expansion	7.3	3.1	3.1	3.0
Contraction	−5.2	0.6	2.4	−6.6
Nondurables				
Expansion	5.3	3.1	3.4	2.0
Contraction	−1.2	0.8	2.3	−3.3
Durables				
Expansion	8.8	3.0	3.0	3.3
Contraction	−8.0	0.5	2.2	−8.6

(continued)

2 Nathaniel Goldfinger, of the AFL-CIO and a member of the NBER Board of Directors' reading committee for this volume, suggests that this can be explained by layoff and equipment-leasing patterns in construction, which differ significantly from those in other industries.

TABLE 5-3 (concluded)

	Real Product	Total Factor Productivity	Real Product per Unit of	
			Labor Input	Capital Input
Transportation				
Expansion	4.6	3.8	3.8	2.8
Contraction	−4.9	2.6	3.2	−6.4
Railroads				
Expansion	3.9	6.2	6.5	3.8
Contraction	−9.6	2.2	3.7	−9.4
Nonrail				
Expansion	5.0	1.9	2.1	−1.0
Contraction	−0.5	3.0	3.4	−6.6
Communication and Public Utilities				
Expansion	7.5	4.0	5.6	1.9
Contraction	5.6	3.5	6.6	−1.0
Communication				
Expansion	7.8	3.9	5.2	1.8
Contraction	4.0	3.6	6.6	−2.8
Electric, gas, & sanitary services				
Expansion	7.2	4.0	6.1	1.8
Contraction	7.1	3.6	6.1	0.4
Trade				
Expansion	5.0	2.8	3.2	0.6
Contraction	1.0	1.4	2.0	−2.4
Wholesale				
Expansion	5.8	2.7	3.3	0.0
Contraction	1.5	1.8	2.4	−1.6
Retail				
Expansion	4.6	2.8	3.0	0.9
Contraction	0.7	1.0	1.6	−2.9
Finance, insurance, and real estate				
Expansion	5.2	n.a.	2.0	n.a.
Contraction	4.6	n.a.	2.2	n.a.
Services				
Expansion	4.1	n.a.	1.2	n.a.
Contraction	1.4	n.a.	1.0	n.a.

Source: Tables A-20, A-22, A-24, A-30–31, A-33, A-35, A-58, A-60, A-62, A-70–71, A-73, A-75–79.

[a] The years 1961-66 were counted as an expansion.

Capital per Unit of Labor Input

Prior to discussing the behavior of the partial productivity ratios, it is helpful to look at capital per unit of labor input by industry segments and groups. Not only is this ratio of intrinsic interest but it explains the difference between movements of the two partial productivity ratios and those of total factor productivity, and between each other. Take, for example, the average annual growth rate of total factor productivity in the private domestic economy—2.5 per cent—which is, in effect, a weighted average of the rates of increase in output per unit of labor input, 3.1, and in the output-capital ratio of 0.5 per cent. The average annual rate of increase in the capital-labor ratio of 2.6 per cent explains the difference between the rates of increase in the partial productivity ratios. Further, if we weight the 2.6 by the base-period factor shares (roughly 0.27 and 0.73), we obtain 0.7 and 1.9, or close to the differences between the rates of increase in the partial productivity ratio and that of total factor productivity. When this approach is applied to industries, of course, differences among the rates of change of productivity ratios would reflect differences not only in rates of increase in capital per unit of labor input but also in the relative weights of the two factor classes.

Capital per unit of labor input increased significantly in all the several industry segments. (See Table 5-4.) The 2.3 per cent average annual rate of increase in manufacturing and 1.6 per cent in mining were somewhat below the business economy average rate of 2.6; in the other segments the rates were above average. This implies that the rate of increase in the uncovered finance and services segments was somewhat below the business economy average. The dispersion of segment rates of change in the capital-labor ratio, as measured by a mean deviation of 1.4 per cent from the economy rate, is 1.75 times as great as that for total factor productivity. The dispersion of rates of change in the subperiods averages 1.9 per cent, or 1.58 times the corresponding measure for total factor productivity.

Capital per unit of labor input increased in all of the industry groups but one—oil and gas. None of the industry average increases was as high as the 6 per cent a year rate in the construction segment. During all of the subperiods but the last one, 1960-66, there was much greater dispersion in industry group rates than in segment rates, with a number of groups showing declining capital-labor ratios in one or two subperiods.

Variability in subperiod rates of change in capital per unit of labor input was moderate. The mean deviation of the subperiod rates from the 1948-66

TABLE 5-4

Private Domestic Business Economy: Capital per Unit of Labor Input,
by Industry Segment and Group, Average Annual Percentage Rates of Change

	1948-66	1948-53	1953-57	1957-60	1960-66	Average Deviation
Private domestic business economy	2.6	3.2	3.8	2.6	1.3	0.9
Farming	5.3	7.3	4.0	3.4	5.6	1.2
Mining	1.6	3.1	1.1	7.2	-2.0	2.7
Metal	3.4	-0.3	9.4	13.4	-2.1	5.9
Coal	5.4	10.2	1.2	11.7	1.3	4.7
Oil and gas	-3.0	-4.7	-3.7	3.8	-4.3	2.2
Nonmetal	3.4	-0.6	6.8	3.5	4.6	2.3
Contract construction	6.0	7.9	5.7	6.0	4.6	1.1
Manufacturing	2.3	1.9	3.6	2.6	1.7	0.7
Nondurables	2.4	2.7	2.4	2.1	2.4	0.1
Foods	1.5	1.0	-0.3	2.3	2.9	1.1
Beverages	1.9	5.7	-2.7	2.3	1.9	2.2
Tobacco	2.8	-1.2	4.2	5.4	3.9	2.2
Textiles	1.6	4.4	4.4	-3.2	-0.2	2.8
Apparel	3.2	3.5	0.1	3.4	4.9	1.4
Paper	2.0	2.4	4.4	0.4	1.1	1.2
Printing, publishing	0.9	0.7	-2.7	1.0	3.6	1.8
Chemicals	3.1	4.1	2.6	2.8	2.8	0.5
Petroleum refining	4.4	1.5	5.8	5.6	5.5	1.7
Rubber products	0.7	-2.1	2.9	2.5	0.7	1.6
Leather products	0.8	0.0	0.0	0.5	2.0	0.8
Durables	2.5	1.7	4.6	2.6	1.5	1.0
Lumber products	3.6	5.2	0.8	0.0	6.0	2.5

Stone, clay, glass products	3.4	3.3	6.3	3.0	1.8	1.3
Primary metals	2.9	2.5	3.1	7.8	0.8	1.7
Fabricated metals	2.4	2.3	3.3	3.0	1.6	0.6
Machinery excluding electric	0.8	1.4	4.0	-1.3	-0.6	1.7
Electric machinery	2.6	1.9	4.6	-0.9	3.8	1.6
Transportation equipment and ordnance	1.7	-3.0	6.6	2.3	2.3	2.7
Instruments	4.4	6.3	6.0	4.0	2.1	1.7
Miscellaneous	3.3	8.9	6.2	0.1	-1.4	4.3
Transportation	3.0	4.6	3.3	4.4	0.9	1.4
Railroads	5.2	6.3	5.2	7.9	3.0	1.5
Nonrail	4.8	8.1	5.1	4.6	2.1	1.9
Local transit and intercity bus lines			n.a.			
Motor freight transportation	2.9	-0.2	-0.3	13.8	2.4	3.6
Water transportation	2.0	-5.7	6.6	9.4	2.1	4.4
Air transportation						
Pipeline transportation			n.a.			
Communication and public utilities	4.5	6.1	4.1	6.3	2.4	1.5
Communication	4.7	4.2	3.7	8.4	4.1	1.2
Electric, gas, and sanitary services	4.5	7.0	5.0	4.4	2.3	1.6
Electric and gas	4.5	7.0	5.0	4.5	2.3	1.5
Trade	2.9	4.1	2.5	1.0	3.2	0.8
Wholesale	3.5	5.5	3.5	1.4	2.8	1.1
Retail	2.7	3.5	2.0	0.8	3.4	0.9
Finance, insurance, and real estate			n.a.			
Services			n.a.			
Average deviation						
7 Industry segments	1.4	2.2	1.0	2.3	2.1	2.1
34 Industry groups[a]	1.4	3.1	2.3	3.0	1.9	1.9

Source: See source for Table 5-1.

a Includes two-digit industries and one-digit industries that are not subdivided. Excludes nondurables, durables, nonrail, and electric and gas subcategories.

TABLE 5-5

Private Domestic Business Economy: Output per Unit of Labor Input,
by Industry Segment and Group, Average Annual Percentage Rates of Change

	1948-66	1948-53	1953-57	1957-60	1960-66	Average Deviation
Private domestic business economy	3.1	3.5	2.6	2.9	3.2	0.3
Farming	5.6	6.4	4.1	5.9	5.8	0.7
Mining	4.6	5.9	3.6	5.1	3.8	0.9
Metal	2.9	1.4	2.8	3.3	4.2	0.9
Coal	5.8	4.7	7.0	5.8	5.8	0.6
Oil and gas	2.3	0.9	0.8	3.8	3.7	1.4
Nonmetal	3.2	2.2	4.7	5.1	2.2	1.3
Contract construction	2.0	4.4	3.2	1.5	-0.5	1.8
Manufacturing	2.9	3.3	2.1	2.5	3.5	0.6
Nondurables	3.2	3.3	3.1	2.9	3.4	0.2
Foods	3.4	2.4	4.0	4.4	3.2	0.6
Beverages	2.9	2.3	3.4	1.9	3.7	0.7
Tobacco	2.7	0.2	3.9	3.6	3.6	1.4
Textiles	4.3	4.2	5.2	4.9	3.6	0.6
Apparel	2.2	1.9	3.3	3.0	1.5	0.7
Paper	3.0	2.5	3.3	2.4	3.7	0.5
Printing, publishing	2.7	2.3	3.9	2.8	2.3	0.5
Chemicals	6.0	6.3	5.4	6.7	5.8	0.4
Petroleum refining	5.5	4.6	4.1	7.7	6.0	1.1
Rubber products	4.0	3.1	5.2	3.7	4.2	0.6
Leather products	1.7	1.4	3.6	1.0	1.1	0.8
Durables	2.8	3.3	1.4	2.1	3.6	0.8
Lumber products	3.9	5.0	3.9	3.7	3.2	0.6
Furniture	2.9	1.8	5.0	3.5	2.2	1.1
Stone, clay, glass products	3.2	3.6	3.6	2.0	3.2	0.4
Primary metals	2.1	1.8	1.7	1.1	3.2	0.7
Fabricated metals	2.2	2.3	1.4	1.8	2.8	0.4
Machinery excluding electric	2.7	3.4	1.7	2.9	2.7	0.4

Electric machinery	4.1	5.4	3.1	4.6	1.1
Transportation equipment and ordnance	3.2	4.0	1.6	3.4	0.7
Instruments	3.7	2.5	3.7	3.2	1.0
Miscellaneous	4.0	3.2	4.4	4.1	0.4
Transportation	3.7	2.4	3.4	5.0	0.9
Railroads	5.8	4.3	4.2	8.2	1.6
Nonrail	2.3	0.6	2.5	3.6	1.0
Local transit	−1.0	0.3	1.3	−1.9	1.7
Intercity bus lines	1.5	4.0	1.0	0.9	1.3
Motor freight transportation	3.1	2.6	2.5	3.5	0.5
Water transportation	0.7	0.7	2.2	−1.5	1.5
Air transportation	8.2	11.8	5.7	10.0	3.1
Pipeline transportation	9.1	10.3	8.2	10.0	1.3
Communication and public utilities	5.8	6.7	4.7	5.2	0.9
Communication	5.5	5.4	3.6	5.7	0.9
Electric, gas, and sanitary services	6.1	7.6	6.3	5.1	0.9
Electric and gas	7.1	8.0	7.9	5.9	0.9
Trade	2.9	2.5	2.7	3.9	0.7
Wholesale	3.1	2.2	3.3	3.7	0.5
Retail	2.7	2.6	2.2	3.8	0.8
Finance, insurance, and real estate	2.1	1.5	2.7	2.6	0.6
Services	1.2	0.5	1.2	1.7	0.4
Average deviation:					
9 industry segments	1.3	1.9	0.8	1.5	1.5
40 industry groups[a]	1.4	1.8	1.5	1.7	1.7

Source: See source for Table 5-1; also, Tables A-64–66, A-69, A-78–79.

[a] Includes two-digit industries and one-digit industries that are not subdivided. Excludes nondurables, durables, nonrail, and electric and gas subcategories.

rate was 0.9 in the business economy as a whole. The average subperiod variability for the segments was somewhat greater, and that for the industry groups much greater—the mean deviations averaging 1.3 and 2.0, respectively. Variability in annual changes would obviously be still larger than subperiod variability, since year-to-year changes in labor input tend to vary much more than the annual changes in real capital stocks and inputs, particularly in recession periods, when stocks continue to grow while man-hours tend to fall, or increase only at much retarded rates.

Output per Unit of Labor Input

Since there was relative substitution of capital for labor in all segments and groups but one, rates of increase in output per unit of labor input were higher than (or equal to) growth rates of total factor productivity in all but one. Although at a higher level, patterns of change were quite similar in the two sets of productivity measures, so our summary of output per unit of labor input can be brief, except for special reference to the groupings for which we have labor productivity but no total factor productivity measures.

In looking at the period as a whole, average annual rates of increase in labor productivity in the segments ranged from 5.8 per cent in communication and public utilities and 5.6 per cent in farming down to 1.2 per cent in services, for which we did not have capital and total factor productivity measures. (See Table 5-5.) In the finance, insurance, and real estate segment, for which total productivity measures are also lacking, labor productivity rose at an average annual rate of 2.1 per cent, very close to that for contract construction, and well below the 3.1 per cent average in the business economy as a whole. At a 2.9 per cent a year growth, manufacturing and trade were only slightly under the business average, while mining and transportation were well above it.

The range of change was greater for the industry groups, varying from a 9.1 per cent a year average increase for pipelines down to a −1.0 for local transit. Neither of these industry groups was included in those for which we had total factor productivity measures. Local transit is the only group showing a productivity drop over the period as a whole, associated with a substantial decline in output and with increasing traffic congestion in metropolitan areas. Oil and gas production was the only group in which labor productivity rose less than total factor productivity, since it is the one with a declining capital-labor ratio.

Even in the subperiods, only three groups other than local transit showed declines in output per unit of labor input, and these for only one subperiod each. Air transportation and pipelines each showed rates of increase of 10 per cent or more in two subperiods each. But in general, the dispersion of rates of change in labor productivity in the subperiods did not average much more than the dispersion of rates for the entire period 1948-66. (See bottom lines of Table 5-5.)

Dispersion of rates of change in output per unit of labor input, by segment and industry group, is significantly greater than that for total factor productivity. This is not surprising in view of the still larger dispersion in rates of change in capital per unit of labor input. (See Table 5-5 for the mean deviations.) The frequency distribution of group rates of labor productivity change (Chart 5-3, panel B) graphically shows the greater dispersion, as well as more skewness to the right. As was true of total factor productivity, dispersion of rates of increase in labor productivity was, on the average, a bit higher in the subperiods than over the 1948-66 period as a whole. It was also slightly higher for the forty industry groups than the nine segments.

In addition to the data for these industry groups and segments, we also had access to index numbers of output per man-hour for 395 four-digit manufacturing industries for the years 1954, 1958, and 1963, based on the Census Bureau production indexes.[3] The years covered were all years of somewhat less than full employment, so the comparisons should not be greatly affected by cyclical factors. As shown in the frequency distribution in Chart 5-4, the dispersion of rates of change for the period 1954-63 is greater than that for the forty industry groups for the period 1948-66. In part, the greater dispersion reflects the fact that the comparison period is only half as long. But more importantly, it reflects the far larger number of four-digit industries available for comparison. The largest number of industries, eighty-one, fell into the 3 to 4 per cent class interval—the mean rate of growth for all 395 industries was 3.5 per cent. About three-quarters of the industries showed average rates of increase between 1 and 5 per cent. There was a definite right skew to the distribution, with over twice as many industries showing rates of increase in excess of 5 per cent as those showing increases of less than 1 per cent. Whereas none of the two-digit groups showed increases of more than 10 per cent, five four-digit industries did: pharmaceutical preparations, cathode ray picture tubes, industrial gases, explosives, and

3 The production indexes were related to indexes of man-hour estimates prepared by Henry Linsert for a master's thesis under my supervision, "An Empirical Study of the Relationships Between Output per Man-Hour and Related Variables in Manufacturing Industries, 1954-1963," June 1970, on file at The George Washington University Library.

Chart 5-4: Frequency Distribution of Average Annual Rates of Change in Output
per Man-Hour, 395 Industries, 1954-63

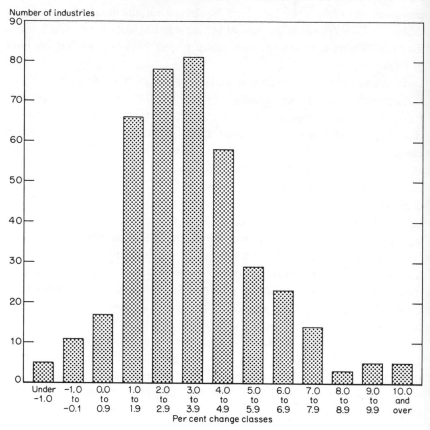

Source: See Chapter 5, footnote 3.

tufted carpets and rugs. While only one two-digit group showed a decline, five
four-digit industries did: raw cane sugar, metal foil and leaf, plating and
polishing, automatic vending machines, and primary nonferrous metals, n.e.c.

Surprisingly, the variability of subperiod rates of change in labor productivity was no greater than that in total factor productivity. The average
deviation in the business economy of subperiod rates of change from the
period mean rate of increase in labor productivity was 0.3 per cent, compared
with 0.4 per cent for total factor productivity. The comparable mean average
deviations for the segments and industry groups were 0.8 and 0.9 per cent,

exactly the same percentages as those for total factor productivity. Annual variability of per cent changes in labor productivity was, of course, much greater than the subperiod variability. The average deviations of annual per cent changes from the long-period rate of change were 2.0 per cent for the segments and 2.6 for the industry groups—somewhat below the comparable measures for total factor productivity, since labor can be more readily adjusted to output changes than capital. (See Table 5-2 above.) In fact, labor productivity in the business economy rose more in contractions than in expansions, although the reverse was true for about one-third of the industry groups. It dropped absolutely during contraction years in three of the groups: primary metal products, local transit, and intercity bus lines. Apparently, firms in these industries had more difficulty in adjusting man-hours worked to declines in output than those in the eighteen other industry groups where output fell in contraction years. (See reference in Table 5-2).

Output per Unit of Capital Input

Despite the substantial and widespread increases in capital per unit of labor input during the postwar period, significant economies in the use of capital per unit of output were also realized at the same time in almost all industry segments and groups. It will be recalled that real product per unit of capital input ("capital productivity") rose at an average annual rate of 0.5 per cent in the business economy. It fell in only one segment, contract construction, remained unchanged in trade as a whole, and averaged annual increases in the other segments ranging from 0.2 per cent in farming to 2.9 per cent in mining (see Table 5-6).

The range of change was wider in the industry groups. About one-third of the groups showed moderate declines in the output-capital ratio. Most of the increases were also moderate, but oil and gas, as well as airlines, showed average gains in capital productivity of more than 5 per cent a year. The average deviations of segment and group rates of change from their means were 1.2 and 1.3 per cent, respectively, about the same as for labor productivity changes. The average deviations in the subperiods were much greater, particularly for the group rates of change from their mean. There were more declines in capital productivity in the first three subperiods than over the period as a whole, and the range of change was greater. By the last subperiod, 1960-66, there was a larger proportion of groups with substantial increases, which was reflected in an accelerated rate of advance in capital productivity averaging 1.8 per cent for the business economy as a whole. Between 1966

TABLE 5-6

Private Domestic Business Economy: Output per Unit of Capital Input,
by Industry Segment and Group, Average Annual Percentage Rates of Change

	1948-66	1948-53	1953-57	1957-60	1960-66	Average Deviation
Private domestic business economy	0.5	0.3	-1.2	0.3	1.8	0.9
Farming	0.2	-0.8	0.1	2.3	0.2	0.7
Mining	2.9	2.7	2.5	-2.0	5.9	2.0
Metal	-0.4	1.7	-6.0	-8.8	6.4	5.5
Coal	0.4	-4.9	5.7	-5.3	4.4	4.9
Oil and gas	5.4	5.9	4.6	0.0	8.3	2.2
Nonmetal	-0.2	2.8	-2.1	1.6	-2.3	2.3
Contract construction	-3.8	-3.3	-2.4	-4.2	-4.9	0.9
Manufacturing	0.8	0.9	-2.1	0.2	3.1	1.5
Nondurables	0.7	0.6	0.6	0.7	1.0	0.2
Foods	1.8	1.4	4.1	2.1	0.3	1.2
Beverages	1.0	-3.2	6.3	-0.4	1.8	2.8
Tobacco	-0.1	1.4	-0.3	-1.8	-0.1	0.7
Textiles	2.7	-0.2	0.8	8.4	3.8	2.6
Apparel	-0.9	-1.6	3.2	-0.3	-3.3	2.0
Paper	1.0	0.1	-1.1	2.0	2.6	1.4
Printing, publishing	1.8	1.7	6.7	1.9	-1.3	2.2
Chemicals	2.8	2.2	2.7	3.8	2.9	0.4
Petroleum refining	1.0	3.0	-1.6	2.0	0.5	1.5
Rubber products	3.3	5.3	2.3	1.2	3.5	1.2
Leather products	1.0	1.4	3.6	0.4	-0.9	1.4
Durables	0.3	1.5	-3.1	-0.6	2.1	1.8
Lumber products	0.3	-0.2	3.1	3.7	-2.7	2.3
Furniture	2.7	4.3	3.0	2.1	1.6	1.0
Stone, clay, glass products	-0.2	0.3	-2.5	-1.0	1.4	1.3
Primary metals	-0.7	-0.6	-1.3	-6.2	2.4	2.1
Fabricated metals	-0.3	-0.1	-2.2	-1.2	1.2	1.1
Machinery excluding electric	1.9	2.0	-1.5	3.4	3.3	1.7

Electric machinery	1.5	3.5	-1.5	3.1	1.0	1.7
Transportation equipment and ordnance	1.5	7.3	-4.8	1.2	1.1	3.2
Instruments	-0.7	-3.6	-2.2	2.7	1.2	3.2
Miscellaneous	0.6	-5.2	-1.6	4.1	5.6	4.4
Transportation	0.6	-2.1	0.0	-0.9	4.1	2.3
Railroads	0.6	-1.9	-0.9	-2.0	5.1	3.0
Nonrail	-2.4	-6.9	-2.5	-2.2	1.5	2.6
Local transit			n.a.			
Intercity bus lines			n.a.			
Motor freight transportation			n.a.			
Water transportation	-2.1	0.9	2.5	-9.4	-3.8	3.6
Air transportation	6.1	18.5	-0.9	-6.2	7.7	7.6
Pipeline transportation			n.a.			
Communication and public utilities	1.2	0.5	0.6	0.4	2.7	1.0
Communication	0.7	1.2	-0.1	-0.7	1.6	0.8
Electric, gas, and sanitary services	1.5	0.6	1.3	1.0	2.7	0.8
Electric and gas	2.4	1.0	2.8	2.0	3.5	0.9
Trade	0.0	-1.6	0.1	0.9	0.6	0.8
Wholesale	-0.3	-3.1	-0.1	1.5	0.9	1.5
Retail	0.0	-0.9	0.2	0.4	0.4	0.5
Finance, insurance, and real estate			n.a.			
Services			n.a.			
Average Deviation						
7 Industry segments	1.2	1.7	1.6	1.6	2.6	2.6
34 Industry groups[a]	1.3	2.7	2.6	2.8	2.3	2.3

Source: See source for Table 5-1.

[a] Includes two-digit industries and one-digit industries that are not subdivided. Excludes nondurables, durables, nonrail, and electric and gas subcategories.

and 1969, however, capital productivity fell in the business economy and in most segments as the growth of output decelerated sharply.

Average deviations of subperiod rates from average period rates of change in capital were well above the corresponding measures for total and labor productivity. (See last column of Table 5-6.) This indicates the problems of adjusting the rate of capital accumulation to the growth of sales and output, even abstracting from cyclical variations in the latter. The average deviations of annual per cent changes in capital productivity from their mean were 3.7 and 5.5 per cent for the segments and groups, respectively. (See Table 5-2 above.) These high mean deviations are not surprising in view of the fact that real capital stocks and inputs rise in most segments and groups even in contractions, when output is falling in most. On the average, output per unit of capital productivity fell by 3.2 per cent during contractions, and rose by an average 1.6 per cent in expansion years (see Table 5-3 above). Of the six segments for which capital productivity changes were available, the rates fell during contraction years in all except farming, which showed no change.

Summary Comparison of
Dispersion and Variability Measures

The average deviations of segment and group rates of change in real product, productivity, and capital-labor ratios from their means are summarized in Table 5-7. It will be noted that the average deviations for total factor

TABLE 5-7

Private Domestic Business Economy: Summary of Measures of Dispersion in Rates of Change in Output, Productivity, and Input Ratios, by Industry Segment and Group, 1948-66 and Subperiods

	Real Product	Total Factor Productivity	Output per Unit of		Capital per Unit of Labor Input
			Labor Input	Capital Input	
Period 1948-66					
Segments	1.4	0.8	1.3	1.2	1.4
Groups	2.2	1.0	1.4	1.3	1.3
Subperiod averages[a]					
Segments	1.8	1.2	1.5	1.9	1.9
Groups	2.8	1.4	1.7	2.6	2.6

Source: Tables 5-1, 5-4–6, 6-1.

[a] Averages of average deviations of rates of change for the four subperiods 1948-53, 1953-57, 1957-60, and 1960-66.

productivity in both segments and groups are well below the corresponding average deviations for the two partial productivity ratios. As demonstrated in *Productivity Trends*,[4] this indicates a positive correlation between rates of change in output per unit of labor input and in capital per unit of labor input. A regression between these two variables for the thirty-two industry groups over the period 1948-66 was run, and the coefficient of correlation was 0.42, significant at the 0.05 level. The correlations for the subperiods were also positive, but less significant.

The dispersion of rates of change for the period 1948-66 in the two partial productivity ratios is almost the same in absolute terms. However, in relative terms, as measured by the coefficient of variation, dispersion in rates of change in capital productivity is much higher, since its secular rate of growth averages only 0.5 per cent a year, compared with 3.1 for output per unit of labor input.

It has been noted that dispersion in the subperiods tends to be higher than dispersion over the entire period covered. This is markedly the case with the output-capital measures, reflecting the long-term nature of the adjustment of capital to output requirements.

With regard to variability of rates of change in the subperiods compared with the average rate of change over 1948-66, average deviations for both total factor productivity and labor productivity averaged 0.8 and 0.9 per cent for the segments and industry groups, respectively. (See Table 5-2, addendum.) This was considerably below the variability prevailing in the earlier decades from 1889 to 1948, reflecting primarily the lesser variability in subperiod rates of growth in real product, by segment and group.[5] For capital productivity, the average mean deviation was considerably higher, at 1.3 per cent, illustrating the difficulties of adjusting real capital stocks to output and the resulting variations in capacity utilization even in peak years. Here, too, variability was smaller than in the decades prior to 1948, a reflection of the smoother pace of economic growth in the postwar period.

The fact that mean deviations of subperiod growth rates in total factor productivity from the 1948-66 average were less than a weighted average of the mean deviations of the two partial productivity ratios from their average rates indicates a positive correlation between subperiod rates of change in labor productivity and capital per unit of labor input. This correlation is not significant with respect to annual changes, however, since the underlying

[4] p. 170.
[5] See *Productivity Trends*, Table 47, p. 173.

relationship is obscured by cyclical factors: since we do not adjust capital stocks and inputs for changes in rates of capital utilization, capital per unit of labor input rises sharply in most industries in recession years, while labor productivity in many segments and groups falls or rises less than in expansion years.

The annual deviation of per cent changes in total factor productivity from the 1948-66 average rate is 2.4 per cent for the industry segments, nearly reaching the average rate of growth itself. For the industry groups, the annual deviation, at 3.0 per cent, surpasses the average rate of growth. In the case of labor productivity changes, average deviations are a bit smaller, and stay below the trend rate for the groups as well as the segments. As to capital productivity changes, average annual deviations from the trend rates are very high for both segments and groups, as would be expected given the concept used in estimating capital. (See Table 5-2, addendum.)

6

INTERRELATIONSHIPS OF PRODUCTIVITY
WITH ASSOCIATED VARIABLES, BY INDUSTRY

Our final chapter starts with an examination of relative changes in output by industry segments and groups and their relationship to relative productivity changes. A positive correlation, working through relative price changes, is found to prevail within—but not across—the broad industry segments. Consequently, while above-average productivity changes are not generally associated with relative declines in employment in the industry groups, the same generalization does not hold for the broader industry segments.

In the latter part of the chapter the chief causal factors that may account for differential industry rates of productivity change are analyzed. In this connection, the results of some experimental regression analyses for twenty-one manufacturing industry groups are also introduced. We emphasize that the results are less than definitive, due to multicollinearity and other statistical problems, but hope that the industry estimates will serve as a basis for further attempts at cross-sectional analysis of causal forces, which provides a useful supplement to aggregative analysis.

Patterns of Output Change, by Industry

Before analyzing the interrelationships between industry productivity and output changes, a look at industry patterns of rates of change in output will be helpful.

It will be recalled that the rate of growth of real product in the private domestic business economy averaged 4.0 per cent a year during the 1948-66 period. Growth rates of the major segments ranged from about 1 per cent in farming to about 7 per cent in communication and public utilities. Manufacturing and trade were close to the business economy average. In terms of the

Chart 6-1: Private Domestic Nonfarm Business Economy, Thirty-two Industry Groups:
Relationship Between Rates of Change in Output and in Total
Factor Productivity, 1948–66

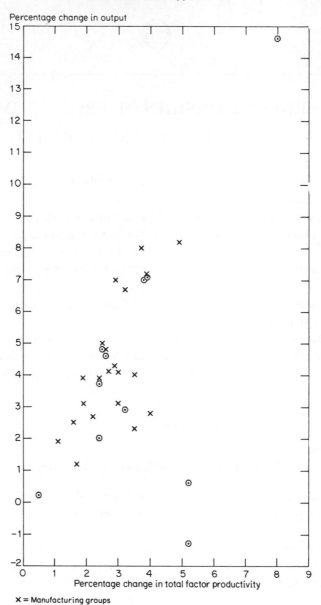

X = Manufacturing groups

Source: Tables 5-1 and 6-1.
a Excludes contract construction; finance, insurance, and real estate; and services.

Chart 6-2: Private Domestic Business Economy, Nine Industry Segments:
Relationship Between Rates of Change in Output and in Labor Productivity, 1948–66

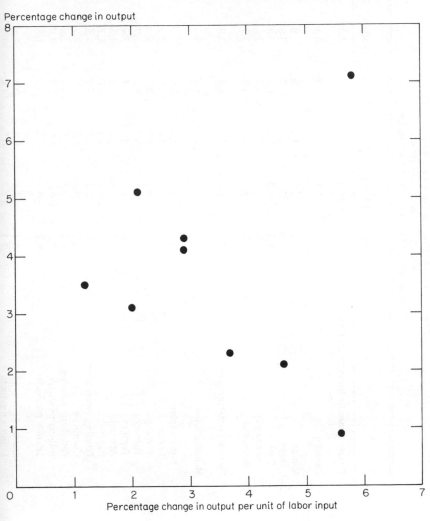

Percentage change in output

Percentage change in output per unit of labor input

Source: Tables 5-5 and 6-1.

TABLE 6-1

Private Domestic Business Economy: Real Product,
by Industry Segment and Group,
Average Annual Percentage Rates of Change

	1948-66	1948-53	1953-57	1957-60	1960-66	Average Deviation
Private domestic business economy	4.0	4.6	2.5	2.6	5.2	1.1
Farming	0.9	1.1	0.2	2.5	0.5	0.6
Mining	2.1	2.3	3.0	-1.0	2.8	1.0
Metal	2.0	2.7	2.3	-1.7	3.0	1.2
Coal	-1.3	-6.3	1.5	-6.1	3.8	4.5
Oil and gas	2.9	4.8	3.5	-0.3	2.6	1.3
Nonmetal	4.6	5.3	6.3	3.8	3.3	1.1
Contract construction	3.1	6.0	2.8	0.9	2.0	1.6
Manufacturing	4.3	6.0	1.1	1.2	6.5	2.4
Nondurables	3.8	3.7	2.7	2.9	5.1	0.9
Foods	3.1	2.4	3.6	3.9	2.9	0.5
Beverages	2.7	0.7	1.8	2.8	5.0	1.5
Tobacco	1.9	1.5	0.7	4.2	1.9	0.8
Textiles	2.8	1.1	0.8	3.4	5.4	1.9
Apparel	3.1	2.3	1.8	3.6	4.3	1.0
Paper	5.0	4.8	4.1	4.0	6.2	0.8
Printing, publishing	4.1	2.7	5.3	4.2	4.5	0.8
Chemicals	8.2	9.6	6.7	6.9	8.7	1.1
Petroleum refining	4.1	5.3	3.6	3.6	3.6	0.7
Rubber products	7.2	6.6	5.9	5.0	9.8	1.7
Leather products	1.2	0.6	2.2	-0.1	1.8	0.8
Durables	4.7	7.6	0.1	0.6	7.5	3.4
Lumber products	2.3	2.2	-0.5	3.8	3.5	1.3

Primary metals	2.9	5.0	0.1	3.0	0.1	3.0
Fabricated metals	3.9	5.4	0.7	1.1	6.3	2.4
Machinery except electric	4.8	6.4	0.8	0.5	8.3	3.2
Electric machinery	8.0	11.4	3.0	5.7	9.8	3.0
Transportation equipment and ordnance	6.7	16.5	-0.4	-0.4	7.5	5.8
Instruments	7.0	9.1	4.8	6.3	7.0	1.2
Miscellaneous	4.0	3.2	1.7	4.8	5.9	1.5
Transportation	2.3	0.5	1.5	0.0	5.6	2.2
Railroads	0.6	-1.1	-1.2	-2.6	4.9	2.8
Nonrail	3.7	2.1	3.6	2.0	5.9	1.5
Local transit	-4.8	-4.0	-5.4	-7.9	-3.5	1.3
Intercity bus lines	0.0	-0.2	-3.2	-2.4	3.6	2.4
Intercity trucking	8.5	12.6	5.3	6.8	8.0	2.3
Water transportation	0.2	0.0	2.9	-4.2	0.8	1.6
Air transportation	14.6	17.9	15.1	7.6	15.3	2.4
Pipeline transportation	6.0	8.9	6.3	1.6	5.8	1.7
Communication and public utilities	7.1	8.4	6.7	6.0	6.8	0.7
Communication	7.0	7.2	6.5	5.5	8.0	0.8
Electric, gas, and sanitary services	7.1	9.2	7.2	6.3	5.8	1.2
Electric and gas	8.0	9.7	8.9	6.9	6.7	1.3
Trade	4.1	3.7	3.7	3.1	5.2	0.6
Wholesale	4.8	3.4	4.8	4.6	6.0	0.8
Retail	3.7	3.8	3.1	2.1	4.7	0.8
Finance, insurance, real estate	5.1	5.2	5.3	4.0	5.3	0.3
Services	3.5	2.0	3.1	3.7	4.8	1.0
Average deviation:						
9 industry segments	1.4	2.2	1.5	1.8	1.7	
40 industry groups	2.2	3.5	2.4	2.9	2.2	

more detailed industry groups, local transit and coal mining showed decline, while positive rates ranged from less than 1 per cent for intercity bus lines, water transportation, and railroads to almost 15 per cent a year for air transportation. (See Table 6-1.)

Dispersion as measured by the average deviation of segment and group rates from their means was 1.4 and 2.2 per cent, respectively. This was well above the dispersion in rates of change of factor productivity in both segments and groups, and above that of the partial productivity rates for the industry groups.

Dispersion of output growth rates averaged considerably higher for subperiods than for the overall period. (See bottom of Table 6-1.) While well above the degree of dispersion for total factor and labor productivity ratios, the average growth rate for subperiods was about the same as that for rates of change in capital productivity and capital per unit of labor input. Output dropped during one or more subperiods in about one-quarter of the industry groups and, of course, showed higher rates of growth in at least one subperiod than the average rate 1948-66. Dispersion was significantly greater in the first subperiod, 1948-53, which was affected both by post-World War II readjustments and the Korean conflict, than in subsequent subperiods. This contrasts with the productivity rates, which generally were as dispersed in the last subperiod, 1960-66, as in the first.

Variability in subperiod rates of growth in real product was somewhat above that in the total factor and labor productivity ratios. The average deviations of subperiod rates from the period rate were 1.2 and 1.5 for segments and groups, respectively (see Table 5-2, addendum). This represented significantly less variability in growth rates than for earlier subperiods, as noted previously.[1]

Average annual mean deviation of output rates for the segments, at 3.1, while much above the subperiod deviations, was still below the trend rate; the comparable deviation for the industry groups, at 4.8 per cent, was greater than the trend rate—reflecting the fact that the majority of groups showed declines in output during contractions, although total and labor productivity declined only in some of them. Variability of annual changes in output was less than that in capital productivity, however.

Interrelation of Output and Productivity Changes

A significant positive correlation between relative industry changes in productivity and in output within broadly similar sectors was found in *Productivity*

---

[1] See *Productivity Trends*, Table 58, pp. 204-05.

Trends, in the earlier studies by Fabricant,[2] and in the more recent work by Fuchs.[3] It has been suggested that the relationship is reciprocal: relative advances in output affect productivity through differential scale economies; and relative changes in productivity, mirrored in relative price changes for the outputs of the various industries, in turn affect relative changes in sales and output.

Fuchs pointed out that the relationship does not hold with respect to ten major one-digit industry segments.[4] Our study confirms his findings, and we suggest some explanations later, following an analysis of the relationship for two-digit industry groups in the "industry" sector (excluding contract construction but including wholesale and retail trade) and for two-digit and four-digit industries in the manufacturing segment alone.

Our results for the period 1948-66 are broadly in line with the results of the earlier studies. The regression between average annual percentage rates of change in output and total factor productivity for thirty-two industry groups yields a coefficient of correlation of 0.55. (The relationship is depicted in the scatter diagram shown in Chart 6-1.) With rates of change in output related to output per man-hour for thirty-six industry groups, the coefficient is 0.60. Finally, the correlation between rates of change in output and capital productivity for thirty-two groups is 0.54. All these correlations are significant at the 0.01 level. (See Table 6-2).

Confining the analysis to manufacturing, for the twenty-one two-digit industry groups the coefficient of correlation between rates of change in output and total factor productivity is higher than in the industry segment including trade: 0.65; using rates of change in output and labor productivity, the coefficient is 0.54. The first correlation is significant at the 0.01 level, and the second, at the 0.05 level. The relationship between relative changes in output and in capital productivity for the manufacturing groups is not significant at the 0.05 level.

Moving down to the correlation between rates of change from 1954 to 1963 in output and in output per man-hour for 395 four-digit manufacturing

[2] Solomon Fabricant, *Employment in Manufacturing, 1899-1939: An Analysis of its Relation to the Volume of Production*, New York, NBER, 1942.

[3] V. R. Fuchs, *The Service Economy*, New York, NBER, 1969, Chapter 4.

[4] Ibid., Chapter 3. In our analysis, we use nine industry segments, combining government enterprises with private service industries. Fuchs combines the segments into three sectors: agriculture, industry, and service (ibid., Table 1, p. 18). His "industry" sector comprises mining, construction, manufacturing, transportation, communications and public utilities, and government enterprises. Our analysis of two-digit industries relates broadly to the "industry sector" so defined, except that in addition to shifting government enterprises to the "services sector," we include wholesale and retail trade. Also, since we do not have any further breakdown of the contract construction segment, we exclude it from our two-digit industry analysis.

TABLE 6-2

Private Domestic Nonfarm Business Economy:[a] Rates of Change, Productivity Ratio Versus Output, Regression Results, 1948-66, by Subperiod

		1948-66	1948-53	1953-57	1957-60	1960-66
		A. Total Factor Productivity Versus Output				
32	Industry groups					
	Coefficient of correlation	0.552b	0.663b	0.343	0.220	0.620b
	t value	3.760b	4.850b	2.000	1.230	4.330b
	Slope	0.261	0.301			0.444
	Intercept	1.971	1.461			0.873
21	Manufacturing groups					
	Coefficient of correlation	0.649b	0.649b	0.490c	0.598b	0.748b
	t value	4.888b	4.888b	2.811c	4.061b	7.411b
	Slope	0.295	0.224	0.312	0.431	0.335
	Intercept	1.538	1.441	2.191	1.567	0.950
		B. Labor Productivity Versus Output				
36	Industry groups					
	Coefficient of correlation	0.595b	0.544b	0.531b	0.445b	0.616b
	t value	4.320b	3.780b	3.650b	2.900b	4.560b
	Slope	0.346	0.271	0.256	0.273	0.479
	Intercept	2.184	2.225	2.861	2.883	1.210
21	Manufacturing groups					
	Coefficient of correlation	0.539b	0.515b	0.606b	0.575b	0.390
	t value	3.315b	3.054b	4.174b	3.747b	2.005
	Slope	0.287	0.189	0.338	0.436	
	Intercept	2.113	2.136	2.705	2.113	

395 Manufacturing industries	(1954-63)	(1954-58)	(1958-63)
Coefficient of correlation	0.505	0.490	0.374
t value	13.49b	12.830b	8.65b
Slope	3.56	2.90	5.35
Intercept	-91.8	-30.5	-53.4

C. Capital Productivity Versus Output

	(1954-63)	(1954-58)	(1958-63)		
32 Industry groups					
Coefficient of correlation	0.544	0.688	0.067	0.561	0.421
t value	4.234b	7.154b	0.368	4.481b	2.803b
Slope	0.932	0.769		0.490	0.412
Intercept	3.300	3.677		2.526	4.777
21 Manufacturing groups					
Coefficient of correlation	0.384	0.491	0.336	0.516	0.549
t value	1.962	2.819c	1.652	3.065b	3.425b
Slope		0.678		0.424	0.594
Intercept		4.219		2.585	4.901

Note: If the coefficient of correlation is not significant at the .05 level, the coefficients of the regression equation (intercept and slope) are not given.

Source: Tables A-26–29, A-37–57, A-60–61, A-64–69, A-71, A-73, A-76–77; and Henry Linsert, "An Empirical Study of the Relationship between Output per Man-Hour and Related Variables in Manufacturing Industries, 1954-1963," June 1970, on file at The George Washington University library.

a Excludes contract construction; finance, insurance, and real estate; and services.

The thirty-six industry groups include all other nonfarm two-digit industries and one-digit industries that are not subdivided.

The thirty-two industry groups exclude local transit, intercity bus lines, intercity trucking, and pipeline transportation.

The 395 manufacturing industries are four-digit industries for which indexes were prepared by H. Linsert.

b Significant at the .01 level.

c Significant at the .05 level.

industries, the coefficient is 0.51, lower than for the twenty-one groups, but still significant at the 0.01 level.

The coefficient of correlation between rates of change in output and in the productivity ratios averages less for the subperiods than for the period as a whole. In the case of total factor productivity and output, the coefficients are higher in the first and last subperiods, 1948-53 and 1960-66, than in the two intervening subperiods. This reflects the fact that relative changes in productivity and in price were also less closely correlated in the subperiods than over the whole period, and that the coefficients were lower in the middle subperiods.

Fuchs also found a significant positive correlation between rates of change in output and output per man-hour within the service sector. Using seventeen service industries (eight service industries proper and nine retail trades) for the periods 1939-63 and 1948-63, he obtained coefficients of rank correlation of 0.91 and 0.69, respectively.[5]

Productivity and Prices of Factors and Products

The general theoretical presupposition behind the associations just described is that, at least over longer periods of time, rates of change in productivity and in factor prices are not correlated to any significant degree, since mobility of resources tends to equalize rates of change in factor prices, including profits. Consequently, relative changes in productivity tend to be reflected in relative price changes, and thus in relative output changes. Actually, if total factor productivity measures are used, it is relative changes in unit value added ("net price") that would be negatively correlated with relative changes in productivity. Relative gross output prices are also affected by relative changes in prices of purchased intermediate products to which value is added.

The hypothesis that relative changes in productivity and in factor prices are not significantly correlated is at least partially confirmed by the evidence shown in Table 6-3. Over the entire eighteen-year period for thirty-two industry groups, the coefficient of correlation between rates of change in total factor productivity and in average (combined) factor prices was only 0.18, not significant at the 0.05 levels. The coefficients in the subperiods averaged almost twice that for the longer period. This indicates that it takes a substantial period of time for shifts of resources in response to relative factor price changes to tend to equalize price changes in similar resources employed by industry groups within the various segments.

[5] Ibid., Table 34, p. 92.

The coefficients of correlation between industry rates of change in the partial productivity ratios and in the corresponding prices of labor and capital are substantially higher—0.34 in both cases—but still not significant at the 0.05 level. This is consistent with the lower degree of correlation on a total factor basis, since relative changes in labor and capital productivity are negatively correlated, and the relative prices of labor and capital therefore tend to show a similar negative association. The table of correlation coefficients also shows that the tendency for coefficients to be higher in the subperiods than over the longer period holds only for the relation between changes in capital productivity and capital price. As we measure it, the price of capital is a compound of the prices of capital goods and the rate of return on net capital assets (see appendix text). It seems reasonable that, over shorter periods, the rate of return component of capital price would tend to reflect rates of change in output (and presumably net income) relative to the stock of capital. But over long periods, movements of capital into areas where rates of return have been rising relatively would tend to bring the increases back down closer to the average rate.

In the case of average hourly labor compensation, labor productivity in specific industries is only one of many influences at work in wage determination, and there is no reason to believe it to be a stronger influence over shorter periods than over longer periods of time. The coefficients of correlation are low for both the 1948-66 period and the subperiods, and are generally not significant at the 0.05 level.

When the industry sample is confined to the twenty-one manufacturing groups, the findings just noted are somewhat more pronounced (see Table 6-3, part B). In the case of the 395 four-digit manufacturing industries for which only labor data are available, the coefficient of correlation between rates of change in output per man-hour and average hourly compensation is only 0.22, and lower when ranks are used. But due to the large size of the sample, the coefficient, while low, is significant at the 0.05 level.

These results make sense; after all, if wage-rate changes in the various industries strongly reflected their productivity changes, the entire wage structure of the economy would be out of kilter within relatively few years. Actually, the ranking of industries by levels of average hourly labor compensation has not generally changed very much since 1948 (see Table 6-4). This confirms evidence with respect to still longer time spans for earlier periods.[6] In other words, rates of change in wage rates show much less dispersion than

6 See *Productivity Trends*, Table 54, p. 197.

TABLE 6-3

Private Domestic Nonfarm Business Economy:[a] Rates of Change, Average Input Price Versus Productivity Ratio, Regression Results, 1948-66, by Subperiod

	1948-66	1948-53	1953-57	1957-60	1960-66
A. Average Price of Total Input Versus Total Factor Productivity					
32 Industry groups					
Coefficient of correlation	0.182	0.388	0.007	0.327	0.452
t value	1.03	2.31[b]	0.38	1.89	2.78[b]
Slope		0.478			0.292
Intercept		3.362			2.968
21 Manufacturing groups					
Coefficient of correlation	-0.203	0.0	-0.016	0.535	-0.077
t value	0.923	0.0	0.070	3.266[b]	0.339
Slope				1.500	
Intercept				-2.029	
B. Average Hourly Earnings Versus Labor Productivity					
32 Industry groups					
Coefficient of correlation	0.339	0.199	-0.104	0.223	0.434
t value	1.97	1.11	0.57	1.25	2.640[c]
Slope					0.138
Intercept					3.018
21 Manufacturing groups					
Coefficient of correlation	0.251	0.208	-0.216	0.264	0.226
t value	1.167	0.948	1.039	1.237	1.038

	(1954-63)		(1954-58)	(1958-63)	
395 Manufacturing industries					
Coefficient of correlation	0.218		0.135	0.470	
t value	4.56[b]		2.74[b]	12.01[b]	
Slope	0.09		0.07	0.21	
Intercept	34.46		18.64	9.47	

C. Price of Capital Versus Capital Productivity

	(1954-63)		(1954-58)	(1958-63)	
32 Industry groups					
Coefficient of correlation	0.340	0.754	0.482	0.556	0.277
t value	2.107[c]	9.565[b]	3.439[b]	4.409[b]	1.645
Slope	0.695	2.261	1.745	1.363	
Intercept	0.609	-3.541	-0.950	-2.266	
21 Manufacturing groups					
Coefficient of correlation	0.195	0.535	0.450	0.549	0.090
t value	0.884	3.266[b]	2.464[c]	3.425[b]	0.396
Slope		1.500	0.660	1.303	
Intercept		-2.029	-0.378	-1.334	

Note: If the coefficient of correlation is not significant at the .05 level, the coefficients of the regression equation (intercept and slope) are not given.

Source: For productivity measures, see source for Tables 6-2. Factor prices derived from Department of Commerce compensation estimates and our factor input estimates.

[a] Excludes contract construction; finance, insurance, and real estate; and services.
[b] Significant at the .01 level.
[c] Significant at the .05 level.

TABLE 6-4
Private Domestic Business Economy: Ranking of Average Hourly Compensation
in Thirty-four Industry Groups,
1948-66, by Subperiod

	1948-66	1948-53	1953-57	1957-60	196
Farming	1	1	1	1	
Mining					
Metal	22	21	26	24	2
Coal	30	33	33	30	2
Oil and gas	16	23	16	15	1
Nonmetal	9	8	9	9	
Contract construction	21	18	18	18	2
Manufacturing					
Foods	11	9	10	11	1
Beverages	25	32	29	23	2
Tobacco	7	3	7	8	1
Textiles	3	5	3	3	
Apparel	4	6	4	4	
Paper	13	14	13	14	1
Printing and publishing	23	26	24	22	2
Chemicals	31	28	30	31	3
Petroleum refining	34	34	34	34	3
Rubber products	17	22	21	19	1
Leather products	6	7	6	6	
Lumber	5	4	5	5	
Furniture	8	10	8	7	
Stone, clay, glass products	14	13	14	16	1
Primary metals	33	30	32	33	3
Fabricated metals	20	20	20	21	1
Machinery, except electric	26	27	28	26	2
Electric machinery	18	19	19	20	1
Transportation equipment and ordnance	32	31	31	32	3
Instruments	24	24	23	25	2
Miscellaneous	10	11	11	10	
Transportation					
Railroads	28	17	25	29	2
Water transportation	27	25	22	28	2
Air transportation	29	29	27	27	3
Communication and public utilities					
Communication	12	12	12	12	1
Electric, gas, sanitary services	19	15	17	17	2
Trade					
Wholesale	15	16	15	13	1
Retail	2	2	2	2	

Note: For 1948-66, rank of absolute hourly earnings in subperiods is weighted by length of
subperiod. Hourly earnings for each subperiod represent an average of hourly earnings in the ter▮
years of the subperiod.

Source: Hourly earnings derived from Department of Commerce labor compensation estimates
our labor input estimates.

rates of productivity change, and relative changes in the two variables are only weakly associated.

Given the weak association between industry rates of change in productivity and in factor prices, one would expect a fairly high degree of correlation between relative industry changes in productivity and in product prices. As noted earlier, unit value added (net price) is the more relevant variable. In computing rates of change, we use two versions of unit value added: one is the implicit price deflator for industry GNP as calculated by OBE; the other is current dollar GNP by two-digit industry, divided by our output measures, which differ somewhat from the OBE real product measures, as explained in the appendix. Our adjusted unit value added (net price) index is thus consistent with our productivity and related measures. Price indexes are available for one group fewer than productivity indexes.

As shown in Table 6-5, the coefficient of correlation between rates of change in total factor productivity and in the implicit industry product price deflator rounds to -0.70 for the period 1948-66, significant at the 0.01 level. The coefficient is substantially lower in most subperiods, which is consistent with the higher correlation between changes in productivity and factor prices in the subperiods than over the period as a whole. The coefficient of correlation between industry rates of change in labor productivity and in the product price deflators during 1948-66 is virtually the same as that obtained when total factor productivity is used. This is to be expected in view of the high degree of correlation between labor productivity and total factor productivity. In the subperiods, however, the coefficients are higher than when total factor productivity is used, though still below the coefficient for the whole period, except in the final subperiod 1960-66, when it is the same.

The coefficients of correlation are higher when the adjusted net output price deflator is used: -0.88 in the regression on total factor productivity, and -0.76 in the regression on labor productivity. The subperiod coefficients are also higher relative to those for the period as a whole. (See Table 6-5.)

Similar results are obtained for the twenty manufacturing groups shown in the table. With regard to the 395 manufacturing industries, the coefficient of correlation between rates of change in output per man-hour and unit value added is lower: -0.60 for the period 1954-63. The shorter length of the period could partially explain the lower coefficient. Also, value added in the Census of Manufactures is more of a gross concept than the OBE industry product concept, which also tends to lead to somewhat different results in correlations.

TABLE 6-5

Private Domestic Nonfarm Business Economy:[a] Rates of Change, Net Price (Unit Value Added) Versus Productivity, Regression Results, 1948-66, by Subperiod

	1948-66	1948-53	1953-57	1957-60	1960-66
A. Net Price Versus Total Factor Productivity					
31 Industry groups					
Coefficient of correlation	-0.695	-0.389	-0.236	-0.048	-0.681
t value	7.23[b]	2.27[c]	1.31	2.59[c]	5.01[b]
Slope	-0.614	-0.388		-0.055	-0.483
Intercept	3.261	3.314		1.343	2.376
20 Manufacturing groups					
Coefficient of correlation	-0.500	-0.205	-0.170	-0.180	-0.050
t value	2.827[c]	1.498	0.741	0.788	0.212
Slope	-0.608				
Intercept	3.375				
B. Adjusted Net Price Versus Total Factor Productivity					
31 Industry groups					
Coefficient of correlation	-0.877	-0.689	-0.408	-0.238	0.813
t value	9.83[b]	5.12[b]	2.40[c]	1.32	7.52[b]
Slope	-1.133	-1.008	-0.693		-0.676
Intercept	4.461	4.533	3.393		2.736
20 Manufacturing groups					
Coefficient of correlation	-0.735	-0.453	-0.552	-0.242	-0.670
t value	6.774[b]	2.416[c]	3.367[b]	1.090	5.156[b]
Slope	-0.946	-0.865	-0.776		-0.894
Intercept	3.952	4.399	3.296		3.252

34 Industry groups					
Coefficient of correlation	-0.696	-0.351	-0.488	-0.302	-0.697
t value	5.48b	2.12c	3.16b	1.79	5.50b
Slope	-0.588	-0.325	-0.811		-0.518
Intercept	3.627	3.535	4.681		2.876
20 Manufacturing groups					
Coefficient of correlation	-0.509	-0.359	-0.419	0.167	-0.012
t value	2.912b	1.747	2.156c	0.728	0.051
Slope	-0.525		-0.902		
Intercept	3.420		5.634		
D. Adjusted Net Price Versus Labor Productivity					
31 Industry groups					
Coefficient of correlation	-0.756	-0.655	-0.596	-0.142	-0.716
t value	6.22b	4.66b	3.99b	1.20	5.43b
Slope	-0.867	-0.888	-1.012		-0.704
Intercept	4.116	4.595	5.078		3.193
20 Manufacturing groups					
Coefficient of correlation	-0.643	-0.570	-0.789	-0.023	-0.483
t value	4.643b	3.580b	8.849b	0.098	2.670c
Slope	-0.703	-0.950	-1.277		-0.593
Intercept	3.633	5.055	5.711		2.794
395 Manufacturing industries	(1954-63)		(1954-58)	(1958-63)	
Coefficient of correlation	-0.60		-0.60	-0.37	
t value	18.66b		18.66b	8.53b	
Slope	-0.35		-0.49	-0.36	
Intercept	24.9		15.5	7.5	

Note: If the coefficient of correlation is not significant at the .05 level, the coefficients of the regression equation (intercept and slope) are not given.

Source: See source for Table 6-3.

a Excludes contract construction; finance, insurance, and real estate; and services.
b Significant at the .01 level.
c Significant at the .05 level.

Unit Value Added, Output, and the Scale Effect

To complete the cycle of relationships, unit value added must be regressed on output. A significant negative relationship between rates of change in these two variables, given the negative relationship between rates of change in productivity and in unit value added, would explain at least part of the positive relationship between output and productivity. It is to be expected that relative changes in average market prices would show a closer relationship to relative changes in output than do relative changes in implicit product price deflators. But there is a fairly close relationship between relative changes in unit value added and in prices, by industry—not only because unit value added is, on the average, the chief component of price but also because there tends to be a positive correlation between relative changes in unit value added and in unit cost of intermediate products, in real terms.[7]

The coefficient of correlation between industry rates of change in the implicit product price deflators and in output is −0.45 when the OBE deflators are used, and −0.49 when the deflators are adjusted as described above. The coefficients are lower in the subperiods, on the average, than over the entire period covered. (See Table 6-6.) Although significant, the coefficients of correlation are not very high for the industry groups, and are even lower for the manufacturing groups and industries. This reflects the fact that sales and output are affected not only by relative changes in prices (given a set of price elasticities of demand) but also by differential income elasticities of demand and by shifts of preferences.

Actually, the degree of correlation between relative industry changes in output and productivity is higher than can be explained by the negative relationships between productivity and net price, and between net price and output. This supports the presumption that scale effects reinforce the positive relationship between relative industry changes in productivity and in output.

Productivity and Inputs

If output increased at the same rate in all industries, inputs would obviously fall relatively in industries with above-average productivity advance and rise relatively in industries with below-average productivity advance. This was not the case in the period 1948-66. The positive association between rates of change in output and in productivity was strong enough to obviate any systematic relationship between relative industry changes in productivity and in the tangible factor inputs, separately or in combination.

[7] See *Productivity Trends*, Table 56, p. 200.

TABLE 6-6

Private Domestic Nonfarm Business Economy:[a] Rates of Change, Output Versus Net Price,
Regression Results, 1948-66, by Subperiod

	1948-66	1948-53	1953-57	1957-60	1960-66
A. Rates of Change: Output Versus Net Price					
Industry groups					
Coefficient of correlation	-0.452	-0.221	-0.356	0.048	-0.266
t value	2.870[b]	1.280	2.160[c]	0.270	1.560
Slope	-0.901		-0.428		
Intercept	5.523		4.011		
Manufacturing groups					
Coefficient of correlation	-0.042	0.045	0.151	-0.302	0.220
t value	0.178	0.191	0.655	1.408	0.980
B. Rates of Change: Output Versus Adjusted Net Price					
Industry groups					
Coefficient of correlation	-0.489	-0.191	-0.477	0.157	-0.503
t value	3.463[b]	1.130	2.920[b]	0.860	3.130[b]
Slope	-0.803		-0.601		-0.828
Intercept	5.080		4.188		5.983
Manufacturing groups					
Coefficient of correlation	-0.182	0.126	-0.403	-0.348	-0.521
t value	0.798	0.543	2.039	1.678	3.030[b]
Slope					-0.818
Intercept					6.339
Manufacturing industries	(1954-63)		(1954-58)	(1958-63)	
Coefficient of correlation	-0.41		-0.42	-0.26	
t value	9.810[b]		10.140[b]	5.55[b]	
Slope	-1.24		-0.72	-0.44	
Intercept	61.4		18.1	20.7	

ote: If the coefficient of correlation is not significant at the .05 level, the coefficients of the re-
on equation (intercept and slope) are not given.
ource: See source for Table 6-3.
Excludes contract construction; finance, insurance, and real estate; and services.
Significant at the .01 level.
Significant at the .05 level.

For the industry groups, the coefficients of correlation between rates of
change in total factor productivity and in total factor input, and in labor and
capital input separately, during 1948-66 have small positive values, but are
not significant (see Table 6-7). It is interesting that, in the subperiods, the
coefficients in the relationships involving total input and labor input have

TABLE 6-7

Private Domestic Nonfarm Business Economy:[a] Rates of Change, Inputs Versus Productivity, Regression Results, 1948-66, by Subperiod

	1948-66	1948-53	1953-57	1957-60	1960-66
A. Total Factor Input Versus Total Factor Productivity					
32 Industry groups					
Coefficient of correlation	0.090	0.245	−0.120	−0.263	−0.121
t value	0.49	1.38	0.66	1.49	0.67
21 Manufacturing groups					
Coefficient of correlation	0.240	0.356	−0.164	−0.157	0.397
t value	1.079	1.777	0.735	0.701	2.055
B. Labor Input Versus Total Factor Productivity					
32 Industry groups					
Coefficient of correlation	0.083	0.260	−0.047	−0.230	−0.066
t value	0.46	1.48	0.260	1.29	0.36
21 Manufacturing groups					
Coefficient of correlation	0.249	0.376	0.061	−0.068	0.388
t value	1.157	1.908	0.297	0.298	1.990
C. Labor Input Versus Labor Productivity					
32 Industry groups					
Coefficient of correlation	0.006	0.091	0.281	−0.332	−0.165
t value	0.033	0.502	1.672	2.044[c]	0.929
Slope				−0.608	
Intercept				1.157	
21 Manufacturing groups					
Coefficient of correlation	0.013	0.163	0.078	0.210	0.127

	(1954-63)		(1954-58)	(1958-63)
395 Manufacturing industries				
Coefficient of correlation	-0.132	-0.329	-0.202	-0.079
t value	2.670[b]	1.607	4.19[b]	1.56
Slope	-0.145		-0.237	
Intercept	12.00		3.51	
D. Capital Input Versus Total Factor Productivity				
32 Industry groups				
Coefficient of correlation	0.177	-0.037	-0.359	-0.225
t value	0.98	0.20	2.11[c]	1.26
Slope			-0.766	
Intercept			4.840	
21 Manufacturing groups				
Coefficient of correlation	0.239	0.173	-0.432	0.026
t value	1.104	0.778	2.317[b]	0.113
Slope			1.015	
Intercept			5.013	

Note: If the coefficient of correlation is not significant at the .05 level, the coefficients of the regression equation (intercept and slope) are not given.

Source: See source for Table 6-2.

[a] Excludes contract construction; finance, insurance, and real estate; and services.

[b] Significant at the .01 level.

[c] Significant at the .05 level.

small negative values (except for the first subperiod), and are negative for all subperiods in the relationship involving capital input. This is consistent with the lesser degree of correlation shown in the subperiods than for the period as a whole between relative changes in output and productivity. In the case of the 395 manufacturing industries, the negative coefficients of correlation for the periods 1954-58 and 1954-63, while quite low, were significant at the 0.01 level.

We stated earlier that, as pointed out by Fuchs, there is virtually no correlation between relative changes in output and in productivity for the major one-digit industry segments (see Chart 6-2). The coefficient of correlation using relative changes in total factor productivity and output during 1948-66 in seven major segments is 0.05; using relative changes in labor productivity and output in all nine segments, it is 0.06. This lack of correlation is not the result of perverse price relationships. As is true of the two-digit industry groups, the coefficient of correlation between relative changes in productivity and input prices is insignificantly small: −0.07. As would be expected, there is a much higher coefficient of correlation between relative changes in productivity and in output prices: −0.43 when total factor productivity is used as the independent variable, and −0.70 when labor productivity is used for all nine segments.

The point where the causal chain breaks is in the relationship between relative changes in output and average prices of output—the coefficient of correlation for the period 1948-66 is a positive 0.49. Although the coefficient is not significant at the 0.05 level due to the small number of segments, it strongly suggests that there is but small cross-elasticity of demand for output across major industry segment lines, and that price elasticities are heavily out-weighed by high income elasticities of demand for products of industries with below-average productivity gains and above-average price increases. In the case of products of industries with above-average productivity gains and below-average price rises, the effects of low price elasticity of demand tend to be accentuated by low income elasticities.

The most striking examples of this effect are farming (or extractive industry as a whole, including mining) on the one hand, and services on the other. Between 1948 and 1966, total factor productivity in farming rose by 3.3 per cent a year on the average, well above the 2.5 per cent average in the private domestic economy as a whole. Despite price support programs, input prices rose somewhat less than in the economy as a whole, and product prices fell by an average 4.2 per cent a year, contrasted with the 1.7 per cent average increase in the private domestic economy as a whole. Despite the relatively favorable price trends, real product in farming rose at only one-quarter the 4.0 per cent growth rate of real domestic business product.

The other extreme is apparent in the case of the services sector, including finance. Here productivity rose less than half as fast as that in the domestic business economy. Despite a somewhat smaller increase in wage rates, average prices of services rose at an average annual rate of 3.2 per cent a year during 1948-66, compared with the 1.7 per cent business economy rate. Nevertheless, real product in the finance and services sector rose at an average annual rate of approximately 4.5 per cent a year, topping the 4.0 per cent average rate in the business economy. It is clear that price elasticities were heavily outweighed by income elasticities of demand and shifts in preferences, which resulted in a relative increase in demand for, and output of, services, despite the relative increase in their average prices.[8]

Productivity and Employment

Given the output changes in the various industry groupings during 1948-66, productivity and associated ratios can explain the changes in labor input and employment, as shown in Table 6-8. With reference to index numbers for 1966 on a 1948 base, by dividing output (*O*, in column 1) by total factor productivity (*O/I*, in column 2), total input (*I*) is obtained. By dividing the total input quotient by the ratio of total input to labor input (*I/L*, column 3), which measures the substitution of capital for labor, labor input (*L*, column 4) is obtained. It will be recalled that labor input is man-hours in component industry groups weighted by base-period average hourly compensation. But our chief interest is in employment change (*E*, column 6), obtained by dividing labor input by the ratio of labor input to employment (*L/E*, column 5), which reflects both changes in average hours worked and the interindustry shift effect.

We shall illustrate the use of the table by tracing through the behavior of the variables for the communication and public utilities group. Real product of this group rose by 242 per cent between 1948 and 1966. Total factor productivity doubled and factor substitution increased by 36 per cent over the period, so labor input rose by 25 per cent. Labor input per person engaged rose by 2 per cent—a drop in average hours having been more than offset by a relative shift of man-hours toward the higher-pay segments of the group. Thus, employment (persons engaged) rose by almost 23 per cent over the eighteen years.

---

[8] Fuchs attempts to estimate roughly the price, income, and substitution elasticities of demand for goods and services in his *The Service Economy*, Chapter 2.

TABLE 6-8

Private Domestic Business Economy: Output, Productivity,
Persons Engaged, and Related Variables, 1966
(index numbers, 1948=100)

	Real Product O (1)	Total Factor Productivity O/I (2)	Factor Substitution I/L (3)	Labor Input L (Col. 1÷Col. 3) (4)	Labor Input per Person L/E (5)	Persons Engaged E (Col. 4÷Col. 5) (6)
Private domestic business economy	203.0	156.6	110.4	117.4	102.9	114.1
Farming	118.1	180.8	147.2	44.4	88.2	50.3
Mining	144.6	209.0	106.7	64.8	100.2	64.7
Contract construction	173.3	130.1	109.5	121.7	97.2	125.2
Manufacturing	213.8	156.6	107.7	126.8	103.2	122.8
Nondurables	195.8	159.0	111.1	110.8	101.2	109.5
Durables	227.2	153.3	106.7	139.0	103.6	134.1
Transportation	150.7	183.8	103.9	78.9	92.6	85.2
Rail	111.5	248.5	111.2	40.4	83.8	48.2
Nonrail	191.1	145.5	103.8	126.6	103.8	121.9
Communication and public utilities	342.2	201.0	136.4	124.9	101.9	122.6
Trade	206.1	156.4	106.7	123.5	97.0	127.3
Finance, insurance, and real estate	243.3	145.9[a]		166.8	101.7	164.1
Services	184.4	123.1[a]		149.8	96.8	154.7

Source: Tables A-20, A-22, A-24, A-30–31, A-33, A-35, A-58, A-60, A-62, A-70, A-75, A-78–79.
[a] Output per unit of labor input.

It is even more informative to view the changes in relation to those for the private domestic business economy. This is done in Table 6-9, where the index numbers for each industry group and segment are divided by those for the private domestic business economy to show the relative changes. To illustrate again by the communication and public utilities group, the 23 per cent increase in employment was 7.4 per cent greater than the 14 per cent increase in the domestic business economy. This explains the expansion in the group's share of total persons engaged from 2.5 per cent in 1948 to 2.7 per cent in 1966 (column 8). The relative change in employment is, of course, the result of the interaction of the relative movements of the several variables we already reviewed in connection with Table 6-8. Thus, the relative output of the industry rose by 69 per cent, while productivity and factor substitution showed relative increases of 28 and 24 per cent, respectively, resulting in a 6.3 per cent relative increase in labor input. This reconciles with the 7.4 per cent increase in persons engaged when account is taken of the 1 per cent relative drop in weighted man-hours per person.

We have also compared proportionate employment changes for the aggregate of industries with above-average productivity advance with the aggregate of those with below-average advance. Looking first at the nine one-digit groupings, the results show a negative relationship. The industrial segments with above-average productivity advance (farming, mining, transportation, and communication and public utilities) registered a 34 per cent drop in employment between 1948 and 1966. The segments with below-average productivity advance (contract construction, finance, and services) showed a 48 per cent rise in employment. Manufacturing and trade, which had the same 2.5 per cent rate of productivity advance as the private domestic business economy, together showed a 25 per cent employment increase, compared with only 14 per cent for all private domestic industries.

The results are quite different when the tabulations are made for the two-digit industries within the manufacturing, mining, transportation, and utility segments. The twenty-one industries with above-average rates of advance in total factor productivity increased employment by 16.5 per cent during 1948-66, while the nine industries with below-average productivity advance raised employment by 11 per cent. The aggregates of the two sets of thirteen and seven manufacturing industries showed somewhat higher rates of increase in employment—26.6 and 12.8 per cent, respectively. One manufacturing industry, paper products, was not included since it showed the average 2.5 per cent rate of productivity advance.

TABLE 6-9

Private Domestic Business Economy, by Industry Segment and Group:[a]
Factors Influencing Relative Changes in Employment, 1948-66

	Real Product O (1)	Total Factor Productivity O/I (2)	Factor Substitution[b] I/L (3)	Labor Input[c] L (4)	Labor Input per Person L/E (5)	Persons Engaged[d] E (6)	Per Cent Distribution of Persons Engaged (PDBE = 100) 1948 (7)	1966 (8)
Farming	58.2	115.4	133.3	37.8	85.7	44.1	15.58	6.87
Mining	71.2	133.5	96.6	55.2	97.4	56.7	2.01	1.14
Metal	69.9	98.2	99.3	71.7	96.4	74.3	0.21	0.15
Coal	39.2	159.4	99.7	24.7	104.3	23.7	1.06	0.25
Oil and gas	82.8	113.3	76.4	95.7	100.7	95.1	0.55	0.52
Nonmetal	110.9	102.0	100.4	108.4	100.2	108.2	0.20	0.22
Contract construction	85.4	83.1	99.2	103.7	94.5	109.7	6.50	7.13
Manufacturing	105.3	100.0	97.6	108.0	100.3	107.6	31.24	33.62
Nondurables	96.5	101.5	100.7	94.4	98.4	95.9	14.42	13.84
Foods	85.0	109.6	95.5	81.2	94.2	86.2	3.14	2.70
Beverages	79.6	94.5	103.0	81.8	94.6	86.5	0.46	0.40
Tobacco	68.9	77.5	120.9	73.5	98.7	74.5	0.20	0.15
Textiles	81.2	130.0	95.7	65.2	103.0	63.3	2.59	1.67
Apparel	84.8	89.5	96.1	98.5	97.4	101.1	2.41	2.44
Paper	117.8	100.1	99.2	118.8	95.6	124.2	0.92	1.14
Printing, publishing	102.2	102.3	92.1	108.6	91.0	119.3	1.58	1.89
Chemicals	203.6	150.1	109.9	123.4	94.9	130.1	1.27	1.65
Petroleum refining	100.9	108.8	138.3	67.1	92.7	72.4	0.44	0.31
Rubber products	172.6	128.0	92.0	146.6	101.4	144.5	0.61	0.87
Leather products	61.4	85.9	91.5	78.2	100.2	78.0	0.80	0.62
Durables	111.9	97.9	96.6	118.4	100.7	117.5	16.82	19.77

Primary metals	76.0	84.7	100.1	90.3	77.1	72.3	2.50	2.31
Fabricated metals	98.4	88.9	95.9	115.3	99.2	116.2	2.02	2.34
Machinery except electric	113.4	101.1	92.5	121.2	100.7	120.4	2.81	3.38
Electric machinery	197.2	123.0	97.5	164.5	98.6	166.9	1.95	3.25
Transportation equipment and ordnance	159.1	111.5	91.6	155.7	102.2	152.3	2.48	3.78
Instruments	165.5	107.2	104.1	148.3	99.6	148.9	0.49	0.74
Miscellaneous	100.0	117.7	98.8	86.0	93.9	91.5	0.86	0.79
Transportation	74.2	117.4	94.1	67.2	90.0	74.7	5.90	4.40
Railroads	54.9	158.7	100.7	34.4	81.5	42.2	2.93	1.24
Nonrail	94.1	92.9	94.0	107.8	100.9	106.8	2.96	3.17
Water transportation	50.9	70.3	93.3	77.6	103.8	74.7	0.50	0.38
Air transportation	575.9	254.7				246.1	0.18	0.44
Pipeline transportation	141.4			51.4	97.7	52.6	0.06	0.03
Communication and public utilities	168.6	128.4	123.6	106.3	99.0	107.4	2.50	2.69
Communication	166.8	126.0	119.7	110.6	101.6	108.9	1.45	1.58
Telephone, telegraph	167.0	131.2	123.7	102.9	99.6	103.3	1.36	1.40
Electric, gas, sanitary services	170.1	127.7	131.7	101.2	96.1	105.3	1.05	1.11
Trade	101.5	99.9	96.6	105.2	94.3	111.6	21.29	23.76
Wholesale	113.8	99.3	100.7	113.8	99.2	114.7	5.23	6.00
Retail	94.1	98.1	94.9	101.1	91.5	110.5	16.07	17.76
Finance, insurance, and real estate	119.8			142.1	98.8	143.8	3.81	5.47
Services	90.8			127.6	94.1	135.6	9.16	12.38

Source: For columns 1-6, Tables A-20, A-22, A-24, A-26–31, A-33, A-35, A-37–58, A-60, A-62, A-64–73, A-75–79; for columns 7 and 8, Table A-7 and Department of Commerce.

a Index numbers (for 1966 on a 1948 base) for the several segments and groups are expressed as percentages of corresponding index numbers for the private domestic business economy.

b Capital for labor.

c Column 1 divided by column 2 divided by column 3.

d Column 4 divided by column 5, or column 8 divided by column 7.

These results are consistent with the mild positive correlation found between rates of change in productivity and in labor input for the thirty-two two-digit industries. So we may conclude that within the industry groups, rates of technological advance as reflected in productivity indexes are at least neutral and possibly positive relative to employment changes. The opposite conclusion for the one-digit industry segments reflects the factors mentioned above in explanation of the lack of correlation between relative changes in productivity and output.

Causal Factors

The estimates of productivity change by industry provide an opportunity for quantitative analysis of causal factors beyond that provided by the global estimates for the private domestic economy. That is, if estimates of those causal forces which are prominent in theoretical explanations can be developed on an industry basis, they can be related through regression analysis to the differential industry rates of productivity change. This will make possible identification of the significant independent variables and quantification of their impacts.

Generally, it would be desirable to measure not only the average levels of the causal variables during the period under consideration but also their rates of change. There are many problems associated with this kind of multivariate analysis, of course, which we shall point out after discussing the chief independent variables it would be desirable to quantify on an industry basis, if possible.

Starting from the general theoretical framework sketched at the end of Chapter 4, it would be essential to try to measure the real stocks of intangible capital embodied in the tangible factors employed in the various industries. In particular, it would be desirable to try to measure the real intangible stocks resulting from research and development designed to improve the quality or productive efficiency of the producers' goods and processes used in the various industries, and the real stocks of knowledge and know-how per employee in the various industries resulting from education and training. It would also be of value to estimate the real stocks per employee resulting from health and mobility outlays, by industry, since these also influence productive efficiency.

Unfortunately, intangible capital stock estimates have not been prepared on an industry basis, so proxy variables have to be used. Another problem is posed by the fact that the intangible investments and resulting capital affecting productive efficiency in a given industry may have been financed in a different industry, or by government. For example, farmers have benefited greatly from research and development outlays by manufacturers of farm machinery, fertilizers, et cetera, as well as by public education, government and university research, extension services, and so on. This complicates the problem of estimating intangible capital *used* in an industry.

Next, attempts would have to be made to measure industry differences and changes in the variables that affect the rate of return on total capital, intangible and tangible, employed in the several industries. As mentioned in Chapter 4, chief among these are differences and changes in the degree of economic efficiency in the allocation of resources among and within industries. If economic efficiency cannot be measured directly, measures can be assembled relating to institutional forms and practices affecting the degree of competition, changing competitiveness, and other elements of efficiency among industries.

The scale factor, as it interacts with changes in productivity, can readily be quantified in terms of differences in levels or rates of change in output or capacity, by industry. The problem here is that scale is not only a causal factor but also a result of productivity advance, as explained earlier in this chapter.

Also of possible significance over cyclical and intermediate time periods are differences in levels, and changes in rates, of capacity utilization. In the period 1948-66, for example, the various industries had different average capacity-utilization rates for the period as a whole, as well as in the first and last years, which may well have influenced the estimated rates of productivity advance, particularly when the compound-interest formula is used to compute the rates of change.

Finally, it would be relevant to attempt to measure possible changes in the average inherent quality of human resources, and of natural resources, especially in extractive industries, used in production. With regard to the former, the content of the labor input unit, the man-hour, may have been influenced by changes in average hours worked per year, as argued by Denison; so this variable might well be included in the regression analysis in lieu of a direct average man-hour quality measure. Similarly, measures of the changing composition of resource stocks and inputs may be associated with changes in average quality.

Even if one had valid estimates for all the variables set forth above, or for those specified in any other theoretical schema, there would inevitably be various qualifications attaching to the empirical results of a multivariate analysis. In the first place, the theoretical framework itself may be deficient, and fail to specify all the significant variables, or the correct form of particular variables with respect to lags, et cetera. Secondly, available econometric techniques may be inadequate to deal with certain difficult problems, particularly collinearity reflecting complex interactions among the independent variables. Finally, alternative models may produce equally good results.

Furthermore, as a practical matter, it may not be possible to compile or prepare direct estimates for all the variables specified in the model. Some of these may be approximated by proxy variables, with varying degrees of accuracy. Even the direct estimates will generally be subject to varying (and often unknown) margins of error.

For all these reasons, the results of multivariate analysis must be interpreted with caution. It is chiefly as a spur to further theoretical and statistical work that we present in the final section the results of some statistical analyses of the rates of productivity change 1948-66 in the twenty-one manufacturing industry groups.

An Experiment with Regression Analysis

The points of departure for the regression experiments described in this concluding section are the theoretical framework discussed above, as well as an earlier cross-sectional regression analysis by Nestor Terleckyj, reported in *Productivity Trends.* Using our earlier estimates of rates of change in factor productivity in twenty manufacturing industry groups for the period 1919-53, Terleckyj regressed a variety of independent variables, and found two to be significantly correlated with the industry rates of productivity change: ratios of research and development outlays to sales, and the cyclical variability of output.[9] In addition to these variables, we use eight others suggested by our theoretical analysis. As will be seen in the following discussion, it was seldom possible to obtain direct estimates of the "ideal" variables, and more or less reasonable proxies were used.

The independent variables will be discussed in the order they are shown in the column headings of Table 6-10, which presents the values of the variables. Following the first column, showing rates of change in total factor productivity, we enter the rates of change in output and in real tangible capital stock (columns 2 and 3). These variables are intended to represent the

---

[9] The findings, and limitations, of Terleckyj's study are pointed out in *Productivity Trends*, pp. 177-88.

scale factor. As mentioned earlier, the problem with using rates of change of output is that it is the result as well as a cause of productivity advance. Because of this interaction, we ran the multiple regressions both including and excluding it. The use of the rate of change in the capital variable was likewise an attempt to get away from the output-productivity interaction by using the volume of fixed capital as a measure of scale.

Variability in rates of change of output is one of the variables found to be significant by Terleckyj, except that we measure it by the average deviation of annual percentage changes in output from the mean per cent change (column 4). This variable would be closely related to the average rate of utilization of capacity, mentioned in the theoretical discussion. We do not have measures of the changes in percentage utilization of capacity, by industry, between 1948 and 1966, which, if marked, could also influence the rates of productivity advance.

Although we did not have estimates of the real stock of educational capital embodied in tangible labor by industry, we were able to obtain estimates of the average number of years of education per employee (column 5) from the 1960 Census 1/1,000 sample. Likewise, although industry estimates of the real stock of knowledge resulting from research and development were not available, industry estimates of ratios of R&D outlays to sales were available for the base period, 1958 (column 6). For neither of these variables were data available to permit calculation of rates of change between 1948 and 1966.

Estimates relating directly to the inherent quality of human resources and inputs are not available. But we do include the variable "average hours worked per year" (column 7), calculated from the Census 1/1,000 sample, which may be relevant to the energy content of each hour worked, as discussed above.

The last three variables are relevant to possible changes in economic efficiency, as well as to the rate of introducing innovations into firms and plants in the various industries. Concentration ratios in the base period (1958) and changes in concentration over the period 1947-66 are computed from Census Bureau data, as detailed in the notes to Table 6-11. The table shows that the average concentration ratio in manufacturing as a whole did not change significantly over the nineteen-year period, so changes in the ratio could hardly have influenced changes in productivity for the segment as a whole. But given the widely different levels of the concentration ratios within the two-digit manufacturing industries, and the frequently significant changes in the degree of concentration within these industries over the period, the

TABLE 6-10

Rates of Change in Total Factor Productivity, 1948-66, and Associated Variables,
Twenty-one U.S. Manufacturing Industry Groups

Manufacturing Industry Groups	Rates of Change 1948-66[a]			Variability of Output Changes[b] (4)	Average Education per Employee, 1959[c] (5)	Ratio of Research and Development to Sales, 1958 (6)	Average Hours Worked, 1959[d] (7)	Concentration Ratios, 1958[e] (8)	Rate of Change in Concentration, 1947-66[f] (9)	Unionization Ratio, 1958[g] (10)
	Total Factor Productivity (1)	Output (2)	Real Tangible Capital Stocks (3)							
Foods	3.0	3.1	1.3	0.5	9.6	0.31	2025	30.36	0.34	48.0[g]
Beverages	2.2	2.7	1.7	1.5	9.9	0.25	1989	32.04	0.98	38.0[g]
Tobacco	1.1	1.9	2.0	0.8	8.4	0.09	1789	73.94	-0.60	55.0
Textiles	4.0	2.8	0.1	1.9	8.7	0.52	1885	26.37	1.45	27.0
Apparel	1.9	3.1	4.0	1.0	8.8	0.06	1669	12.95	1.66	52.0
Lumber products	3.5	2.3	2.0	1.3	8.1	0.32	1756	20.63	1.72	37.0
Furniture	2.9	4.3	1.6	0.9	8.9	0.55	1939	15.75	-0.64	40.0
Paper	2.5	5.0	4.0	0.8	10.0	0.70	2000	39.23	-0.30	60.0
Printing, publishing	2.7	4.1	2.3	0.8	11.0	0.24	1624	21.41	-0.72	40.0

Chemicals	4.9	8.2	5.4	1.1	11.5	3.80	1966	43.31	-0.66	41.0
Petroleum refining	3.0	4.1	3.1	0.7	11.6	1.10	2024	31.87	-0.73	60.0
Rubber products	3.9	7.2	3.9	1.7	10.3	1.80	1925	68.29	-1.00	60.0
Leather products	1.7	1.2	0.2	0.8	8.8	0.50	1716	23.85	-0.62	44.0
Stone, clay, glass	2.4	3.9	4.1	0.4	9.6	1.40	1977	51.30	0.23	60.0
Primary metals	1.6	2.5	3.2	3.0	9.5	0.70	1784	46.16	0.16	71.0
Fabricated metals	1.9	3.9	4.2	2.4	10.1	1.70	1968	32.55	-1.25	53.0
Machinery except electric	2.6	4.8	2.9	3.2	10.5	3.60	2010	40.86	0.00	47.0
Electric machinery	3.7	8.0	6.5	3.0	11.0	10.50	1902	61.43	0.18	48.0
Transportation equipment and ordnance	3.2	6.7	5.2	5.8	10.5	4.20	1946	63.94	0.59	61.0
Instruments	2.9	7.0	7.7	1.2	11.1	7.50	1954	59.19	0.49	34.0
Miscellaneous	3.5	4.0	3.4	1.5	9.8	2.90	1889	26.95	0.61	40.0

Source: Tables 6-1, 6-11, A-37–A-57; 1/1000 sample of 1960 Census tabulated by NBER; the National Science Foundation's *Funds for Development in Industry 1959*, Table XIII; and H. G. Lewis, *Unions and Relative Wages in the United States*, 1963, Table 79.

a Average annual percentage rates of change computed by compound interest method.

b Average deviation from mean value of output.

c Average number of years of education per employee.

d Average hours worked per employee per year.

e Percentage of concentration by largest four companies in four-digit industries weighted by value of shipments.

f Average annual percentage rates of change in concentration ratio computed by compound interest method.

g Percentage of unionization weighted by value of shipments.

cross-sectional analysis provides a means of testing the effect of concentration on innovation. The direction of the effect is controversial in the literature. Some economists claim that a high degree of competition spurs innovation and productivity advance; others follow the lead of Schumpeter in arguing that a small number of large firms in an industry are in a better position to engage in the research, development, and engineering activities that result in innovation. Terleckyj found no significant influence of the degree of concentration on interindustry rates of productivity advance. But since we have a somewhat different collection of independent variables, and for a more recent period, we have included the concentration variables.

Finally, we include estimates of the percentage of employees belonging to unions in the base period, 1958, a variable not included by Terleckyj. As in the case of concentration, there appears to have been little trend in the unionization ratio for all manufacturing over the period.[10] We did not have the data for estimating changes in unionization ratios by industry, but the differences in ratios in 1958 are considerable and make it possible to test for a possible effect of these differences in rates of productivity advance.

Here, again, views differ on possible effects of unionization. The work rules of some unions may affect productivity levels. But, unless the relative incidence of these practices changes significantly, they would presumably not affect rates of productivity change. But to the extent that unions are able to affect rates of innovation in the plants of an industry out of their understandable concern about immediate employment impacts, they obviously could have an effect on rates of productivity advance. Unions may also take actions which promote productivity advance. To the extent that wage rates may rise faster in more heavily unionized industries, for example, this could spur a higher rate of substitution of capital for labor and thus a faster growth of labor productivity, if not of total factor productivity. Only quantitative analysis can indicate what has been the *net* effect of unionization on productivity.

We have had to confine our regression analyses to the twenty-one manufacturing industry groups shown in Table 6-10, since some of the variables are not available for the nonmanufacturing groups. As the first step in the analysis, we ran simple correlations between the average annual percentage rates of change in total factor productivity, as the dependent variable, against

[10] See H. G. Lewis, *Unionism and Relative Wages in the United States*, Chicago, The University of Chicago Press, 1963, Table 72, p. 244. Lewis estimates that union membership as a percentage of persons engaged in the U.S. civilian economy was 25.6 in both 1947 and 1960.

TABLE 6-11

Concentration Ratios in
Manufacturing, by Industry Group,[a]
1947, 1958, and 1966[b]

	Weights (1958)[c]		Percentage Concentration		
	(A) Value of Shipments (In Millions of Dollars)	(B) Value Added (In Millions of Dollars)	1947	1958	1966
s	23,615	14,696	28.94	30.36	30.86
ages	5,024	2,836	30.76	32.04	36.99
cco	3,722	1,413	83.45	73.94	74.45
es	6,812	4,858	23.57	26.37	30.90
rel	7,983	6,004	13.57	12.95	18.55
er products	1,431	3,177	15.42	20.63	21.26
ture	2,355	2,349	18.93	15.75	16.78
	375	5,707	43.57	39.23	41.12
ng, publishing	7,756	7,923	23.64	21.41	20.63
icals	12,658	12,270	47.40	45.51	41.89
eum refining	15,110	2,518	36.91	31.87	32.17
er products	257	3,277	81.44	68.29	67.43
er products	3,401	1,897	26.52	23.85	23.57
, clay, glass	5,256	5,529	49.42	51.30	51.58
ry metals	9,463	11,671	42.73	46.16	44.02
cated metals	7,340	9,412	36.41	32.55	28.79
nery except electric	4,040	12,391	40.29	40.86	40.07
ic machinery	6,351	10,395	60.75	61.43	62.91
portation equipment					
ordnance	13,518	15,284	58.38	63.94	65.34
ments	1,790	2,906	55.40	59.19	60.82
llaneous manufacturing	3,814	4,754	27.13	26.95	30.50
weights manufacturing	142,071		38.18	38.10	38.56
weights		141,267	40.88	41.07	41.28

urce: Computed from *Annual Survey of Manufactures–1966: Value of Shipment Concentration s by Industry,* U.S. Department of Commerce, Bureau of the Census. The (B) weights, value l, come from *1958 Census of Manufactures,* Volume II, U.S. Department of Commerce, Bureau e Census.

Average percentages of shipments in each of the selected groups originating in the largest four of the component four-digit industries.

1954 ratios were used for 1947 in twenty-one cases, and 1963 ratios were used for 1966 enty cases out of 225 industries in the total for all of the three years.

The (A) weights represent the value of shipments of the sample of industries in each group. B) weights represent total value added in each of the groups as a whole.

each of the nine independent variables. The results are summarized in the matrix of coefficients of correlation in Table 6-12.

Some of the simple correlation results are of considerable interest. The only independent variable showing a significant direct degree of correlation with rates of productivity change is the rate of change in output. To the extent that there are errors in the output variable, the correlation may be spurious in part, since output is the numerator of the productivity ratio. As also noted earlier, the correlation reflects an interaction, the relative output changes being a result (through associated relative price changes) as well as a cause of the relative productivity changes.

It should also be noted that the output changes are rather highly correlated with rates of change in real capital stocks (the other scale variable), average education, the research and development ratios, and, to a lesser degree, with concentration ratios. The same intercorrelations exist for capital changes.

Because of collinearity, and the reciprocal aspect of the relationship, we ran the multiple correlations described below both with and without the output-change variables.

With regard to the other variables, average education per employee shows a significant degree of correlation, at the 0.05 level, with average hours worked and, at the 0.01 level, with the rates of change in output and capital as well as with the R&D ratio. The latter is not only significantly correlated with all the independent variables mentioned previously but also with the concentration ratio (at the 0.05 level). Average hours worked per year is significantly correlated only with average education, as cited above, while the concentration ratio is correlated, also at the 0.05 level, with the three variables already cited. No significant correlation with any of the other variables is shown for variability of output change, rate of change in concentration, and unionization ratio.

The multicollinearity among the several independent variables makes it difficult to arrive at meaningful multiple regression equations. When the rate of change of output is included in the correlations, its influence tends to suppress that of other variables to which it is related, such as R&D, or to give them the "wrong" sign. Nevertheless, the final outcome of a stepwise trial using all the independent variables is of interest:[11]

---

[11] We progressively eliminated variables with the lowest t values, until we were left with variables whose t values were significant at the 0.05 level.

TABLE 6-12

Twenty-one U.S. Manufacturing Industry Groups: Matrix of Simple Correlation Coefficients, Rates of Change in Total Factor Productivity, 1948-66, Versus Nine Independent Variables

	(1)	(2)	(3)	(4)	(5)	(6)	(7)	(8)	(9)	(10)
1. Rate of change in productivity	1.000	0.649[a]	0.248	0.106	0.397	0.397	0.327	0.044	0.112	-0.387
2. Rate of change in output	0.649[a]	1.000	0.801[a]	0.341	0.745[a]	0.762[a]	0.430	0.513[b]	-0.237	0.050
3. Rate of change in real capital	0.248	0.801[a]	1.000	0.311	0.633[a]	0.777[a]	0.270	0.541[b]	-0.075	0.229
4. Variability of output changes	0.106	0.341	0.311	1.000	0.201	0.431	0.125	0.372	0.133	0.249
5. Average education per employee	0.397	0.745[a]	0.633[a]	0.201	1.000	0.571[a]	0.437[b]	0.315	-0.413	0.124
6. Ratio of R&D to sales	0.397	0.762[a]	0.777[a]	0.431	0.571[a]	1.000	0.282	0.510[b]	-0.004	-0.100
7. Average hours worked	0.327	0.430	0.270	0.125	0.437[b]	0.282	1.000	0.292	-0.188	0.103
8. Concentration ratio	0.044	0.513[b]	0.541[b]	0.372	0.315	0.510[b]	0.292	1.000	-0.264	0.425
9. Rate of change in concentration	0.112	-0.237	-0.075	0.133	-0.413	-0.004	-0.188	-0.264	1.000	-0.350
10. Unionization ratio	-0.387	0.050	0.229	0.249	0.124	-0.100	0.103	0.425	-0.350	1.000

Source: Table 6-10.
[a] Significant at .01 level.
[b] Significant at .05 level.

$$P\dot{t}y = 3.179 + 0.305\,O - 0.035\,U$$
$$\qquad\qquad (4.475)\quad\ (2.810)$$

where $P\dot{t}y$ is the average annual percentage change 1948-66 in total factor productivity; $O^{\cdot}$ is the average annual percentage rate of change in output over the same period; and U is the percentage of employees of the industries belonging to labor unions in our base period, 1958.

The coefficient of multiple correlation of 0.773 is significant at the 0.01 level. The t value for the rate of change in output is likewise significant at the 0.01 level, while that for the degree of unionization is significant at the 0.05 level (just under the 0.01 value). It must be remembered that, in part, the rate of output change also stands for the R&D ratio and average education per employee, with which it is highly correlated. It should also be borne in mind, in interpreting the regression results, that output change is correlated with the concentration ratio. In the first step of the analysis, concentration did appear with a negative sign, indicating that the less the degree of concentration (as with unionization), the higher the rate of growth of productivity. But the t value for the concentration ratio was only 0.706, and it dropped out in later steps.

When the rate of change in output is dropped from the multiple regressions, for reasons adduced above, the coefficients of multiple correlation are lower, but the equations are interesting. The final result of the stepwise procedure is as follows:

$$P\dot{t}y = 0.568 + 0.407\,Ed - 0.037\,U.$$
$$\qquad\qquad (2.364)\quad\ (2.319)$$

The variables are as before, except that average education of employees replaces output change as the significant independent variable in addition to the degree of unionization, which continues to show a negative relationship to the rate of productivity advance. The coefficient of multiple correlation is 0.593, significant at the 0.05 level.

At an earlier stage in the analysis, the R&D ratio and average hours worked (H) also showed up in the multiple regressions with positive signs:

$$P\dot{t}y = -1.084 + 0.254\,Ed + 0.046\,R\&D + 0.002\,H - 0.037\,U.$$
$$\qquad\quad (1.102)\quad\ (0.554)\qquad (0.976)\ (2.156)$$

But the t values for these variables (except for unionization) are not significant at the 0.05 level. However, the coefficient of multiple regression of 0.633 is significant at that level.

The results of the multivariate analyses must be interpreted in the light of our earlier theoretical discussion. The positive influence of the scale factor as measured by rates of output change is to be expected; but the numerical result is ambiguous because of the reciprocal reaction of productivity change on output change. The positive influence of average education per employee (and the related R&D ratios) is in accord with growth theory. It would have been desirable to include rates of change in average education and R&D ratios, but the data did not permit it. The negative influence of the degree of unionization tells us that apparently the influence of unions with regard to the rate of innovation and changes in economic efficiency has outweighed possible positive union influences mentioned earlier. Even this result is not unambiguous, of course, in view of the possible correlations between unionization ratios and other parameters.

In conclusion, we emphasize again that the results of our cross-sectional analyses are intended to be suggestive, not definitive. It is hoped that eventually more satisfactory estimates can be prepared of the variables included in the theoretical construct for the full range of industry groups. In particular, it would be desirable to compile time series of the several relevant types of real intangible capital stocks on an industry basis, as well as additional estimates relating to institutional forms and practices that affect economic and technological efficiency.

Other analysts, of course, will use somewhat different theoretical approaches than the one we have employed, and will therefore have a somewhat different set of independent variables for empirical implementation. But regardless of the precise theoretical model, the cross-sectional analysis of productivity change will be an important supplement to macroeconomic analysis in the continuing effort to explain the causes of productivity advance. It is hoped that the estimates presented in this volume will make a useful contribution to these studies.

APPENDIX

SOURCES AND METHODS

Introduction

This appendix describes in some detail the data sources and methodology underlying the estimates of outputs, inputs, and productivity presented and analyzed in this study. Part I covers the national economy, by major sector. Part II covers the various industry groups (one-digit SIC codes) and component industries within the private domestic business economy, around which most of the analysis is centered. Part III presents Tables A-1 through A-80—the basic statistical tables for this study.

Part I corresponds to Appendix A in *Productivity Trends in the United States* (hereafter referred to as *Productivity Trends*); Part II covers the areas comprising Appendixes B through K in the earlier volume. The appendix material in this monograph is considerably shorter than that in *Productivity Trends*, for two reasons. First, where substantially the same sources and methods are used as in the prior work, we summarize them briefly, with appropriate references. Second, and more important, the estimates presented in *Productivity Trends* generally extend back to the latter part of the nineteenth century, whereas the series revised and extended to 1966 or 1969 for this study begin with 1929 for the national economy by major sector, plus farming and manufacturing, and with 1948 for the other industries.

Appendix tables A-1 through A-21 relate to the national economy by major sectors, while tables beginning with A-22 relate to the various industry segments and groups. In all cases in which the tables presented here have the same or similar coverage as those contained in *Productivity Trends*, references to the specific table numbers in the latter source are noted. For all practical purposes, most of the time series presented here can be extrapolated back by the corresponding earlier series, although it should be mentioned that in many cases sector and industry definitions have been modified—usually to a minor degree—since the preparation of the estimates contained in *Productivity Trends*.

With respect to the weighting of industry and sector outputs and inputs required to obtain aggregates, we have revised and extended the previous system. That is, for the period 1948-53, we used the Marshall-Edgeworth formula, applying an average of revised relative weights in the first and last years of the period to the component series for each of the six annual values. The series so obtained were then linked in 1953 to the corresponding series for the period 1953-66, obtained by applying 1958 relative weights to the components. For the several aggregates that we revised back to 1929, we used the same weighting procedures for the period 1929-48 as those described in *Productivity Trends*.

As indicated in the text, we also introduce two new sets of series in the present volume. First, we have made use of the OBE real product estimates for the various industry groups and subgroups, beginning with 1948. These are not available prior to 1947, except for farming, but we also present gross output series and the corresponding productivity estimates which are consistent with the historical nonfarm industry series. Second, we include gross as well as net real capital stock series for the sectors and various industries, and the associated gross factor input and productivity estimates. These variant measures are not contained in *Productivity Trends*, and comparisons of movement with the net measures are limited to the period covered in the current study. Both the gross and the net input series include labor input measured as weighted man-hours.

PART I

THE NATIONAL ECONOMY

The dimensions of the national economy, and the broad sectors into which it is divided for purposes of production and productivity estimates, are largely based on the definitions of the National Income Division, Office of Business Economics (OBE) of the U.S. Department of Commerce.[1] Because of shortcomings in the estimates of real product originating in the nonbusiness sectors, the analysis in the text relates primarily to the private domestic business sector, in the aggregate and by major industry groupings.

Nevertheless, for some aspects of the analysis of U.S. economic growth, we have made use of real national product, factor input, and productivity estimates for the economy as a whole and for levels between the latter and the private domestic business sector, as shown in the following text table (A-i). The adjustments made to the OBE estimates, described in the following section on output, largely comprise depreciation and imputed interest on capital goods employed in the nonbusiness sectors. OBE estimates product originating in the nonbusiness sectors in terms of labor compensation alone, but, since a major aim of this study is to measure the inputs of nonhuman capital as well as of labor, we have prepared capital estimates for the nonbusiness sectors and, for the sake of consistency, include gross return on these capital assets as part of gross product originating outside of business.

Even with the upward adjustments to nonbusiness product, it can be seen from the table that the private domestic business economy accounts for more than four-fifths of gross national product. We focus on this broad sector of the economy in order to avoid the downward bias to productivity estimates inherent in the OBE approach of estimating real product in general government, households and nonprofit institutions, and the rest of the world in terms of real factor cost.

[1] The OBE is now the Bureau of Economic Analysis (BEA); see footnote 1, p. xx.

TABLE A-i

Gross Product, 1958,
by Sectors of the National Economy

	Gross Product Originating, 1958		
	OBE Estimates	OBE Adjusted	OBE Adjusted
	(Billions of Dollars)		(Percentage Distribu
Private domestic nonfarm business	371.0	367.8	76.0
Farm	20.8	22.5	4.7
Private domestic business	391.8	390.3	80.7
Households and private nonprofit institutions	11.4	14.4	3.0
Private domestic economy	403.2	404.7	83.7
General government, civilian	31.6	46.4	9.6
Domestic civilian economy	434.8	451.1	93.3
Rest of the world	2.0	2.0	0.4
National civilian economy	436.8	453.1	93.7
General government, military (federal)	10.5	30.7	6.3
National economy	447.3	483.8	100.0

This is not the place to discuss the concepts of national income and product in detail. But it may be helpful to remind the nonspecialist that the OBE estimates are largely confined to final market transactions (with the major exceptions of food produced and consumed on farms, payments in kind, the rental value of owner-occupied houses, and certain financial services for which no explicit charges are made). Altogether, the imputations amounted to 6 per cent of GNP in 1966. By a broader definition of economic activities and the economy, valuations could be imputed to the services of housewives and other unpaid household labor, volunteer labor, schoolwork by students of labor-force age, and the services of household durable goods as well as durables used in government and nonprofit institutions.

In another National Bureau study in progress, we are experimenting with imputations for nonmarket final output.[2] But the estimates are in terms of

[2] See *Forty-seventh Annual Report*, NBER, June 1967, pp. 9-15, and p. 54.

current dollar costs, since data on the physical volume of final product involved are generally not available now. Therefore, the broader estimates, when available, will not add to our knowledge of changes in the total real volume of economic activity. Further, most of the additional imputations relate to the household sector of the economy; the private domestic business sector, on which we focus attention in this study, would be but little affected by a broader definition of economic activity.

Output

The chief changes in this study's real product estimates, by major sector, from the estimates in *Productivity Trends* are the incorporation of subsequent conceptual and statistical revisions in the Commerce Department estimates, plus our own adjustments; the addition of estimates for the private domestic business sector and its major industry divisions; and the dropping of the real national product series of Simon Kuznets.

The Kuznets series, which we used in the previous volume in addition to the official estimates, was dropped because it is not available for years beyond the period ending in 1955, as published in *Capital in the American Economy: Its Formation and Financing,* New York, NBER, 1961. Further, Kuznets, Variant III, which was statistically consistent with the Commerce series, showed virtually the same trend as the Commerce Department estimates when adjusted to include national security outlays, despite several conceptual differences. Finally, a special use for the Kuznets estimates in the earlier volume was to extend the Commerce estimates back to 1869 by means of estimating and adjusting for the several reconciliation items. Since the pre-1929 estimates are available in *Productivity Trends*, it is not necessary to reproduce them here.

In August 1965, OBE presented a major revision of the official income and product accounts, involving both conceptual and statistical changes. The revised estimates are "benchmarked" on the results of the 1958 Census of Manufactures, Business, and Mineral Industries, and the 1960 Census of Population and Housing. The latest revision is the most systematic of its kind, embodying, in addition to the latest Census data, the improved data sources and estimating methods used by OBE in the preparation of the 1958 input-output matrix. With a complete accounting for all product, the input-output work provides a powerful cross-check which improves the accuracy of the GNP estimates. In the light of the thorough 1965 revisions, the estimates for the prior benchmark years of 1954 and 1947 were reviewed and adjusted whenever necessary. Other improvements, particularly in the construction estimates, were also made; and the price deflators were reworked and converted to a 1958 base.

Although most of the revisions relate to the postwar period, estimates for 1929-45 were revised by OBE to the extent required for continuity. However, there is a break in continuity in respect to the industrial classification of national income and product in 1948; beginning with that year, the 1957 Standard Industrial Classification (SIC) is used by OBE, while for years prior to 1948, the 1942 SIC is used, with modifications. Estimates of national income for 1948 are presented on both bases to show the quantitative differences. Since the estimates used in this study are on the later basis while those in *Productivity Trends* followed the earlier SIC, the differences in industry classifications should be kept in mind by those wishing to link the new to the old output, input, and productivity index numbers as of 1948.

On balance, the statistical revisions served to raise estimates of growth in total GNP by approximately 3 per cent in 1964 relative to 1948. The average annual percentage rate of growth over the period in real GNP was raised to 3.7 per cent, compared with 3.6 per cent based on the old estimates. The upward revision was relatively most marked in the first subperiod, 1948-53, and the last, 1960-64. The amplitude of the cyclical contractions during the period was somewhat lessened by the revised estimates. As emphasized by Rosanne Cole in a recent National Bureau study, the general tendency of successive revisions in GNP estimates has been to raise the apparent secular growth rate and to diminish amplitudes of fluctuations, so the 1965 revisions were no exception.[3] Subsequent statistical revisions for recent years, as published in the July 1968 *Survey of Current Business*, have been incorporated in the estimates presented in this volume.

The effect of the statistical revisions was reduced by one percentage point between 1948 and 1964 by the net impact of several conceptual revisions. The largest of these, by far, was the exclusion of consumer interest payments from national income and product. This was desirable, since debt financing had risen relative to stocks of consumer goods; thus, consumer interest payments overstated the increase in services furnished by real household wealth. It is hoped that OBE will eventually impute a rental value to stocks of household durables, just as we have for stocks held by governments and nonprofit institutions. We have not done so for consumer durables, however,

---

[3] Rosanne Cole, *Errors in Provisional Estimates of Gross National Product*, New York, NBER, 1970.

since we have not included household assets in our capital estimates, although they definitely belong in more comprehensive wealth estimates. Nonbusiness capital goods yield a stream of services through time, even though they are generally not monetized, and imputations are necessary to indicate their contribution to economic product, broadly defined. Also important is the fact that shifts in ownership of capital goods between the business and nonbusiness sectors distort the movements of GNP, according to present estimating methodology, as practices with respect to owning versus leasing capital goods or buying their services change with time. Changes in these practices also affect the industry composition of business product, as noted below.

The other conceptual changes are relatively less important: Capital outlays charged to current expense are excluded from gross private domestic investment and GNP; commissions arising from transactions in tangible assets, principally real estate, are now capitalized; transactions in secondhand fixed assets among the several sectors are now recorded; certain nontax receipts of government are reclassified as sales and netted against total government purchases; and personal remittances to and from foreigners and government nonmilitary grants are uniformly treated as transfer payments rather than purchases. Since these changes have been discussed extensively elsewhere and have virtually no effect on the productivity movements, it is unnecessary to comment on them further.[4]

The estimates of real GNP by sector contained in Table A-1, which underlie our broad productivity measures, represent the revised OBE estimates,[5] with a number of modifications. The estimates of real product originating in the private domestic business sector are adjusted only to exclude the depreciation on fixed assets owned by private nonprofit institutions which is included with nonfarm business depreciation in the OBE estimates. In addition to shifting these capital consumption allowances out of the private domestic nonfarm business sector (service industry) to the households and private nonprofit institutions sector, we have also shifted "gross rents paid to nonfarm landlords" from the nonfarm sector (real estate) to the farm sector. Our estimates of farm capital include the assets owned by nonfarm landlords. In principle, we would prefer to count capital and its

[4] See John W. Kendrick, "Recent Revisions and Long-Term Trends in the National Economic Accounts," *1966 Proceedings of the Business and Economic Statistics Section,* American Statistical Association, pp. 117-19.

[5] Taken from Table 1.8 of *The National Income and Product Accounts of the United States, 1929-1965,* Statistical Tables (1966) for the period 1929-62, and for 1963-66 from the July 1967 and July 1968 *Survey of Current Business.*

earnings in the industry where used. But it was possible to make the adjustment only in the case of farming; for other private industry groups, plant and equipment rentals are counted as expenses to the leasee industry, and the assets and rentals received are counted in the lessor industries. The estimates of gross rents paid to nonfarm landlords (and the estimates of gross farm product generally) are based on U.S. Department of Agriculture estimates, as shown in OBE's *National Income and Product Accounts*, 1929-65, Table 1.18.

The gross product of households and institutions includes not only labor compensation, as shown in the OBE tables, but also the capital consumption allowances mentioned above, plus an imputed net interest using an average base-period interest rate times the real stock of capital employed by the institutions shown in Table A-15. No allowance is made for the rental value of household capital, nor for unpaid household work. Thus, gross private domestic product (Table A-1, column 7) differs from the OBE estimates only to the extent of imputed interest on institutional capital (1.4 billion dollars in 1958, as shown in Table A-3), since the several intersectoral shifts do not affect the aggregates.

For gross product originating in general government, civilian and military (Table A-1, columns 2 and 6), we have added to the OBE compensation of employees capital consumption allowances and imputed net interest on the real stock of capital owned by general government, as shown in Table A-3. The estimates were made separately for federal, state, and local governments, and the imputed interest was computed on the basis of the average borrowing rates for the two governmental sectors.

The estimates of real net factor income originating in the rest of the world (Table A-1, column 4), which largely represent net property income, are the same as those published by OBE.

Thus, the total GNP series in Table A-1 (column 1) represents the revised OBE estimates adjusted upward to include capital consumption on real fixed assets of general government, and an imputed interest return on the real capital stocks of general government and private nonprofit institutions. These adjustments, summarized in Table A-3, make the nonbusiness sectors consistent with the business sector by including factor income accruing to property as well as to labor.

With respect to the constant dollar estimates, it must be stressed that adjusted real product originating in the nonbusiness sectors, no less than the unadjusted OBE estimates, is not appropriate for productivity analysis. That is, the real gross property income of these sectors is estimated as a by-product of the nonbusiness real capital stock estimates, described below, and represents capital input, just as the real nonbusiness labor compensation estimates of OBE essentially represent labor input.

Table A-2 presents estimates of real *net* product originating in the various sectors covered in Table A-1. OBE estimates total capital consumption allowances neither in current nor in constant prices, relying on book depreciation for the nonfarm business sector. We have supplied rough estimates, prepared as described in the later section on capital, for those readers who prefer to work with real net product. Since the ratios of real net to gross product (Table A-2, columns 7 to 12) have not changed substantially over the period, and because of the lesser accuracy of the real net product estimates, our productivity measures are generally based on real gross product estimates. These may, of course, be converted to a net basis by use of the factors given in Table A-2.

Finally, it is necessary to make a few comments on the effects of the OBE price deflation procedures on the estimates of real product originating in the private domestic business sector. Unlike the implicit deflators for the imputed value of products originating in the nonbusiness sectors, the price indexes used to deflate the final products of the business economy are generally based on prices of the goods and services sold to consumers, to business on capital account (including inventory accumulation), to governments, and to the rest of the world (less deflated imports of goods and services). Thus, real business product generally represents, in effect, a base-period price-weighted aggregate of the physical quantities of goods produced. An output aggregate of this type may be related to a consistently weighted input aggregate in order to obtain a measure of productivity change.

Yet even real business product, and the associated productivity estimates, are subject to well-known qualifications as a result of inadequacies of the price deflators. Even in the business sector, some of the price deflators are really based on input price indexes. This is notably true of some of the construction cost indexes used to deflate the value of new structures put in place, and some of the deflators used for private services.[6] The value of the outputs involved is not large, but some small downward bias is imparted to the real business product and productivity estimates.

More generally, the price deflators and thus the real product estimates do

[6] These issues are discussed in *A Critique of the United States Income and Product Accounts*, Studies in Income and Wealth, Volume Twenty-two, Princeton University Press for NBER, 1958, and more recently, with respect to the service industries, in *Six Papers on the Size Distribution of Wealth and Income*, Lee Soltow, ed., Volume Thirty-three of the same series.

not reflect changes in quality of particular goods and services over time. Shifts in purchases among different price lines or "qualities" of products are reflected in the deflated value figures, in the same manner as some quality improvements associated with higher real unit costs. It is widely believed that there has been a net improvement in quality of goods in the same price lines. To the extent that this is true, it can likewise be argued that there is some (indeterminate) downward bias in the productivity estimates. These, and other qualifications that attach to the real product and productivity series, have been discussed in more detail in *Productivity Trends*.

In concluding this section on output, reference is made to Table A-4. The estimates of real product originating by industry groups shown there have been developed in recent years by OBE on a basis broadly consistent with total real business product. These and the other industry measures will be described in Part II of the appendix. For present purposes it will suffice to call attention to the last line of Table A-4, which shows the differences between the real aggregate final purchases and the sum of real industry products in the private domestic business economy. The residuals, and the changes in the residuals, are generally not large. Thus, between 1948 and 1966, the residual drops from -4.7 to -1.9, indicating that aggregate real industry product grew by about 1.3 per cent less over the period than real sector product as presented in Table A-1. Since this is almost negligible when reduced to average annual rates, we can say that our analysis of aggregate economic growth based on real final expenditure estimates is broadly consistent with our analysis of growth by industry groups based on the real product originating estimates.

In accordance with our basic weighting scheme, in the productivity tables we use index numbers of real product in 1958 dollars for the period 1953-66. We then reweight real product by broad industry groups and sectors using average unit product weights for the first and last years of the periods 1948-53, 1937-48, and 1929-37 for the annual estimates contained in each of these periods, linking back from 1953 at each overlapping year. The movements of the real product aggregates are not affected very much by this system of occasionally changing weights, which is consistent with the procedures followed in *Productivity Trends*.

Labor Input

Overall estimates for the national economy and its broad sectors of persons engaged, average hours, man-hours, and weighted man-hours (which we call "labor input") are built from the industry estimates. Thus, there is no question as to consistency between the aggregate estimates and the estimates for industry and sector components. Further, since the weights for persons engaged and average compensation are based largely on OBE estimates—which come from social security data consistent with income and product estimates—it follows that our labor input estimates are consistent to a high degree with the real product estimates to which they are related.

The components of labor input have been estimated, with few exceptions, by the methods described for the post-1948 period in *Productivity Trends*, so the summary presented here is brief. The estimates of nonfarm persons engaged are largely those of OBE representing full-time equivalent employees plus proprietors (not necessarily full-time), to which we have added Census Bureau estimates of unpaid family workers, distributed for nonfarm industries in proportion to the distribution of proprietors. The farm worker estimates are from the Department of Agriculture, adjusted to a full-time equivalent basis by methods described in *Productivity Trends*.

The class-of-worker estimates are shown in Table A-5. There it may be seen that proprietors and family workers dropped from approximately 23 per cent of total persons engaged in 1948 to 15 per cent in 1966, continuing the long-term decline from 42 per cent in 1889, as shown in the earlier study. Note also that full-time equivalents have risen about 3 per cent less rapidly between 1948 and 1966 than full- and part-time employment.

Annual estimates of persons engaged for the national economy by major sector are shown in Table A-6; the distribution by major industry segments in key years is presented in Table A-7. Annual estimates may be interpolated in the latter table by use of the index numbers shown in the industry tables.

An important external check on the aggregate of industry and sector estimates of persons engaged is provided by the decennial Census of Population data on the labor force, adjusted to an employment basis. As shown in Table A-8, our industry aggregate was only 2 per cent less than the Census-based estimates in 1960, compared with 1 per cent in 1950, and a virtual identity in 1930. One would not expect the two series to show precisely the same levels and movements for reasons detailed in the previous study (*Productivity Trends*, pp. 252-59). Neither would one expect widely divergent trends in the two series, so the general consistency shown by Table A-8 is reassuring as to the validity of both series (which are largely independent of each other).

The next step in deriving man-hours estimates is to multiply the average number of persons engaged each year by the average hours worked. In the industries in which proprietors and unpaid family workers are a significant fraction of total persons, we used separate average hours worked estimates based on special Census Bureau tabulations. For employees in these industries, and all persons in the industries where proprietors and family workers are negligible, we multiplied by average hours of employees, except in a few cases in which direct man-hour data were available.

In principle, our objective is to obtain estimates of average hours, and thus of total man-hours, *worked* rather than paid for. We succeeded in obtaining hours worked estimates for the nonbusiness sectors, and for farming, manufacturing, railroads, finance, and services. Data are from the economic censuses and Census surveys, including unpublished industry detail from the *Monthly Report on the Labor Force* (MRLF), from the Department of Agriculture, and from the Interstate Commerce Commission. For the remaining industries, we had to use average hours estimates from the Bureau of Labor Statistics (BLS), which relate to time paid for. Since time paid for but not worked has shown a relative rise since World War II, one might expect our average hours estimates to have a mild upward bias for a true average hours worked series. This appears to have been the case based on the comparisons shown in Table A-12 (columns 4, 5, and 6), in which our industry composite is compared with average hours worked in the civilian economy, based on the BLS *Monthly Report on the Labor Force* (MRLF). The latter series drops by half an hour, or 1.1 percentage point, more than our industry composite between 1948 and 1966, and the trend of the annual ratios between the two series is clearly but mildly in the expected direction. Despite the slight bias, the industry composite suits our purposes better, since it comprises greater industry detail than that available from the MRLF series. Also, the average hours estimates for industry groups based on establishment data are more stable than those from MRLF because of the larger samples from which the establishment data are drawn. And, as we shall see in the next paragraphs, the bias is not apparent in total man-hour comparisons.

Total man-hours are shown annually for the national economy by major sector in Table A-10, and by industrial segment for key years in Table A-11. Again, the annual numbers can be interpolated in the latter table by the man-hour index numbers presented in the industry tables. Composite hours worked per week are estimated for key years in Table A-9.

Table A-12 contains an important comparison of our man-hour estimates with several other series. First, we compare them with man-hours worked computed from the MRLF employment and hours data. Between 1948 and 1966, our estimates drop by 0.8 percentage points relative to those based on

MRLF. It will be recalled that our average hours series showed a mild relative increase, but this was more than offset by the decline in the ratio of our employment series to that of MRLF. Next, we compare our man-hour estimates with the two private economy series compiled by the Bureau of Labor Statistics for its productivity studies. Our industry man-hour composite rises by 1.3 percentage points more than the BLS estimates based on MRLF data; it falls by 0.7 percentage points relative to the BLS series based largely on establishment data. Not only the trend but also the annual movements of our series are closer to the BLS establishment-based series than to those of the MRLF-based series. The close correspondence of our man-hour estimates to the BLS establishment-based series represents a check on the accuracy of the computations underlying both series, and it means that our real product per man-hour estimates for the private economy are very close to the "official" estimates.[7] In fact, our prior series have been used in BLS publications to extrapolate their private economy estimates for the pre-1947 period.

It will be recalled that, in addition to estimating straight man-hours, we have weighted industry man-hours by base-period average hourly labor compensation to obtain weighted "labor input" measures for broad industry segments, sectors, and the economy as a whole. In Table A-13, we present index numbers for key years of both man-hours and weighted labor input for the national economy, by major sector, to show the effect of relative interindustry man-hour shifts. Between 1948 and 1966, labor input at the national level rose by 6.7 per cent more than unweighted man-hours, at an average annual rate of increase of 0.4 per cent, reflecting the relative shift of man-hours to higher-pay industries. Virtually all of this effect was due to the continuing relative shift of manpower from the farm to the nonfarm economy. If, however, it had been possible to estimate and weight man-hours in finer industry detail, and by occupational groupings, the shift effect might well have been more pronounced.

The final table on labor, A-14, shows, for 1948, 1957, and 1966, the percentage distribution among sectors and industry segments of persons engaged, of man-hours, and of labor input. The trends indicated by the three distributions are generally about the same, but the levels differ, particularly for labor input. For example, in 1948 the farm proportion accounted for 15.5 per cent of man-hours, 13.2 per cent of persons engaged, but only for 6.1 per cent of labor input (weighted man-hours) due to the much lower

---

[7] See *Trends in Output per Man-Hour in the Private Economy, 1909-1958*, Bulletin No. 1249, Bureau of Labor Statistics, U.S. Department of Labor.

average hourly compensation in farming. All three percentages showed much the same drop from 1948 to 1966 because of the relative stability of interindustry differentials with respect to average hours worked and average earnings.

Real Stocks of Capital

The real capital stock estimates were built up from the same sectors as the national product. The private domestic business economy stocks comprise farm and nonfarm business, and the latter is split again between residential and nonresidential components, and manufacturing and nonmanufacturing, but no further. The nonfarm business total is compared with the independently estimated figures for component industries, and the residual is assessed for reasonableness in Part II.

The real capital stock estimates have been reworked since those presented in *Productivity Trends*, primarily in order to incorporate estimates for the private economy prepared by OBE. Although the revised and extended real net stock estimates show virtually the same trends as the earlier series, we have extended them back to 1929 (see Table A-15), since this could be done with relatively little additional work, and it is useful to have a completely consistent series for the longer period. We have also provided real stock estimates gross of depreciation for the period 1929-66 (Table A-16), consistent with the net series.

Private Domestic Business

For the revised and extended estimates of real reproducible capital in this sector for the period 1929-66, we have shifted from primary reliance on the estimates prepared by Raymond Goldsmith in *Productivity Trends* to those prepared by the Office of Business Economics.[8] The OBE estimates are available for the entire period, whereas Goldsmith's most recent estimates end in 1958. Further, OBE has presented a number of variants of the fixed capital stock estimates, which permits us to select those most appropriate for our purposes and to indicate the difference in movement of the variant chosen compared with other plausible alternatives.

The underlying OBE estimates were first adjusted to conform to our sectoral definition. That is, from the OBE estimates of real fixed reproducible

---

[8] "Fixed Business Capital in the United States, 1925-66," *Survey of Current Business,* December 1967.

capital stocks for the private nonfarm economy we deducted estimates for private nonprofit institutions in order to arrive at the *business* sector, and added estimates for government enterprises which are not in the OBE private economy figures. We also added estimates for the real stock of farm residential structures, since the OBE estimates of farm structures are confined to service buildings and other producers' structures. OBE estimates were also used for farm and nonfarm inventories, which are consistent with the real net change in the business inventory component of GNP. We added estimated inventories of government enterprises, but did not make a deduction for nonprofit institutions' inventories, which are negligible.

The estimates for the nonfarm reconciliation items are based on those described below for private nonprofit institutions (see pp. 162-63); and for government enterprises, on those presented through 1958 by Raymond Goldsmith.[9] These series were extended to 1966 by basically the same sources and methods as those used by Goldsmith. The farm residential stocks are based on those estimated in an earlier OBE study (*Survey of Current Business*, November 1962), and are revised and updated.

Under the heading of land, for nonfarm site land the 1958 estimate of Goldsmith was taken as the benchmark; following the procedure used in *Productivity Trends*, the 1958 ratio of the value of site land to the gross value of structures was applied to the latter series in constant dollars in order to approximate movements in the physical volume of site land. Goldsmith's estimates of the real value of private forest and mineral lands were used and extended to 1966 by the same procedures. For real farm land values we used the method developed by Alvin Tostlebe, whose estimates were employed in *Productivity Trends*.[10] Department of Agriculture annual estimates of the acreage of farm land, by ten regions, were weighted by 1958 values per acre (for farm land only). The Department's estimates are benchmarked on Census data.

Now let us return to describe and appraise the OBE estimates of private structures and equipment. The variants we have chosen are based on Treasury Bulletin "F" service lives, less 15 per cent, with the Winfrey S-3 retirement curve and an adjustment to real nonfarm structures to correct for the upward bias of the construction cost deflator ("constant cost 2"). The net stock

9 See R. Goldsmith, *The National Wealth of the United States in the Postwar Period*, Princeton University Press for NBER, 1962, Tables B-149, B-154, and B-156.

10 A. Tostlebe, *Capital in Agriculture: Its Formation and Financing since 1870*, NBER, 1957.

estimates are those calculated using straight-line depreciation. (See the *Survey of Current Business*, December 1966 and December 1967.)

In the *Productivity Trends* estimates of real net stocks in the private domestic sector, the underlying Goldsmith estimates were also calculated using straight-line depreciation. The recent OBE estimates were computed not only on the basis of straight-line depreciation but also on the basis of the double-declining balance method, which some economists believe to give a more accurate representation of the pattern of decline in value of fixed assets as they age. The sum-of-the-years' digits variant was not present in the December 1967 *Survey of Current Business*, since its results were almost identical with those obtained using the double-declining balance method. Actually, the straight-line and double-declining balance methods result in closely similar movements of the total private net fixed stock estimates. Use of the straight-line basis would result in a somewhat larger growth in *total* capital stock, since land and inventories have grown less than fixed capital and the *level* of the latter (and thus its relative importance) is greater by the straight-line than by the declining-balance approach.

Both the gross and net stock estimates of OBE chosen for use in our series differ from the previous series in three methodological aspects. We indicate the differences in growth rates obtained by use of alternative methods in these areas in Table A-ii.

In the first place, we use the series in which lengths of lives for retirement and depreciation calculations are distributed around the mean life according to the Winfrey S-3 curve. This curve was based on studies of the age distribution of retirements for various types of producers' durable goods in the 1930s. Even if it is a stylized picture of retirements, it seems more accurate to apply a mortality curve rather than make the "one-hoss shay" assumption that all items of each type of asset are retired at the end of their average life. The real gross stock estimates computed using the Winfrey S-3 retirement pattern show somewhat less growth in both the 1929-48 and 1948-66 periods than estimates using average-age retirement for 180 types of structures and equipment.

The Goldsmith estimates used in *Productivity Trends* were based on the average lengths of life for structures and equipment shown in Treasury Bulletin "F," which were based on engineering studies made around 1940. Studies made after World War II, cited in the Commerce article,[11] indicate

11 "New Estimates of Fixed Capital in the United States, 1925-66," *Survey of Current Business*, December 1966, p. 34.

TABLE A-ii

Effect of Alternative Methods of Estimating Real Net Fixed Capital Stocks for the
Private Economy (Exclusive of Residential Structures)

	Per Cent Change	
Estimating Method	1929-48	1948-66
Retirement pattern: Winfrey S-3 versus "basic"[a]	–1.7	–3.5
Average lengths of life: Bulletin "F" - 15% versus Bulletin "F"[a]	–1.7	+3.5
Construction cost deflator: Adjusted versus unadjusted	+4.0	+5.3
Net difference	+0.6	+5.3
Depreciation pattern: Straight-line versus double-declining balance[a]	–0.4	–0.3
Revised estimates versus estimates in *Productivity Trends*	–0.4	+2.3[b]

[a] See Appendix text for definitions.
[b] Period 1948-57, since 1957 is the last year covered in *Productivity Trends*.

that somewhat shorter lives were prevalent. The OBE suggests that lives averaging 15 per cent less than the Bulletin "F" lives are more appropriate. As the table above indicates, real stock estimates using the shorter lives rose by 1.7 per cent less than real stocks based on Bulletin "F" in the period 1929-48, but by 3.5 per cent more in 1948-66.

The third adjustment relates to the well-known upward bias of construction cost deflators (see *Productivity Trends*, Appendix E). Commerce presents a "constant cost 2" variant for the real stock of structures and total fixed capital. This variant increased by 4.0 per cent more than the "constant cost 1" variant of volume of fixed capital stocks during 1929-48, and by 5.3 per cent more in the period 1948-66.

The *net* difference in growth of real stocks obtained via the new method versus the old is negligible in terms of average annual rates of growth for the period 1929-48, and only about 0.1 percentage point a year for 1948-66, in respect to total capital (including land and inventories, as well as fixed reproducible capital). When one considers that the weight of capital is only about one-fourth the weight of labor in the total factor input and productivity measures, it is clear that the differences in method affect the postwar growth rates of these variables very little. To the extent that they do have a perceptible effect, the new methods would seem to work in the right direction.

The estimates of real net stock of nonfarm residential structures are based on estimates by the Commerce Department, adjusted to take account of subsequent revisions in the new residential construction estimates and extended to 1966 by the same procedure. Basically, the estimates were made by the perpetual inventory method, using the Commerce Department's new residential construction estimates, assuming a seventy-year life (Bulletin "F" plus 40 per cent), and depreciation calculated according to the double-declining balance method (which would mean a 2.86 per cent annual rate). The estimates presented in *Productivity Trends* were those developed by Grebler, Blank, and Winnick, which also used the declining balance method of calculating depreciation, but at a 2 per cent average annual rate. The lower rate would, of course, produce a somewhat faster rate of growth in net stock.

The gross stock estimates were obtained by applying the gross-net stock ratios obtained from Goldsmith (in *National Wealth*), extended through 1966. The site-land estimate for 1958 was also obtained from Goldsmith and extrapolated forward, and back to 1929, by the real gross stock estimates, in line with the procedure used for nonresidential site land.

Private Nonprofit Institutions

To go from the estimates for private domestic business to the total private domestic economy, we reinserted the estimates for structures and equipment of private nonprofit institutions, which had been deducted from the OBE estimates, as noted above. The institutional plant estimates are based on accumulating real investment, assuming fifty-year average life and using straight-line depreciation to arrive at net stock consistent with the OBE private economy totals. The equipment expenditures were cumulated on the basis of a fourteen-year average life and, again, straight-line depreciation. The real stock of structures were marked up by 15.65 per cent to include site land, based on Goldsmith's 1958 ratio (in *National Wealth*).

The gross expenditure estimates, from which stocks are calculated, were obtained as follows. For institutional plant and equipment outlays, the following categories of OBE's breakdown of private nonresidential construction were counted as institutional plants: (a) religious buildings, (b) educational buildings, (c) hospital and institutional buildings, and (d) social and recreational buildings, the latter accounting for one-third of expenditures (OBE, e.g., the 1962 Jaszi study).[12] These estimates are available back to 1920 from the Commerce Department's *Construction Review,* 1955 Statistical Supplement. They are extrapolated to 1879 on the basis of Goldsmith's *A Study of Saving in the United States* (Princeton University, 1955-56), Table R-27, column 9 and Table R-17, column 1.

For the period 1946 to 1966, estimates of institutional equipment outlays consist of expenditures for institutional plant and equipment from the Federal Reserve Board flow-of-funds accounts (*Federal Reserve Bulletin,* April 1965, Flow of Funds, Table 4(A), category 14) less expenditures for institutional construction. The resulting series is extrapolated back to 1915 by percentage changes shown for institutional construction expenditures from Goldsmith's *Saving* (Table R-17, column 1).

The deflator for private nonprofit institutional plant is the American Appraisal Company's average construction cost index (*Survey of Current Business,* July 1967, pp. 5-9); for years prior to 1915, this index was linked to an index in *Saving,* Table R-20, column 5. For institutional equipment, the OBE implicit price deflator for producers' durable equipment was used back to 1929 (*Survey of Current Business,* July 1967, Table 8-8, line 1), linked to the implicit deflator from *Saving* (Table P-5, column 1, divided by P-6, column 1).

General Government

In general, the real capital stock estimates for federal as well as state and local general governments are based on Raymond Goldsmith's *National Wealth* for the period 1945-58, extended back to 1929 by the estimates contained in his earlier work, *Saving* (see above). Goldsmith's estimates were converted to 1958 dollars by minor categories. They were extended to 1966 usually by the same sources and methods he employed. In the case of reproducibles, we used the perpetual inventory method to extend Goldsmith's estimates and, in some cases, to obtain the entire stock series. End-of-year estimates were averaged to obtain mid-year values compatible with the annual flows.

Federal Government—Civilian

Structures. The stock of federal civilian structures at the end of 1929 is taken from *Saving* (Table W-43, sum of lines I,1 and I,2), converted to 1958 prices. Constant dollar stocks for subsequent year-ends are estimated by

---

[12] "National Income and Product Accounts," *Survey of Current Business,* July 1962, Table 35.

cumulating annual net investment. The gross federal outlays for new construction (excluding military and government enterprises, but adjusted to include work relief construction 1933-43) are Commerce Department estimates, adjusted to constant 1958 prices by means of the American Appraisal Company construction cost index converted to a 1958 base. An average fifty-year life is used and 1-1/2 declining-balance depreciation, which means that 3 per cent of the previous year's real stock is deducted from real gross investment to obtain the net investment and thus the real stock at the end of each successive year through 1966.

Land. Estimates of the value of federal forest land and other land for civilian use in current and constant dollars for 1945-58 are from Goldsmith's *National Wealth* (Table B-151, columns 3 and 4, and Table B-152, columns 3 and 4; the latter is converted to 1958 prices). In constant prices, federal land is assumed to remain at the 1958 levels through 1966, but the price indexes used to convert to current dollars are extrapolated as follows. Nonforest land prices are extended by the price index for grazing land in western states from the U.S. Department of Agriculture's *Farm Real Estate Developments* (October 1964, Table 3, p. 11). Federal forest land prices are extended from 1956 by an average of stumpage price for Douglas fir, southern pine, and ponderosa pine from the *Statistical Abstract of the United States* (1964 edition, Table 979).

To go back to 1929, the value of federal land was added to that of state and local government land (see below), and extrapolated by the series for total public land from *Saving* (Table W-1, column 24 for current dollars, and W-3, column 25 for constant dollars). The total public land estimates were split into 68 per cent for federal, and 32 per cent for state and local, based on the average 1945-58 proportions.

Equipment. The real stock of federal civilian equipment is estimated by the perpetual inventory method, benchmarked on the Goldsmith stock estimate for 1958 contained in *National Wealth* (Table B-155, column 2). The current dollar gross outlay estimates for 1946-58 are taken from the same source (Table B-159), and for 1929-45, from *Saving* (Table F-16, column 9). For the period 1959 to 1966, calendar year estimates are obtained up to 1962 from two-year moving averages of fiscal year estimates by Ira A. Hunt, Jr.,[13] and for subsequent years from *The Budget of the United States*

---

[13] Ira A. Hunt, Jr., "National Security Contributions to Post-World War II United States Economic Growth," D.B.A. dissertation, The George Washington University, August 1964.

Government (for fiscal year ending June 30, 1968, Table D-2, p. 431).

We followed Goldsmith's procedure in deflating the equipment expenditure series by the OBE implicit deflator for total producers' durable equipment on a 1958 base. We also adopted Goldsmith's estimate of a twelve-year average life for equipment, but used the double-declining balance depreciation method. Thus, in extending the estimates forward from the benchmark, we subtracted 16.67 per cent of the real stock at the previous year-end, and added real gross investment. The reverse procedure was applied for going back in time.

Inventories–Monetary Metals. Goldsmith's estimates of federal inventories (other than monetary metals) are confined to those held by public corporations, which we include with government enterprises in the business sector. Presumably the inventories held by federal general government civilian agencies are quite small, and we do not estimate them. Consequently, our inventory estimates for the federal government sector are confined to monetary gold and silver. The total stock is equivalent to the sum of (1) the stock of monetary gold, from *Saving* (Table W-8, column 2), for 1928-44, and thereafter from *National Wealth* (Table B-182, column 2), with an adjustment to current dollar estimates for the 1934 change in price to obtain constant (1958) price estimates for 1929-34; and, (2) the stock of silver dollars and bullion and subsidiary silver outstanding, taken from *National Wealth* (Table B-182, column 5 for current prices, and column 6 for constant prices, shifted to a 1958 base) for the period 1945-58, extrapolated to 1942 and to 1966 from the *Federal Reserve Bulletin* (February 1968, p. A-15) and for 1928-41 from *Banking and Monetary Statistics* (pp. 419-20). No attempt has been made to distribute silver coins (and gold coin prior to 1934) held outside the Treasury to the various sectors holding the money. In any case, the federal government holds most monetary gold and silver, and there are some advantages to counting the entire stock in one sector.

State and Local Governments

Structures. These estimates are prepared entirely by the perpetual inventory method for highways and other structures separately. For structures other than highways, an average life of fifty years is assumed. This means that a construction outlay series had to be extended back to 1879 in order to obtain stock estimates beginning with 1929. The current dollar estimates

1929-66 are those of OBE for state and local government purchases of structures, plus construction force account compensation from the *Survey of Current Business* (August 1965, Table 9, lines 27 and 29), less expenditures for highway construction (see below), plus that portion of work relief construction 1933-43 allocated to state and local governments on the basis of wage-salary proportions. This series was linked in 1929 to the sum of two series from *Saving*: (1) for state government, 80 per cent of Table G-15, column 3, converted to calendar years, and (2) for local governments, column 6 of Table G-6. Since the *Saving* estimates go back only to 1896, expenditures for the previous seventeen years were assumed to average $100 million, based on the trends. The current dollar estimates were converted to constant prices by the American Appraisal Company's construction cost index on a 1958 base, linked in 1915 to the index used by Goldsmith (*Saving*, Table R-20, column 8).

Depreciation was estimated by the double-declining balance formula. Thus, to obtain real net stock, 4 per cent of the stock at the previous year-end was deducted, and real gross investment added each year. The real stock estimates were deflated to current prices by the price index noted above.

In the case of highways, a thirty-year average life was used, which means that the investment series had to be carried back to 1899. From 1945 forward, OBE estimates of state and local highway construction were obtained from worksheets. They were linked in 1945 to the sum of Goldsmith's separate estimates for state and for local government highway construction going back to 1899 in *Saving* (Table G-15, column 2 and Table G-16, column 2), converted to a calendar year basis.

The deflator from 1915 forward was the Bureau of Public Road's highway construction cost index, on a 1958 base. This was linked in 1915 to Goldsmith's index from *Saving* (Table R-20, column 6) and carried back to 1899.

Depreciation was estimated by the 1-1/2 declining balance formula, which means that 6.67 per cent of the previous year-end real stock was deducted from the current year's real gross investment to obtain real net investment for the purposes of cumulation.

Land. The value of state and local land in current and constant prices 1945-58 was obtained from *National Wealth* (Table B-151, column 6 and B-152, column 6). To the 1958 figure, estimated state and local net land purchases were added through 1966. It was assumed that state and local government purchases of land comprised 80 and 50 per cent, respectively, of the purchases of land plus existing structures by each. Purchases data for fiscal years are available from the U.S. Bureau of the Census (*Government Finances in 1963*, Table 5). The price deflator was extrapolated by the average annual value per acre of farm real estate from *Farm Real Estate Market Developments* (1967).

The state and local, plus federal, land values were extrapolated from 1945 back to 1929 by the total land series from *Saving* and allocated as described above.

Equipment. The same procedures were used here as in deriving federal equipment. Expenditures series 1945-58 are from *National Wealth* (Table B-136 and B-140, columns 5). They are extended forward by the U.S. Bureau of the Census data (e.g., *Government Finances in 1963*, p. 20) converted to a calendar year basis. They are linked in 1945 and extrapolated back by Goldsmith's estimates in *Saving* (20 per cent of the series in Table G-15, column 3, plus the series for local government in Table G-6, column 5). The deflator is the OBE overall deflator for producers' durable equipment.

As in the case of federal equipment, a twelve-year average life and double-declining balance depreciation are assumed in deriving real net stock by the perpetual inventory method.

Inventories. For 1946-58, state and local inventories in current and constant prices are from *National Wealth* (Table B-156, columns 4 and 3). The constant dollar series in 1958 prices was extended to 1966 based on the trend from 1948 to 1958, and converted to current dollars by use of the BLS wholesale price index for all commodities. The estimates from 1945 back are from *Saving* (Table W-1, column 17 less Table F-14, column 10).

Federal Government—Military

Structures. For regular military structures inside the continental United States, Goldsmith's estimates for the period 1945-58 were used (Table B-175, column 2 for current prices, and B-174, column 2 for constant prices, adjusted to a 1958 base). The estimates were extended forward and backward in time by the perpetual inventory method. The basic series on gross expenditures for military facility construction is that of OBE (*The National Income and Product Accounts of the United States, 1929-1965*, Table 5.2, line 41), deflated by the Commerce composite construction cost index, also used by Goldsmith. A depreciation rate of 8 per cent was applied for the period since

1958; 10 per cent for the period 1929-40; 15 per cent for 1941; 25 per cent for 1942-44; and 12 per cent for 1945.

Current dollar estimates of Atomic Energy Commission plant for 1943-45 are taken from *National Wealth* (Table B-177, column 11 plus Table B-178, column 11). Estimates for subsequent years were derived by the perpetual inventory method. The current dollar gross expenditure estimates for fiscal years are from *The Budget of the United States Government* (for fiscal year ending June 30, 1965, Table D-2, p. 358), converted to a calendar year basis. The Turner Construction Company cost index on a 1958 base was used to deflate the current expenditure estimates, as well as the 1943-45 current dollar stock. A depreciation rate of 3 per cent was applied to the real stock at the end of each year to obtain depreciation for the subsequent year. This was based on the assumption of a fifty-year average life, and 1-1/2 declining balance depreciation.

Equipment. The current dollar stock of regular military equipment for 1945-51 is taken from *National Wealth* (Table B-175, column 1). The price deflator for this stock, and for the entire gross military equipment expenditure series used in the extensions of the stock estimates, is the BLS wholesale price index for machinery and motive products, 1939-66 on a 1958 base, extended from 1939 to 1929 by the wholesale price index for metals and metal products, following Goldsmith's procedure. The military equipment expenditure estimates for 1929-51 are from *National Wealth* (Table B-166, column 4); for 1952-63, from *Survey of Current Business*, July 1964, Table 26, extrapolated forward by unpublished OBE estimates, which were somewhat lower in 1963 than the published estimates due to a definitional change. In extending Goldsmith's 1951 stock estimates forward by the perpetual inventory method, a depreciation rate of 22 per cent was used. For the pre-1945 period, depreciation rates were chosen so that total stock of regular military equipment and structures was consistent with the current dollar value for 1939 given in *Saving* (Vol. III, p. 6). The rates used were 20 per cent, 1929-35; 24 per cent, 1936-37; 27 per cent, 1938-39; 25 per cent, 1940-43; and 40 per cent for 1944.

Atomic Energy Commission equipment stock in current dollars 1943-45 is from *National Wealth* (Table B-178A, column 11). The price deflator for these stocks, and for subsequent AEC equipment expenditures used to extend the stock estimates, is the wholesale price index for machinery and motive products. The expenditure estimates for calendar years 1946-66 are derived from fiscal year data given in *The Budget of the United States Government* (e.g., for fiscal year ending June 30, 1965, Table D-2, p. 359). The depreciation rate applied to successive end-of-year stock estimates is 9 per cent.

Inventories. Military inventories are assumed equal to AEC and General Services Administration stockpiles. Ideally, the series should also include nondurable stock, but paucity of data precludes more extended coverage.

AEC stockpiles are taken from *National Wealth* (Table B-175, column 7) for 1945-58. Stockpiles for 1959-64 are derived by cumulating additions to stock from the 1958 figure. Additions to stock for 1959-66 are fiscal year figures for AEC additions to "other physical assets" from *The Budget of the United States Government* (for fiscal year ending June 30, 1965, Table D-2, p. 359), converted to a calendar year basis. Constant dollar and current dollar values are assumed to be the same.

GSA stockpiles are taken from *National Wealth* (Table B-175, column 6) for 1945-58. Additions to GSA stock for 1959-63 are taken from the *Survey of Current Business* (July 1964, Table 26). The 1964-66 figures are derived by linking 1963 to a new unpublished OBE series. Stock additions are deflated by the wholesale price index for nonferrous metals and are added cumulatively to the 1958 stock in constant dollars.

Net Assets Abroad

The productive nonhuman capital of the nation comprises not only the tangible assets located in the geographical area of the United States, but also the assets and investments abroad owned by U.S. residents, less foreign assets and investments in the United States. The net U.S. assets abroad give rise to the net property income originating in the rest of the world, which (together with a very small labor income from abroad) must be added to net and gross domestic income and product to arrive at national income and product.

Official estimates of the international investment position of the United States have been made annually by the OBE since year-end 1947. Estimates for the period 1950-60 were published in the *Balance of Payments Statistical Supplement Revised Edition,* a 1963 supplement to the *Survey of Current Business.* Estimates for earlier years to 1947, and subsequent years through 1966, were obtained from annual articles in the *Survey of Current Business* (September 1967, p. 40). The year-end differences between total U.S. assets and investments abroad, not including gold stock, and total foreign assets and investment in the United States were averaged to center the estimates at mid-year. Following Goldsmith's procedure, net U.S. assets abroad were deflated by the implicit price deflator for total GNP, as estimated by the OBE on a 1958 base.

The estimates from 1929 through 1947 were from Goldsmith (*Saving,* Table W-1, column 25), converted to 1958 prices and put on a mid-year basis. The Goldsmith estimates were based on Robert Sammons's "Foreign Investment Aspects of Measuring National Wealth" (in *Studies in Income and Wealth, Volume Twelve,* NBER, 1950, pp. 563-67), plus Sammons's unpublished worksheets, supplemented for 1945-48 by the Commerce Department's *The Balance of International Payments of the United States* (both the 1940-45 and 1946-48 versions). The levels of the Goldsmith estimates differ somewhat from the later, revised official estimates for the overlapping period after 1947. Rather than attempt to adjust the earlier series through 1947 without adequate data, we used the Goldsmith estimates as they stand, recognizing the possibility of a minor discontinuity, in absolute terms, between 1947 and 1948.

Capital Weighting System

The index numbers of real net capital stock for the various sectors were assigned the weights shown in Table A-iii. Stocks within the several sectors are unweighted. Capital weights were obtained by dividing estimated capital compensation in the various sectors for the weight-base years by the index numbers of real stock to obtain "capital compensation per unit." The sum of these estimates for successive pairs of key years, and for the final weight-base year of 1958, were used to derive the percentage weights shown in the table. This procedure parallels that used in weighting the index numbers of labor input described earlier. It gives the same results as would be obtained by applying average rates of return in weight-base years to the real stock estimates themselves for each weighting period shown in the table, and linking back from 1953.

For the private business sectors, net capital compensation was obtained by subtracting labor compensation (including the imputed labor compensation of proprietors described above) from total national income originating. For the nonbusiness sectors, capital compensation was imputed by the methods indicated earlier. Gross capital compensation, needed for weighting the real gross stock estimates, was obtained by adding capital consumption allowances for each sector to the net capital compensation estimates described above. Since the levels and movements of the ratios of gross to net capital compensation in the several domestic economy sectors do not differ greatly, we do

National Economy: Relative Weight of Real Net Capital Input, by Major Sector, Subperiods, 1929-58
(per cent based on 1958 dollars)

	1929-37 Weights		1937-48 Weights		1948-53 Weights		1958 Weights	
	Sector	Total	Sector	Total	Sector	Total	Sector	Total
Manufacturing	33.8	24.7	41.2	32.0	40.9	32.1	33.2	24.4
Nonmanufacturing nonresidential business	49.3	36.0	47.9	37.2	44.0	34.6	47.3	34.7
Residential	16.9	12.4	10.9	8.4	15.1	11.9	19.5	14.3
Private domestic nonfarm business	100.0		100.0		100.0		100.0	
Private domestic nonfarm business	87.8	73.1	87.8	77.6	89.0	78.6	88.0	73.4
Farm	12.2	10.2	12.2	10.8	11.0	9.7	12.0	10.0
Private domestic business	100.0		100.0		100.0		100.0	
Private domestic business	98.4	83.3	98.8	88.4	98.7	88.3	97.6	83.4
Households and nonprofit institutions	1.6	1.4	1.2	1.1	1.3	1.2	2.4	2.1
Private domestic economy	100.0		100.0		100.0		100.0	
Private domestic economy	90.1	84.7	93.9	89.5	93.5	89.5	91.1	85.5
General government	9.9	9.3	6.1	5.8	6.5	6.2	8.9	8.4
Domestic civilian economy	100.0		100.0		100.0		100.0	
Domestic civilian economy	97.9	94.0	97.8	95.3	97.9	95.7	97.4	93.9
Net income from abroad	2.1	2.0	2.2	2.1	2.1	2.0	2.6	2.5
National civilian economy	100.0		100.0		100.0		100.0	
National civilian economy	96.0	96.0	97.4	97.4	97.7	97.7	96.4	96.4
General government, military	4.0	4.0	2.6	2.6	2.3	2.3	3.6	3.6
National economy	100.0	100.0	100.0	100.0	100.0	100.0	100.0	100.0

Note: This table corresponds to Table A-7 in *Productivity Trends*.

not present a separate table showing the relative gross capital weights. The capital weights relative to labor weights are significantly larger on a gross basis, however, as shown in Table A-v.

The weighted and unweighted net aggregates are compared in Table A-iv. Between 1929 and 1966, the weighted series rises by 5.7 per cent more than the unweighted, an average annual shift effect of 0.15 per cent. The result is in the same direction as that shown in a comparison of weighted with unweighted labor input. The shift effect is considerably less in the case of capital, due in part to the fact that capital is weighted in far less detail than labor.

TABLE A-iv

Private Domestic Economy: Weighted Versus Unweighted Capital Measures
(index numbers, 1958=100)

Year	Weighted (1)	Unweighted (2)	Ratio (Col. 1÷Col. 2) (3)
1929	61.3	64.3	0.953
1937	56.4	60.1	0.938
1948	68.7	69.1	0.994
1957	98.0	97.8	1.002
1966	128.7	127.8	1.007

Source: Tables A-15 and A-19.

Total Factor Input

The indexes of labor input (weighted man-hours) and of capital input (weighted real stock, gross and net) in major sectors, and in the national economy as a whole, were combined in the several subperiods by the weights shown in Table A-v. The indexes so obtained were linked back in time beginning with 1953 as of the terminal year of each subperiod. The relative weights for the base year were obtained for each sector from the quotients of total labor compensation and the index of labor input, and of total capital compensation and the index of capital input on both the gross and net bases. This method yields the same aggregate results as those obtained by weighting total input indexes of component sectors by relative sector weights. (See the more detailed discussion of weights in *Productivity Trends*, Appendix A, pp. 284-88 and 232-34.)

It is not possible to obtain a completely unweighted total factor input index, since man-hours and capital are not additive without the use of a

TABLE A-v

National Economy by Major Sector: Relative Weights of Capital Input,
Gross and Net, as Proportion of Factor Cost
(per cent)

	1929-37	1937-48	1948-53	1958
National economy				
Gross	41.5	38.6	38.0	33.0
Net	29.8	28.2	28.1	21.2
Civilian domestic economy				
Gross	39.5	36.3	35.8	30.5
Net	29.3	28.0	28.4	21.2
Private domestic economy				
Gross	39.8	36.4	35.7	30.0
Net	30.3	29.3	28.9	21.2
Private domestic business				
Gross	40.3	37.0	36.3	30.3
Net	30.8	29.9	29.6	21.5
Farm				
Gross	70.2	61.2	54.2	52.6
Net	65.6	55.8	46.0	42.9
Private domestic nonfarm business				
Gross	38.2	34.8	34.9	28.8
Net	28.8	28.3	28.3	20.2

Note: The labor input weights are, of course, 100 per cent minus the capital
input percentage weights given in the table.

common denominator. But it is possible to combine unweighted man-hours
and unweighted real capital stock by means of their relative unit compensations in the base year 1958. This represents the minimum weighting possible.
The variant is calculated for the private domestic business economy, and is
shown as a supplement, Table A-19b. This total input index increases far less
than total input calculated with internal weights for labor and capital, and
thus total factor productivity based on unweighted inputs increases more—by
around 0.3 per cent a year, on the average. The ratios of weighted to
unweighted input indexes reflect the relative shift of input from lower- to
higher-paying uses, as pointed out in connection with the discussions of each
factor class. The indexes of total input are shown in the summary tables
beginning with A-17.

Productivity Ratios: Summary Tables

Summary tables beginning with A-17 present indexes of output, partial and total inputs, and partial and total factor productivity ratios for the national economy and major broad sectors of the economy. Consistent with *Productivity Trends*, we base the productivity ratios on real *gross* product measures, even when relating to real capital and total input measures *net* of real depreciation allowances. We do this because real gross product measures are somewhat more reliable than real net product measures, and because, in the sectors for which we have both, the movements of gross and net product do not diverge significantly. Further, for most nonfarm industries, we have only real gross product estimates from OBE, not real net product. Therefore, we use real gross product throughout the sectors and industries as a proxy for real net product.

The alternative is to measure real capital and total input *gross* of depreciation reserves, and to include depreciation along with net property income in obtaining the weight of real gross capital input relative to the weight of real labor input. As noted in the text, labor compensation is inclusive of depreciation on human capital, so the gross capital input indexes and gross capital weights are actually more consistent with the labor input indexes and weights, as well as with the real gross product numerators of the productivity ratios. This alternative is presented for the broad economy, its sectors, and, subsequently, major industry segments. In these tables, we have an "a" part of each, showing indexes of real gross capital input, the ratio of real gross product to real gross capital input, total gross input, and total gross factor productivity.

Table A-17 covers the total national economy, and Table A-18, the civilian domestic economy. It will be recalled that the real product and productivity index numbers for these broadest segments of the economy are subject to downward bias due to the absence of a productivity-advance element in the estimates of real government product (civilian as well as military) and of real product originating in the rest of the world.

Table A-19 relates to the private domestic economy. This series is continuous with the main series relied on in *Productivity Trends*, and we have extrapolated the component series on the revised basis 1929-66 prior to 1929 using the previous estimates. Thanks to new estimates of real product originating, we are able to present series for the private domestic business economy in Table A-20 going back to 1929.

For some purposes analysts are interested in the nonfarm sector of the private domestic business economy. We present estimates for that variant in Table A-21, obtained by subtracting estimates for the farm economy (Table A-22) from the broader totals. For all these broad sectors, as noted earlier, we present gross capital, gross input, and total gross factor productivity estimates.

Productivity Trends, Appendix A (pp. 287-88), included some discussion of the consistency of the weighting patterns for the output and input measures. In the period covered by this study the weighting systems are entirely consistent, at least in a formal sense. We also discussed the reliability of the estimates. There is no need to repeat this here, except to point out that the productivity ratios may well be more reliable than either the output or input indexes alone. To the extent that the output and input data come from the same sources and are subject to the same errors or biases, the ratios will be less affected than the component series.

PART II

INDUSTRY GROUPS

Rather than treat each industry segment separately (as was done in *Productivity Trends*, Appendixes B through K), we shall discuss them together here, since many of the same sources and methods were used for each individually. Following the initial section on classification, we shall look at the estimates of gross output, real product, labor input, capital input, total input, and productivity indexes. The index numbers of outputs, inputs, and productivity ratios for the various industry groups and components are presented consecutively beginning with Table A-22.

Classification

The industry classifications in terms of which the output, input, and productivity estimates are presented from 1948 forward follow the 1957 Standard Industrial Classification (SIC). This is in line with the 1965-66 revisions of the OBE national income and product accounts.[14] In our earlier work, the industry estimates conformed to the 1942 SIC, with the modifications described in OBE's *National Income*, 1954 edition. The new OBE estimates for years prior to 1948 are still based on the old classification, since the data for earlier years could not be adapted to the revised SIC.

Estimates of national income and other variables presented by industry are shown according to both classifications for 1948 by OBE in order to indicate the magnitudes of the differences occasioned by the classification revision. Among major industry groupings, the changes resulted primarily in shifting income and product from trade to manufacturing and services. Many two-digit industries were affected little or not at all. A few of the former two-digit

---

[14] See *Survey of Current Business,* August 1965; and *The National Income and Product Accounts of the United States,* 1929-1965, Statistical Tables (1966).

groups were merged, notably the bituminous and anthracite coal groups and the ferrous and nonferrous primary metals groups. Conversely, instruments were broken out of the miscellaneous manufactures group and added as a separate two-digit group.

The conceptual revisions described in Part I above affected several industries significantly. The 1958 gross product for services including households was reduced by $5.9 billion because of the elimination of interest paid by consumers from income. The total for real estate, on the other hand, was raised by $12 billion, reflecting the capitalization of real estate commissions. The totals for manufacturing, mining, and contract construction decreased slightly due to exclusion of small tools and similar outlays charged to current expense from capital consumption allowances. Other conceptual revisions resulted in only minor changes, or none at all, in industry estimates. The statistical revisions generally had little effect.

Output

First on the agenda are the OBE real industry product estimates. These have become available for major nonfarm industries since *Productivity Trends* appeared, and we now use them for productivity comparisons since they are conceptually consistent with the overall estimates of real product in the private domestic economy. But we use gross output indexes for two-digit industry groups, for which real product estimates are not published (and may be less stable, as explained below). We also present alternative productivity estimates based on gross output indexes for some broader groupings in order to continue series given in the earlier study, even though real product estimates are also shown. In the second section below, we describe the gross output estimates used, and compare their trends with those of real product where both sets of series are available.

Real Industry Product

The OBE estimates of gross product originating in broad industry groupings, in current and constant prices, were first published for the private nonfarm economy in October 1962. The estimates were revised to conform to the 1965-66 conceptual and statistical changes in the income and product accounts, and presented to the public in April 1967. The initial and revised estimates were described in considerable detail in *Survey of Current Business* articles and in supplementary documents made available by OBE on request; further detailed descriptions of the estimates for the manufacturing and service groups were prepared by staff members of OBE in connection with the Conference on Research in Income and Wealth. In view of the more or less extensive documentation concerning sources and methods used in making the OBE estimates, we shall only summarize briefly the technical aspects of the series, and attempt to point out some of the limitations and qualifications that must attach to their use for production and productivity analysis.

In principle, real industry product estimates represent the gross value of output less the cost of intermediate products consumed in the production process, each deflated by appropriate price indexes. Given perfectly consistent value estimates and price deflators for intermediate and final products, the sum of real industry product would equal real product obtained by deflating purchases of final goods and services, by type. Even perfect consistency would not mean that the aggregate and industry estimates were necessarily correct. In the case of the OBE estimates, as noted above, some of the price deflators, particularly in the new construction and finance-services area, are subject to upward bias, which is also true of the gross industry output deflators in these areas. This means that both real final expenditures and real industry product estimates may consistently tend to understate growth. Further, both sets of current value estimates could be subject to errors in the same direction which would not necessarily show in reconciliation tables— although we have no reason to believe this to be the case.

More to the point, the preferred double-deflation method could be applied only in industries accounting for about 50 per cent of total product originating in the private domestic business economy in 1958—directly applied in farming, and indirectly in contract construction, manufacturing, railroads, and gas and electric utilities. In farming, the basic estimates (drawn from Department of Agriculture data) of value of output less intermediate product purchases equaled gross product originating as the sum of factor costs plus nonfactor charges against product.[15] In this industry, then, real product could be obtained directly by the double-deflation approach. In the other industries listed above, the available estimates of gross values of output and of intermediate product purchases did not reconcile with gross product originating, built up from the income side, due primarily to incomplete information on intermediate costs obtained, for example, from the Census of Manufactures. In these cases, the implicit deflators obtained as quotients of the differences in current and constant dollar flows were applied to the OBE gross product originating estimates. Since the two sets of current-price esti-

15 See Table A-vi below.

mates did not match precisely, the implicit deflator is subject to possible error. Moreover, the deflators for intermediate product purchases generally did not incorporate annually changing quantity weights, as is ideally desirable.[16]

There are greater possible sources of errors and inconsistencies with aggregate measures in the other industry real product estimates, for which the double-deflation method was not applied even in modified form. For some of these industries, base-period gross product was extrapolated by physical output series, or by the deflated value of gross output. This was the procedure used for fisheries, mining, trade, insurance, most transportation groups other than railroads, telephone and telegraph, and some of the service industries (private and public enterprises). The use of gross output extrapolators involves the assumption that the net-gross ratios did not change, or that, if they did, the changes are offsetting each other. The larger the net-gross ratio, the less the influence of changing ratios.

For most of the remaining industries, current gross product originating was directly deflated by price indexes, including average wage-salary (or, what amounts to the same thing, base period product was extrapolated by employment). Direct deflation of gross product by gross output price indexes involves the assumption that the ratios of prices received to prices paid have not changed. Actually, in the case of real estate, a rent index was averaged with prices of intermediate inputs (appropriately weighted) in order to approximate the implicit deflator. Average wage-salary indexes for deflators (or extrapolation of base-period gross product by employment) does not, of course, allow for productivity change. Fortunately, this procedure was confined to some of the service industries and a few minor residual industries such as agricultural services, brokerage, radio broadcasting, and TV. Once the "household and nonprofit institutions" sector is removed from the services industry grouping, the remaining proportion of the private services industries deflated by average pay is not large. Nevertheless, real product and productivity estimates in this grouping are subject to some downward bias.[17] Yet the industry aggregate is reasonably consistent with the final expenditure aggregate, since some of the service expenditure categories were likewise deflated by average compensation per full-time equivalent employee.

---

[16] See J. J. Gottsegen and R. C. Ziemer, "Comparison of Federal Reserve and OBE Measures of Real Manufacturing Output, 1947-64," *The Industrial Composition of Income and Product,* Studies in Income and Wealth, John W. Kendrick, ed., Volume Thirty-two, NBER, 1968.

[17] See *Production and Productivity in the Service Industries,* Victor R. Fuchs, ed., Studies in Income and Wealth, Volume Thirty-four, NBER, 1969.

Despite the possibilities for inconsistency between the sum of the real industry product estimates and the private domestic business aggregate obtained by the final expenditure approach, it will be recalled from Part I (and reference to Table A-4) that the statistical discrepancy between the two aggregates is not large and does not fluctuate markedly. This does not prove the accuracy of the industry estimates since there may be offsetting errors. But at least it means that the aggregate measure is close to a weighted average of the industry measures, and that industry-aggregate comparisons may be made on a statistically consistent basis. This was also true of the industry estimates used in the earlier volume, which were largely based on gross output extrapolators.[18]

Gross Output

Farming. Farming is the only industry group, as noted in the preceding section, in which the estimates of the real total value of output are completely consistent with the real gross product estimates. In this industry, therefore, the differences in movement between the estimates of gross output and real gross product (inclusive of capital consumption allowances, but not of intermediate product consumption) may be interpreted as reflecting changes in real purchases of intermediate products relative to gross (or net) output.

The relationships are shown for selected years in Table A-vi, which reproduces the OBE estimates drawn, in turn, from Department of Agriculture estimates rearranged in accordance with the OBE industry product concepts. We have modified the OBE concept only to the extent of including gross rents paid to nonfarm landlords in gross farm income and product, rather than excluding them along with intermediate purchases. This is consistent with our treatment of farm capital in terms of capital goods *used* in the sector.

In the table only the implicit deflator for total farm output is shown. Actually, the current dollar estimates were deflated in great detail: Cash receipts from farm marketings were deflated by indexes of prices received for all the various types of crops and livestock; farm products consumed directly in farm households were deflated by the corresponding prices received indexes; net change in farm inventories were obtained in constant prices by multiplying physical changes, by category, and base-period average prices; and the gross rental value of farm homes was deflated by a rent index. Similarly,

---

[18] See *Productivity Trends*, Appendix A, pp. 250-51.

TABLE A-vi

Farming: Total Output and Gross Product Originating in
Current and Constant Prices, Selected Years, 1929-66

	1929	1948	1958	1966
	Billions of Current Dollars			
al value of farm output	13.82	36.20	37.65	46.21
Cost of intermediate products consumed[a]	3.32	11.20	15.14	19.38
als: Farm gross product	10.49	25.00	22.51	26.83
or costs, net of capital consumption[b]				
d business indirect taxes	9.09	22.66	18.60	23.12
tal consumption allowances	0.86	1.85	3.79	4.95
rect business taxes less subsidies	0.54	0.49	0.11	−1.24
	Implicit Price Deflators			
al value of farm output	58.1	115.0	100.0	108.1
of intermediate products consumed	60.4	101.8	100.0	104.2
n gross product	57.0	122.0	100.0	110.9
	Billions of Constant Dollars			
al value of farm output	23.8	31.5	37.6	42.7
Cost of intermediate products consumed[a]	5.5	11.0	15.1	18.6
als: Farm gross product	18.4	20.5	22.5	24.2
	Per Cent in Terms of Constant Dollars			
endum:				
atio of real gross product to total output	77.3	65.1	59.8	56.7

Source: Rearrangement of OBE estimates contained in *The National Income and Product Accounts
the United States, 1929-1965, Statistical Tables,* Tables 1.17 and 1.18; and July 1968 *Survey
Current Business,* Tables 1.17 and 1.18

[a] Exclusive of gross rents paid to nonfarm landlords, which are included as part of gross product
inating; inclusive of "other items," a small adjustment required in the OBE estimates to reconcile
s product estimates as total output less intermediate costs with the sum of factor costs and other
rges against product.

[b] Except for a small amount of depreciation included in gross rents paid to nonfarm landlords.

the intermediate product purchases were broken down by type and deflated
by the corresponding indexes of prices paid by farmers, based on Department
of Agriculture estimates. The implicit deflators for total output and intermediate costs represent the quotients of the current and constant dollar
aggregates. Real product is the difference between the real value of total
output and real intermediate costs. The implicit deflator for gross farm
product is obtained by dividing the constant dollar series into the current
dollar estimates; it may also be viewed as a weighted average of the current
dollar estimates, or as a weighted average of the implicit deflators for gross

output and intermediate purchases. Note also that gross farm product in current dollars derived as the difference between the total value of output and intermediate costs equals the sum of factor costs, capital consumption allowances, and indirect business taxes less subsidies.

It can be seen in Table A-vi that the ratio of intermediate costs to the total value of farm output in real terms rose from about 35 per cent in 1948 to 44 per cent in 1966. This continued the rising trend evident in prior decades, reflecting the transfers of various activities from the farm to nonfarm sectors, and the increasing use of various nonfarm inputs required to operate tractors, farm trucks, et cetera.

This trend is reflected, of course, in a significantly smaller rate of increase in real farm product than in total gross output. The latter measure should really be related not only to factor inputs but to total input inclusive of intermediate inputs as well, which would reduce the apparent rate of productivity advance. Generally, we use gross output measures as a proxy for real product measures, and so relate only to factor inputs. In the case of farming, however, it is clear that gross output has a persistent upward bias as a proxy for real product and cannot be so interpreted.

In the analyses, we used the real product estimates and the corresponding productivity estimates with all industry groups for which both sets of output estimates are available. The gross output estimates are presented to serve as supplementary information and to continue the gross output series presented in *Productivity Trends*.

Mining. The gross output index numbers for the mining group, and the four component industries, are the Census Bureau-Federal Reserve Board benchmark indexes for 1947, 1954, and 1958, interpolated and extrapolated by the corresponding FRB annual production indexes for the corresponding groupings. As described in greater detail below for manufacturing, the Census-FRB benchmark indexes represent the value of production, deflated by unit value or price indexes in terms of five-digit product classes. The 1947-54 indexes were combined using 1954 unit value weights, while the 1954-58 indexes employ 1958 unit value weights, which is roughly consistent with our general weighting procedure. The crude petroleum and natural gas production index includes the physical volume of oil and gas drilling activity, which is consistent with our earlier industry definition and with the coverage of the input measures.

The benchmark index numbers for 1963 relative to 1958 were not available at the time of writing, but we are informed that the changes are fairly close to those indicated by the annual FRB indexes, according to preliminary results.

The gross production index shows closely similar movements to the real gross product measure for the mining group. This is not surprising when it is realized that OBE extrapolated base period gross product originating in the component industries forward, and back to 1947, from 1958 by the FRB annual indexes. The slight deviations in movement are due to the following factors. The component FRB mining industry indexes were not yet tied into the 1958 and 1963 benchmark indexes. This means that the 1954-58 movements of the industry indexes, and thus of the group index, differ somewhat from our gross output indexes. Specifically, the real product measures for metal and nonmetallic mining rise a bit less. On balance, the group gross output index falls by 1.0 percentage point relative to the real product measure during 1948-54, rises by 1.5 percentage point in 1954-58, and shows virtually the same movement thereafter. Some small part of the difference is due to the different weighting procedure implicit in the group real product measure. The real gross output index is the more up-to-date measure. Since the real product measures are not published for the four industry components, we use the gross output indexes exclusively for these industries.

The 1957 SIC combined anthracite and bituminous coal mining into one two-digit industry. In *Productivity Trends* we showed the components separately; in the present study our measures relate to the combined coal industry.

Manufacturing. The manufacturing gross output indexes for total manufacturing and its components—durables and nondurables—and the twenty-one two-digit groups are based on the Census-FRB benchmark production indexes for 1947, 1954, 1958, and 1963, interpolated and extrapolated to 1966 by the FRB indexes of manufacturing production.[19] In summarizing the construction of the benchmark indexes, we shall refer chiefly to the indexes for 1954, 1958, and 1963, which differ in a few respects from the earlier indexes in ways that will be indicated.

In all the benchmark indexes, the detailed quantity and value data for manufacturing products (published in Tables 6 of Volume II of each manufacturing Census) are basic. Weighted indexes of the quantity of products are not directly used, however. Rather, for the 1954-58 and 1958-63 indexes, the

---

[19] See, particularly, the *Census of Manufactures, 1963,* Bureau of the Census, Vol. IV, *Indexes of Production,* 1968. The indexes through 1954 are described in *Productivity Trends.*

value of output of every industry was deflated in five-digit detail, using the breakdowns of industry shipments, adjusted for inventory change, published in Table 5B of Census Volume II. Thus, secondary products were more appropriately deflated than in earlier benchmark calculations, in which they were implicitly deflated by the unit values of the primary products of each industry.

The deflators were based primarily on unit values, derived as quotients of the value and quantity data available for about 5,000 products in more than 1,000 Census seven-digit product lines. The unit values give accurate measures of price change to the extent that changes in product mixes at the seven-digit level were not significant, or did not affect unit value, on balance. The unit value indexes were reviewed, and in some cases rejected, if external evidence or criteria indicated that their movements were significantly distorted. The Census unit value indexes were supplemented by the BLS wholesale price index series, and to some extent by price or unit value data from other sources, such as the Tariff Commission and Bureau of Mines.

Indexes of the deflated value of production were weighted by value-added at the four-digit industry level up to 1954; since 1954, value-added weights were applied at the five-digit product class level. The more detailed weighting makes little difference in the movements of the two-digit industry indexes. The choice of weight base or bases does make a difference in movements, however, as a result of the significant negative correlation between relative changes in prices or unit value-added and in quantities. For example, the total manufacturing index increased by a 0.6 percentage point a year faster from 1954 to 1958 with 1958 weights than with 1954 weights, and by a 0.2 percentage point a year less from 1958 to 1963 with 1958 weights than with 1963 weights.[20] For the period 1954-66 as a whole, our use of 1958 price and unit value weights would result in little difference in movement in comparison with the use of average 1954-66 weights.

Finally, we must note the differences in movement of the Census-FRB gross production indexes and the OBE real product measures and consider the chief factors that could account for them. The gross output index for total manufacturing rises by about 8 per cent more than the real product estimates between 1948 and 1960, and thereafter shows little difference in trend. The relative increase is somewhat greater in nondurables than in durables. Although OBE does not regularly publish its estimates of real product by two-digit industries, they were published for the period 1947-64 as part of an

[20] Ibid., Table B, p. 4.

article analyzing the differences between the OBE and FRB indexes.[21] The relative increase in the gross output indexes is evident in all industries but tobacco products, fabricated metal products, and petroleum refining. The differences in annual changes were frequently significant. This is believed to reflect to an important extent the sensitivity of real product estimates to differential changes in the output and input deflators.[22] In fact, even if real product estimates by two-digit industries were available for use, we might well have chosen to use the gross output indexes anyway because of their lesser short-term instability.

There are several reasons for the differences in trend between the OBE real product and the Census-FRB gross output indexes. The first is conceptual. As noted earlier, the OBE estimates are approximations of true net output measures, while the Census-FRB indexes, in effect, extrapolate base-period value-added by gross output measures at the five-digit level. To the extent that real intermediate costs have risen in relation to gross output in these industries, real product would rise less than gross output, as in the case of agriculture.

Yet it is doubtful whether this is the main explanation of the divergence in trend between the two measures, since there are a number of statistical and methodological differences between the series. In the first place, OBE relied primarily on BLS wholesale price indexes as deflators, while Census-FRB relied primarily on a larger range of unit value indexes. Since the latter set of indexes tended to show a lesser increase over the period, this appears to be a major factor explaining the greater increase in the Census-FRB measures.[23] The 1954 value-added weights used for the Census-FRB indexes underlying our measures result in a somewhat higher rate of increase for 1948-54 than would the 1958 weight base employed by OBE throughout. A further small difference arises from the fact that the Census-FRB weights are gross value-added while the OBE weights are net value-added, inclusive of excise taxes and depreciation.

The possibilities of divergence between the two measures in the annual changes and the 1963-66 trend are even greater than in the trends between Census benchmarks. The OBE estimates, based on the Census annual survey of manufactures, are subject to sampling errors in the value estimates as well as to cyclical biases in the price deflators. The implicit deflator for gross

21 *The Industrial Composition of Income and Product,* Studies in Income and Wealth, Vol. 32, pp. 225-346.

22 Ibid., Comment by Frank Garfield on the Gottsegen-Ziemer paper, pp. 367-70.

23 Ibid., Comment by Vivian Spencer on the Gottsegen-Ziemer paper, pp. 355-56.

product is particularly sensitive to errors in the component deflators since it is a weighted difference between the output and intermediate input deflators. The FRB index by which we have interpolated and extrapolated the benchmark indexes relied on quantity series and proxies for output, particularly productivity-adjusted man-hours, for about half the series. Although the proxies are based on careful study of their relationship to actual output measures for benchmark years, it is obvious that errors will occur and may cumulate in the extrapolation period. They may be particularly significant in some of the two-digit industries, but tend to offset each other in the broader group measures. Fortunately, our estimates extend only three years beyond the latest (1963) benchmark, so the biases should be limited.

Transportation. Gross output for the transportation industry as a whole is based on estimates of gross output in each of the covered sectors described below, weighted by base-period (1958) GNP originating. In practice the estimates were made by taking the estimates prepared by the Office of Business Economics of average current dollar GNP originating in 1958 for each industry and extrapolating by the appropriate output indexes for the period 1948-66. The GNP originating in the covered segment was adjusted to include a residual sector that comprises transportation services not covered in the individual industries for which estimates could be made. The adjustment factor was based on a ratio of persons engaged in the covered industries to OBE estimates of persons engaged for the whole transportation industry. Estimated real GNP was divided by these adjustment ratios annually for the years 1948-66 in order to derive an estimate for real GNP for the transportation industry, including the residual sector. This procedure implied that GNP per person engaged in the uncovered sector showed the same movements as that in the covered sector. The uncovered sector comprised 21.9 per cent of industry GNP in 1948 and 23.5 per cent in 1966.

A separate series of real GNP originating in the nonrailroad sector was obtained by subtracting real GNP originating in railroads from total real GNP. Both series were transformed into output indexes using 1958 as the comparison base.

Except for the use of new weighting and comparison bases, the railway output index constructed for this study is based on the same procedures as those described in *Productivity Trends.* The index shown in Table A-60 covers all phases of railroad passenger and freight operations. It is based on statistics compiled by the Interstate Commerce Commission and published under the title *Statistics of Railways in the United States* for the years

1948-53 and as *Transport Statistics in the United States* from 1954 to the present.

The index of freight output was based on revenue ton-miles weighted by average revenue per ton-mile in cents. An output index was prepared for each of the three classes of line-haul railroads. The output of Class I, II, and III line-haul railroads omits a small fraction of total railway output, that of switching and terminal companies and of the Railway Express Company. In order to account for this segment of coverage, adjustment based on total operating revenues to operating revenues of the covered segment was calculated for each year of the period. The adjustment ratio fluctuated only narrowly between 1.045 and 1.052.

In 1956, the three-division classification of line-haul railroads was changed. Before that date, Class I line-haul railroads were those with annual operating revenues over $1,000,000, Class II, between $100,000 and $1,000,000, and Class III, below $100,000. The 1956 reclassification eliminated Class III and redefined Class I as railroads having $3,000,000 or over in annual operating revenues and Class II as having under $3,000,000. Because of the relatively small size of Class III, Classes II and III were combined for the years 1953-55 in order to assure weighting-base comparability.

For the period 1948-53, we calculated weights for each of the three classes and used the average of 1948 and 1953 as a weight base. The separately weighted output indexes were then combined into an aggregate and linked in 1953 to the aggregate employing average 1958 weights. The index for the entire period 1948-66 was expressed on the comparison base of 1958=100.

The ICC transportation statistics give passenger-miles for Class I railroads in commutation, coaches, and parlor and sleeping cars. For Class II and Class III and for the Pullman Company, only the total number of revenue passenger-miles are given. Each of the available divisions of passenger traffic was weighted separately by average revenue per passenger per mile using the same weight bases as in freight traffic. The aggregate passenger output is the sum of the individual weighted outputs on a comparison base of 1958=100. The 1956 change in the classification scheme was treated in the same manner as it was for freight output.

Total output was obtained by weighting the freight and passenger output indexes together by their proportionate shares in total operating revenues in the two base periods, linking in 1953, and using the 1958 comparison base throughout.

For air transportation, the index of output which appears in Table A-68 is the BLS composite index based on the quantities of passenger and cargo services combined with unit revenue weights for the average of the years 1957-59. This output index is separated into eight categories. The various outputs are domestic and international territorial operations (measured by passenger-miles), freight ton-miles, express ton-miles, and U.S. and foreign mail ton-miles for both scheduled and nonscheduled services. Unit revenue weights for the outputs are generally based on revenue derived from scheduled services only.

The major source of the output data is the Civil Aeronautics Board (CAB). Data collected from the different carriers were published in 1963 in a *Handbook of Airline Statistics*. A CAB monthly publication, *Air Carrier Traffic Statistics*, is another important source for output data.

For pipeline transportation, the ICC reports contain data on barrel-miles of crude and refined oils having trunkline movement.[24] These were converted to ton-miles, using Barger's conversion factors: one barrel crude = 0.15 ton; one barrel refined = 0.13 ton.[25] Oil movement through the gathering lines operated by interstate carriers is not reported. The trunkline estimates were adjusted by dividing by the ratio of depreciation and amortization for trunk-pipelines to the total for all lines. This ratio rose gradually from 81.5 per cent in 1948 to over 87 per cent in 1966. Thus, total estimated output rises less rapidly than that based on trunkline data only, and is consistent with the employment data. No such adjustment was made in the earlier output and productivity estimates, which, as was noted, may have resulted in some upward bias on this account.

Water transportation output (Table A-67) is the sum of the weighted outputs of freight traffic and of international and other passenger traffic, as shown in Table A-vii. Relative 1957-59 weights were calculated by revising the 1929 weights used in *Productivity Trends* (Table G-5) to reflect the relative changes in volume since then.

Freight output statistics were gathered for five types of traffic: coastwise and intercoastal; internal (inland); noncontiguous; domestic Great Lakes; and international.[26] These data have been tied to the estimates in *Producti-*

[24] See Interstate Commerce Commission, *Annual Report on the Statistics of Railways in the United States*, Tables 175-76, for the period 1948-53; from 1954 onward, ICC's *Transport Statistics in the United States, Part 6, Oil Pipe Lines*.

[25] See Harold Barger, *The Transportation Industries, 1889-1946: A Study of Output, Employment, and Productivity*, New York, National Bureau of Economic Research, 1951, p. 251, footnote C.

[26] Ibid., p. 17, note C.

TABLE A-vii

Water Transportation,
Percentage Weights by Category, 1957-59

Freight	86.6
International	26.8
Great Lakes	5.5
Internal	20.5
Noncontiguous	9.2
Coastwise and intercoastal	24.6
Passenger	13.4
International	6.2
Other[a]	7.2

[a] Includes passenger traffic on ferry, Great Lakes, and other inland vessels, also on coastwise, intercoastal, and noncontiguous vessels.

vity Trends. Unit revenue weights from Barger (Table 30, p. 128) were used throughout.

Ton-mile figures for coastwise and intercoastal traffic are not available prior to 1955. Therefore, the period 1948-54 was extrapolated by linking with the *Productivity Trends* data on the basis of tons of freight carried. For 1955-61, ton-mile statistics published in ICC Statement 6501 were used, and for the remainder of the period, U.S. Corps of Army Engineers ton-mile data. Two adjustments are necessary to make the series internally consistent. First, a comparison of our estimate for the year 1955 with the ICC ton-mile data shows that the level of the former is somewhat higher than the ICC figures for that year. The ratio of the ICC figure to our estimate in 1955 was used to adjust the level of our estimates for 1948-54 to that of the ton-mile data. Second, the Army ton-mile data published since 1961 include noncontiguous traffic. In order to maintain comparability with the data prior to 1961, noncontiguous traffic as published in ICC Statement 6501 was subtracted from the Army coastwise statistics.

Estimates for noncontiguous traffic are an extrapolation of the previous data on the basis of short tons of freight carried.

The series for internal waterways is a departure from the earlier Kendrick-Barger output statistics. The basic series used by Kendrick and Barger overstates the level of output because the Army statistics published before 1961 include a certain amount of foreign flag traffic on internal waterways. Beginning in 1961 the ton-mile data published in the U.S. Department of Commerce publication *Waterborne Commerce of the United States* (Supplement 2 to Part 5, National Summaries) are given by type of carrier and exclude foreign flag vessels. Private information from the Corps of Engineers established the fact that the portion of foreign flag traffic included in the inland traffic statistics has been about the same since the end of World War II. Therefore, the ratio of new data in 1961 to the old in 1961 was applied to the statistics between 1948 and 1960 in order to adjust for the inclusion of foreign flag traffic prior to 1961.

The level of output for Great Lakes traffic used in this study is below that of the series used in *Productivity Trends* because domestic Great Lakes traffic data were available, while the earlier series includes foreign as well as domestic traffic.

Because there are no ton-mile figures available for international freight traffic of U.S. flag vessels, we extended the earlier Barger-Kendrick ton-mile output figures on the basis of short tons of freight carried by U.S. flag vessels.

The passenger output sector of the water transportation industry suffers from a shortage of usable statistical information. The primary source for the Barger study was the Corps of Engineers' *Annual Report*, Part 2. All of the information published by the Corps on passengers carried in the various noninternational modes of water transportation was discontinued in 1947 because of incomplete information. As far as we have been able to ascertain, no new studies concerning miles traveled by various types of passengers have been made since Barger published his findings. As a result our estimates are exact extensions of the methods used in *Productivity Trends*.

Passenger-mile estimates for international travel were prepared on the basis of the number of passengers arriving in and departing from U.S. ports as published in the *Annual Report of the Immigration and Naturalization Service* (Tables 31 and 32), linked up with the earlier Kendrick-Barger passenger-mile estimates.

The "other" category includes coastwise, internal, and ferry traffic. Because the Corps of Engineers stopped publication of passenger data in these categories, estimates were extended on the basis of vessel tonnages engaged in domestic trade.

The local transit industry includes electric railways and local bus lines, as described below. It presents a more accurate measure of productivity than either of the component parts—electric railways and local buses. This is so because it was necessary to apply average hours in the whole industry to employment in each of the individual sectors to obtain man-hour figures, and split output estimates between public and private sectors based on total industry data.

The separate output indexes were combined on the basis of relative revenue weights. These weights reflect the relative contribution of electric railways and local buses to total revenue. For the years 1948-53 electric railways accounted for 43.5 per cent of total revenue, and local buses provided the remainder. In the period 1957-59 the importance of local bus operations increased, accounting for 65.6 per cent of total revenue, while electric railways produced 34.4 per cent of total revenue. It must be noted that the roles of electric railways and local buses have almost reversed themselves since 1939, the weight base year used by Barger in *The Transportation Industries* (Tables 3 and 4). At that time electric railways were the dominant sector in the industry.

The combined output index shown in Table A-64 was placed on a 1958 comparison basis. Despite the declining importance of electric railways relative to local bus lines, the irregularity of the final output for the former transmitted itself to some extent to the index of output for the local transit group as a whole.

The local bus lines portion of the local transit industry is composed of companies primarily engaged in operating street and suburban passenger bus lines, within the confines of a single municipality, contiguous municipalities, or a municipality and its suburban areas (see *Productivity Trends*, p. 516). Again, we are considering only private companies in calculating the productivity indexes.

The output index is based on the number of revenue passengers carried by private bus lines. A ratio of private employment to total employment for the local transit group applied to the number of revenue passengers carried on public plus private local bus lines provides an estimate of output for the private sector of local bus lines. The series of private employment for the local transit industry is the same one described in the local transit section. The series of total employment (private and public) can be obtained from the American Transit Association's *Transit Fact Book*. This is also the source of the number of revenue passengers carried on private and public bus lines. This extrapolation was necessary for the years 1954-66 only. For the period prior to 1954 we used the basic data given in *Productivity Trends*. The output estimates were then weighted by unit revenues in the two weight periods (1948-53 and 1957-59) and an index was calculated and put on a 1958 comparison base.

The electric railway portion of the local transit industry includes local street and interurban railway systems, elevated or subway lines, and trolley buses. It does not include the electrified portion of steam railroads. Output and productivity measures were confined to the private sector.

The traffic output indexes for the 1948-66 period are based on a weighted aggregate of revenue passengers and freight car-miles on electric railways. The traffic indexes of the 1948-53 period are derived in the same manner as those appearing in *Productivity Trends*. Differences between the former estimates and those shown here resulted from a change in the weight base from 1939 to 1948-53 and 1958, and a change in the comparison base from 1929 to 1958. For the remainder of the period 1953-66 a new method was used to estimate the number of revenue passengers carried.

For freight output (car-miles) the ICC was the primary source of data: for the 1948-53 period, *Statistics of Railways in the United States*, and for the 1953-66 period, *Transport Statistics in the U.S.*, Part 4, *Electric Railways*. A weighted output was calculated by applying a unit revenue weight (freight revenue per car-mile) to car-mile data. The irregular behavior of output as reported by the ICC can be explained in part by the fact that the number of carriers reporting to the ICC between 1956 and 1960 decreased from forty-one to twenty-five. This decrease is a result of two factors. On the one hand, some carriers have been reclassified as Class II line-haul railroads. Because freight output is relatively more important than passenger output, the total output index was affected by the irregular behavior of the freight sector. This behavior can also be noted in *Productivity Trends*, Table G-V, for the 1948-53 period.

For passenger output the basic series is the number of revenue passengers carried. The *Transit Fact Book* is the major source of data. These include revenue passengers carried on both private and municipally owned systems. The number of revenue passengers carried for the years 1948-53 on privately owned systems was derived on the basis of the method presented by Ulmer,[27] which is based on unpublished data from the American Transit Association. It was not feasible to obtain the data for this study after 1953. Therefore, for the period 1954-66 the number of revenue passengers carried was adjusted by the ratio of employment in the private sector to employment in the whole sector, applied to the number of revenue passengers carried on electric railways as reported by the ATA. According to this extrapolation,

---

[27] Melville J. Ulmer, *Capital in Transportation, Communications, and Public Utilities: Its Formation and Financing,* Princeton University Press for NBER, 1960, Table I-26.

output per employee in the private sector moved in the same relative fashion as did output in the whole sector. Freight and passenger outputs were weighted by 1948-53 and 1958 unit revenues and then combined.

The estimates of productivity in intercity motor carriers of passengers (bus), given in Table A-65, cover all classes rather than Class I alone. Following the method in *Productivity Trends* (pp. 519-21), revenue passenger-miles were used as the output measure of intercity bus lines. This was obtained from *Bus Facts* (33rd edition, 1965, p. 6). Figures for the 1957-64 period also appear in the *Statistical Abstract* (1965, p. 559, Table 780). The revenue passenger-mile figures for 1965-66 were supplied by the National Association of Motor Bus Owners.

Output and productivity estimates for intercity trucking shown in Table A-66 were based on Class I and II intercity carriers. For the period 1950-66, ton-mile data provided by the American Trucking Association's *American Trucking Trends* were used as output. First, the number of carriers, Class I and II, is multiplied by average power units operated per carrier. This result is multiplied by ton-miles per power unit to get total ton-miles. Secondly, figures for 1948 and 1949 are extrapolated from 1950 by the intercity tonnage index, Classes I and II, in the American Trucking Association's *Intercity Truck Tonnage*, (1965, p. 4). This extrapolation is necessary as separate figures on Class II and III are not available prior to 1950.

For the transportation segment as a whole, gross output rose by about 10 per cent more than real product between 1948 and 1966. This was due to a relatively large increase in the gross-net ratio in the nonrailway transport segment more than offsetting a modest decline in the gross-net ratio in the railway industry. Based on independent estimates by the author, savings of more than 4 per cent appear to have been achieved in the consumption of fuels and other intermediate inputs per unit of output by the railroads over the period. In the nonrailroad segment, the 20 per cent increase in gross output relative to real product may largely reflect an underestimate by OBE of the growth in real product. For example, the OBE estimate of the increase in airlines real product falls significantly below the increase in the gross output estimates of BLS used in this study, despite the fact that the airlines also achieved some savings in the use of fuels and other intermediate inputs per unit of output. But in the face of the inadequacy of basic production data for a large portion of nonrailroad transportation, we cannot definitely conclude that the gross output measures are superior to the real product estimates. More and better data are needed to improve both sets of estimates.

Electric and Gas Utilities. For this industry we employ the output index prepared by the Bureau of Labor Statistics for its productivity studies.[28] The component electricity and gas output measures are very similar to the indexes prepared for *Productivity Trends* (Appendix H).

Electricity output is measured in terms of kilowatt-hours sold, by class of service: residential, commercial, and industrial, and other ultimate consumers for privately owned class A and B electric utilities and for Rural Electrification Administration borrowers (by type of service beginning in 1957).

The basic sources are the Federal Power Commission's *Statistics of Electric Utilities in the United States, Privately Owned,* and REA's *Annual Statistical Reports.* Weights are the average 1957-59 revenue per KWH for each class of service.

Gas production (sales) is measured in terms of therms, by type of service—residential, commercial, industrial, and other—for privately owned gas utilities and pipelines. Sales cover natural, manufactured, mixed, and liquified petroleum gas. The source of the basic data is the American Gas Association. Average 1957-59 revenues per therm, by class of service, are used as weights.

The separate electric and gas output indexes were combined, using a harmonic mean, with the current employment weights. It should be noted that the products not covered by the combined index amounted to about 3.5 per cent in 1947 and to about 1 per cent in 1961.

The BLS gross output index for electric and gas utilities rose by almost 20 per cent more than the OBE estimates of real gross product originating in the electric, gas, and sanitary services group. Presumably, this reflects a much lower rate of output growth in the sanitary and other local utility services which are not included in the BLS measure. Part of the difference could be due to different methodology, since OBE deflated sales to each class of customer by corresponding wholesale and consumer price indexes. OBE also deflated costs of fuels and certain other intermediate purchases to deduct from gross output, but the double-deflation approach would have worked in the opposite direction, since fuel requirements per unit of output declined over the period. Differences in the weighting procedures to combine the two component industry indexes may have accounted for a small part of the difference in trends.

Industry Composites.

It is apparent from the foregoing industry discussion that the gross output indexes rose somewhat faster over the period 1948-66 than the real product

---

[28] *Indexes of Output per Man-Hour, Gas and Electric Utilities Industry, 1932-62,* U.S. Department of Labor, April 1964. These estimates are updated annually by the BLS.

measures in the groups for which we have both. Weighted averages for the two sets of indexes for the relevant nonfarm industry segments—mining, manufacturing, transportation, communication and public utilities, and trade—indicate that the composite gross output index rose by about 9 per cent more over the eighteen-year period than the real product composite. As implied earlier, this discrepancy is probably the result of different sources and methods underlying the two sets of estimates rather than of an increase in real intermediate costs relative to gross output.

In the text, we discuss the relative movements of output and productivity in thirty-two industry groups for which we have capital, total input, and total productivity indexes.[29] In this collection of industries, we use gross output and derived total factor productivity indexes for twenty-seven of the industries; for the others—railroads, communication, electric, gas, and sanitary services, wholesale and retail trade—we use real product indexes. This composite rises by 113 per cent between 1948 and 1966, compared with a 103 per cent increase using real product indexes for all of the corresponding groups. The average annual percentage rates of change for the two composites are 4.3 and 4.0, respectively. Thus, it should be borne in mind in interpreting the behavior of the thirty-two industries that their composite output rises by 0.3 per cent a year more than the composite that forms a major portion of the real product index for the private domestic business economy as a whole. It so happens that the latter index also rose by 103 per cent, or 4.0 per cent a year, over the period. This means that the industries for which we do not have capital estimates—agricultural service, forestry and fisheries, certain nonrail transportation groups, finance and services, including government enterprises but excluding households and nonprofit institutions—grew at about the same rate as the industries for which capital estimates could be prepared.

Labor Input

In Part I it was pointed out that the persons-engaged, man-hours, and labor-input (weighted man-hours) series for the economy were built up from estimates for the component two-digit industries, with subtotals for the one-digit industry groups. There we summarized the basic sources and methods used to obtain the industry and aggregate estimates. For more detailed descriptions, the labor sections of the appendixes in *Productivity*

---

[29] Two groups which are complete segments—farming and contract construction—are omitted.

TABLE A-viii

Private Domestic Business Economy: Persons Engaged, Man-Hours,
and Labor Compensation by Industry, 1958

Industry Group	Persons Engaged (Thousands)	Man-Hours (Millions)	Labor Compensation (Millions $)	(Percent Distribution)
Agriculture, forestry, fisheries	6,085	13,249	11,702	4.
Farming	5,777	12,579	10,614	4.
Agricultural service, forestry, fisheries	308	670	1,088	0.
Mining	788	1,609	4,506	1.
Metal	95	191	570	0.
Coal	226	388	1,275	0.
Oil and gas	344	753	2,013	0.
Nonmetal	123	277	648	0.
Contract construction	3,586	7,082	17,535	7.
Manufacturing	16,308	31,747	88,162	36.
Nondurables	7,230	13,987	35,433	14.
Foods	1,576	3,166	7,681	3.
Beverages	214	419	1,219	0.
Tobacco	93	179	385	0.
Textiles	925	1,790	3,329	1.
Apparel	1,186	2,111	4,013	1.
Paper	559	1,164	3,099	1.
Printing, publishing	947	1,781	5,240	2.
Chemicals	798	1,599	5,258	2.
Petroleum refining	227	444	1,968	0.
Rubber products	347	681	1,941	0.
Leather products	358	653	1,300	0.
Durables	9,078	17,760	52,729	21.
Lumber products	711	1,350	2,664	1.
Furniture	386	759	1,693	0.
Stone, clay, glass products	580	1,150	3,102	1.
Primary metals	1,161	2,195	7,553	3.
Fabricated metals	1,099	2,168	6,265	2.
Machinery except electric	1,407	2,746	8,535	3.
Electric machinery	1,234	2,426	7,075	2.
Transportation equipment and ordnance	1,766	3,539	11,996	5.
Instruments	329	648	2,002	0.
Miscellaneous	405	779	1,844	0.
Transportation	2,554	5,804	15,609	6.
Railroads	956	1,946	6,103	2.
Nonrail	1,598	3,858	9,506	3.
Local, suburban, and highway passenger transportation	313	728	1,492	0.
Motor freight transportation and warehousing	803	2,097	4,994	2.

TABLE A-viii (concluded)

Industry Group	Persons Engaged (Thousands)	Man-Hours (Millions)	Labor Compensation	
			(Millions $)	(Percentage Distribution)
ter transportation	213	450	1,342	0.56
transportation	169	360	1,085	0.45
eline transportation	25	53	172	0.07
nsportation services	75	170	421	0.18
unication and public utilities	1,483	3,066	8,308	3.47
munication	854	1,728	4,477	1.87
ephone and telegraph	774	1,552	3,877	1.62
dio broadcasting and levision	80	176	600	0.25
tric, gas, and sanitary services	629	1,338	3,831	1.60
	12,117	28,143	52,814	22.03
lesale	2,992	6,639	17,572	7.33
ail	9,125	21,504	35,242	14.70
ce, insurance, real estate	2,675	5,521	13,265	5.53
ance and insurance	1,962	4,049	10,466	4.36
l estate	713	1,472	2,799	1.17
es (excluding households nonprofit institutions, uding government enterprises)	6,492	13,716	27,834	11.61
rvices	5,566	11,929	23,064	9.62
overnment enterprises	926	1,787	4,770	1.99
Federal	600	1,094	3,250	1.36
State and local	326	693	1,520	0.63
e domestic business economy	52,088	109,937	239,735	100.00

Trends may be consulted, since the same sources and methodology are used in the present work. In this section, therefore, it is only necessary to refer to a few supplementary matters relevant to the industry and group estimates.

First, since the tables referred to in Part I give estimates for only the broad industry segments of the economy, in Table A-viii above we present estimates of persons engaged, man-hours, and labor compensation by two- or three-digit industries within the major industrial divisions of the private domestic business economy for the base year 1958. By applying the index numbers for persons engaged and man-hours from the later industry tables to the 1958 figures, the reader can derive annual estimates for the period 1948-66 and compute average hours worked per year as a quotient if desired. It will be recalled that the persons-engaged estimates are based on the OBE series, raised to include unpaid family workers where significant. The man-hours and labor compensation estimates also allow for unpaid family workers as well as for proprietors. The labor compensation estimates are relevant to the derivation of base-period relative weights used to combine man-hours when aggregating to obtain labor input by industry group.

Table A-ix compares the movement of weighted and unweighted man-hours by industry segment between 1948 and 1966. The table makes the point noted in Part I that weighted man-hours (labor input) in the private domestic business economy as a whole increased by 7.2 per cent more than straight man-hours. This is due entirely to the farm-nonfarm shift, since within the nonfarm economy weighted and unweighted man-hours show virtually the same increase. Table A-ix indicates that this is the result of offsetting shift effects among the several industry groups. Internal weights result in a larger increase in labor input than in man-hours in most groups. But in mining and transportation the shift effect works in the opposite direction. In the latter group, the relative decline in the highly paid railroad industry is the reason. In the mining group the relative decline in the highly paid coal mining industry is the chief factor. Otherwise, the tendency has been for workers to shift towards higher-paying industries.

In concluding this section, we stress that the labor estimates are consistent with the gross product estimates, on the basis of an individual industry as well as the economy as a whole. This is because the employment data and the labor compensation portion of the industry product estimates are drawn from the same sources, chiefly social security records. The reader should be reminded, however, that the average hours estimates by industry are not entirely consistent. Whereas the bulk of these estimates are drawn from Census sources and represent hours worked, in several industries—notably wholesale and retail trade—we relied on BLS estimates, which represent hours paid for and decline somewhat less than hours worked.

Real Capital Stock and Input

The estimates of real gross and net capital stocks for the various industries come from several different sources, but are based on broadly consistent methodology. They are available for all the industry groups except finance and services. After summarizing the underlying sources and methods, we shall compare the sum of the industry estimates for the private domestic nonfarm business economy, and assess the residual for reasonableness. The methods whereby the group capital estimates were combined with each other to obtain

TABLE A-ix

Private Domestic Business Economy: Man-Hours, Weighted
Man-Hours, and Shift Effect by Industry Group

Industry Group[a]	Index Numbers, 1966 (1948=100)		
	Man-Hours (1)	Weighted Man-Hours (2)	Shift Effect (Col. 2)÷(Col. 1) (3)
Mining	69.3	64.8	0.935
Manufacturing	123.9	126.8	1.023
Nondurables	108.6	110.8	1.020
Durables	136.7	139.0	1.017
Transportation	82.5	78.9	0.956
Nonrail	124.2	126.6	1.019
Communication and public utilities	124.0	124.9	1.007
Communication	128.2	129.9	1.013
Trade	122.2	123.5	1.011
Finance	162.5	166.8	1.026
Services (excluding households and nonprofit institutions, including government enterprises)	149.8	149.8	1.000
Private domestic business economy	109.5	117.4	1.072
Nonfarm	123.7	123.5	0.998

[a] Excludes groups such as contract construction, for which internal weights
were not applied because of lack of breakdowns.

aggregates for the private domestic business economy were described in Part
I; the only groups where internal industry weights were used to combine the
capital estimates were mining and manufacturing. The final sections describe
the weighting system by which the capital and labor input measures were
combined for component industries, and introduce the productivity summary
tables beginning with A-22.

Farming. The sources and methods used in estimating the real capital
stock employed in farming were described in Part I. To summarize briefly, we
used the OBE estimates of real structures and equipment based on Bulletin F

service lives less 15 per cent, with the Winfrey S-3 retirement curve used for estimating gross stock and straight-line depreciation rates used for calculating net stock. The farm inventory estimates are also from OBE, which multiplied physical units of various types of crops and livestock on hand at the end of each period by average base-period prices. For agricultural land, we multiplied Department of Agriculture estimates of acreage for ten regions by the estimated 1958 values per acre. All year-end estimates were adjusted to annual averages.

Mining. Our basic procedure for this group was to deflate the corporate book-value data given in *Statistics of Income* for the four component industries, adjusted where necessary for continuity and raised to total industry coverage.[30] The Internal Revenue Service data were available separately for gross and net depreciable and depletable assets, land, and inventories, and the corresponding sales data were also taken as a basis for the coverage adjustments. The data were available for each of the four industry groups, except for the period 1957-62, when anthracite coal was combined with nonmetallic mining instead of with bituminous coal. For this period, 1957 data for anthracite coal alone were extrapolated by data for "other nonmetallic mining excluding dimension stone, including anthracite," and then subtracted from nonmetallic mining and quarrying and added back into the coal group. Also, it was necessary to interpolate linearly betwen 1961 and 1963 to obtain estimates for land and depletable capital, since only depreciable assets data were provided for 1962.

End-of-year balance sheet data were transformed to mid-year ones by two-year moving averages. The corporate assets data were adjusted to total coverage by multiplying by the 1953-64 ratio of Bureau of Mines data on the value of total mineral production to the IRS corporate sales data, by industry. The average ratios for the period are as follows: metal mining, 1.0618; coal mining, 0.9605; crude petroleum and natural gas, 2.1032; and nonmetallic mining and quarrying, 2.3163.

The fixed capital estimates were deflated by Daniel Creamer's implicit price deflator for the net book value of manufacturing capital (see next section). This deflator was extrapolated back to 1948 by the OBE implicit deflator for private domestic nonresidential investment, using the following weighting pattern: given year, t, $\times$ 5; t-1 $\times$ 4; t-2 $\times$ 3; t-3 $\times$ 2; and t-4 $\times$ 1.

---

[30] We generally follow the method described in D. Creamer, S. Dobrovolsky, and I. Borenstein, *Capital in Manufacturing and Mining: Its Formation and Financing*, New York, NBER, 1960, Appendix B.

Inventories were deflated by a composite of two indexes. For each mining industry, a unit value of output index was weighted 0.75. The other component was the BLS wholesale price index for industrial commodities, weighted 0.25.

In the case of crude petroleum and natural gas, we extrapolated the 1953 estimate to 1948 by the series presented in *Productivity Trends*, Appendix C, and interpolated annually by the series obtained as described above. The capital estimates for the other industries were obtained directly for the period 1948-53 by the sources and methods described above. The estimates for the mining group are the weighted sum of the estimates for the four components; the relative weights are presented in Table A-xi below.

The capital estimates for the mining industries are obviously subject to a considerable margin of error, and are probably the least reliable of the industry series. For this reason, we show the index numbers for capital and the output-capital ratios only for key years, while using the annual series in deriving annual estimates for total input and total factor productivity.

Manufacturing. The estimates of real capital stock in manufacturing industries are taken from Daniel Creamer of the Conference Board. The key-year estimates of net capital for this class and its two-digit industries presented in *Productivity Trends* were also taken from Creamer.[31] The net capital input estimates for the group as a whole, shown for the period since 1929 in this study, are bench-marked prior to 1948 by the estimates for key years given in the earlier volume, interpolated annually by the OBE real net capital stock estimates for manufacturing, described in Part I, and presented in Table A-15. Gross capital inputs for the key years 1929-48 are obtained by applying ratios of real gross to net capital inputs based on OBE estimates, with annual interpolations made by use of the OBE real gross capital stock estimates (Table A-16).

Creamer's method consists essentially in assembling asset data from the IRS *Statistics of Income* balance-sheet aggregates for manufacturing industries, making a number of adjustments, and then converting the various major categories of assets from book values to constant dollars. Although Creamer treats all types of assets, including the financial items, we use only the real asset categories—equipment, structures, land, and inventories. Creamer's estimates were available only through 1963, so we extended his series through 1966, using similar sources and methods.

[31] See *Productivity Trends*, Appendix D, and *Capital in Manufacturing and Mining*, NBER, 1960.

For the period since 1953-63, Creamer has used more elaborate and somewhat revised procedures compared with those described in his earlier published works.[32] In particular, he used balance sheet data for three-digit industries, and summed to two-digit industry and manufacturing group totals. Creamer's three-digit estimates of fixed capital (structures and equipment) start with the balance sheet data for fixed capital from the IRS Source Book. Industry classifications were rearranged to provide a reasonably comparable set of industry classification. Fixed capital in each three-digit industry was partitioned into separate estimates of the stock of structures and the stock of equipment on the basis of Patrick Huntley's separate estimates of the stock of structures and stock of equipment by three-digit industries.[33] Adjusting the book-value data and deflating by three-digit detail presumably increases the accuracy of the two-digit industry and group estimates. The chief adjustments are for inclusion of government-owned but privately-operated manufacturing facilities, and to normalize the accelerated depreciation allowed on emergency facilities acquired during World War II and the Korean conflict. The estimates do not include an upward adjustment for manufacturing plants rented from nonmanufacturing firms, which amounted to about 3.5 per cent of the book value of structures in 1957.

Asset totals for corporations submitting balance sheets were raised to the total corporate level, by industry, by the ratio of gross sales of the former to the total group given in *Statistics of Income*. To achieve coverage for unincorporated manufacturing enterprises, the relationship of value of product for all establishments, as given in the *Census of Manufactures*, to the value of product of corporate establishments was applied to the corporate totals, with straight-line interpolation of the ratios between census years.

With respect to deflation of book values to constant prices, Creamer was able to treat structures and equipment separately. The underlying price indexes were those developed by OBE for manufacturing structures (constant cost 2) and equipment, described in Part I. By reference to the average lengths of life and annual plant and equipment expenditures (from Huntley), Creamer estimated the proportions of the depreciated book values of struc-

---

[32] See D. Creamer, *Capital Expansion and Capacity in Postwar Manufacturing*, Studies in Business Economics No. 72, National Industrial Conference Board, 1961, Appendixes; and *Recent Changes in Manufacturing Capacity*, Studies in Business Economics No. 79, NICB, 1962.

[33] See the unpublished manuscript by Patrick Huntley "Capital Assets: The Wellspring for Economic Growth—A Study in Estimation of Manufacturers' Depreciable Capital Assets. . . ," University of Arkansas.

tures and equipment in each year acquired in previous years. These proportions were used to weight the price index values for the current and prior years, and the weighted index for each year was applied to book values in order to convert from original costs to constant prices.[34] For structures, an average life of forty-five years was used throughout. Average equipment lives were based on the IRS's (1962) *Depreciation Guidelines and Rules*. The weights for the price indexes differed by industry depending on the annual expenditure services, which were based on the *Census of Manufactures* and the *Annual Survey of Manufactures* for intercensal years after 1948.

For inventories, a different index was compiled for each industry, composed of a weighted average of the appropriate BLS wholesale price indexes.

The 1958 ratio of the value of land to the value of structures, by industry, was applied to the estimated values of structures in constant prices for the entire period. The value of land is reported by IRS. For all manufacturing, land values represented about 4 per cent of the value of structures in 1958.

As compared with the OBE perpetual inventory method of estimating the fixed depreciable capital stock, Creamer sees some advantages in using the method of adjusting balance sheet data. In particular, the balance sheets reflect actual company practice, and changes in practices, with respect to retirements and discards.[35] Despite the differences in methods, however, the real net stock estimates of Creamer and OBE show much the same movements over the period, particularly after 1953. (Table A-x, columns 1, 2, and 4.) The levels of the estimates differ significantly, however. Creamer suggests that the higher level of his estimates is due in part to a faster rate of retirement used by OBE in the perpetual inventory method than that implicit in the balance sheet approach. Upward revaluations and inclusion of some nonmanufacturing facilities would also have affected the balance sheet data to some extent, but part of the differences in level remains unexplained.

In order to obtain our estimates of capital input for all manufacturing, and the durables and nondurables subsegments, we weighted the real stock estimates for the twenty-one two-digit industries by the unit compensation in 1958 for 1953-66, and by average unit compensation in 1948 and 1953 for

---

[34] For a more detailed description, see Creamer, *Capital Expansion and Capacity*, NICB, 1961, Appendix A.

[35] For a detailed discussion of the alternative sources and methods, see Creamer, "Some Notes for Users of Capital Stock Estimates in Manufacturing," *Proceedings of the Business and Economic Statistics Section of the American Statistical Association,* 1968.

TABLE A-x

Alternative Capital Stock Estimates,
Total Manufacturing, 1929-66
(index numbers, 1958=100)

Year	Real Net Stock OBE (1)	Real Net Stock Creamer (2)	Weighted Net Stock (Based on Creamer) (3)	Real Net Stock (Col. 2÷ Col. 1) (4)	Weighted Vs. Unweighted (Col. 3÷Col. 2) (5)
1929	55.3	62.2	59.1	1.125	0.950
1930	57.6	63.1	61.2	1.095	0.970
1931	57.1	62.3	60.3	1.091	0.968
1932	53.6	59.6	56.3	1.112	0.945
1933	50.0	56.3	52.2	1.126	0.927
1934	48.0	53.9	49.8	1.123	0.924
1935	47.2	52.4	48.7	1.110	0.929
1936	47.6	51.7	48.8	1.086	0.944
1937	49.6	52.0	50.5	1.048	0.971
1938	49.9	52.7	50.9	1.056	0.966
1939	48.9	52.2	50.1	1.067	0.960
1940	50.1	53.4	51.4	1.066	0.963
1941	54.0	56.7	55.6	1.050	0.981
1942	57.7	59.3	59.6	1.028	1.005
1943	58.5	59.3	60.6	1.014	1.022
1944	57.4	58.2	59.6	1.014	1.024
1945	55.8	57.2	58.1	1.025	1.016
1946	59.2	60.1	61.8	1.015	1.028
1947	64.5	66.6	67.5	1.033	1.014
1948	68.0	73.2	71.4	1.076	0.975
1949	70.5	75.2	73.3	1.067	0.975
1950	72.2	75.5	73.8	1.046	0.977
1951	77.5	79.4	78.3	1.025	0.986
1952	83.3	86.2	85.5	1.035	0.992
1953	87.0	89.1	88.8	1.024	0.997
1954	88.9	89.6	89.2	1.008	0.996
1955	90.5	90.1	89.9	0.996	0.998
1956	90.8	95.4	95.1	1.051	0.997
1957	99.0	99.0	98.7	1.000	0.997
1958	100.0	100.0	100.0	1.000	1.000
1959	100.9	101.2	101.6	1.003	1.004
1960	103.0	102.8	103.7	0.998	1.009
1961	104.4	103.5	104.9	0.991	1.014
1962	106.3	104.9	106.6	0.987	1.016
1963	108.6	109.1	111.1	1.005	1.018
1964	111.6				
1965	116.7				
1966	125.3				

this period. The relative weights are shown in Table A-xi. The weighted index for all manufacturing rises a bit faster than the unweighted total real capital stock, as shown in Table A-x, columns 2, 3, and 5.

Transportation. The real capital stock estimates for total transportation are the sum of estimates for the railroads and the aggregate nonrail components.

TABLE A-xi

Manufacturing and Mining Industries,
Relative Weights for Gross and Net Real Capital,
1948-53 and 1958
(per cent)

	Gross Capital		Net Capital	
	1948-53	1958	1948-53	1958
Total Manufacturing	100.0	100.0	100.0	100.0
Nondurables	48.7	50.1	50.2	52.5
Foods	6.0	8.3	5.4	8.4
Beverages	2.9	2.8	2.6	2.8
Tobacco	1.1	1.9	1.3	2.5
Textiles	3.7	2.9	4.1	2.7
Apparel	1.8	1.7	1.7	2.1
Paper	5.1	5.2	4.9	4.9
Printing, publishing	2.0	2.7	1.7	2.5
Chemicals	11.9	12.9	11.2	13.1
Petroleum refining	11.5	8.9	14.9	10.7
Rubber products	2.0	2.3	1.7	2.2
Leather products	0.7	0.5	0.7	0.6
Durables	51.3	49.9	49.8	47.5
Lumber products	2.0	2.0	1.5	1.3
Furniture	0.6	0.7	0.5	0.6
Stone, clay, glass products	4.0	5.0	3.9	5.0
Primary metals	11.1	11.3	10.4	10.0
Fabricated metals	4.9	4.8	4.8	4.8
Machinery except electric	7.4	7.4	6.7	6.9
Electric machinery	5.1	6.1	5.6	6.8
Transportation equipment and ordnance	12.3	8.9	12.6	8.2
Instruments	1.9	2.2	2.0	2.4
Miscellaneous	2.0	1.5	1.8	1.5
Total Mining	100.0	100.0	100.0	100.0
Metal	11.0	7.7	22.1	12.3
Coal	10.7	8.2	13.8	10.3
Oil and gas	66.4	75.6	47.5	65.3
Nonmetal	11.9	8.5	16.6	12.1

Railroads. The 1948 current dollar net stock of road and equipment was taken from Ulmer's *Capital in Transportation, Communications, and Public Utilities*, Table C-1, page 256. This base stock was converted to 1958 constant dollars by the *Railroad Construction Price Index* published by the Bureau of Accounts of the ICC. The 1948 stock estimate was then extended by cumulation of real net investment data.

The series on gross outlays for new plant and equipment by railroads is from the investment surveys conducted by the OBE and SEC (see, for example, Genevieve B. Wimsatt, "Business Expects Plant and Equipment Expansion and Larger Sales in 1964," *Survey of Current Business,* March 1964, Table 7, p. 13), and was converted to 1958 constant dollars by the above deflator. The average ratio of depreciation to the preceding end-of-year stock for 1945-58 was applied to the yearly stocks to get yearly depreciation. The 1949 net stock was accumulated by adding gross expenditures in 1949 to Ulmer's 1948 stock less depreciation in 1949, all in constant 1958 dollars. This process was continued to build up the net stock through 1966. Gross stock was obtained by applying the ratios of real gross to net stock, as estimated by M. Gort. (Gort's sources and methods are described below in the section covering capital in "other industries.")

Nonrail Transportation. For the nonrailway transportation component, the base stock for 1948 was also taken from Ulmer's *Capital in Transportation* (Table B-7, p. 244). It is the sum of the following industries: local transit, trucking, other motor vehicles, pipelines, water transportation, air transportation, transportation services, and miscellaneous transportation. The expenditure series on plant and equipment for transportation other than railway is from the OBE-SEC survey mentioned above for railroads. The price deflator used was a simple average of the implicit price deflators for ships and boats, aircraft, and trucks and buses. The estimation process was the same as that explained for railroads: applying the depreciation ratio to the preceding year-end stock to get the yearly depreciation, then adding the yearly capital expenditure to the preceding year-end stock and subtracting the depreciation, all in constant 1958 dollars. The process was continued to cumulate the stock from 1948 to 1966.

The real gross stock was obtained by applying the ratios of real gross to net stock for the sum of water and air transportation, as estimated by Gort (see below).

As just implied, we have separate and independent estimates of real capital stocks for two of the nonrail industries. The capital estimates for the water transportation industry were based entirely on Gort's estimates, extended to 1966 by his sources and methods as described below.

The real net capital stock estimates for airlines were also based on Gort for the period 1948-57. In 1957 they were linked to the estimates of Joseph E. Dragonette, described in his master's thesis (1966) on file at The George Washington University. Briefly, he used book-value data from the FAA, converted to current replacement costs by appropriately weighted price indexes for aircraft, other equipment, and buildings and then deflated to constant (1958) prices. Gort's real gross-to-net ratios were applied to the net stock estimates for the entire period in order to obtain the gross series.

Other Industries. The real gross and net capital stock estimates for the remaining industries—contract construction, wholesale and retail trade, communication and public utilities—are based on the estimates prepared by Gort for the period 1948-63.[36] They were extended to 1966 by the author, using methods and sources similar to those employed by Gort where possible.

Gort's basic methodology was to derive real gross and net stock estimates from deflated gross investment estimates by means of the perpetual inventory approach. He derived several variants of the net stock series, of which we chose the variant based on straight-line depreciation for consistency with our private economy aggregates.

The gross investment estimates for all of his industries (including mining and manufacturing, which we did not use), except the regulated areas, were obtained from the successive balance sheets and income accounts for corporations compiled by the Internal Revenue Service (IRS).[37]

He calculated the annual changes in net fixed assets from year-end balance sheet totals, and added depreciation, depletion, and amortization from the income statement compilations. He also made a number of adjustments to the published data: For years in which it was apparent that significant revaluations had been made, particularly in the 1930s, he interpolated the published data. He extrapolated the series prior to 1927 or 1931, when the IRS compilations began. He adjusted for occasional changes in accounting methods, particularly with regard to consolidation of returns, as well as for occasional changes in industry classifications (by means of transition tables in 1948 and 1958), and switched from a company to an establishment basis where indicated. Finally, he adjusted the industry estimates to cover unincor-

---

36 See R. Boddy and M. Gort, "The Derivation of Investment Expenditures," and "The Derivation of Capital Stocks," mimeograph.

37 IRS, *Statistics of Income* and *Source Book of the Statistics of Income.*

porated as well as corporate enterprises, except for contract construction and wholesale and retail trade. In these three industries we made the required coverage adjustment to the stock estimates by dividing by the ratio of corporate to total national income originating, based on OBE estimates.

For purposes of price deflation and cumulation over estimated average lives, Gort broke down the gross investment estimates into structures and eleven types of equipment. Structures were deflated by the OBE implicit deflator for new private nonresidential construction, and the equipment categories were deflated by various OBE equipment price indexes, published and unpublished.

Average lives for the structures and various types of equipment were based on the Treasury Department study *Life of Depreciable Assets Survey*. Published in 1962, the IRS survey reflects actual tax lives in use during the period 1954-59. The lives are somewhat shorter than those contained in Bulletin "F," but somewhat longer than those permitted by the more recent IRS *Depreciation Guidelines and Rules*.

Retirements for each type of investment were made at the end of the average life of each, rather than being spread over a mortality curve. But since the investment estimates were prepared by a dozen types, there is a considerable spread of retirements resulting from each year's investment. The same is true of depreciation, which was also calculated separately for structure and equipment by type.

Gort's estimates cover fixed capital. For wholesale and retail trade we added constant dollar estimates of inventories, based on the OBE series used for private economy aggregates. In the other nonfarm nonmanufacturing industries we did not include inventories since they are small relative to fixed capital and data are not readily available.

Year-end stock estimates were averaged to approximate annual averages. All series were shifted to a 1958 base.

Industry and Sector Aggregates

In table A-xii we summarize the real net stock estimates for all industry groups within the private business economy, excluding farming, manufacturing and residential real estate, for which we have estimates. These estimates are deducted from the independent estimates for the sector as a whole (see Table A-15), and the residual is shown in the last line.

The residual comprises primarily finance, insurance, and real estate (other than residential); service, including government enterprises but excluding households and nonprofit institutions; and the small group of agricultural services, forestry, and fisheries.

TABLE A-xii

Private Domestic Nonfarm Business Economy, Excluding Manufacturing and Residential,
Real Net Stocks of Capital, by Industry, Including Residual Sector:
Selected Years, 1948-66
(billions of 1958 dollars)

	1948	1953	1958	1963	1966
private nonfarm, nonresidential, nmanufacturing business	203.4	249.5	305.8	360.2	416.4
ng	18.6	18.2	18.8	19.3	18.0
ract construction	2.1	3.7	5.5	7.7	9.1
sportation	62.3	70.8	75.8	78.6	83.7
munication	11.3	15.0	20.9	27.5	33.6
tric and gas utilities	28.8	43.4	53.6	68.6	76.2
.e	49.7	64.4	75.1	87.9	103.3
dual[a]	30.6	34.0	56.1	70.6	92.5

Residual relates chiefly to finance and services, obtained by subtracting covered industry totals
sector totals

Over the period 1948-66, the real net capital stock in the residual sector approximately tripled, while only doubling in the sector as a whole. This 10.8 per cent faster growth resulted in an increase in the residual sector's share of capital in the sector as a whole from 15 per cent in 1948 to about 22 per cent in 1966. This may be compared with a relative growth of real product in the residual industries from 26.7 per cent of real product in the sector in 1948 to 27.4 per cent in 1966. These figures imply that the capital coefficient in the residual sector is lower than in the sector as a whole, but that it has increased relatively.

On its face, the behavior of the real capital stock in the residual industries is not unreasonable. We may conclude, therefore, that the capital estimates for the various covered industries are broadly consistent with the estimates for the private domestic business economy as a whole. We have not made use of the residual capital estimates other than for this rough check on the consistency of the estimates for the covered industries with those for the entire business sector.

Total Inputs

For the various industry segments and groups, the index numbers of real capital and labor inputs were combined according to relative unit compensation in the base periods. Table A-xiii gives the percentage weights in 1958, and during 1948-53, for both the net and gross capital variants. Since the

TABLE A-xiii

Private Domestic Business Economy, by Industry Segment and Group: Gross and Net Capital Weights, 1948-53 and 1958, Based on Capital Shares of Unit Factor Income
(per cent)

Industry Segments and Groups	Gross Capital Input 1948-53	Gross Capital Input 1958	Net Capital Input 1948-53	Net Capital Input 1958
Farming	54.2	52.6	46.0	42.9
Mining	47.6	46.1	30.9	20.9
Metal	45.9	34.4	46.5	20.4
Coal	25.9	19.9	18.5	8.8
Oil and gas	56.3	59.1	31.9	27.9
Nonmetal	44.4	33.5	36.0	18.2
Contract construction	21.2	13.2	15.4	7.7
Manufacturing	33.9	24.5	29.6	18.2
Nondurables	37.4	28.8	33.8	22.5
Foods	26.7	23.7	21.3	17.6
Beverages	48.8	39.7	41.1	31.4
Tobacco	58.3	57.6	57.0	56.2
Textiles	29.6	19.9	28.0	13.9
Apparel	14.4	11.0	11.9	9.0
Paper	42.4	32.5	37.0	23.7
Printing, publishing	14.7	13.0	10.6	8.5
Chemicals	51.8	41.3	45.6	32.8
Petroleum refining	73.4	56.5	74.6	51.7
Rubber products	30.5	24.9	24.5	18.1
Leather products	17.2	10.0	15.2	7.7
Durables	31.1	21.4	26.5	15.0
Lumber products	24.1	17.4	17.1	9.0
Furniture	12.5	9.9	9.2	6.0
Stone, clay, glass products	37.2	31.9	32.2	23.9
Primary metals	42.1	30.1	35.9	20.6
Fabricated metals	26.1	18.1	22.0	13.1
Machinery except electric	28.5	20.0	22.9	13.6
Electric machinery	24.8	20.0	22.8	15.9
Transportation equipment and ordnance	33.0	17.6	29.4	11.8
Instruments	31.0	23.3	28.4	19.1
Miscellaneous	32.2	18.6	26.6	13.5
Transportation	26.5	18.0	15.5	4.7
Railroads	34.9	21.2	25.4	9.5
Nonrail	26.2	16.9	10.3	2.5
Water transportation	25.2	10.5	12.2	5.7
Air transportation	42.6	9.4	10.3	2.5
Communication and public utilities	50.6	52.1	44.5	42.5
Communication	38.4	42.7	31.2	36.1
Telephone and telegraph	40.5	44.2	32.6	38.0
Electric, gas and sanitary services	60.3	59.8	55.2	48.5
Electric and gas utilities	61.0	59.7	56.2	48.7
Trade	25.9	15.6	20.3	9.3
Wholesale	30.8	20.7	24.4	15.3
Retail	24.0	12.5	18.4	6.0

quantity units are index numbers, the relative weights for 1958 are the factor proportions of net and gross national income originating; for 1948-53, however, the average factor compensations are divided by the average factor input indexes for the two years, and weights are based on the proportions of total unit factor compensation (net and gross) so derived. The indexes of real total inputs are presented in the summary tables referred to below.

Industry Summary Tables

Summary data on output, input, and productivity for the various industry segments, subsegments, and two-digit groups are presented in Tables A-22 through A-80. For several of the groups and industries, capital series are not available as noted above, and only output, labor input, and labor productivity index numbers are shown for these. For all the groups and industries where capital estimates are available, the gross capital and associated gross factor input and productivity series are shown in the "a" supplements to the basic tables which contain the net capital series. For the segments and groups with both gross output and real product estimates, both variants of the productivity ratios are presented. For the two-digit industries, it will be recalled, only the gross output and associated productivity measures are available. Similarly, for some of the industry groups only the real product and associated productivity measures are presented.

PART III

BASIC TABLES

TABLE A-1

Gross National Product, by Sector, 1929-66
(billions of 1958 dollars)

Year	Gross National Product (1)	Gross Govt. Product, Military (2)	Gross National Civilian Product (3)	Net Factor Income from Abroad (4)	Gross Domestic Civilian Product (5)	Gross Govt. Product, Civilian (6)	Gross Private Domestic Product (7)	Gross Product of Households & Institutions (8)	Gross Domestic Business Product (9)	Gross Farm Product (10)	Gross Nonfarm Business Product (11)
1929	212.8	2.7	210.1	1.4	208.7	17.7	191.0	10.1	180.9	18.4	162.5
1930	192.8	2.5	190.3	1.6	188.7	18.7	170.0	9.9	160.1	17.4	142.7
1931	179.0	2.4	176.6	1.4	175.2	19.3	155.9	9.5	146.4	19.7	126.7
1932	154.2	2.2	152.0	1.3	150.7	19.4	131.3	8.8	122.5	19.2	103.3
1933	151.8	2.2	149.6	1.2	148.4	20.5	127.9	8.5	119.4	18.7	100.7
1934	164.5	2.1	162.4	1.0	161.4	22.7	138.7	8.8	129.9	15.6	114.3
1935	179.9	2.1	177.8	1.1	176.7	24.0	152.7	8.9	143.8	17.6	126.2
1936	203.9	2.2	201.7	1.0	200.7	27.1	173.6	9.3	164.3	16.1	148.2
1937	214.6	2.4	212.2	0.8	211.4	26.5	184.9	9.6	175.3	19.0	156.3
1938	204.4	2.4	202.0	1.1	200.9	28.2	172.7	9.2	163.5	19.0	144.5
1939	221.5	2.6	218.9	0.9	218.0	28.8	189.2	9.5	179.7	19.5	160.2
1940	240.2	3.7	236.5	1.0	235.5	29.5	206.0	10.0	196.0	18.9	177.1
1941	278.3	9.5	268.8	0.9	267.9	31.0	236.9	9.8	227.1	20.4	206.7
1942	316.7	23.4	293.3	0.8	292.5	34.7	257.8	10.2	247.6	22.2	225.4
1943	366.3	53.1	313.2	0.8	312.4	39.1	273.3	9.4	263.9	21.1	242.8
1944	420.9	93.0	327.9	0.9	327.0	39.8	287.2	9.2	278.0	20.8	257.2
1945	437.4	115.6	321.8	0.8	321.0	38.2	282.8	9.1	273.7	19.5	254.2
1946	355.7	45.4	310.3	0.9	309.4	34.1	275.3	9.1	266.2	20.2	246.0
1947	347.1	31.9	315.2	1.1	314.1	32.6	281.5	9.6	271.9	18.6	253.3

Year											
1948	356.1	26.4	329.7	1.2	328.5	33.4	295.1	10.0	285.1	20.5	264.6
1949	353.1	23.3	329.8	1.2	328.6	34.5	294.1	10.4	283.7	19.9	263.8
1950	382.1	21.3	360.8	1.3	359.5	35.4	324.1	11.0	313.1	20.9	292.2
1951	409.7	26.1	383.6	1.2	382.4	37.8	344.6	11.2	333.4	19.9	313.5
1952	420.5	26.9	393.6	1.2	392.4	39.1	353.3	11.3	342.0	20.6	321.4
1953	442.1	30.0	412.1	1.3	410.8	39.6	371.2	11.6	359.6	21.6	338.0
1954	439.4	31.7	407.7	1.6	406.1	40.1	366.0	11.7	354.3	21.9	332.4
1955	471.9	31.6	440.3	1.8	438.5	41.6	396.9	12.7	384.2	22.5	361.7
1956	480.4	30.9	449.5	2.0	447.5	43.2	404.3	13.4	390.9	22.4	368.5
1957	487.6	30.7	456.9	2.1	454.8	44.8	410.0	13.9	396.1	21.8	374.3
1958	483.8	30.7	453.1	2.0	451.1	46.4	404.7	14.4	390.3	22.5	367.8
1959	513.3	30.6	482.7	2.2	480.5	47.7	432.8	14.9	417.9	22.7	395.2
1960	526.2	30.8	495.4	2.3	493.1	49.6	443.5	15.5	428.0	23.5	404.5
1961	535.7	30.7	505.0	2.9	502.1	50.9	451.2	15.9	435.3	23.9	411.4
1962	569.3	31.7	537.6	3.4	534.2	52.6	481.6	16.6	465.0	23.8	441.2
1963	591.2	31.7	559.5	3.4	556.1	54.2	501.9	17.1	484.8	24.5	460.3
1964	622.1	31.9	590.2	3.9	586.3	56.0	530.3	17.8	512.5	24.1	488.4
1965	659.1	31.6	627.5	4.1	623.4	58.3	565.1	18.2	546.9	25.7	521.2
1966	698.6	32.5	666.1	4.0	662.1	61.5	600.6	19.2	581.4	24.2	557.2

Note: Relates to *Productivity Trends*, Table A-III.

Source: The following adjustments were made to the published OBE real gross product estimates (*Survey of Current Business*, July 1968), as described more fully in the appendix text: *col. 2* and *6*: general government product adjusted to include imputed rent on government capital and capital consumption allowances; *col. 7* (Cols. 8 + 9): gross private domestic product adjusted to include imputed rent on nonprofit institutions' capital; *col. 8*: gross product of households and institutions adjusted to include imputed rent on nonprofit institutions' capital and capital consumption allowances; *col. 9*: gross private domestic business product, OBE Table 1.8, adjusted to exclude capital consumption allowances of households and institutions; *col. 10*: gross farm product adjusted to include gross rents paid to nonfarm landlords, OBE Table 1.18 (line 10 + line 8); *col. 11*: gross nonfarm business product adjusted to exclude rents paid by farmers to nonfarm landlords.

TABLE A-2

Net National Product and Relationship of Net to Gross National Product,
by Sector, 1929-66

(cols. 1–6 in billions of 1958 dollars; cols. 7–12 are ratios, net to gross product)

Year	Net National Product (1)	Net Domestic Civilian Product (2)	Net Private Domestic Product (3)	Net Domestic Business Product			National Economy (7)	Domestic Civilian Economy (8)	Private Domestic Economy (9)	Domestic Business Economy		
				Total (4)	Farm (5)	Nonfarm (6)				Total (10)	Farm (11)	Nonfarm (12)
1929	188.3	185.6	170.8	161.9	16.8	145.1	.885	.889	.894	.895	.913	.893
1930	168.0	165.1	149.5	140.9	15.8	125.1	.871	.875	.879	.880	.908	.877
1931	154.8	152.1	136.1	127.9	18.1	109.8	.865	.868	.873	.874	.919	.867
1932	131.2	128.7	112.8	105.3	17.7	87.6	.851	.854	.859	.860	.922	.848
1933	130.0	127.6	110.7	103.4	17.4	86.0	.856	.860	.866	.866	.930	.854
1934	143.3	141.1	122.2	114.6	14.3	100.3	.871	.874	.881	.882	.917	.878
1935	158.9	156.6	136.5	128.7	16.3	112.4	.883	.886	.894	.895	.926	.891
1936	182.3	180.0	157.0	148.8	14.7	134.1	.894	.897	.904	.906	.913	.905
1937	192.0	189.8	167.7	159.2	17.6	141.6	.895	.898	.907	.908	.926	.906
1938	181.5	179.0	155.4	147.3	17.5	129.8	.888	.891	.900	.901	.921	.898
1939	198.6	196.2	172.2	163.7	18.0	145.7	.897	.900	.910	.911	.923	.909
1940	216.2	212.8	188.3	179.4	17.4	162.0	.900	.904	.914	.915	.921	.915
1941	252.0	244.1	218.3	209.5	18.8	190.7	.905	.911	.921	.923	.922	.923
1942	286.9	268.5	239.2	230.1	20.6	209.5	.906	.918	.928	.929	.928	.929
1943	328.4	289.3	255.7	247.3	19.5	227.8	.897	.926	.936	.937	.924	.938
1944	354.2	304.4	270.1	261.8	19.3	242.5	.842	.931	.940	.942	.928	.943
1945	347.7	298.0	265.2	257.0	17.9	239.1	.795	.928	.938	.939	.918	.941
1946	302.7	284.8	255.9	247.6	18.5	229.1	.851	.920	.930	.930	.916	.931
1947	296.7	286.4	259.1	250.4	16.7	233.7	.855	.912	.920	.921	.898	.923

1948	307.6	298.2	270.1	261.0	18.3	242.7	.864	.908	.915	.915	.893	.917
1949	305.9	296.3	267.3	257.9	17.4	240.5	.866	.902	.909	.909	.874	.912
1950	335.4	325.6	295.8	285.9	18.1	267.8	.878	.906	.913	.913	.866	.916
1951	361.9	346.7	314.8	304.7	16.8	287.9	.883	.907	.914	.914	.844	.918
1952	373.1	355.6	322.5	312.4	17.4	295.0	.887	.906	.913	.913	.845	.918
1953	390.5	372.8	339.5	329.0	18.3	310.7	.883	.907	.915	.915	.847	.919
1954	384.2	366.8	333.3	322.7	18.5	304.2	.874	.903	.911	.911	.845	.915
1955	414.1	397.6	362.8	351.3	19.1	332.2	.878	.907	.914	.914	.849	.918
1956	420.7	404.6	368.5	356.4	19.0	337.4	.876	.904	.912	.911	.848	.916
1957	426.1	410.2	372.9	360.4	18.4	342.0	.874	.902	.910	.910	.844	.914
1958	420.9	405.5	367.2	354.2	19.0	335.2	.870	.899	.908	.907	.844	.911
1959	449.1	433.9	394.7	381.3	19.2	362.1	.875	.903	.912	.912	.846	.916
1960	460.2	444.9	404.2	390.2	20.0	370.2	.875	.902	.912	.911	.851	.915
1961	468.9	452.6	411.0	396.7	20.5	376.2	.875	.901	.911	.911	.858	.914
1962	500.9	483.3	440.3	425.4	20.4	405.0	.880	.905	.915	.914	.857	.918
1963	520.7	503.3	458.9	443.6	21.0	422.6	.881	.905	.915	.914	.857	.918
1964	549.0	531.1	485.2	469.3	20.5	448.8	.882	.906	.916	.915	.851	.919
1965	583.0	565.0	517.2	501.0	22.0	479.0	.885	.906	.916	.915	.856	.919
1966	619.4	599.8	549.3	532.1	20.4	511.7	.887	.906	.915	.915	.843	.918

TABLE A-3

Nonbusiness Sectors of the National Economy: Capital Consumption Allowances
and Property Income, 1929-66

(billions of 1958 dollars)

Year	Capital Consumption Allowances			Imputed Net Rentals		
	General Government		Private Nonprofit Institutions	General Government		Private Nonprofit Institutions
	Military	Civilian		Military	Civilian	
1929	1.4	2.9	1.2	0.3	3.1	1.5
1930	1.2	3.1	1.3	0.2	3.3	1.5
1931	1.1	3.3	1.3	0.2	3.5	1.6
1932	1.0	3.5	1.3	0.2	3.7	1.6
1933	1.0	3.6	1.2	0.2	3.8	1.5
1934	0.9	3.8	1.2	0.2	3.9	1.5
1935	0.9	3.9	1.1	0.2	4.1	1.4
1936	0.9	4.1	1.1	0.2	4.2	1.4
1937	1.0	4.4	1.1	0.2	4.4	1.4
1938	1.0	4.6	1.1	0.2	4.6	1.4
1939	1.1	4.8	1.0	0.2	4.8	1.3
1940	1.3	5.0	1.1	0.2	5.1	1.3
1941	2.5	5.2	1.0	0.3	5.4	1.3
1942	5.8	5.4	1.1	1.0	5.4	1.3
1943	14.8	5.5	1.0	2.3	5.4	1.2
1944	44.1	5.5	0.9	3.5	5.3	1.2
1945	66.7	5.4	0.9	3.8	5.2	1.1
1946	28.4	5.2	0.8	3.3	5.1	1.1
1947	22.7	5.3	0.9	2.7	5.1	1.1

Year						
1948	18.2	5.3	0.9	2.3	5.2	1.2
1949	14.9	5.5	1.0	2.0	5.4	1.2
1950	12.8	5.6	1.1	1.8	5.5	1.2
1951	12.0	5.9	1.1	1.7	5.6	1.3
1952	10.6	6.0	1.2	1.8	5.7	1.3
1953	13.6	6.3	1.1	1.8	5.8	1.4
1954	15.9	6.6	1.1	2.2	6.0	1.4
1955	16.9	6.8	1.2	2.5	6.1	1.5
1956	16.8	7.1	1.3	2.6	6.3	1.5
1957	16.9	7.5	1.4	2.7	6.5	1.6
1958	17.4	8.1	1.4	2.8	6.7	1.7
1959	17.6	8.5	1.5	2.9	6.8	1.7
1960	17.8	8.9	1.5	2.9	7.0	1.8
1961	17.3	9.3	1.6	3.0	7.1	1.9
1962	17.5	9.6	1.7	3.0	7.3	2.0
1963	17.7	9.8	1.8	3.1	7.5	2.1
1964	17.9	10.1	1.9	3.1	7.6	2.2
1965	17.7	10.5	2.0	3.1	7.9	2.3
1966	16.9	11.0	2.0	3.0	8.1	2.4

Note: These estimates make it possible to go from gross to net product in the nonbusiness sectors, and also provide the adjustments required to go from the published OBE real GNP estimates to those given in Table A-1.

TABLE A-4

Gross Private Domestic Business Product by Industry Segment,
Key Years, 1948-66

	Billions of 1958 Dollars					Percentage of Total				
	1948	1953	1957	1960	1966	1948	1953	1957	1960	1966
Private domestic business economy[a]	285.1	359.6	396.1	428.0	581.4	100.0	100.0	100.0	100.0	100.0
Agriculture, forestry, and fisheries[b]	21.5	22.8	23.0	24.7	25.5	7.5	6.3	5.8	5.8	4.4
Farms[b]	20.5	21.6	21.8	23.5	24.2	7.2	6.0	5.5	5.5	4.2
Mining	10.7	12.0	13.6	13.1	15.5	3.8	3.3	3.4	3.1	2.7
Contract construction	14.1	18.9	21.1	21.7	24.4	4.9	5.3	5.3	5.1	4.2
Manufacturing	96.3	128.6	134.6	140.9	205.7	33.8	35.8	34.0	32.9	35.4
Nondurable goods industries	41.3	49.5	54.9	59.9	80.8	14.5	13.8	13.9	14.0	13.9
Durable goods industries	55.0	79.1	79.6	81.0	124.9	19.3	22.0	20.1	18.9	21.5
Transportation	20.7	21.2	22.5	22.5	31.2	7.3	5.9	5.7	5.3	5.4
Railroads	10.5	9.9	9.5	8.7	11.7	3.7	2.8	2.4	2.0	2.0

Communication	4.7	6.7	8.5	10.0	15.9	1.6	1.9	2.1	2.3	2.7
Telephone and telegraph	4.4	6.1	7.7	9.1	14.8	1.5	1.7	1.9	2.1	2.5
Electric, gas, and sanitary services	5.0	7.8	10.3	12.4	17.3	1.8	2.2	2.6	2.9	3.0
Wholesale and retail trade	54.2	64.9	75.1	82.3	111.7	19.0	18.0	19.0	19.2	19.2
Finance, insurance, and real estate[c]	35.0	45.2	55.5	62.5	85.2	12.3	12.6	14.0	14.6	14.6
Finance and insurance	9.9	11.9	14.1	14.9	16.4	3.5	3.3	3.6	3.5	2.8
Services (including government enterprises)	27.6	30.5	34.5	38.5	50.9	9.7	8.5	8.7	9.0	8.7
Residual[d]	-4.7	1.0	-2.6	-0.6	-1.9	-1.6	0.3	-0.7	-0.1	-0.3

Source: "Revised Estimates of GNP by Major Industries," *Survey of Current Business*, April 1967, and "1967 GNP by Major Industries," ibid., April 1968, with adjustments described in footnotes. Details may not add to totals because of rounding.

[a] Table A-1, column 9.
[b] Includes gross rents paid to nonfarm landlords by farmers.
[c] Excludes gross rents paid to nonfarm landlords by farmers.
[d] Residual differs slightly from OBE numbers in several years due to rounding.

TABLE A-5

Private Domestic Economy: Persons Engaged by Class of Worker,
Key Years, 1948-66

(cols. 1–4 are in thousands; cols. 5–6 are percentages)

| Year | Proprietors and Unpaid Family Workers[a] (1) | Employees | | Persons Engaged (4) | Proprietors and Family Workers as Proportion of Persons Engaged (5) | Full and Part-Time Employees as Proportion of Full-Time Equivalents (6) |
		Full-Time Equivalent (2)	Full and Part-Time (3)			
1948	12,382	41,963	44,254	54,345	22.8	105.5
1953	11,610	45,791	48,688	57,401	20.2	106.3
1957	10,947	47,060	50,551	58,007	18.9	107.4
1960	10,675	47,324	51,201	57,999	18.4	108.2
1966	9,734	53,925	58,626	63,659	15.3	108.7

Note: Relates to *Productivity Trends*, Table A-V.

[a] For the farm sector, proprietors and family workers are adjusted to full-time equivalents

TABLE A-6

National Economy: Persons Engaged by Sector, 1948-66
(thousands)

Year	Total[a] Including Military	Total[a] Civilian	General Government Total	General Government Military	General Government Civilian	Households and Nonprofit Institutions	Private Domestic Business Economy Total	Private Domestic Business Economy Farm	Private Domestic Business Economy Nonfarm
1948	60,452	58,984	6,107	1,468	4,639	3,128	51,217	7,980	43,237
1949	58,938	57,334	6,425	1,604	4,821	3,211	49,302	7,672	41,630
1950	60,668	58,974	6,650	1,694	4,956	3,425	50,593	7,643	42,950
1951	64,699	61,575	8,505	3,124	5,381	3,462	52,732	7,350	45,382
1952	65,785	62,147	9,217	3,638	5,579	3,381	53,187	7,045	46,142
1953	66,582	63,037	9,181	3,545	5,636	3,439	53,962	6,825	47,137
1954	64,569	61,243	9,007	3,326	5,681	3,405	52,157	6,661	45,496
1955	65,771	62,746	8,879	3,025	5,854	3,718	53,174	6,452	46,722
1956	66,905	64,057	8,951	2,848	6,103	3,897	54,057	6,047	48,010
1957	67,099	64,313	9,092	2,786	6,306	3,988	54,019	5,852	48,167
1958	65,374	62,742	9,131	2,632	6,499	4,155	52,088	5,777	46,311
1959	66,643	64,100	9,204	2,543	6,661	4,264	53,175	5,653	47,522
1960	67,449	64,933	9,450	2,516	6,934	4,409	53,590	5,434	48,156
1961	67,244	64,646	9,730	2,598	7,132	4,506	53,008	5,327	47,681
1962	68,578	65,778	10,182	2,800	7,382	4,655	53,741	5,159	48,582
1963	69,262	66,539	10,364	2,723	7,641	4,770	54,128	5,019	49,109
1964	70,522	67,802	10,635	2,720	7,915	4,886	55,001	4,705	50,296
1965	72,494	69,762	11,001	2,732	8,269	5,008	56,485	4,320	52,165
1966	75,674	72,518	12,015	3,156	8,859	5,201	58,458	4,015	54,443

Note: Relates to *Productivity Trends*, Table A-VI.
a With respect to labor, the national and domestic economies are practically identical.

TABLE A-7

National Economy: Persons Engaged, by Sector and by
Industry Segment, Key Years, 1948-66
(thousands)

	1948	1953	1957	1960	1966
National economy	60,452	66,582	67,099	67,449	75,674
National civilian economy	58,984	63,037	64,313	64,933	72,518
General government, civilian	4,639	5,636	6,306	6,934	8,859
Private domestic economy	54,345	57,401	58,007	57,999	63,659
Households and nonprofit institutions	3,128	3,439	3,988	4,409	5,201
Private domestic business economy	51,217	53,962	54,019	53,590	58,458
Farm	7,980	6,825	5,852	5,434	4,015
Nonfarm	43,237	47,137	48,167	48,156	54,443
Private domestic business, nonfarm					
Agricultural services, forestry, fisheries	286	313	311	302	327
Mining	1,033	916	881	737	668
Contract construction	3,330	3,646	3,706	3,671	4,169
Manufacturing	16,001	18,046	17,651	17,163	19,652
Transportation	3,021	2,976	2,783	2,559	2,575
Communication and public utilities	1,282	1,409	1,518	1,466	1,571
Trade	10,908	11,644	12,233	12,546	13,888
Finance, insurance, real estate	1,949	2,322	2,632	2,791	3,199
Services	4,694	4,992	5,550	5,953	7,235
Government enterprises	733	873	902	968	1,159

Note: Relates to *Productivity Trends*, Table A-VII.

TABLE A-8

National and Civilian Economy: Persons Engaged—Comparison of Industry
Aggregate and Census-based Series, Decennial, 1930-60

National Economy			National Civilian Economy		
Based on Census of Population (millions)	Industry Aggregate	Ratio: Industry Aggregate to Census	Based on Census of Population (millions)	Industry Aggregate	Ratio: Industry Aggregate to Census
45.7	45.5	1.00	45.5	45.2	0.99
48.1	49.6	1.03	47.5	49.1	1.03
61.4	60.7	0.99	59.7	59.0	0.99
68.9	67.4	0.98	66.4	64.9	0.98

Source: *Census data: Economic Report of the President*, January 1967, p. 236. 1950 and 1960
not strictly comparable with 1930 and 1940 due to new definitions of employment. In *Productivity Trends*, Table A-VIII, Clarence D. Long's estimates of employment were used. Here we
ge to labor force data. *Industry aggregate:* 1950 and 1960, Table A-6; 1930 and 1940, *Productivity Trends*, Table A-VI.

TABLE A-9

National Economy: Average Hours Worked per Week, by Sector
and by Industry Segment, Key Years, 1948-66

	1948	1953	1957	1960	1966
National economy	41.8	40.3	39.7	39.8	39.6
National civilian economy	42.0	40.7	39.9	40.0	39.8
General government, civilian	34.5	34.3	34.0	33.9	33.6
Private domestic economy	42.6	41.3	40.6	40.7	40.7
Households and nonprofit organizations	38.1	37.5	35.1	35.4	35.1
Private domestic business economy	42.9	41.5	41.0	41.1	41.2
Farm	49.2	44.4	44.6	43.6	43.4
Nonfarm	41.7	41.1	40.6	40.8	41.0
Private domestic business, nonfarm					
Agricultural services, forestry, fisheries	43.1	42.8	42.2	42.4	43.2
Mining	39.7	39.1	40.2	40.6	42.6
Contract construction	39.8	39.4	38.2	37.9	38.7
Manufacturing	39.0	38.6	37.8	38.2	39.3
Transportation	47.1	43.9	44.1	43.9	45.5
Communication and public utilities	40.7	40.0	40.1	40.4	41.2
Trade	45.3	45.0	44.6	44.9	43.5
Finance, insurance, real estate	40.7	40.6	39.3	39.7	40.3
Services	42.4	42.3	41.4	41.8	40.9
Government enterprises	37.5	37.2	37.1	37.1	37.4

Note: Relates to *Productivity Trends*, Table A-IX.

Source: Man-hour estimates (Table A-11) divided by corresponding estimates of
persons engaged (Table A-7) and 52 (weeks in the year).

TABLE A-10

National Economy: Man-Hours by Sector, 1948-66
(millions)

Year	Total		General Government			Households and Nonprofit Institutions	Private Domestic Business		
	Including Military	Civilian	Total	Military	Civilian		Total	Farm	Nonfarm
1948	131,390	128,783	10,924	2,607	8,317	6,203	114,263	20,407	93,856
1949	127,537	124,688	11,448	2,849	8,599	6,240	109,849	20,463	89,386
1950	129,917	126,908	11,874	3,009	8,865	6,626	111,417	18,864	92,553
1951	137,322	131,774	15,159	5,548	9,611	6,643	115,520	17,850	97,670
1952	139,575	133,027	16,548	6,548	10,000	6,541	116,486	16,947	99,539
1953	139,709	133,328	16,445	6,381	10,064	6,712	116,552	15,756	100,796
1954	134,269	128,282	16,083	5,987	10,096	6,413	111,773	15,269	96,504
1955	138,157	132,712	15,870	5,445	10,425	6,934	115,353	15,527	99,826
1956	139,996	134,870	15,962	5,126	10,836	7,166	116,868	14,821	102,047
1957	138,586	133,571	16,152	5,015	11,137	7,278	115,156	13,575	101,581
1958	133,653	128,915	16,190	4,738	11,452	7,526	109,937	12,579	97,358
1959	137,696	133,119	16,367	4,577	11,790	7,712	113,617	12,556	101,061
1960	139,504	134,975	16,767	4,529	12,238	8,125	114,612	12,329	102,283
1961	138,076	133,400	17,279	4,676	12,603	8,227	112,570	11,536	101,034
1962	141,143	136,103	18,092	5,040	13,052	8,403	114,648	11,259	103,389
1963	142,457	137,556	18,385	4,901	13,484	8,655	115,417	10,640	104,777
1964	145,345	140,449	18,840	4,896	13,944	8,784	117,721	10,232	107,489
1965	150,001	145,083	19,449	4,918	14,531	9,122	121,430	9,964	111,466
1966	155,741	150,060	21,166	5,681	15,485	9,497	125,078	9,056	116,022

Note: Relates to *Productivity Trends*, Table A-X.

TABLE A-11

National Economy: Man-Hours by Sector and by
Industry Segment, Key Years, 1948-66
(millions)

	1948	1953	1957	1960	1966
National economy	131,390	139,709	138,586	139,504	155,741
National civilian economy	128,783	133,328	133,571	134,975	150,060
General government, civilian	8,317	10,064	11,137	12,238	15,485
Private domestic economy	120,466	123,264	122,434	122,737	134,575
Households and nonprofit institutions	6,203	6,712	7,278	8,125	9,497
Private domestic business economy	114,263	116,552	115,156	114,612	125,078
Farm	20,407	15,756	13,575	12,329	9,056
Nonfarm	93,856	100,796	101,581	102,283	116,022
Private domestic business, nonfarm					
Agricultural services, forestry, fisheries	641	696	682	666	735
Mining	2,135	1,863	1,842	1,557	1,480
Contract construction	6,898	7,462	7,363	7,228	8,395
Manufacturing	32,459	36,215	34,744	34,059	40,177
Transportation	7,396	6,799	6,378	5,837	6,098
Communication and public utilities	2,715	2,934	3,163	3,082	3,369
Trade	25,704	27,249	28,341	29,279	31,406
Finance, insurance, real estate	4,124	4,902	5,380	5,761	6,705
Services	10,356	10,989	11,948	12,945	15,405
Government enterprises	1,428	1,687	1,740	1,869	2,252

Note: Relates to *Productivity Trends*, Table A-XI.

TABLE A-12

Employment, Average Hours, and Man-Hours:
Comparison of Industry Composite with Census and BLS Estimates, 1948-66

A. Civilian Economy

Year	Employment (thousands)			Avg. Hours Worked per Week			Man-Hours (millions)		
	MRLF[a] (1)	Industry Composite (2)	Ratio (2)÷(1) (3)	MRLF[b] (4)	Industry Composite (8)÷(2)÷52 (5)	Ratio (5)÷(4) (6)	MRLF (1)×(4)×52 (7)	Industry Composite (8)	Ratio (8)÷(7) (9)
1948	58,344	58,984	1.011	43.2	42.0	.972	132,800	128,783	.970
1949	57,649	57,334	.995	42.6	41.8	.981	129,419	124,688	.963
1950	58,920	58,974	1.001	42.4	41.4	.976	131,732	126,908	.963
1951	59,962	61,575	1.027	42.5	41.2	.969	134,333	131,774	.981
1952	60,254	62,147	1.031	42.4	41.2	.972	134,570	133,027	.989
1953	61,181	63,037	1.030	42.2	40.7	.964	135,932	133,328	.981
1954	60,110	61,243	1.019	41.6	40.3	.969	131,717	128,282	.974
1955	62,171	62,746	1.009	41.8	40.7	.974	136,815	132,712	.970
1956	63,802	64,057	1.004	41.6	40.5	.974	139,976	134,870	.964
1957	64,071	64,313	1.004	41.1	39.9	.971	138,942	133,571	.961
1958	63,036	62,742	.995	40.7	39.5	.971	135,378	128,915	.952
1959	64,630	64,100	.992	40.8	39.9	.978	139,137	133,119	.957
1960	65,778	64,933	.987	40.8	40.0	.980	141,470	134,975	.954
1961	65,746	64,646	.983	40.5	39.7	.980	140,672	133,400	.948
1962	66,702	65,778	.986	40.6	39.8	.980	143,236	136,103	.950
1963	67,762	66,539	.982	40.6	39.8	.980	145,270	137,556	.947
1964	69,305	67,802	.978	40.4	39.8	.985	147,806	140,449	.950
1965	71,088	69,762	.981	40.7	40.0	.983	152,760	145,083	.950
1966	72,895	72,518	.995	40.5	39.8	.983	155,981	150,060	.962

B. Private Economy

| Year | Man-Hours (millions) BLS Series | | | Man-Hour Ratios Industry Composite to | |
	Establishment Basis (10)	Labor Force Basis (11)	Industry Composite (12)	BLS, Establishment Basis (12)÷(10) (13)	BLS, Labor Force Basis (12)÷(11) (14)
1948	124,688	118,978	120,466	.966	1.013
1949	120,551	115,977	116,089	.963	1.001
1950	122,900	117,151	118,043	.960	1.008
1951	126,840	119,120	122,163	.963	1.026
1952	127,611	118,509	123,027	.964	1.038
1953	128,681	119,025	123,264	.958	1.036
1954	124,086	114,349	118,186	.952	1.034
1955	128,920	118,923	122,287	.949	1.028
1956	131,153	121,258	124,034	.946	1.023
1957	129,253	119,715	122,434	.947	1.023
1958	123,855	115,624	117,463	.948	1.016
1959	127,856	118,925	121,329	.949	1.020
1960	128,956	120,501	122,737	.952	1.019
1961	127,064	119,493	120,797	.951	1.011
1962	129,595	121,284	123,051	.950	1.015
1963	130,361	122,197	124,072	.952	1.015
1964	132,567	124,662	126,505	.954	1.015
1965	136,868	128,613	130,552	.954	1.015
1966	140,291	131,132	134,575	.959	1.026

Note: Relates to *Productivity Trends*, Table A-XII.
[a]Household data from *Employment and Earnings* and *Monthly Report on the Labor Force*, July 1967, Table A-1, persons 16 years and over.
[b]Adjusted for holiday weeks.

TABLE A-13

National Economy: Real Labor Input and Man-Hours—Effect of
Interindustry Man-Hour Shifts by Sector, Key Years, 1948-66
(1958 = 100)

	1948	1953	1957	1960	19
National economy					
Labor input	95.2	104.6	104.3	104.8	120
Man-hours	98.3	104.5	103.7	104.4	116
Ratio (1)÷(2)	0.968	1.001	1.006	1.004	1
Private economy					
Labor input	99.7	105.3	105.1	104.9	118
Man-hours	102.6	104.9	104.2	104.5	114
Ratio (4)÷(5)	0.972	1.004	1.009	1.004	1
Private business economy					
Labor input	100.6	106.0	105.5	104.8	118
Man-hours	103.9	106.0	104.7	104.3	113
Ratio (7)÷(8)	0.968	1.000	1.008	1.005	1
Private nonfarm business economy					
Labor input	97.3	105.1	105.4	105.1	120
Man-hours	96.4	103.5	104.3	105.1	119
Ratio (10)÷(11)	1.009	1.015	1.011	1.000	1
Effect of government-private shifts (3)÷(6)	0.996	0.997	0.997	1.000	1
Effect of farm-nonfarm shifts (9)÷(12)	0.959	0.985	0.997	1.005	1

Note: Relates to *Productivity Trends,* Table A-XIII.

National Economy: Distribution of Labor Input, Man-Hours, and Persons Engaged by Sector and by Industry Segment, 1948, 1957, and 1966
(per cent)

	1948			1957			1966		
	Persons Engaged	Man-Hours	Labor Input[a]	Persons Engaged	Man-Hours	Labor Input[a]	Persons Engaged	Man-Hours	Labor Input[a]
National economy	100.0	100.0	100.0	100.0	100.0	100.0	100.0	100.0	100.0
Military	2.4	2.0	2.1	4.2	3.6	3.6	4.2	3.7	3.5
Civilian	97.6	98.0	97.9	95.8	96.4	96.4	95.8	96.3	96.5
General government, civilian	7.7	6.3	8.2	9.4	8.0	10.0	11.7	9.9	12.1
Private economy	89.9	91.7	89.7	86.4	88.4	86.4	84.1	86.4	84.4
Households and nonprofit institutions	5.2	4.7	3.3	5.9	5.3	3.6	6.9	6.1	4.0
Private business economy	84.7	87.0	86.4	80.5	83.1	82.8	77.2	80.3	80.3
Farm	13.2	15.5	6.1	8.7	9.8	3.7	5.3	5.8	2.1
Nonfarm	71.5	71.5	80.3	71.8	73.3	79.1	71.9	74.5	78.2
Private business, nonfarm									
Agricultural services, forestry, fisheries	0.5	0.5	0.4	0.5	0.5	0.4	0.4	0.5	0.3
Mining	1.7	1.6	2.3	1.3	1.3	1.7	0.9	0.9	1.2
Contract construction	5.5	5.3	6.9	5.5	5.3	6.7	5.5	5.4	6.6
Manufacturing	26.5	24.7	31.7	26.3	25.1	31.5	26.0	25.8	31.7
Transportation	5.0	5.6	7.3	4.2	4.6	5.6	3.4	3.9	4.5
Communication and public utilities	2.1	2.1	2.6	2.3	2.3	2.8	2.1	2.2	2.6
Trade	18.0	19.6	17.2	18.2	20.4	17.2	18.3	20.2	16.7
Finance, insurance, real estate	3.2	3.1	3.4	3.9	3.9	4.2	4.2	4.3	4.5
Services	7.8	7.9	7.1	8.3	8.6	7.5	9.6	9.9	8.4
Government enterprises	1.2	1.1	1.4	1.3	1.3	1.5	1.5	1.4	1.7

Note: Relates to *Productivity Trends*, Table A-XIV.

[a] Absolute figures on which these percentages are based were derived by multiplying 1958 labor compensation by labor input indexes and summing to sector totals.

TABLE A-15

National Economy: Real Net Capital Stocks, by Sector, 1929-66
(billions of 1958 dollars)

Year	National Economy (1)	National Civilian Economy (2)	Net Foreign Assets (3)	Domestic Civilian Economy (4)	General Govt., Civilian (5)	Private Domestic Economy (6)	Nonpr Institut (7)
1929	788.0	777.9	23.9	754.0	101.1	652.9	32.8
1930	806.2	797.0	25.0	772.0	109.1	662.9	33.8
1931	811.5	803.1	25.2	777.9	118.8	659.1	34.4
1932	803.8	796.0	24.2	771.8	126.9	644.9	34.4
1933	785.6	778.3	22.1	756.2	129.6	626.6	33.9
1934	769.7	762.8	19.9	742.9	131.2	611.7	33.0
1935	763.8	757.2	16.8	740.4	136.6	603.8	32.6
1936	766.8	760.4	12.7	747.7	143.8	603.9	31.2
1937	779.2	773.0	9.7	763.3	152.4	610.9	30.6
1938	790.8	784.7	7.8	776.9	162.6	614.3	30.1
1939	798.3	792.0	5.6	786.4	172.7	613.7	29.6
1940	815.3	807.1	2.9	804.2	183.4	620.8	29.1
1941	843.3	830.5	2.8	827.7	190.3	637.4	28.7
1942	884.9	847.8	3.8	844.0	195.3	648.7	28.1
1943	935.6	847.3	3.7	843.6	198.2	645.4	27.2
1944	977.2	841.4	3.2	838.2	199.2	639.0	26.2
1945	980.4	834.0	2.3	831.7	196.0	635.7	25.6
1946	974.7	847.7	5.7	842.0	193.7	648.3	25.2
1947	989.0	883.4	12.2	871.2	194.7	676.5	25.2
1948	1,004.8	915.8	15.4	900.4	198.8	701.6	25.4
1949	1,027.1	950.9	16.8	934.1	203.5	730.6	26.0
1950	1,050.3	982.8	16.9	965.9	205.9	760.0	26.8
1951	1,090.3	1,026.8	16.4	1,010.4	211.0	799.4	27.7
1952	1,137.3	1,066.2	16.3	1,049.9	217.3	832.6	28.9
1953	1,186.9	1,101.0	16.8	1,084.2	222.5	861.7	29.3
1954	1,228.1	1,132.4	17.0	1,115.4	225.4	890.0	30.3
1955	1,270.8	1,170.8	16.3	1,154.5	231.0	923.5	31.4
1956	1,318.1	1,216.1	17.3	1,198.8	237.2	961.6	32.6
1957	1,362.6	1,257.5	20.5	1,237.0	243.8	993.2	34.0
1958	1,399.9	1,291.1	23.0	1,268.1	252.1	1,016.0	35.6
1959	1,435.2	1,323.4	22.8	1,300.6	258.0	1,042.6	37.2
1960	1,473.8	1,360.8	24.1	1,336.7	262.2	1,074.5	39.0
1961	1,508.1	1,394.1	27.0	1,367.1	267.5	1,099.6	40.8
1962	1,545.6	1,429.2	30.1	1,399.1	273.8	1,125.3	42.7
1963	1,588.1	1,469.3	33.2	1,436.1	280.0	1,156.1	44.6
1964	1,635.1	1,515.3	36.6	1,478.7	287.3	1,191.4	46.8
1965	1,692.6	1,574.6	40.8	1,533.8	295.6	1,238.2	49.6
1966	1,763.5	1,647.2	44.0	1,603.2	305.2	1,298.0	52.6

Note: Relates to *Productivity Trends,* Table A–XV.

Private Domestic Business Economy

| | | | | Nonfarm | | |
| | | | | | Nonresidential | |
tal (8)	Farm (9)	Total (10)	Residential (11)	Total (12)	Manufacturing (13)	Nonmanufacturing (14)
20.1	148.0	472.1	204.6	267.5	79.2	188.2
29.1	147.8	481.3	207.7	273.6	82.6	190.9
24.7	147.5	477.2	207.8	269.4	81.8	187.6
0.5	147.4	463.1	206.5	256.6	76.8	179.7
2.7	146.4	446.3	203.7	242.6	71.6	171.0
8.7	143.8	434.9	200.5	234.4	68.8	165.6
1.8	142.7	429.1	198.4	230.7	67.6	163.1
2.7	142.8	429.9	197.7	232.2	68.2	164.0
0.3	143.3	437.0	197.8	239.2	71.1	168.1
4.2	144.4	439.8	198.2	241.6	71.5	170.0
4.1	144.6	439.5	199.8	239.7	70.1	169.6
1.7	145.2	446.5	203.1	243.4	71.8	171.6
8.7	146.5	462.2	207.2	255.0	77.4	177.5
0.6	148.2	472.4	209.2	263.2	82.7	180.6
8.2	148.9	469.3	207.7	261.6	83.8	177.8
2.8	148.4	464.4	205.2	259.2	82.3	176.9
0.1	147.8	462.3	202.1	260.2	79.9	180.4
23.1	148.0	475.1	203.5	271.6	84.8	186.8
1.3	149.1	502.2	212.2	290.0	92.4	197.5
6.2	151.8	524.4	223.5	300.9	97.4	203.4
4.6	155.5	549.1	235.4	313.7	101.0	212.8
3.2	158.8	574.4	250.6	323.8	103.4	220.4
1.7	162.4	609.3	266.4	342.9	111.0	231.9
4.1	165.2	638.9	278.9	360.0	119.3	240.8
2.4	166.7	665.7	291.5	374.2	124.7	249.5
9.7	167.7	692.0	305.6	386.4	127.4	259.0
2.1	168.5	723.6	322.8	400.8	129.7	271.0
9.0	168.2	760.8	339.6	421.2	135.9	285.4
9.2	167.6	791.6	352.2	439.4	141.8	297.5
0.4	167.8	812.6	363.4	449.2	143.3	305.8
5.4	168.2	837.2	377.8	459.4	144.6	314.8
5.5	168.4	867.1	392.7	474.4	147.6	326.8
8.8	168.6	890.2	404.0	486.2	149.6	336.6
2.6	169.4	913.2	414.0	499.2	152.3	347.0
1.5	170.5	941.0	425.2	515.8	155.6	360.2
4.6	170.8	973.8	438.4	535.4	159.9	375.6
8.6	171.1	1,017.5	456.2	561.3	167.2	394.2
5.4	171.6	1,073.8	477.8	596.0	179.6	416.4

TABLE A-16

National Economy: Real Gross Capital Stocks,
by Sector, 1929-66
(billions of 1958 dollars)

Year	National Economy (1)	National Civilian Economy (2)	Net Foreign Assets (3)	Domestic Civilian Economy (4)	General Govt., Civilian (5)	Private Domestic Economy (6)	Nonpro Organiza (7)
1929	1,092.3	1,064.7	23.9	1,040.8	145.6	895.2	52.2
1930	1,118.9	1,093.7	25.0	1,068.7	154.9	913.8	53.9
1931	1,134.5	1,111.5	25.2	1,086.3	166.5	919.8	55.2
1932	1,137.2	1,116.0	24.2	1,091.8	176.6	915.2	56.1
1933	1,128.5	1,108.6	22.1	1,086.5	180.8	905.7	56.3
1934	1,121.6	1,102.8	19.9	1,082.9	184.4	898.5	56.0
1935	1,123.0	1,104.9	16.8	1,088.1	191.5	896.6	55.8
1936	1,133.0	1,115.4	12.7	1,102.7	201.0	901.7	55.6
1937	1,152.1	1,135.0	9.7	1,125.3	211.4	913.9	55.4
1938	1,170.2	1,153.3	7.8	1,145.5	222.9	922.6	55.1
1939	1,182.2	1,164.8	5.6	1,159.2	233.9	925.3	54.8
1940	1,208.4	1,186.4	2.9	1,183.5	249.7	933.8	54.2
1941	1,249.1	1,215.8	2.8	1,213.0	258.6	954.4	53.7
1942	1,339.1	1,246.3	3.8	1,242.5	266.2	976.3	52.8
1943	1,472.3	1,260.3	3.7	1,256.6	271.3	985.3	51.4
1944	1,573.1	1,265.1	3.2	1,261.9	273.0	988.9	50.1
1945	1,573.3	1,261.2	2.3	1,258.9	270.7	988.2	49.0
1946	1,564.5	1,277.9	5.7	1,272.2	271.6	1,000.6	48.6
1947	1,605.5	1,323.0	12.2	1,310.8	277.6	1,033.2	48.8
1948	1,639.7	1,374.3	15.4	1,358.9	286.9	1,072.0	49.0
1949	1,660.6	1,424.0	16.8	1,407.2	296.8	1,110.4	49.7
1950	1,686.7	1,473.0	16.9	1,456.1	303.8	1,152.3	50.6
1951	1,742.2	1,534.7	16.4	1,518.3	313.1	1,205.2	51.4
1952	1,811.4	1,589.9	16.3	1,573.6	323.4	1,250.2	51.9
1953	1,880.4	1,640.8	16.8	1,624.0	332.6	1,291.4	52.5
1954	1,936.5	1,689.9	17.0	1,672.9	340.2	1,332.7	53.6
1955	1,996.8	1,746.8	16.3	1,730.5	350.0	1,380.5	54.9
1956	2,073.3	1,810.3	17.3	1,793.0	359.6	1,433.4	56.1
1957	2,149.7	1,868.9	20.5	1,848.4	370.6	1,477.8	57.4
1958	2,203.6	1,919.8	23.0	1,896.8	382.9	1,513.9	59.2
1959	2,256.3	1,970.1	22.8	1,947.3	392.4	1,554.9	61.0
1960	2,315.9	2,025.2	24.1	2,001.1	400.0	1,601.1	63.0
1961	2,366.5	2,075.5	27.0	2,048.5	408.6	1,639.9	65.0
1962	2,422.7	2,127.1	30.1	2,097.0	418.8	1,678.2	67.0
1963	2,485.6	2,185.4	33.2	2,152.2	430.0	1,722.2	69.0
1964	2,551.6	2,250.5	36.6	2,213.9	442.3	1,771.6	71.0
1965	2,628.3	2,331.9	40.8	2,291.1	455.1	1,836.0	74.4
1966	2,722.6	2,430.4	44.0	2,386.4	470.0	1,916.4	78.9

Private Domestic Business Economy

		Nonfarm				
				Nonresidential		
al	Farm (9)	Total (10)	Residential (11)	Total (12)	Manufacturing (13)	Nonmanufacturing (14)
0	185.4	657.6	244.1	413.5	116.4	297.1
9	186.0	673.9	251.2	422.7	120.8	301.9
6	186.8	677.8	256.4	421.4	121.0	300.5
1	187.8	671.3	260.6	410.7	116.8	293.8
4	187.6	661.8	263.7	398.1	112.2	285.9
5	185.6	656.9	266.1	390.8	109.8	280.9
8	184.8	656.0	268.4	387.6	109.0	278.6
1	184.7	661.4	271.4	390.0	109.8	280.2
5	184.6	673.9	275.3	398.6	112.8	285.8
5	185.0	682.5	279.8	402.7	113.3	289.4
5	184.5	686.0	284.8	401.2	111.8	289.3
6	184.4	695.2	290.6	404.6	113.4	291.2
7	185.1	715.6	298.8	416.8	119.0	297.9
5	186.4	737.1	309.5	427.6	124.2	303.4
9	186.4	747.5	318.9	428.6	125.1	303.5
8	185.3	753.5	325.8	427.7	123.2	304.6
2	184.4	754.8	325.2	429.6	120.6	309.0
0	184.2	767.8	327.6	440.2	125.4	314.9
4	184.7	799.7	342.6	457.1	133.2	323.8
0	187.4	835.6	361.2	474.4	139.1	335.4
7	192.1	868.6	380.0	488.6	143.8	344.8
7	196.6	905.1	403.5	501.6	147.9	353.8
8	201.4	952.4	427.5	524.9	157.4	367.6
3	205.3	993.0	446.2	546.8	167.6	379.2
9	208.2	1,030.7	465.0	565.7	175.2	390.5
1	210.6	1,068.5	486.0	582.5	180.2	402.2
6	213.0	1,112.6	510.6	602.0	185.1	417.0
3	214.3	1,163.0	534.6	628.4	193.9	434.4
4	215.0	1,205.4	552.6	652.8	202.7	450.1
7	216.2	1,238.5	569.5	669.0	206.9	462.1
9	217.6	1,276.3	590.9	685.4	210.8	474.6
1	219.2	1,318.9	612.0	706.9	216.2	490.6
9	221.0	1,353.9	627.6	726.3	220.8	505.4
2	222.9	1,388.3	641.1	747.2	226.1	521.2
2	224.7	1,428.5	656.5	772.0	231.6	540.4
6	225.4	1,475.2	674.6	800.6	238.0	562.7
6	226.2	1,535.4	699.8	835.6	247.5	588.0
5	227.3	1,610.2	730.6	879.6	262.6	617.1

TABLE A-17

National Economy: Real Gross Product, Inputs, and Productivity Ratios,[a] 1929-66

(1958=100)

Year	Real Gross Product[a]	Persons Engaged	Real Product per Person	Man-Hours	Real Product per Man-Hour	Labor Input	Real Product per Unit of Labor Input	Net Capital Input	Real Product per Unit of Net Capital Input	Total Factor Input	Total Factor Productivity
1929	45.0	72.9	61.7	90.0	50.0	79.6	56.5	58.8	76.5	74.7	60.2
1930	40.8	69.6	58.6	84.2	48.5	73.6	55.4	60.4	67.5	70.9	57.5
1931	38.1	65.2	58.4	77.6	49.1	66.5	57.3	60.5	63.0	65.8	57.9
1932	33.0	60.1	54.9	69.1	47.8	58.2	56.7	58.5	56.4	59.3	55.6
1933	32.2	60.7	53.0	69.2	46.5	58.4	55.1	56.3	57.2	58.8	54.8
1934	34.9	65.4	53.4	69.3	50.4	59.7	58.5	55.7	62.7	59.5	58.7
1935	37.8	67.7	55.8	73.1	51.7	63.4	59.6	54.0	70.0	61.7	61.3
1936	42.7	72.1	59.2	79.9	53.4	70.3	60.7	54.1	78.9	66.7	64.0
1937	44.8	73.8	60.7	83.3	53.8	73.1	61.3	55.2	81.2	69.0	64.9
1938	42.9	71.0	60.4	77.6	55.3	67.4	63.6	55.5	77.3	64.9	66.1
1939	46.5	73.1	63.6	81.2	57.3	71.2	65.3	55.3	84.1	67.6	68.8
1940	50.0	76.0	65.8	84.8	59.0	75.0	66.7	55.9	89.4	70.5	70.9
1941	57.7	82.8	69.7	92.9	62.1	85.5	67.5	58.4	98.8	79.0	73.0
1942	64.8	90.4	71.7	103.4	62.7	98.3	65.9	60.9	106.4	89.0	72.8
1943	73.5	99.3	74.0	116.9	62.9	115.4	63.7	62.0	118.5	101.8	72.2
1944	83.5	101.1	82.6	119.7	69.8	118.9	70.2	62.5	133.6	104.4	80.0
1945	86.7	98.5	88.0	112.2	77.3	111.0	78.1	62.4	138.9	98.6	87.9
1946	73.0	90.4	80.8	98.5	74.1	94.9	76.9	64.1	113.9	87.4	83.5
1947	71.6	90.9	78.8	97.6	73.4	94.1	76.1	67.4	106.2	87.8	81.5

Year											
1948	73.8	92.5	79.8	98.3	75.1	95.2	77.5	69.6	106.0	89.2	82.7
1949	73.3	90.2	81.3	95.4	76.8	91.7	79.9	72.0	101.8	87.4	83.9
1950	79.4	92.8	85.6	97.2	81.7	94.3	84.2	74.0	107.3	89.9	88.3
1951	84.9	99.0	85.8	102.7	82.7	101.5	83.6	77.7	109.3	96.1	88.3
1952	87.0	100.6	86.5	104.4	83.3	103.8	83.8	81.6	106.6	99.0	87.9
1953	91.4	101.8	89.8	104.5	87.5	104.6	87.4	84.7	107.9	100.4	91.0
1954	90.8	98.8	91.9	100.5	90.3	99.8	91.0	87.4	103.9	97.2	93.4
1955	97.5	100.6	96.9	103.4	94.3	103.0	94.7	90.2	108.1	100.3	97.2
1956	99.3	102.3	97.1	104.7	94.8	104.7	94.8	94.1	105.5	102.5	96.9
1957	100.8	102.6	98.2	103.7	97.2	104.3	96.6	97.6	103.3	102.9	98.0
1958	100.0	100.0	100.0	100.0	100.0	100.0	100.0	100.0	100.0	100.0	100.0
1959	106.1	101.9	104.1	103.0	103.0	103.4	102.6	102.2	103.8	103.1	102.9
1960	108.8	103.2	105.4	104.4	104.2	104.8	103.8	105.2	103.4	104.9	103.7
1961	110.7	102.9	107.6	103.3	107.2	104.0	106.4	107.8	102.7	104.8	105.6
1962	117.7	104.9	112.2	105.6	111.5	106.8	110.2	110.5	106.5	107.6	109.4
1963	122.2	105.9	115.4	106.6	114.6	108.3	112.8	113.7	107.5	109.4	111.7
1964	128.6	107.9	119.2	108.7	118.3	110.8	116.1	117.6	109.4	112.2	114.6
1965	136.2	110.9	122.8	112.2	121.4	114.7	118.7	122.5	111.2	116.4	117.0
1966	144.4	115.8	124.7	116.5	123.9	120.3	120.0	128.8	112.1	122.1	118.3

Note: The real product and productivity estimates for the national economy are subject to downward bias because of the inclusion of real government product estimates, which do not allow for productivity changes in general government.

a For productivity comparisons, real product is weighted by the Marshall-Edgeworth formula, as described in the appendix text, so its movements differ somewhat from the estimates presented in Table A-1. This is also the case with real product indexes at the various sectoral levels, presented in subsequent tables.

TABLE A-17a

National Economy: Gross Capital Input and Gross Productivity Ratios,[a]
in Terms of Real Product, 1929-66

(1958=100)

Year	Gross Capital Input	Real Product per Unit of Gross Capital Input	Gross Factor Input	Gross Factor Productivity
1929	49.9	90.2	68.8	65.4
1930	51.2	79.7	65.7	62.1
1931	51.5	74.0	61.6	61.9
1932	51.5	64.1	56.6	58.3
1933	50.9	63.3	56.5	57.0
1934	50.5	69.1	57.1	61.1
1935	50.4	75.0	59.3	63.7
1936	50.6	84.4	63.5	67.2
1937	51.5	87.0	65.5	68.4
1938	52.1	82.3	62.2	69.0
1939	52.4	88.7	64.6	72.0
1940	52.2	95.8	67.0	74.6
1941	54.9	105.1	74.6	77.3
1942	59.0	109.8	84.1	77.1
1943	65.2	112.7	97.1	75.7
1944	69.7	119.8	101.1	82.6
1945	69.9	124.0	96.2	90.1
1946	69.6	104.9	86.1	84.8
1947	71.6	100.0	86.4	82.9
1948	73.2	100.8	87.7	84.2
1949	74.3	98.7	86.0	85.2
1950	75.7	104.9	88.1	90.1
1951	78.4	108.3	93.7	90.6
1952	81.6	106.6	96.4	90.2
1953	84.8	107.8	98.1	93.2
1954	87.5	103.8	95.7	94.9
1955	90.3	108.0	98.8	98.7
1956	93.9	105.8	101.1	98.2
1957	97.5	103.4	102.1	98.7
1958	100.0	100.0	100.0	100.0
1959	102.4	103.6	103.1	102.9
1960	105.2	103.4	104.9	103.7
1961	107.6	102.9	105.2	105.2
1962	110.3	106.7	108.0	109.0
1963	113.2	108.0	109.9	111.2
1964	116.3	110.6	112.6	114.2
1965	119.9	113.6	116.4	117.0
1966	124.4	116.1	121.7	118.7

[a] Index numbers of real gross product are the same as those shown in Table A-17.

TABLE A-17b

National Economy: Real Net National Product and Productivity Ratios,[a] 1929-66
(1958=100)

Year	Real Net Product	Net Product per Person Engaged	Net Product per Man-Hour	Net Product per Unit of Labor Input	Net Product per Unit of Net Capital Input	Net Product per Unit of Factor Input
1929	45.7	62.7	50.8	57.4	77.7	61.2
1930	40.8	58.6	48.5	55.4	67.5	57.5
1931	37.9	58.1	48.8	57.0	62.6	57.6
1932	32.3	53.7	46.7	55.5	55.2	54.5
1933	31.7	52.2	45.8	54.3	56.3	53.9
1934	34.9	53.4	50.4	58.5	62.7	58.7
1935	38.4	56.7	52.5	60.6	71.1	62.2
1936	43.9	60.9	54.9	62.4	81.1	65.8
1937	46.0	62.3	55.2	62.9	83.3	66.7
1938	43.8	61.7	56.4	65.0	78.9	67.5
1939	47.9	65.5	59.0	67.3	86.6	70.9
1940	51.7	68.0	61.0	68.9	92.5	73.3
1941	60.1	72.6	64.7	70.3	102.9	76.1
1942	67.5	74.7	65.3	68.7	110.8	75.8
1943	75.7	76.2	64.8	65.6	122.1	74.4
1944	80.8	79.9	67.5	68.0	129.3	77.4
1945	79.2	80.4	70.6	71.4	126.9	80.3
1946	71.4	79.0	72.5	75.2	111.4	81.7
1947	70.4	77.4	72.1	74.8	104.5	80.2
1948	73.3	79.2	74.6	77.0	105.3	82.2
1949	73.0	80.9	76.5	79.6	101.4	83.5
1950	80.1	86.3	82.4	84.9	108.2	89.1
1951	86.2	87.1	83.9	84.9	110.9	89.7
1952	88.7	88.2	85.0	85.5	108.7	89.6
1953	92.8	91.2	88.8	88.7	109.6	92.4
1954	91.3	92.4	90.8	91.5	104.5	93.9
1955	98.4	97.8	95.2	95.5	109.1	98.1
1956	100.0	97.8	95.5	95.5	106.3	97.6
1957	101.2	98.6	97.6	97.0	103.7	98.3
1958	100.0	100.0	100.0	100.0	100.0	100.0
1959	106.7	104.7	103.6	103.2	104.4	103.5
1960	109.3	105.9	104.7	104.3	103.9	104.2
1961	111.4	108.3	107.8	107.1	103.3	106.3
1962	119.0	113.4	112.7	111.4	107.7	110.6
1963	123.7	116.8	116.0	114.2	108.8	113.1
1964	130.4	120.9	120.0	117.7	110.9	116.2
1965	138.5	124.9	123.4	120.7	113.1	119.0
1966	147.2	127.1	126.4	122.4	114.3	120.6

Note: Relates to *Productivity Trends*, Table A-XXI. The real product and productivity estimates for the national economy are subject to downward bias because of the inclusion of real government product estimates, which do not allow for productivity changes in general government.

[a] Index numbers of inputs are the same as those shown in Table A-17.

TABLE A-18

Domestic Civilian Economy: Real Gross Product, Inputs, and Productivity Ratios, 1929-66

(1958=100)

Year	Real Gross Product	Persons Engaged	Real Product per Person	Man-Hours	Real Product per Man-Hour	Labor Input	Real Product per Unit of Labor Input	Net Capital Input	Real Product per Unit of Net Capital Input	Total Factor Input	Total Factor Productivity
1929	46.9	75.5	62.1	92.9	50.5	82.5	56.8	59.3	79.1	76.9	61.0
1930	42.5	72.1	58.9	86.9	48.9	76.3	55.7	60.8	69.9	72.9	58.3
1931	39.6	67.5	58.7	80.1	49.4	68.9	57.5	61.0	64.9	67.6	58.6
1932	34.3	62.2	55.1	71.3	48.1	60.2	57.0	59.0	58.1	60.7	56.5
1933	33.6	62.8	53.5	71.4	47.1	60.4	55.6	56.9	59.1	60.3	55.7
1934	36.4	67.8	53.7	71.5	50.9	61.8	58.9	56.4	64.5	61.1	59.6
1935	39.5	70.1	56.3	75.4	52.4	65.7	60.1	55.0	71.8	63.6	62.1
1936	44.6	74.6	59.8	82.4	54.1	72.9	61.2	55.5	80.4	68.9	64.7
1937	46.9	76.4	61.4	86.0	54.5	75.7	62.0	56.9	82.4	71.3	65.8
1938	44.7	73.4	60.9	80.0	55.9	69.7	64.1	57.4	77.8	67.2	66.5
1939	48.6	75.6	64.3	83.7	58.1	73.7	65.9	57.4	84.7	70.0	69.4
1940	52.1	78.2	66.6	87.1	59.8	77.3	67.4	58.3	89.4	73.0	71.4
1941	59.2	83.6	70.8	93.8	63.1	86.3	68.6	60.8	97.4	80.3	73.7
1942	64.2	87.5	73.4	100.6	63.8	94.8	67.7	62.7	102.4	87.0	73.8
1943	68.1	89.0	76.5	104.9	64.9	101.6	67.0	62.6	108.8	91.9	74.1
1944	71.5	87.2	82.0	103.5	69.1	100.4	71.2	62.0	115.3	90.8	78.7
1945	70.8	84.6	83.7	97.7	72.5	94.4	75.0	61.7	114.7	86.3	82.0
1946	68.9	88.6	77.7	97.4	70.7	93.5	73.7	63.7	108.2	86.3	79.8
1947	69.9	92.1	75.9	99.0	70.6	95.5	73.2	67.0	104.3	88.7	78.8

Year											
1948	73.2	94.0	77.9	99.9	73.3	96.9	75.5	69.5	105.3	90.4	81.0
1949	73.2	91.4	80.1	96.7	75.7	93.0	78.7	72.1	101.5	88.3	82.9
1950	80.1	94.0	85.2	98.4	81.4	95.6	83.8	74.4	107.7	90.9	88.1
1951	85.0	98.1	86.6	102.2	83.2	101.0	84.2	78.4	108.4	96.0	88.5
1952	87.1	99.1	87.9	103.2	84.4	102.6	84.9	82.3	105.8	98.2	88.7
1953	91.1	100.5	90.6	103.4	88.1	103.5	88.0	85.2	106.9	99.7	91.4
1954	90.0	97.6	92.2	99.5	90.5	98.8	91.1	87.8	102.5	96.5	93.3
1955	97.2	100.0	97.2	102.9	94.5	102.6	94.7	90.6	107.3	100.1	97.1
1956	99.2	102.1	97.2	104.6	94.8	104.6	94.8	94.6	104.9	102.5	96.8
1957	100.8	102.5	98.3	103.6	97.3	104.2	96.7	97.9	103.0	102.9	98.0
1958	100.0	100.0	100.0	100.0	100.0	100.0	100.0	100.0	100.0	100.0	100.0
1959	106.5	102.2	104.2	103.3	103.1	103.7	102.7	102.3	104.1	103.4	103.0
1960	109.3	103.5	105.6	104.7	104.4	105.1	104.0	105.2	103.9	105.1	104.0
1961	111.3	103.0	108.1	103.5	107.5	104.2	106.8	107.6	103.4	104.9	106.1
1962	118.4	104.8	113.0	105.6	112.1	106.8	110.9	110.1	107.5	107.5	110.1
1963	123.3	106.1	116.2	106.7	115.6	108.5	113.6	113.1	109.0	109.5	112.6
1964	130.0	108.1	120.3	108.9	119.4	111.1	117.0	116.8	111.3	112.3	115.8
1965	138.2	111.2	124.3	112.5	122.8	115.1	120.1	121.5	113.7	116.4	118.7
1966	146.8	115.6	127.0	116.4	126.1	120.3	122.0	128.0	114.7	121.9	120.4

Note: The real product and productivity estimates for the domestic civilian economy are subject to downward bias because of the inclusion of real government product estimates, which do not allow for productivity changes in general government.

TABLE A-18a

Domestic Civilian Economy: Gross Capital
Input and Gross Productivity Ratios,[a] in Terms of Real Product, 1929-66

(1958=100)

Year	Gross Capital Input	Real Product per Unit of Gross Capital Input	Gross Factor Input	Gross Factor Productivity
1929	55.5	84.5	73.2	64.1
1930	56.9	74.7	69.9	60.8
1931	57.5	68.9	65.6	60.4
1932	57.5	59.7	60.2	57.0
1933	57.1	58.8	60.2	55.8
1934	56.8	64.1	60.9	59.8
1935	56.9	69.4	63.4	62.3
1936	57.4	77.7	68.1	65.5
1937	58.6	80.0	70.2	66.8
1938	59.5	75.1	66.7	67.0
1939	59.9	81.1	69.4	70.0
1940	60.8	85.7	72.0	72.4
1941	62.3	95.0	78.4	75.5
1942	63.9	100.5	84.5	76.0
1943	64.7	105.3	89.1	76.4
1944	64.9	110.2	88.4	80.9
1945	64.9	109.1	84.6	83.7
1946	65.7	104.9	84.3	81.7
1947	67.9	102.9	86.4	80.9
1948	70.5	103.8	88.2	83.0
1949	73.0	100.3	86.6	84.5
1950	75.8	105.7	89.3	89.7
1951	79.2	107.3	94.1	90.3
1952	82.3	105.8	96.2	90.5
1953	85.1	107.1	97.9	93.1
1954	87.8	102.5	95.4	94.3
1955	91.0	106.8	99.1	98.1
1956	94.4	105.1	101.5	97.7
1957	97.4	103.5	102.1	98.7
1958	100.0	100.0	100.0	100.0
1959	102.8	103.6	103.4	103.0
1960	105.7	103.4	105.3	103.8
1961	108.3	102.8	105.5	105.5
1962	111.0	106.7	108.1	109.5
1963	113.9	108.3	110.1	112.0
1964	117.3	110.8	113.0	115.0
1965	121.5	113.7	117.1	118.0
1966	126.8	115.8	122.3	120.0

a Index numbers of real gross product are the same as those in Table A-18.

TABLE A-19

Private Domestic Economy: Real Gross Product, Inputs, and Productivity Ratios, 1929-69

(1958=100)

Year	Real Gross Product	Persons Engaged	Real Product per Person	Man-Hours	Real Product per Man-Hour	Labor Input	Real Product per Unit of Labor Input	Net Capital Input	Real Product per Unit of Net Capital Input	Total Factor Input	Total Factor Productivity
1929	47.5	79.7	59.6	97.8	48.6	88.8	53.5	61.3	77.5	82.2	57.8
1930	42.6	75.7	56.3	91.1	46.8	81.4	52.3	62.6	68.1	77.3	55.1
1931	39.4	70.4	56.0	83.5	47.2	72.9	54.0	62.4	63.1	71.2	55.3
1932	33.6	64.6	52.0	74.0	45.4	63.1	53.2	59.8	56.2	63.4	53.0
1933	32.6	64.2	50.8	73.2	44.5	62.6	52.1	57.4	56.8	62.3	52.3
1934	35.3	68.3	51.7	72.0	49.0	62.8	56.2	56.8	62.1	62.3	56.7
1935	38.4	70.5	54.5	75.9	50.6	66.4	57.8	55.0	69.8	64.2	59.8
1936	43.4	73.6	59.0	81.6	53.2	73.3	59.2	55.2	78.6	69.2	62.7
1937	46.0	76.8	59.9	86.7	53.1	77.6	59.3	56.4	81.6	72.7	63.2
1938	43.3	72.4	59.8	79.2	54.7	70.4	61.5	56.7	76.4	67.6	64.1
1939	47.4	74.9	63.3	83.3	56.9	74.7	63.5	56.5	83.9	70.6	67.1
1940	51.1	78.0	65.5	87.3	58.5	78.7	64.9	57.2	89.3	73.7	69.3
1941	58.5	84.2	69.5	94.7	61.8	88.2	66.3	59.6	98.2	81.2	72.0
1942	63.3	88.7	71.4	102.1	62.0	96.3	65.7	61.5	102.9	87.6	72.3
1943	66.7	90.0	74.1	105.8	63.0	101.4	65.8	61.4	108.6	91.3	73.1
1944	70.2	88.0	79.8	104.4	67.2	100.1	70.1	60.7	115.7	90.2	77.8
1945	69.8	85.3	81.8	98.7	70.7	94.3	74.0	60.4	115.6	85.9	81.3
1946	68.5	90.5	75.7	99.7	68.7	95.5	71.7	62.6	109.4	87.4	78.4
1947	69.9	94.7	73.8	101.8	68.7	98.4	71.0	66.2	105.6	90.6	77.2

(continued)

TABLE A-19 (concluded)

Year	Real Gross Product	Persons Engaged	Real Product per Person	Man-Hours	Real Product per Man-Hour	Labor Input	Real Product per Unit of Net Capital Input	Net Capital Input	Real Product per Unit of Net Capital Input	Total Factor Input	Total Factor Productivity
1948	73.3	96.6	75.9	102.6	71.4	99.7	73.5	68.7	106.7	92.2	79.5
1949	73.1	93.4	78.3	98.8	74.0	95.2	76.8	71.4	102.4	89.7	81.5
1950	80.5	96.0	83.9	100.5	80.1	97.8	82.3	73.8	109.1	92.4	87.1
1951	85.3	99.9	85.4	104.0	82.0	102.9	82.9	77.9	109.5	97.2	87.8
1952	87.4	100.6	86.9	104.7	83.5	104.3	83.8	81.9	106.7	99.4	87.9
1953	91.7	102.1	89.8	104.9	87.4	105.3	87.1	84.9	108.0	101.0	90.8
1954	90.4	98.8	91.5	100.6	89.9	100.1	90.3	87.6	103.2	97.4	92.8
1955	98.1	101.2	96.9	104.1	94.2	103.9	94.4	90.5	108.4	101.1	97.0
1956	99.9	103.0	97.0	105.6	94.6	105.8	94.4	94.6	105.6	103.4	96.6
1957	101.3	103.1	98.3	104.2	97.2	105.1	96.4	98.0	103.4	103.6	97.8
1958	100.0	100.0	100.0	100.0	100.0	100.0	100.0	100.0	100.0	100.0	100.0
1959	106.9	102.1	104.7	103.3	103.5	103.8	103.0	102.3	104.5	103.5	103.3
1960	109.6	103.1	106.3	104.5	104.9	104.9	104.5	105.3	104.1	105.0	104.4
1961	111.5	102.3	109.0	102.8	108.5	103.5	107.7	107.7	103.5	104.4	106.8
1962	119.0	103.8	114.6	104.8	113.5	105.9	112.4	110.2	108.0	106.8	111.4
1963	124.0	104.7	118.4	105.6	117.4	107.3	115.6	113.3	109.4	108.6	114.2
1964	131.0	106.5	123.0	107.7	121.6	109.7	119.4	117.1	111.9	111.3	117.7
1965	139.6	109.3	127.7	111.1	125.7	113.6	122.9	121.9	114.5	115.4	121.0
1966	148.4	113.2	131.1	114.6	129.5	118.3	125.4	128.7	115.3	120.5	123.2
1967	151.8	114.8	132.2	115.4	131.5	118.9	127.7	134.6	112.8	122.2	124.2
1968	159.0	117.4	135.4	117.6	135.2	121.4	131.0	140.1	113.5	125.4	126.8
1969	163.4	120.7	135.4	120.5	135.6	124.8	130.9	145.7	112.1	129.2	126.5

Note: Relates to *Productivity Trends*, Table A-XXII.

TABLE A-19a

Private Domestic Economy: Gross Capital
Input and Gross Productivity Ratios,[a] in Terms of Real Product, 1929-66

(1958=100)

Year	Gross Capital Input	Real Product per Unit of Gross Capital Input	Gross Factor Input	Gross Factor Productivity
1929	57.7	82.3	78.1	60.8
1930	59.0	72.2	74.2	57.4
1931	59.3	66.4	69.0	57.1
1932	58.9	57.0	62.8	53.5
1933	58.3	55.9	62.3	52.3
1934	57.8	61.1	62.2	56.8
1935	57.7	66.6	64.3	59.7
1936	58.0	74.8	68.7	63.2
1937	58.9	78.1	71.8	64.1
1938	59.5	72.8	67.4	64.2
1939	59.7	79.4	70.2	67.5
1940	60.2	84.9	73.1	69.9
1941	61.6	95.0	79.6	73.5
1942	63.2	100.2	85.5	74.0
1943	63.9	104.4	89.1	74.9
1944	64.1	109.5	88.3	79.5
1945	64.1	108.9	84.5	82.6
1946	65.0	105.4	85.6	80.0
1947	67.3	103.9	88.4	79.1
1948	69.9	104.9	90.2	81.3
1949	72.4	101.0	88.2	82.9
1950	75.3	106.9	90.9	88.6
1951	78.8	108.2	95.5	89.3
1952	82.0	106.6	97.5	89.6
1953	84.8	108.1	99.2	92.4
1954	87.7	103.1	96.4	93.8
1955	90.9	107.9	100.0	98.1
1956	94.5	105.7	102.4	97.6
1957	97.5	103.9	102.8	98.5
1958	100.0	100.0	100.0	100.0
1959	102.8	104.0	103.5	103.3
1960	105.9	103.5	105.2	104.2
1961	108.5	102.8	105.0	106.2
1962	111.2	107.0	107.5	110.7
1963	114.1	108.7	109.3	113.4
1964	117.5	111.5	112.0	117.0
1965	121.9	114.5	116.1	120.2
1966	127.4	116.5	121.0	122.6

[a] Index numbers of real gross product are the same as those in Table A-19.

TABLE A-19b

Private Domestic Economy, Supplement: Productivity Ratios
Based on Unweighted Real Product and Unweighted Inputs, 1929-66
(1958=100)

Year	Real Gross Product (Measured in 1958 Prices)	Man-Hours	Real Product per Man-Hour	Unweighted Net Capital Input (Measured in 1958 Prices)	Real Product per Unit of Unweighted Capital Input	Unweighted Factor Input (Measured in 1958 Prices)	Unweighted Factor Productivity
1929	47.2	97.8	48.3	64.3	73.4	90.7	52.0
1930	42.0	91.1	46.1	65.2	64.4	85.6	49.1
1931	38.5	83.5	46.1	64.9	59.3	79.6	48.4
1932	32.4	74.0	43.8	63.5	51.0	71.8	45.1
1933	31.6	73.2	43.2	61.7	51.2	70.8	44.6
1934	34.3	72.0	47.6	60.2	57.0	69.5	49.4
1935	37.7	75.9	49.7	59.4	63.5	72.4	52.1
1936	42.9	81.6	52.6	59.4	72.2	76.9	55.8
1937	45.7	86.7	52.7	60.1	76.0	81.1	56.4
1938	42.7	79.2	53.9	60.5	70.6	75.2	56.8
1939	46.8	83.3	56.2	60.4	77.5	78.4	59.7
1940	50.9	87.3	58.3	61.1	83.3	81.7	62.3
1941	58.5	94.7	61.8	62.7	93.3	87.9	66.6
1942	63.7	102.1	62.4	63.8	99.8	94.0	67.8
1943	67.5	105.8	63.8	63.5	106.3	96.8	69.7
1944	71.0	104.4	68.0	62.9	112.9	95.6	74.3
1945	69.9	98.7	70.8	62.6	111.7	91.0	76.8
1946	68.0	99.7	68.2	63.8	106.6	92.1	73.8
1947	69.6	101.8	68.4	66.6	104.5	94.3	73.8

Year							
1948	72.9	102.6	71.1	69.1	105.5	95.5	76.3
1949	72.7	98.8	73.6	71.9	101.1	93.1	78.1
1950	80.1	100.5	75.7	74.8	107.1	95.1	84.2
1951	85.1	104.0	81.8	78.7	108.1	98.6	86.3
1952	87.3	104.7	83.4	81.9	106.6	99.9	87.4
1953	91.7	104.9	87.4	84.8	108.1	100.6	91.2
1954	90.4	100.6	89.9	87.6	103.2	97.8	92.4
1955	98.1	104.1	94.2	90.9	107.9	101.3	96.8
1956	99.9	105.6	94.6	94.6	105.6	103.3	96.7
1957	101.3	104.2	97.2	97.8	103.6	102.8	98.5
1958	100.0	100.0	100.0	100.0	100.0	100.0	100.0
1959	106.9	103.3	103.5	102.6	104.2	103.3	103.5
1960	109.6	104.5	104.9	105.8	103.6	104.8	104.6
1961	111.5	102.8	108.5	108.2	103.0	103.9	107.3
1962	119.0	104.8	113.5	110.8	107.4	106.1	112.2
1963	124.0	105.6	117.4	113.8	109.0	107.3	115.6
1964	131.0	107.7	121.6	117.3	111.7	109.7	119.4
1965	139.6	111.1	125.7	121.9	114.5	113.4	123.1
1966	148.4	114.6	129.5	127.8	116.1	117.4	126.4

Note: Relates to *Productivity Trends*, Table A-XXII, Supplement. Note that the productivity measures in Table A-XXII, Supplement, were based on Marshall-Edgeworth weighted output and M-E weighted average of man-hours and unweighted capital input.

TABLE A-20

Private Domestic Business Economy: Real Gross Product, Inputs, and Productivity Ratios, 1929-66

(1958=100)

Year	Real Gross Product	Persons Engaged	Real Product per Person	Man-Hours	Real Product per Man-Hour	Labor Input	Real Product per Unit of Labor Input	Net Capital Input	Real Product per Unit of Net Capital Input	Total Factor Input	Total Factor Productivity
1929	46.8	79.9	58.6	96.2	48.6	88.3	53.0	61.0	76.7	81.6	57.4
1930	41.8	75.8	55.1	89.6	46.7	80.9	51.7	62.3	67.1	76.8	54.4
1931	38.6	70.7	54.6	82.4	46.8	72.4	53.3	61.6	62.7	70.6	54.7
1932	32.8	64.9	50.5	73.2	44.8	62.6	52.4	59.4	55.2	62.9	52.1
1933	31.8	64.8	49.1	72.8	43.7	62.3	51.0	57.0	55.8	62.0	51.3
1934	34.5	68.8	50.1	71.2	48.5	62.4	55.3	55.4	62.3	61.5	56.1
1935	37.7	70.9	53.2	75.0	50.3	65.9	57.2	54.6	69.0	63.7	59.2
1936	42.8	73.9	57.9	80.7	53.0	72.9	58.7	54.8	78.1	68.7	62.3
1937	45.4	77.1	58.9	85.8	52.9	77.2	58.8	56.1	80.9	72.2	62.9
1938	42.7	72.7	58.7	78.4	54.5	69.9	61.1	56.5	75.6	67.1	63.6
1939	46.8	75.2	62.2	82.4	56.8	74.3	63.0	56.3	83.1	70.2	66.7
1940	50.6	78.1	64.8	86.1	58.8	78.2	64.7	57.0	88.8	73.2	69.1
1941	58.2	84.9	68.6	94.5	61.6	88.2	66.0	59.4	98.0	81.1	71.8
1942	63.1	89.7	70.3	102.2	61.7	96.6	65.3	61.4	102.8	87.7	71.9
1943	66.7	91.8	72.7	107.0	62.3	102.3	65.2	61.3	108.8	91.7	72.7
1944	70.4	89.7	78.5	105.6	66.7	101.0	69.8	60.6	116.2	90.6	77.7
1945	70.0	86.8	80.6	99.6	70.3	95.0	73.7	60.4	115.9	86.3	81.1
1946	68.7	92.4	74.4	100.9	68.1	96.3	71.3	62.6	109.7	87.8	78.2
1947	70.0	96.5	72.5	103.1	67.9	99.3	70.5	66.2	105.7	91.1	76.8

1948	73.4	98.3	74.7	103.9	70.6	100.6	73.0	68.8	106.7	92.8	79.1
1949	73.1	94.7	77.2	99.9	73.2	95.8	76.3	71.5	102.2	90.1	81.1
1950	80.6	97.1	83.0	101.3	79.6	98.3	82.0	73.9	109.1	92.7	86.9
1951	85.5	101.2	84.5	105.1	81.4	103.6	82.5	78.0	109.6	97.6	87.6
1952	87.7	102.1	85.9	106.0	82.7	105.1	83.4	82.0	107.0	100.0	87.7
1953	92.1	103.6	88.9	106.0	86.9	106.0	86.9	85.0	108.4	101.5	90.7
1954	90.8	100.1	90.7	101.7	89.3	100.8	90.1	87.7	103.5	98.0	92.7
1955	98.4	102.1	96.4	104.9	93.8	104.4	94.3	90.6	108.6	101.4	97.0
1956	100.2	103.8	96.5	106.3	94.3	106.3	94.3	94.7	105.8	103.8	96.5
1957	101.5	103.7	97.9	104.7	96.9	105.5	96.2	98.1	103.5	103.9	97.7
1958	100.0	100.0	100.0	100.0	100.0	100.0	100.0	100.0	100.0	100.0	100.0
1959	107.1	102.1	104.9	103.3	103.7	103.9	103.1	102.2	104.8	103.5	103.5
1960	109.7	102.9	106.6	104.3	105.2	104.8	104.7	105.2	104.3	104.9	104.6
1961	111.5	101.8	109.5	102.4	108.9	103.2	108.0	107.5	103.7	104.1	107.1
1962	119.1	103.2	115.4	104.3	114.2	105.6	112.8	110.0	108.3	106.5	111.8
1963	124.2	103.9	119.5	105.0	118.3	106.9	116.2	113.0	109.9	108.2	114.8
1964	131.3	105.6	124.3	107.1	122.6	109.4	120.0	116.7	112.5	111.0	118.3
1965	140.1	108.4	129.2	110.5	126.8	113.3	123.7	121.5	115.3	115.1	121.7
1966	149.0	112.2	132.8	113.8	130.9	118.1	126.2	128.2	116.2	120.3	123.9

TABLE A-20a

Private Domestic Business Economy: Gross Capital
Input and Gross Productivity Ratios,[a] in Terms of Real Product, 1929-66

(1958=100)

Year	Gross Capital Input	Real Product per Unit of Gross Capital Input	Gross Factor Input	Gross Factor Productivity
1929	57.2	81.8	77.4	60.5
1930	58.4	71.6	73.3	57.0
1931	58.7	65.8	68.3	56.5
1932	58.3	56.3	62.2	52.7
1933	57.6	55.2	61.7	51.5
1934	57.1	60.4	61.6	56.0
1935	57.1	66.0	63.7	59.2
1936	57.4	74.6	68.1	62.8
1937	58.3	77.9	71.1	63.9
1938	58.9	72.5	66.7	64.0
1939	59.1	79.2	69.6	67.2
1940	59.7	84.8	72.4	69.9
1941	61.1	95.3	79.3	73.4
1942	62.7	100.6	85.2	74.1
1943	63.5	105.0	89.1	74.9
1944	63.7	110.5	88.4	79.6
1945	63.8	109.7	84.6	82.7
1946	64.7	106.2	85.7	80.2
1947	67.0	104.5	88.5	79.1
1948	69.7	105.3	90.4	81.2
1949	72.2	101.2	88.3	82.8
1950	75.1	107.3	91.0	88.6
1951	78.7	108.6	95.8	89.2
1952	81.9	107.1	97.9	89.6
1953	84.7	108.7	99.5	92.6
1954	87.6	103.7	96.8	93.8
1955	90.8	108.4	100.3	98.1
1956	94.5	106.0	102.7	97.6
1957	97.5	104.1	101.3	100.2
1958	100.0	100.0	100.0	100.0
1959	102.8	104.2	103.6	103.4
1960	105.9	103.6	105.1	104.4
1961	108.5	102.8	104.8	106.4
1962	111.1	107.2	107.3	111.0
1963	114.0	108.9	109.1	113.8
1964	117.4	111.8	111.8	117.4
1965	121.8	115.0	115.9	120.9
1966	127.2	117.1	120.9	123.2

[a] Index numbers of real gross product are the same as those in Table A-20.

TABLE A-21

Private Domestic Nonfarm Business Economy: Real Gross Product, Inputs, and Productivity Ratios, 1929-66

(1958=100)

Year	Real Gross Product	Persons Engaged	Real Product per Person	Man-Hours	Real Product per Man-Hour	Labor Input	Real Product per Unit of Labor Input	Net Capital Input	Real Product per Unit of Net Capital Input	Total Factor Input	Total Factor Productivity
1929	43.9	68.7	63.9	81.1	54.1	80.8	54.3	57.5	76.3	74.7	58.8
1930	38.9	64.6	60.2	74.1	52.5	73.6	52.9	58.9	66.0	69.9	55.6
1931	34.9	58.3	59.9	65.5	53.3	64.9	53.8	58.2	60.0	63.5	55.0
1932	29.0	51.7	56.1	56.2	51.6	55.4	52.3	55.7	52.1	55.9	51.9
1933	28.1	51.7	54.4	55.8	50.4	55.0	51.1	53.0	53.0	54.8	51.3
1934	31.7	56.4	56.2	56.7	55.9	55.9	56.7	51.4	61.7	55.0	57.6
1935	34.6	58.6	59.0	60.0	57.7	59.2	58.4	50.6	68.4	57.1	60.6
1936	40.3	62.7	64.3	66.9	60.2	66.3	60.8	50.8	79.3	62.3	64.7
1937	42.3	66.8	63.3	70.8	59.7	70.1	60.3	52.2	81.0	65.4	64.7
1938	39.4	62.5	63.0	64.2	61.4	63.2	62.3	52.6	74.9	60.6	65.0
1939	43.6	65.7	66.4	68.6	63.6	67.8	64.3	52.4	83.2	63.8	68.3
1940	48.0	69.6	69.0	72.6	66.1	71.9	66.8	53.1	90.4	67.1	71.5
1941	55.6	77.8	71.5	82.7	67.2	82.7	67.2	55.7	99.8	75.6	73.5
1942	60.3	83.5	72.2	90.4	66.7	91.2	66.1	57.9	104.1	82.4	73.2
1943	64.6	85.9	75.2	95.9	67.4	97.3	66.4	57.7	112.0	86.7	74.5
1944	68.7	83.9	81.9	94.5	72.7	96.0	71.6	57.0	120.5	85.6	80.3
1945	68.7	81.0	84.8	89.4	76.8	90.4	76.0	56.8	121.0	81.4	84.4
1946	67.1	86.9	77.2	91.6	73.3	92.1	72.9	59.3	113.2	83.4	80.5
1947	69.1	91.4	75.6	94.9	72.8	95.7	72.2	63.3	109.2	87.1	79.3

(continued)

TABLE A-21 (concluded)

Year	Real Gross Product	Persons Engaged	Real Product per Person	Man-Hours	Real Product per Man-Hour	Labor Input	Real Product per Unit of Labor Input	Net Capital Input	Real Product per Unit of Net Capital Input	Total Factor Input	Total Factor Productivity
1948	72.1	93.4	77.2	96.4	74.8	97.3	74.1	66.0	109.2	89.0	81.0
1949	72.0	89.9	80.1	91.8	78.4	92.2	78.1	68.8	104.7	87.2	82.6
1950	79.7	92.7	86.0	95.1	83.8	95.6	83.4	71.3	111.8	90.3	88.3
1951	85.4	98.0	87.1	100.3	85.1	101.6	84.1	75.6	113.0	95.9	89.1
1952	87.5	99.6	87.9	102.2	85.6	103.6	84.5	79.8	109.6	98.7	88.7
1953	91.9	101.8	90.3	103.5	88.8	105.1	87.4	83.1	110.6	100.7	91.3
1954	90.4	98.2	92.1	99.1	91.2	99.8	90.6	86.0	105.1	97.0	93.2
1955	98.3	100.9	97.4	102.5	95.9	103.5	95.0	89.3	110.1	100.6	97.7
1956	100.2	103.7	96.6	104.8	95.6	105.8	94.7	93.9	106.7	103.4	96.9
1957	101.8	104.0	97.9	104.3	97.6	105.4	96.6	97.8	104.1	103.9	98.0
1958	100.0	100.0	100.0	100.0	100.0	100.0	100.0	100.0	100.0	100.0	100.0
1959	107.4	102.6	104.7	103.8	103.5	104.1	103.2	102.5	104.8	103.8	103.5
1960	110.0	104.0	105.8	105.1	104.7	105.1	104.7	105.8	104.0	105.2	104.6
1961	111.9	103.0	108.6	103.8	107.8	103.7	107.9	108.4	103.2	104.6	107.0
1962	120.0	104.9	114.4	106.2	113.0	106.3	112.9	111.2	107.9	107.3	111.8
1963	125.1	106.0	118.0	107.6	116.3	107.9	115.9	114.6	109.2	109.3	114.5
1964	132.8	108.6	122.3	110.4	120.3	110.7	120.0	118.7	111.9	112.3	118.3
1965	141.7	112.6	125.8	114.5	123.8	114.9	123.3	124.2	114.1	116.8	121.3
1966	151.5	117.6	128.8	119.2	127.1	120.2	126.0	131.7	115.0	122.5	123.7

TABLE A-21a

Private Domestic Nonfarm Business Economy:
Gross Capital Input and Gross Productivity Ratios,[a]
in Terms of Real Product, 1929-66

(1958=100)

Year	Gross Capital Input	Real Product per Unit of Gross Capital Input	Gross Factor Input	Gross Factor Productivity
1929	53.1	82.7	71.7	61.2
1930	54.4	71.5	67.6	57.5
1931	54.7	63.8	62.3	56.0
1932	54.2	53.5	56.1	51.7
1933	53.4	52.6	55.6	50.5
1934	53.0	59.8	56.0	56.6
1935	53.0	65.3	58.0	59.7
1936	53.4	75.5	62.7	64.3
1937	54.4	77.8	65.5	64.6
1938	55.1	71.5	61.2	64.4
1939	55.4	78.7	64.4	67.7
1940	56.1	85.6	67.3	71.3
1941	57.8	96.2	75.0	74.1
1942	59.5	101.3	81.3	74.2
1943	60.4	107.0	85.7	75.4
1944	60.8	113.0	85.0	80.8
1945	60.9	112.8	81.2	75.0
1946	62.0	108.2	82.7	81.1
1947	64.6	107.0	86.1	80.3
1948	67.5	106.8	88.1	81.8
1949	70.1	102.7	85.7	84.0
1950	73.1	109.0	89.0	89.6
1951	76.9	111.1	94.3	90.6
1952	80.2	109.1	96.8	90.4
1953	83.2	110.5	98.8	93.0
1954	86.3	104.8	95.9	94.3
1955	89.8	109.5	99.6	98.7
1956	93.9	106.7	102.4	97.9
1957	97.3	104.6	103.1	98.7
1958	100.0	100.0	100.0	100.0
1959	103.1	104.2	103.8	103.5
1960	106.5	103.3	105.5	104.3
1961	109.3	102.4	105.3	106.3
1962	112.1	107.0	108.0	111.1
1963	115.3	108.5	110.0	113.7
1964	119.1	111.5	113.1	117.4
1965	124.0	114.3	117.5	120.6
1966	130.0	116.5	123.0	123.2

[a] Index numbers of real gross product are the same as those in Table A-21.

TABLE A-22

Farm Segment: Real Product, Inputs, and Productivity Ratios, 1929-69

(1958=100)

Year	Real Gross Product	Persons Engaged	Real Product per Person	Man-Hours	Real Product per Man-Hour	Net Capital Input	Real Product per Unit of Net Capital Input	Total Factor Input	Total Factor Productivity
1929	81.8	170.1	48.1	219.5	37.3	88.2	92.7	155.5	52.6
1930	77.3	166.6	46.4	217.2	35.6	88.1	87.7	154.4	50.1
1931	87.6	169.9	51.6	222.0	39.5	87.9	99.7	156.2	56.1
1932	85.3	170.8	49.9	214.2	39.8	87.8	97.2	153.0	55.8
1933	83.1	169.8	48.9	213.7	38.9	87.2	95.3	152.3	54.6
1934	69.3	168.3	41.2	191.7	36.2	85.7	80.9	142.4	48.7
1935	78.2	169.7	46.1	199.5	39.2	85.0	92.0	145.0	53.9
1936	71.6	164.4	43.6	193.7	37.0	85.1	84.1	142.8	50.1
1937	84.4	159.7	52.8	209.4	40.3	85.4	98.8	149.3	56.5
1938	84.4	154.9	54.5	195.0	43.3	86.1	98.0	142.9	59.1
1939	86.7	151.1	57.4	196.0	44.2	86.2	100.6	143.4	60.5
1940	84.0	146.3	57.4	196.8	42.7	86.5	97.1	144.0	58.3
1941	90.7	142.2	63.8	190.0	47.7	87.3	103.9	141.3	64.2
1942	98.7	140.0	70.5	197.6	49.9	88.3	111.8	145.4	67.9
1943	93.8	139.2	67.4	196.0	47.9	88.7	105.7	144.9	64.7
1944	92.4	136.2	67.8	194.1	47.6	88.4	104.5	143.8	64.3
1945	86.7	133.3	65.0	181.1	47.9	88.1	98.4	137.6	63.0
1946	89.8	137.2	65.5	174.6	51.4	88.2	101.8	134.6	66.7
1947	82.7	138.4	59.8	166.7	49.6	88.9	93.0	131.3	63.0

Year									
1948	91.1	138.1	66.0	162.2	56.2	90.5	100.7	130.1	70.0
1949	88.4	132.8	66.6	162.7	54.3	92.7	95.4	131.4	67.3
1950	92.9	132.3	70.2	150.0	61.9	94.6	98.2	125.4	74.1
1951	88.4	127.2	69.5	141.9	62.3	96.8	91.3	122.1	72.4
1952	91.6	121.9	75.1	134.7	68.0	98.5	93.0	118.8	77.1
1953	96.0	118.1	81.3	125.3	76.6	99.3	96.7	114.1	84.1
1954	97.3	115.3	84.4	121.4	80.1	99.9	97.4	112.2	86.7
1955	100.0	111.7	89.5	123.4	81.0	100.4	99.6	113.5	88.1
1956	99.6	104.7	95.1	117.8	84.6	100.2	99.4	110.2	90.4
1957	96.9	101.3	95.7	107.9	89.8	99.9	97.0	104.5	92.7
1958	100.0	100.0	100.0	100.0	100.0	100.0	100.0	100.0	100.0
1959	100.9	97.9	103.1	99.8	101.1	100.2	100.7	100.0	100.9
1960	104.4	94.1	110.9	98.0	106.5	100.4	104.0	99.0	105.4
1961	106.2	92.2	115.2	91.7	115.8	100.5	105.7	95.5	111.2
1962	105.8	89.3	118.5	89.5	118.2	101.0	104.8	94.4	112.1
1963	108.9	86.9	125.3	84.6	128.7	101.6	107.2	91.9	118.5
1964	107.1	81.4	131.6	81.3	131.7	101.8	105.2	90.1	118.9
1965	114.2	74.8	152.7	79.2	144.2	102.0	112.0	89.0	128.3
1966	107.6	69.5	154.8	72.0	149.4	102.3	105.2	85.0	126.6
1967	114.6	65.3	175.5	69.6	164.7				
1968	112.4	63.3	177.6	68.0	165.3				
1969P	116.1	61.2	189.7	63.8	182.0				

Note: Relates to *Productivity Trends*, Table B-I.

P Preliminary (as of July 1971 *Survey of Current Business*).

TABLE A-23

Farm Segment: Output and Productivity Ratios,[a] 1929-66
(1958=100)

Year	Output	Output per Person	Output per Man-Hour	Output per Unit of Net Capital Input	Total Factor Productivity
1929	63.3	37.2	28.8	71.8	40.7
1930	59.8	35.9	27.5	67.9	38.7
1931	64.9	38.2	29.2	73.8	41.5
1932	62.5	36.6	29.2	71.2	40.8
1933	62.2	36.6	29.1	71.3	40.8
1934	53.7	31.9	28.0	62.7	37.7
1935	59.8	35.2	30.0	70.4	41.2
1936	57.2	34.8	29.5	67.2	40.1
1937	65.7	41.1	31.4	76.9	44.0
1938	66.2	42.7	33.9	76.9	46.3
1939	69.1	45.7	35.3	80.2	48.2
1940	69.7	47.6	35.4	80.6	48.4
1941	74.7	52.5	39.3	85.6	52.9
1942	82.2	58.7	41.6	93.1	56.5
1943	80.3	57.7	41.0	90.5	55.4
1944	80.3	59.0	41.4	90.8	55.8
1945	79.3	59.5	43.8	90.0	57.6
1946	81.7	59.5	46.8	92.6	60.7
1947	78.5	56.7	47.1	88.3	59.8
1948	83.8	60.7	51.7	92.6	64.4
1949	82.2	61.9	50.5	88.7	62.6
1950	86.4	65.3	57.6	91.3	68.9
1951	85.9	67.5	60.5	88.7	70.4
1952	87.8	72.0	65.2	89.1	73.9
1953	89.9	76.1	71.8	90.5	78.8
1954	92.3	80.1	76.0	92.4	82.3
1955	94.9	85.0	76.9	94.5	83.6
1956	96.0	91.7	81.5	95.8	87.1
1957	95.5	94.3	88.5	95.6	91.4
1958	100.0	100.0	100.0	100.0	100.0
1959	101.9	104.1	102.1	101.7	101.9
1960	104.3	110.8	106.4	103.9	105.4
1961	106.1	115.1	115.7	105.6	111.1
1962	108.2	121.2	120.9	107.1	114.6
1963	111.7	128.5	132.0	109.9	121.5
1964	109.6	134.6	134.8	107.7	121.6
1965	115.2	154.0	145.5	112.9	129.4
1966	113.6	163.5	157.8	111.0	133.6

Note: Relates to *Productivity Trends*, Table B-II (gross output revised).

[a] Index numbers of the inputs are the same as those shown in Table A-22.

TABLE A-23a

Farm Segment: Gross Capital Input and Gross Productivity
Ratios[a] in Terms of Real Product and Output, 1929-66

(1958=100)

Year	Gross Capital Input	Real Product per Unit of Gross Capital Input	Gross Factor Input	Real Product per Unit of Gross Factor Input	Output per Unit of Gross Capital Input	Output per Unit of Gross Factor Input
1929	85.8	95.3	143.8	56.9	73.8	44.0
1930	86.0	89.9	143.2	54.0	69.5	41.8
1931	86.4	101.4	145.1	60.4	75.1	44.7
1932	86.9	98.2	142.8	59.7	71.9	43.8
1933	86.8	95.7	142.6	58.3	71.7	43.6
1934	85.8	80.8	134.4	51.6	62.6	40.0
1935	85.5	91.5	136.8	57.2	69.9	43.7
1936	85.4	83.8	134.7	53.2	67.0	42.5
1937	85.4	98.8	140.1	60.2	76.9	46.9
1938	85.6	98.6	134.3	62.8	77.3	49.3
1939	85.3	101.6	134.6	64.4	81.0	51.3
1940	85.3	98.5	134.9	62.3	81.7	51.7
1941	85.6	106.0	132.3	68.6	87.3	56.5
1942	86.2	114.5	135.8	72.7	95.4	60.5
1943	86.2	108.8	135.1	69.4	93.2	59.4
1944	85.7	107.8	134.1	68.9	93.7	59.9
1945	85.3	101.6	128.5	67.5	93.0	61.7
1946	85.2	105.4	125.8	71.4	96.1	65.1
1947	85.4	96.8	122.6	67.5	91.9	64.0

(continued)

TABLE A-23a (concluded)

Year	Gross Capital Input	Real Product per Unit of Gross Capital Input	Gross Factor Input	Real Product per Unit of Gross Factor Input	Output per Unit of Gross Capital Input	Output per Unit of Gross Factor Input
1948	86.7	105.1	121.7	74.9	96.7	68.9
1949	88.9	99.4	123.1	71.8	92.5	66.8
1950	90.9	102.2	118.4	78.5	95.0	73.0
1951	93.2	94.8	115.9	76.3	92.2	74.1
1952	95.0	96.4	113.6	80.6	92.4	77.3
1953	96.3	99.7	110.0	87.3	93.4	81.7
1954	97.4	99.9	108.8	89.4	94.8	84.8
1955	98.5	101.5	110.3	90.7	96.3	86.0
1956	99.1	100.5	108.0	92.2	96.9	88.9
1957	99.4	97.5	103.4	93.7	96.1	92.4
1958	100.0	100.0	100.0	100.0	100.0	100.0
1959	100.6	100.3	100.2	100.7	101.3	101.7
1960	101.4	103.0	99.8	104.6	102.9	104.5
1961	102.2	103.9	97.2	109.3	103.8	109.2
1962	103.1	102.6	96.7	109.4	104.9	111.9
1963	103.9	104.8	94.8	114.9	107.5	117.8
1964	104.3	102.7	93.4	114.7	105.1	117.3
1965	104.6	109.2	92.6	123.3	110.1	124.4
1966	105.1	102.4	89.4	120.4	108.1	127.1

a Index numbers of real product and output are the same as those shown in Tables A-22 and A-23.

TABLE A-24

Mining: Real Product, Inputs, and Productivity Ratios, 1948-69

(1958=100)

Year	Real Gross Product	Persons Engaged	Real Product per Person	Man-Hours	Real Product per Man-Hour	Labor Input	Real Product per Unit of Labor Input	Net Capital Input	Real Product per Unit of Net Capital Input	Total Factor Input	Total Factor Productivity
1948	86.9	131.1	66.3	132.7	65.5	140.5	61.9	100.9	86.1	130.5	66.6
1949	77.5	122.1	63.5	114.4	67.7	119.7	64.7			117.2	66.1
1950	86.4	122.5	70.5	119.4	72.4	125.1	69.1			122.1	70.8
1951	95.0	124.2	76.5	123.1	77.2	127.9	74.3			124.6	76.2
1952	94.3	121.3	77.7	120.4	78.3	124.2	75.9			121.3	77.7
1953	97.5	116.2	83.9	115.8	84.2	118.5	82.3	99.1	98.4	114.4	85.2
1954	94.3	106.9	88.2	105.3	89.6	106.4	88.6			103.7	90.9
1955	103.9	107.5	96.7	111.3	93.4	112.6	92.3			109.0	95.3
1956	109.7	112.2	97.8	116.8	93.9	118.2	92.8			114.5	95.8
1957	109.7	111.8	98.1	114.5	95.8	115.6	94.9	101.0	108.6	112.5	97.5
1958	100.0	100.0	100.0	100.0	100.0	100.0	100.0			100.0	100.0
1959	104.0	95.9	108.4	99.5	104.5	99.1	104.9			99.6	104.4
1960	106.4	93.5	113.8	96.8	109.9	96.5	110.3	104.0	102.3	98.1	108.5
1961	107.3	89.3	120.2	92.6	115.9	91.9	116.8			95.1	112.8
1962	109.9	87.2	126.0	91.4	120.2	90.7	121.2			94.4	116.4
1963	112.8	84.9	132.9	90.4	124.8	89.7	125.8			92.1	122.5
1964	116.6	84.5	138.0	90.5	128.8	89.7	130.0			91.2	127.9
1965	120.0	85.3	140.7	91.9	130.6	91.1	131.7			91.4	131.3
1966	125.7	84.8	148.2	92.0	136.6	91.1	138.0	87.2	144.2	90.3	139.2
1967	129.2	82.6	156.4	89.6	144.2	88.8	145.5				
1968	132.0	82.1	160.8	89.2	148.0	88.3	149.5				
1969P	136.1	83.9	162.2	92.1	147.8	91.2	149.2				

P Preliminary (as of July 1971 *Survey of Current Business*).

TABLE A-25

Mining: Output and Productivity Ratios,[a] 1948-66
(1958=100)

Year	Output	Output per Person	Output per Man-Hour	Output per Unit of Labor Input	Output per Unit of Capital Input	Total Factor Productivity
1948	86.5	66.0	65.2	61.6	85.7	66.3
1949	76.7	62.8	67.0	64.1		65.4
1950	85.7	70.0	71.8	68.5		70.2
1951	94.0	75.7	76.4	73.5		75.4
1952	93.2	76.8	77.4	75.0		76.8
1953	95.7	82.4	82.6	80.8	96.6	83.7
1954	92.9	86.9	88.2	87.3		89.6
1955	102.6	95.4	92.2	91.1		94.1
1956	108.8	97.0	93.2	92.0		95.0
1957	109.0	97.5	95.2	94.3	107.9	96.9
1958	100.0	100.0	100.0	100.0		100.0
1959	104.3	108.8	104.8	105.2		104.7
1960	106.3	113.7	109.8	110.2	102.2	108.4
1961	107.3	120.2	115.9	116.8		112.8
1962	109.8	125.9	120.1	121.1		116.3
1963	112.9	133.0	124.9	125.9		122.6
1964	116.6	138.0	128.8	130.0		127.9
1965	120.1	140.8	130.7	131.8		131.4
1966	126.0	148.6	137.0	138.3	144.5	139.5

Note: Relates to *Productivity Trends,* Table C-II.

[a] Index numbers of inputs are the same as those shown in Table A-24.

TABLE A-25a

Mining: Gross Capital Input and Gross Productivity Ratios,[a]
in Terms of Real Product and Output, 1948-66
(1958=100)

	Gross Capital Input	Real Product per Unit of Gross Capital Input	Gross Factor Input	Real Product per Unit of Gross Factor Input	Output per Unit of Gross Capital Input	Output per Unit of Gross Factor Input
8	101.0	86.0	122.0	71.2	85.6	70.9
9			113.4	68.3		67.6
0			117.3	73.7		73.1
1			118.6	80.1		79.3
2			115.5	81.6		80.7
3	96.4	101.1	108.3	90.0	99.2	88.4
4			99.3	95.0		93.6
5			103.5	100.4		99.1
6			108.8	100.8		100.0
7	99.2	110.6	108.0	101.6	109.9	100.9
8			100.0	100.0		100.0
9			100.2	103.8		104.1
0	103.6	102.7	99.8	106.6	102.6	106.5
1			99.1	108.3		108.3
2			100.0	109.9		109.8
3			96.2	117.3		117.4
4			93.9	124.2		124.2
5			92.4	129.9		130.0
6	82.5	152.4	87.1	144.3	152.7	144.7

[a] Index numbers of real product and output are the same as those shown in Tables A-24 and
25.

TABLE A-26

Metal Mining: Output, Inputs, and Productivity Ratios, 1948-66
(1958=100)

Year	Output	Persons Engaged	Output per Person	Man-Hours	Output per Man-Hour	Net Capital Input	Output per Unit of Net Capital Input	Total Factor Input	Total Factor Productivity
1948	98.7	111.6	88.4	122.5	80.6	66.2	149.1	111.3	88.7
1949	88.7	104.2	85.1	110.5	80.3			104.8	84.6
1950	102.2	106.3	96.1	115.7	88.3			107.0	95.5
1951	109.9	111.6	98.5	125.7	87.4			115.2	95.4
1952	101.4	112.6	90.1	127.7	79.4			118.4	85.6
1953	112.8	116.8	96.6	130.9	86.2	69.6	162.1	118.4	95.3
1954	92.4	110.5	83.6	116.8	79.1			109.0	84.8
1955	115.1	113.7	101.2	124.1	92.7			118.1	97.5
1956	119.1	121.1	98.3	131.9	90.3			124.9	95.4
1957	123.5	122.1	101.1	128.3	96.3	97.7	126.4	122.1	101.1
1958	100.0	100.0	100.0	100.0	100.0			100.0	100.0
1959	93.5	90.5	103.3	94.2	99.3			97.4	96.0
1960	117.3	102.1	114.9	110.5	106.2	122.6	95.7	113.0	103.8
1961	117.5	95.8	122.7	102.6	114.5			107.2	109.6
1962	118.2	90.5	130.6	97.4	121.4			103.1	114.6
1963	117.8	87.4	134.8	93.2	126.4			98.5	119.6
1964	123.2	87.4	141.0	93.7	131.5			94.9	129.8
1965	130.3	91.6	142.2	98.4	132.4			96.8	134.6
1966	140.0	94.7	147.8	103.1	135.8	100.9	138.8	102.7	136.3

Note: Relates to *Productivity Trends*, Table C-III.

TABLE A-26a

Metal Mining: Gross Capital
Input and Gross Productivity Ratios,[a] 1948-66

(1958=100)

Year	Gross Capital Input	Output per Unit of Gross Capital Input	Gross Factor Input	Gross Factor Productivity
1948	86.5	114.1	112.6	87.7
1949			106.9	83.0
1950			108.5	94.2
1951			114.7	95.8
1952			114.1	88.9
1953	74.7	151.0	111.6	101.1
1954			105.1	87.9
1955			114.1	100.9
1956			119.7	99.5
1957	98.8	125.0	118.2	104.5
1958			100.0	100.0
1959			98.9	94.5
1960	118.8	98.7	113.4	103.4
1961			107.8	109.0
1962			103.7	114.0
1963			100.5	117.2
1964			95.9	128.5
1965			95.6	136.3
1966	97.0	144.3	101.0	138.6

[a] Index numbers of output are the same as those shown in Table A-26.

TABLE A-27

Coal Mining: Output, Inputs, and Productivity Ratios, 1948-66
(1958=100)

Year	Output	Persons Engaged	Output per Person	Man-Hours	Output per Man-Hour	Net Capital Input	Output per Unit of Net Capital Input	Total Factor Input	Total Factor Productivity
1948	157.5	240.7	65.4	274.2	57.4	125.9	125.1	253.2	62.2
1949	116.2	215.5	53.9	208.8	55.7			198.5	58.5
1950	133.7	213.7	62.6	221.9	60.3			209.9	63.7
1951	137.1	201.3	68.1	208.5	65.8			199.0	68.9
1952	120.7	181.4	66.5	183.5	65.8			177.0	68.2
1953	113.9	156.6	72.7	157.5	72.3	117.3	97.1	154.0	74.0
1954	98.2	123.0	79.8	119.6	82.1			118.7	82.7
1955	116.4	115.5	100.8	128.6	90.5			126.3	92.2
1956	124.8	120.8	103.3	135.3	92.2			132.1	94.5
1957	121.1	118.1	102.5	127.8	94.8	100.0	121.1	125.4	96.6
1958	100.0	100.0	100.0	100.0	100.0			100.0	100.0
1959	99.8	88.9	112.3	95.4	104.6			95.7	104.3
1960	100.3	83.2	120.6	89.4	112.2	97.5	102.9	90.1	111.3
1961	96.5	74.3	129.9	80.7	119.6			82.0	117.7
1962	102.0	71.2	143.3	79.6	128.1			80.3	127.0
1963	109.7	69.0	159.0	81.2	135.1			81.2	135.1
1964	116.2	67.3	172.7	79.4	146.3			80.0	145.2
1965	121.3	66.4	182.7	80.2	151.2			81.5	148.8
1966	125.3	65.0	192.8	79.4	157.8	93.8	133.6	80.7	155.3

Note: Relates to *Productivity Trends*, Table C-III.

TABLE A-27a

Coal Mining: Gross Capital
Input and Gross Productivity Ratios,[a] 1948-66

(1958=100)

Year	Gross Capital Input	Output per Unit of Gross Capital Input	Gross Factor Input	Gross Factor Productivity
1948	126.6	124.4	240.0	65.6
1949			190.4	61.0
1950			201.1	66.5
1951			191.2	71.7
1952			170.8	70.7
1953	117.1	97.3	149.5	76.2
1954			118.0	83.2
1955			124.2	93.7
1956			128.7	97.0
1957	100.6	120.4	122.4	98.9
1958			100.0	100.0
1959			96.1	103.9
1960	98.1	102.2	91.1	110.1
1961			83.9	115.0
1962			82.3	123.9
1963			81.6	134.4
1964			80.7	144.0
1965			82.8	146.5
1966	92.4	135.6	82.0	152.8

[a] Index numbers of output are the same as those shown in Table A-27.

TABLE A-28

Crude Petroleum and Natural Gas Mining: Output, Inputs, and
Productivity Ratios, 1948-66
(1958=100)

Year	Output	Persons Engaged	Output per Person	Man-Hours	Output per Man-Hour	Net Capital Input	Output per Unit of Net Capital Input	Total Factor Input	Total Factor Productivity
1948	73.1	81.7	89.5	79.9	91.5	112.9	64.7	90.0	81.2
1949	69.1	79.7	86.7	78.4	88.1			91.5	75.5
1950	75.8	80.5	94.2	79.9	94.9			94.5	80.2
1951	85.6	88.7	96.5	88.7	96.5			100.6	85.1
1952	88.5	94.2	93.9	94.7	93.5			103.3	85.7
1953	92.6	96.8	95.7	96.8	95.7	107.6	86.1	99.8	92.8
1954	92.6	99.1	93.4	98.1	94.4			98.0	94.5
1955	99.6	103.2	96.5	102.5	97.2			100.9	98.7
1956	105.4	106.7	98.8	106.9	98.6			105.8	99.6
1957	106.1	107.6	98.6	107.6	98.6	103.1	102.9	106.3	99.8
1958	100.0	100.0	100.0	100.0	100.0			100.0	100.0
1959	105.4	100.0	105.4	101.2	104.2			100.9	104.5
1960	105.2	95.6	110.0	95.5	110.2	102.2	102.9	97.4	108.0
1961	107.4	93.9	114.4	93.2	115.2			96.9	110.8
1962	109.9	92.7	118.6	92.6	118.7			97.0	113.3
1963	112.4	89.8	125.2	90.3	124.5			92.3	121.8
1964	115.0	90.1	127.6	91.0	126.4			91.4	125.8
1965	117.0	90.1	129.9	90.7	129.0			89.1	131.3
1966	122.9	88.7	138.6	89.8	136.9	73.7	166.8	85.3	144.1

Note: Relates to *Productivity Trends*, Table C-III.

TABLE A-28a

Crude Petroleum and Natural Gas Mining: Gross
Capital Input and Gross Productivity Ratios,[a] 1948-66

(1958=100)

Year	Gross Capital Input	Output per Unit of Gross Capital Input	Gross Factor Input	Gross Factor Productivity
1948	104.2	70.2	93.7	78.0
1949			96.7	71.5
1950			99.0	76.6
1951			102.3	83.7
1952			103.6	85.4
1953	99.3	93.3	98.3	94.2
1954			94.1	98.4
1955			96.4	103.3
1956			101.8	103.5
1957	99.4	106.7	102.8	103.2
1958			100.0	100.0
1959			101.3	104.0
1960	102.9	102.2	99.9	105.3
1961			101.7	105.6
1962			103.8	105.9
1963			97.3	115.5
1964			93.2	123.4
1965			88.9	131.6
1966	71.8	171.2	79.2	155.2

[a] Index numbers of output are the same as those shown in Table A-28.

TABLE A-29

Nonmetallic Mining and Quarrying: Output, Inputs, and Productivity Ratios, 1948-66
(1958=100)

Year	Output	Persons Engaged	Output per Person	Man-Hours	Output per Man-Hour	Net Capital Input	Output per Unit of Net Capital Input	Total Factor Input	Total Factor Productivity
1948	61.5	82.9	74.2	84.8	72.5	59.9	102.7	80.7	76.2
1949	59.5	82.9	71.8	82.7	71.9			80.2	74.2
1950	68.1	84.6	80.5	85.6	79.6			82.5	82.5
1951	74.4	91.9	81.0	94.9	78.4			89.6	83.0
1952	77.6	93.5	83.0	96.8	80.2			91.7	84.6
1953	79.7	95.9	83.1	98.6	80.8	67.6	117.9	93.0	85.7
1954	87.8	95.9	91.6	97.1	90.4			92.6	94.8
1955	95.2	100.0	95.2	102.2	93.2			98.5	96.6
1956	102.5	104.9	97.7	107.6	95.3			104.1	98.5
1957	101.9	104.1	97.9	105.1	97.0	93.9	108.5	103.1	98.8
1958	100.0	100.0	100.0	100.0	100.0	100.0		100.0	100.0
1959	109.7	101.6	108.0	104.3	105.2			103.7	105.8
1960	113.9	100.0	113.9	101.1	112.7		113.9	100.9	112.9
1961	113.5	99.2	114.4	100.7	112.8			101.3	112.0
1962	113.8	98.4	115.7	100.7	113.0			102.3	111.2
1963	116.3	98.4	118.2	101.4	114.7			104.5	111.3
1964	123.1	98.4	125.1	102.5	120.1			107.4	114.6
1965	131.2	101.6	129.1	107.2	122.4			112.2	116.9
1966	138.5	102.4	135.3	107.9	128.4	140.1	98.9	113.8	121.7

Note: Relates to *Productivity Trends*, Table C-III.

TABLE A-29a

Nonmetallic Mining and Quarrying: Gross
Capital Input and Gross Productivity Ratios,[a] 1948-66

(1958=100)

Year	Gross Capital Input	Output per Unit of Gross Capital Input	Gross Factor Input	Gross Factor Productivity
1948	61.1	100.7	77.0	79.9
1949			77.0	77.3
1950			79.0	86.2
1951			85.2	87.3
1952			87.5	88.7
1953	70.4	113.2	89.2	89.3
1954			89.8	97.8
1955			96.1	99.1
1956			102.3	100.2
1957	96.8	105.3	102.3	99.6
1958			100.0	100.0
1959			103.0	106.5
1960	101.1	112.7	101.1	112.7
1961			102.9	110.3
1962			105.9	107.5
1963			110.9	104.9
1964			117.4	104.9
1965			122.7	106.9
1966	155.4	89.1	123.8	111.9

[a] Index numbers of output are the same as those shown in Table
A-29.

TABLE A-30

Contract Construction: Real Product, Inputs, and Productivity Ratios, 1948-69

(1958=100)

Year	Real Gross Product	Persons Engaged	Real Product per Person	Man-Hours	Real Product per Man-Hour	Net Capital Input	Real Product per Unit of Net Capital Input	Total Factor Input	Total Factor Productivity
1948	68.2	92.9	73.4	97.4	70.0	48.2	141.5	91.8	74.3
1949	70.9	89.2	79.5	92.7	76.5	56.2	126.2	89.1	79.6
1950	78.3	96.7	81.0	99.6	78.6	58.4	134.1	95.4	82.1
1951	88.2	103.3	85.4	107.8	81.8	68.2	129.3	104.0	84.8
1952	88.7	103.3	85.9	109.9	80.7	75.0	118.3	106.9	83.0
1953	91.4	101.7	89.9	105.4	86.7	76.3	119.8	103.2	88.6
1954	93.4	98.3	95.0	99.7	93.7	76.4	122.3	97.9	95.4
1955	100.4	101.1	99.3	102.0	98.4	77.8	129.0	100.1	100.3
1956	105.6	105.3	100.3	107.2	98.5	84.5	125.0	105.5	100.1
1957	102.2	103.3	98.9	104.0	98.3	94.0	108.7	103.2	99.0
1958	100.0	100.0	100.0	100.0	100.0	100.0	100.0	100.0	100.0
1959	106.6	103.4	103.1	103.9	102.6	104.0	102.5	103.9	102.6
1960	105.1	102.4	102.6	102.1	102.9	109.9	95.6	102.7	102.3
1961	103.5	101.5	102.0	101.9	101.6	115.8	89.4	103.0	100.5
1962	104.9	103.4	101.5	104.1	100.8	123.0	85.3	105.6	99.3
1963	105.9	105.7	100.2	107.1	98.9	132.5	79.9	109.1	97.1
1964	112.9	109.0	103.6	110.1	102.5	143.1	78.9	112.6	100.3
1965	113.6	113.6	100.0	115.2	98.6	154.7	73.4	118.2	96.1
1966	118.2	116.3	101.6	118.5	99.7	167.3	70.7	122.3	96.6
1967	111.6	114.4	97.6	116.9	95.5				
1968	115.3	117.2	98.4	118.5	97.3				
1969p	116.6	123.2	94.6	126.4	92.2				

Note: Relates to *Productivity Trends*, Table E-I.

p Preliminary (as of July 1971 *Survey of Current Business*)

TABLE A-30a

Contract Construction: Gross Capital Input and Gross Productivity Ratios,[a]
in Terms of Real Product, 1948-66

(1958=100)

Year	Gross Capital Input	Real Product per Unit of Gross Capital Input	Gross Factor Input	Gross Factor Productivity
1948	44.1	154.5	88.1	77.4
1949	51.0	139.0	85.8	82.6
1950	54.4	143.9	92.1	85.0
1951	64.4	137.0	100.9	87.4
1952	72.1	123.0	104.3	85.0
1953	77.1	118.5	101.7	89.9
1954	81.6	114.5	97.3	96.0
1955	82.9	121.1	99.5	100.9
1956	86.9	121.5	104.5	101.1
1957	93.6	109.2	102.6	99.6
1958	100.0	100.0	100.0	100.0
1959	105.2	101.3	104.1	102.4
1960	110.1	95.5	103.2	101.8
1961	116.4	88.9	103.8	99.7
1962	124.2	84.5	106.8	98.2
1963	134.3	78.9	110.7	95.7
1964	145.7	77.5	114.8	98.3
1965	158.0	71.9	120.8	94.0
1966	171.3	69.0	125.5	94.2

[a] Index numbers of real product are the same as those shown in Table A-30.

TABLE A-31

Manufacturing: Real Product, Inputs, and Productivity Ratios, 1948-69

(1958=100)

Year	Real Gross Product	Persons Engaged	Real Product per Person	Man-Hours	Real Product per Man-Hour	Labor Input	Real Product per Unit of Labor Input	Net Capital Input	Real Product per Unit of Net Capital Input	Total Factor Input	Total Factor Productivity
1948	77.8	98.1	79.3	102.2	76.1	100.8	77.2	71.4	109.0	94.7	82.2
1949	73.5	91.3	80.5	92.9	79.1	91.7	80.2	73.3	100.3	88.7	82.9
1950	85.3	96.1	88.8	99.6	85.6	98.4	86.7	73.8	115.6	93.6	91.1
1951	93.9	103.7	90.5	107.7	87.2	107.2	87.6	78.3	119.9	101.4	92.6
1952	96.0	105.6	90.9	109.7	87.5	109.6	87.6	85.5	112.3	105.4	91.1
1953	104.0	110.7	93.9	114.1	91.1	114.4	90.9	88.8	117.1	109.8	94.7
1954	96.6	103.2	93.6	104.5	92.4	104.4	92.5	89.2	108.3	101.7	95.0
1955	108.0	106.6	101.3	109.7	98.5	109.8	98.4	89.9	120.1	106.2	101.7
1956	108.4	108.8	99.6	111.2	97.5	111.5	97.2	95.1	114.0	108.5	99.9
1957	108.8	108.2	100.6	109.4	99.5	110.3	98.6	98.7	110.2	108.2	100.6
1958	100.0	100.0	100.0	100.0	100.0	100.0	100.0	100.0	100.0	100.0	100.0
1959	112.4	104.5	107.6	107.1	104.9	107.1	104.9	101.6	110.6	106.1	105.9
1960	113.9	105.2	108.3	107.3	106.2	107.4	106.1	103.7	109.8	106.7	106.7
1961	113.5	102.5	110.7	104.3	108.8	104.3	108.8	104.9	108.2	104.4	108.7
1962	125.0	105.9	118.0	109.0	114.7	109.2	114.5	106.6	117.3	108.7	115.0
1963	131.3	106.6	123.2	110.0	119.4	110.4	118.9	111.1	118.2	110.5	118.8
1964	140.4	108.5	129.4	113.5	123.7	114.0	123.2	115.6	121.5	114.3	122.8
1965	154.1	113.3	136.0	118.5	130.0	119.2	129.3	123.4	124.9	120.0	128.4
1966	166.3	120.5	138.0	126.6	131.4	127.8	130.1	136.4	121.9	129.3	128.6
1967	166.1	121.7	136.5	125.5	132.4	124.9	133.0				
1968	177.3	123.9	143.1	128.1	138.4	127.6	138.9				
1969p	182.6	126.3	144.6	130.3	140.1	129.8	140.7				

p Preliminary (as of July 1971 *Survey of Current Business*).

TABLE A-31a

Manufacturing: Gross Capital Input and Gross
Productivity Ratios,[a] in Terms of Real Product, 1948-66

(1958=100)

Year	Gross Capital Input	Real Product per Unit of Gross Capital Input	Gross Factor Input	Gross Factor Productivity
1948	70.8	109.9	92.8	83.8
1949	73.2	100.4	87.4	84.1
1950	74.2	115.0	92.3	92.4
1951	77.6	121.0	99.5	94.4
1952	84.1	114.1	103.4	92.8
1953	87.7	118.6	107.8	96.5
1954	88.8	108.8	100.6	96.0
1955	89.7	120.4	104.9	103.0
1956	94.3	115.0	107.3	101.0
1957	97.8	111.2	107.3	101.4
1958	100.0	100.0	100.0	100.0
1959	102.9	109.2	106.1	105.9
1960	106.6	106.8	107.2	106.2
1961	109.7	103.5	105.6	107.5
1962	112.9	110.7	110.1	113.5
1963	116.7	112.5	111.9	117.3
1964	121.7	115.4	115.9	121.1
1965	129.7	118.8	121.8	126.5
1966	142.0	117.1	131.3	126.7

a Index numbers of real product are the same as those shown in Table A-31.

TABLE A-32

Manufacturing: Output, Inputs, and Productivity Ratios, 1929-66
(1958=100)

Year	Output	Persons Engaged	Output per Person	Man-Hours	Output per Man-Hour	Labor Input	Output per Unit of Labor Input	Net Capital Input	Output per Unit of Net Capital Input	Total Factor Input	Total Factor Productivity
1929	40.0	67.0	59.7	76.9	52.0	73.6	54.3	59.1	67.7	71.3	56.1
1930	34.2	59.7	57.3	65.4	52.3	62.7	54.5	61.2	55.9	63.8	53.6
1931	28.8	50.6	56.9	53.3	54.0	51.2	56.3	60.3	47.8	55.0	52.4
1932	21.5	42.8	50.2	42.6	50.5	40.9	52.6	56.3	38.2	46.3	46.4
1933	25.1	46.1	54.4	45.7	54.9	44.0	57.0	52.2	48.1	47.4	53.0
1934	27.6	53.5	51.6	48.1	57.4	46.5	59.4	49.8	55.4	48.6	56.8
1935	33.1	57.0	58.1	54.1	61.2	52.3	63.3	48.7	68.0	52.5	63.0
1936	38.7	61.7	62.7	62.8	61.6	60.7	63.8	48.8	79.3	58.8	65.8
1937	41.3	67.8	60.9	68.0	60.7	65.8	62.8	50.5	81.8	63.1	65.5
1938	32.4	58.5	55.4	54.1	59.9	52.5	61.7	50.9	63.7	53.7	60.3
1939	41.0	63.9	64.2	62.7	65.4	60.9	67.3	50.1	81.8	59.5	68.9
1940	47.5	69.8	68.1	69.1	68.7	67.3	70.6	51.4	92.4	64.4	73.8
1941	63.2	84.2	75.1	88.8	71.2	86.6	73.0	55.6	113.7	79.5	79.5
1942	78.9	97.8	80.7	109.0	72.4	106.5	74.1	59.6	132.4	95.0	83.1
1943	95.3	111.4	85.5	129.9	73.4	127.0	75.0	60.6	157.3	109.9	86.7
1944	93.0	109.2	85.2	128.3	72.5	125.7	74.0	59.6	156.0	108.6	85.6
1945	78.6	97.4	80.7	109.9	71.5	107.9	72.8	58.1	135.3	95.5	82.3
1946	64.3	93.1	69.1	97.7	65.8	96.1	66.9	61.8	104.0	88.3	72.8
1947	71.3	97.7	73.0	102.5	69.6	100.9	70.7	67.5	105.6	93.5	76.3

Year											
1948	73.7	98.1	75.1	102.2	72.1	100.8	73.1	71.4	103.2	94.7	77.8
1949	69.6	91.3	76.2	92.9	74.9	91.7	75.9	73.3	95.0	88.7	78.5
1950	81.1	96.1	84.4	99.6	81.4	98.4	82.4	73.8	109.9	93.6	86.6
1951	87.6	103.7	84.5	107.7	81.3	107.2	81.7	78.3	111.9	101.4	86.4
1952	91.1	105.6	86.3	109.7	83.0	109.6	83.1	85.5	106.5	105.4	86.4
1953	99.1	110.7	89.5	114.1	86.9	114.4	86.6	88.8	111.6	109.8	90.3
1954	92.3	103.2	89.4	104.5	88.3	104.4	88.4	89.2	103.5	101.7	90.8
1955	104.1	106.6	97.7	109.7	94.9	109.8	94.8	89.9	115.8	106.2	98.0
1956	107.3	108.8	98.6	111.2	96.5	111.5	96.2	95.1	112.8	108.5	98.9
1957	108.1	108.2	99.9	109.4	98.8	110.3	98.0	98.7	109.5	108.2	99.9
1958	100.0	100.0	100.0	100.0	100.0	100.0	100.0	100.0	100.0	100.0	100.0
1959	113.7	104.5	108.8	107.1	106.2	107.1	106.2	101.6	111.9	106.1	107.2
1960	116.7	105.2	110.9	107.3	108.8	107.4	108.7	103.7	112.5	106.7	109.4
1961	117.4	102.5	114.5	104.3	112.6	104.3	112.6	104.9	111.9	104.4	112.5
1962	127.1	105.9	120.0	109.0	116.6	109.2	116.4	106.6	119.2	108.7	116.9
1963	133.7	106.6	125.4	110.0	121.5	110.4	121.1	111.1	120.3	110.5	121.0
1964	142.5	108.5	131.3	113.5	125.6	114.0	125.0	115.6	123.3	114.3	124.7
1965	155.2	113.3	137.0	118.5	131.0	119.2	130.2	123.4	125.8	120.0	129.3
1966	169.9	120.5	141.0	126.6	134.2	127.8	132.9	136.4	124.6	129.3	131.4

Note: Relates to *Productivity Trends*, Tables D-I and D-II.

TABLE A-32a

Manufacturing: Gross Capital Input and Gross
Productivity Ratios,[a] in Terms of Output, 1929-66

(1958=100)

Year	Gross Capital Input	Output per Unit of Gross Capital Input	Gross Factor Input	Gross Factor Productivity
1929	60.4	66.2	71.0	56.3
1930	62.3	54.9	64.1	53.4
1931	62.0	46.5	56.1	51.3
1932	59.5	36.1	48.2	44.6
1933	56.7	44.3	49.4	50.8
1934	55.2	50.0	50.6	54.5
1935	54.5	60.7	54.4	60.8
1936	54.5	71.0	60.0	64.5
1937	55.6	74.3	64.0	64.5
1938	56.1	57.8	55.1	58.8
1939	55.4	74.0	60.6	67.7
1940	56.4	84.2	65.2	72.9
1941	59.4	106.4	79.2	79.8
1942	62.1	127.1	93.5	84.4
1943	62.8	151.8	107.5	88.7
1944	62.0	150.0	106.4	87.4
1945	60.9	129.1	94.0	83.6
1946	63.5	101.3	87.1	73.8
1947	67.7	105.3	91.8	77.7
1948	70.8	104.1	92.8	79.4
1949	73.2	95.1	87.4	79.6
1950	74.2	109.3	92.3	87.9
1951	77.6	112.9	99.5	88.0
1952	84.1	108.3	103.4	88.1
1953	87.7	113.0	107.8	91.9
1954	88.8	103.9	100.6	91.7
1955	89.7	116.1	104.9	99.2
1956	94.3	113.8	107.3	100.0
1957	97.8	110.5	107.3	100.7
1958	100.0	100.0	100.0	100.0
1959	102.9	110.5	106.1	107.2
1960	106.6	109.5	107.2	108.9
1961	109.7	107.0	105.6	111.2
1962	112.9	112.6	110.1	115.4
1963	116.7	114.6	111.9	119.5
1964	121.7	117.1	115.9	123.0
1965	129.7	119.7	121.8	127.4
1966	142.0	119.6	131.3	129.4

[a] Index numbers of output are the same as those shown in
Table A-32.

TABLE A-33

Manufacturing, Nondurable Goods: Real Product, Inputs, and Productivity Ratios, 1948-66

(1958=100)

Year	Real Gross Product	Persons Engaged	Real Product per Person	Man-Hours	Real Product per Man-Hour	Labor Input	Real Product per Unit of Labor Input	Net Capital Input	Real Product per Unit of Net Capital Input	Total Factor Input	Total Factor Productivity
1948	76.4	102.2	74.8	106.6	71.7	104.4	73.2	77.7	98.3	97.1	78.7
1949	74.8	98.5	75.9	101.3	73.8	99.5	75.2	81.9	91.3	95.3	78.5
1950	82.8	101.1	81.9	105.2	78.7	103.3	80.2	82.2	100.7	97.9	84.6
1951	87.4	103.7	84.3	106.9	81.8	105.3	83.0	84.2	103.8	100.0	87.4
1952	87.4	103.4	84.5	107.2	81.5	105.8	82.6	89.1	98.1	102.0	85.7
1953	91.5	105.4	86.8	107.4	85.2	106.1	86.2	90.4	101.2	102.6	89.2
1954	89.3	102.0	87.5	102.6	87.0	101.9	87.6	90.7	98.5	99.4	89.8
1955	97.8	104.0	94.0	105.8	92.4	105.0	93.1	91.8	106.5	102.0	95.9
1956	101.1	105.0	96.3	106.5	94.9	106.0	95.4	95.6	105.8	103.7	97.5
1957	101.7	103.9	97.9	104.5	97.3	104.5	97.3	98.0	103.8	103.0	98.7
1958	100.0	100.0	100.0	100.0	100.0	100.0	100.0	100.0	100.0	100.0	100.0
1959	109.2	102.7	106.3	104.7	104.3	104.3	104.7	102.5	106.5	103.9	105.1
1960	110.9	103.3	107.4	104.6	106.0	104.6	106.0	104.5	106.1	104.6	106.0
1961	112.3	102.3	109.8	103.7	108.3	103.8	108.2	105.7	106.2	104.2	107.8
1962	119.6	104.0	115.0	106.1	112.7	106.0	112.8	108.0	110.7	106.4	112.4
1963	123.7	104.1	118.8	106.3	116.4	106.2	116.5	111.1	111.3	107.3	115.3
1964	131.9	105.2	125.4	109.3	120.7	109.2	120.8	115.0	114.7	110.5	119.4
1965	140.1	108.0	129.7	111.3	125.9	111.1	126.1	121.9	114.9	113.5	123.4
1966	149.6	111.9	133.7	115.8	129.2	115.7	129.3	133.1	112.4	119.6	125.1

TABLE A-34

Manufacturing, Nondurable Goods:
Output and Productivity Ratios,[a] 1948-66

(1958=100)

Year	Output	Output per Person	Output per Man-Hour	Output per Unit of Labor Input	Output per Unit of Capital Input	Total Factor Productivity
1948	70.9	69.4	66.5	67.9	91.2	73.0
1949	69.7	70.8	68.8	70.1	85.1	73.1
1950	77.5	76.7	73.7	75.0	94.3	79.2
1951	80.1	77.2	74.9	76.1	95.1	80.1
1952	81.6	78.9	76.1	77.1	91.6	80.0
1953	85.3	80.9	79.4	80.4	94.4	83.1
1954	85.3	83.6	83.1	83.7	94.0	85.8
1955	93.8	90.2	88.7	89.3	102.2	92.0
1956	97.9	93.2	91.9	92.4	102.4	94.4
1957	99.6	95.9	95.3	95.3	101.6	96.7
1958	100.0	100.0	100.0	100.0	100.0	100.0
1959	110.0	107.1	105.1	105.5	107.3	105.9
1960	113.1	109.5	108.1	108.1	108.2	108.1
1961	116.7	114.1	112.5	112.4	110.4	112.0
1962	123.8	119.0	116.7	116.8	114.6	116.4
1963	129.5	124.4	121.8	121.9	116.6	120.7
1964	137.0	130.2	125.3	125.5	119.1	124.0
1965	145.5	134.7	130.7	131.0	119.4	128.2
1966	155.9	139.3	134.6	134.7	117.1	130.4

Note: Relates to *Productivity Trends,* Table D-III.

[a] Index numbers of inputs are the same as those shown in Table A-33.

TABLE A-34a

Manufacturing, Nondurable Goods: Gross Capital Input and
Gross Productivity Ratios,[a] in Terms of Real Product and Output, 1948-66

(1958=100)

Year	Gross Capital Input	Real Product per Unit of Gross Capital Input	Gross Factor Input	Real Product per Unit of Gross Factor Input	Output per Unit of Gross Capital Input	Output per Unit of Gross Factor Input
1948	75.7	100.9	95.0	80.4	93.7	74.6
1949	79.5	94.1	93.3	80.2	87.7	74.7
1950	80.6	102.7	96.1	86.2	96.2	80.6
1951	82.3	106.2	98.1	89.1	97.3	81.7
1952	87.3	100.1	100.3	87.1	93.5	81.4
1953	89.8	101.9	101.4	90.2	95.0	84.1
1954	90.9	98.2	98.7	90.5	93.8	86.4
1955	92.1	106.2	101.3	96.5	101.8	92.6
1956	95.5	105.9	103.0	98.2	102.5	95.0
1957	97.8	104.0	102.6	99.1	101.8	97.1
1958	100.0	100.0	100.0	100.0	100.0	100.0
1959	103.3	105.7	104.0	105.0	106.5	105.8
1960	106.5	104.1	105.1	105.5	106.2	107.6
1961	108.8	103.2	105.2	106.7	107.3	110.9
1962	112.1	106.7	107.8	110.9	110.4	114.8
1963	115.7	106.9	108.9	113.6	111.9	118.9
1964	120.2	109.7	112.4	117.3	114.0	121.9
1965	127.4	110.0	115.8	121.0	114.2	125.6
1966	138.0	108.4	122.1	122.5	113.0	127.7

[a] Index numbers of real product and output are the same as those shown in Tables A-33 and A-34.

TABLE A-35

Manufacturing, Durable Goods: Real Product, Inputs, and Productivity Ratios, 1948-66

(1958=100)

Year	Real Gross Product	Persons Engaged	Real Product per Person	Man-Hours	Real Product per Man-Hour	Labor Input	Real Product per Unit of Labor Input	Net Capital Input	Real Product per Unit of Net Capital Input	Total Factor Input	Total Factor Productivity
1948	78.9	94.9	83.1	98.8	79.9	97.8	80.7	65.1	121.2	92.1	85.7
1949	72.5	85.5	84.8	86.4	83.9	85.7	84.6	64.9	111.7	82.9	87.5
1950	87.3	92.2	94.7	95.2	91.7	94.4	92.5	65.5	133.3	89.7	97.3
1951	99.0	103.7	95.5	108.3	91.4	108.2	91.5	72.3	136.9	102.1	97.0
1952	102.6	107.4	95.5	111.6	91.9	111.9	91.7	81.9	125.3	107.6	95.4
1953	113.7	114.8	99.0	119.3	95.3	120.0	94.8	87.1	130.5	115.1	98.8
1954	102.2	104.2	98.1	105.9	96.5	106.1	96.3	87.6	116.7	103.3	98.9
1955	115.9	108.8	106.5	112.7	102.8	113.0	102.6	87.9	131.9	109.2	106.1
1956	114.1	111.8	102.1	114.9	99.3	115.3	99.0	94.6	120.6	112.2	101.7
1957	114.3	111.7	102.3	113.3	100.9	114.2	100.1	99.4	115.0	112.0	102.1
1958	100.0	100.0	100.0	100.0	100.0	100.0	100.0	100.0	100.0	100.0	100.0
1959	114.8	106.0	108.3	108.9	105.4	108.9	105.4	100.6	114.1	107.7	106.6
1960	116.3	106.8	108.9	109.4	106.3	109.3	106.4	102.8	113.1	108.3	107.4
1961	114.5	102.6	111.6	104.8	109.3	104.7	109.4	104.1	110.0	104.6	109.5
1962	129.2	107.4	120.3	111.3	116.1	111.4	116.0	105.1	122.9	110.5	117.2
1963	137.3	108.6	126.4	112.9	121.6	113.1	121.4	111.2	123.5	112.8	121.7
1964	147.0	111.0	132.4	116.9	125.7	117.1	125.5	116.3	126.4	117.0	125.6
1965	164.9	117.5	140.3	124.1	132.9	124.7	132.2	125.0	131.9	124.7	132.2
1966	179.3	127.3	140.8	135.1	132.7	135.9	131.9	140.1	128.0	136.5	131.4

TABLE A-36

Manufacturing, Durable Goods:
Output and Productivity Ratios,[a] 1948-66

(1958=100)

Year	Output	Output per Person	Output per Man-Hour	Output per Unit of Labor Input	Output per Unit of Capital Input	Total Factor Productivity
1948	74.3	78.3	75.2	76.0	114.1	80.7
1949	67.5	78.9	78.1	78.8	104.0	81.4
1950	82.1	89.0	86.2	87.0	125.3	91.5
1951	92.6	89.3	85.5	85.6	128.1	90.7
1952	98.1	91.3	87.9	87.7	119.8	91.2
1953	110.7	96.4	92.8	92.2	127.1	96.2
1954	98.0	94.0	92.5	92.4	111.9	94.9
1955	112.9	103.8	100.2	99.9	128.4	103.4
1956	115.2	103.0	100.3	99.9	121.8	102.7
1957	115.2	103.1	101.7	100.9	115.9	102.9
1958	100.0	100.0	100.0	100.0	100.0	100.0
1959	116.8	110.2	107.3	107.3	116.1	108.4
1960	119.8	112.2	109.5	109.6	116.5	110.6
1961	118.0	115.0	112.6	112.7	113.4	112.8
1962	129.9	120.9	116.7	116.6	123.6	117.6
1963	137.0	126.2	121.3	121.1	123.2	121.5
1964	146.9	132.3	125.7	125.4	126.3	125.6
1965	163.3	139.0	131.6	131.0	130.6	131.0
1966	181.3	142.4	134.2	133.4	129.4	132.8

Note: Relates to *Productivity Trends,* Table D-III.

[a] Index numbers of inputs are the same as those shown in Table A-35.

TABLE A-36a

Manufacturing, Durable Goods: Gross Capital Input and
Gross Productivity Ratios,[a] in Terms of Real Product and Output, 1948-66
(1958=100)

Year	Gross Capital Input	Real Product per Unit of Gross Capital Input	Gross Factor Input	Real Product per Unit of Gross Factor Input	Output per Unit of Gross Capital Input	Output per Unit of Gross Factor Input
1948	66.2	119.2	90.7	87.0	112.2	81.9
1949	67.2	107.9	82.3	88.1	100.4	82.0
1950	68.0	128.4	88.8	98.3	120.7	92.5
1951	73.0	135.6	100.2	98.8	126.8	92.4
1952	81.0	126.7	105.4	97.3	121.1	93.1
1953	85.6	132.8	112.6	101.0	129.3	98.3
1954	86.7	117.9	101.9	100.3	113.0	96.2
1955	87.2	132.9	107.5	107.8	129.5	105.0
1956	93.0	122.7	110.5	103.3	123.9	104.3
1957	97.7	117.0	110.7	103.3	117.9	104.1
1958	100.0	100.0	100.0	100.0	100.0	100.0
1959	102.5	112.0	107.5	106.8	114.0	108.7
1960	106.7	109.0	108.7	107.0	112.3	110.2
1961	110.6	103.5	106.0	108.0	106.7	111.3
1962	113.8	113.5	111.8	115.6	114.1	116.2
1963	117.8	116.6	114.0	120.4	116.3	120.2
1964	123.3	119.2	118.4	124.2	119.1	124.1
1965	132.0	124.9	126.3	130.6	123.7	129.3
1966	146.1	122.7	138.1	129.8	124.1	131.3

[a] Index numbers of real product and output are the same as those shown in Tables A-35 and A-36.

TABLE A-37

Manufacturing, Food and Kindred Products Excluding Beverages:
Output, Inputs, and Productivity Ratios, 1948-66
(1958=100)

Year	Output	Persons Engaged	Output per Person	Man-Hours	Output per Man-Hour	Net Capital Input	Output per Unit of Net Capital Input	Total Factor Input	Total Factor Productivity
1948	74.4	102.0	72.9	106.4	69.9	97.6	76.2	104.6	71.1
1949	75.7	101.3	74.7	103.9	72.9	99.9	75.8	103.1	73.4
1950	78.2	101.8	76.8	104.3	75.0	102.3	76.4	104.0	75.2
1951	80.0	104.4	76.6	107.0	74.8	104.3	76.7	106.5	75.1
1952	82.7	104.4	79.2	107.4	77.0	105.0	78.8	107.0	77.3
1953	83.6	104.6	79.9	106.3	78.6	102.5	81.6	105.6	79.2
1954	86.1	103.4	83.3	105.3	81.8	100.5	85.7	104.5	82.4
1955	90.4	103.4	87.4	105.1	86.0	100.5	90.0	104.3	86.7
1956	95.2	104.4	91.2	106.3	89.6	101.3	94.0	105.4	90.3
1957	96.3	103.0	93.5	104.7	92.0	99.6	96.7	103.8	92.8
1958	100.0	100.0	100.0	100.0	100.0	100.0	100.0	100.0	100.0
1959	104.6	100.6	104.0	102.0	102.5	103.6	101.0	102.3	102.2
1960	107.9	101.7	106.1	103.0	104.8	104.8	103.0	103.3	104.5
1961	111.8	100.9	110.8	102.2	109.4	105.7	105.8	102.8	108.8
1962	115.2	100.3	114.9	101.6	113.4	108.0	106.7	102.7	112.2
1963	118.4	99.4	119.1	100.6	117.7	109.0	108.6	102.1	116.0
1964	121.8	99.4	122.5	102.6	118.7	112.6	108.2	104.4	116.7
1965	124.0	99.6	124.5	100.7	123.1	117.1	105.9	103.6	119.7
1966	128.3	100.3	127.9	101.4	126.5	122.6	104.6	105.1	122.1

Note: Relates to *Productivity Trends*, Table D-IV.

TABLE A-37a

Manufacturing, Food and Kindred Products, Excluding Beverages:
Gross Capital Input and Gross Productivity Ratios,[a] 1948-66

(1958=100)

Year	Gross Capital Input	Output per Unit of Gross Capital Input	Gross Factor Input	Gross Factor Productivity
1948	89.9	82.8	102.3	72.7
1949	92.1	82.2	101.0	75.0
1950	93.9	83.3	101.8	76.8
1951	96.5	82.9	104.5	76.6
1952	98.5	84.0	105.3	78.5
1953	97.4	85.8	104.2	80.2
1954	97.0	88.8	103.3	83.3
1955	97.9	92.3	103.4	87.4
1956	98.6	96.6	104.5	91.1
1957	97.4	98.9	103.0	93.5
1958	100.0	100.0	100.0	100.0
1959	105.0	99.6	102.7	101.9
1960	106.2	101.6	103.8	103.9
1961	106.7	104.8	103.3	108.2
1962	109.5	105.2	103.4	111.4
1963	111.0	106.7	103.1	114.8
1964	114.7	106.2	105.5	115.5
1965	120.2	103.2	105.3	117.8
1966	126.1	101.7	107.3	119.6

[a] Index numbers of output are the same as those shown in Table A-37.

TABLE A-38

Manufacturing, Beverages: Output, Inputs, and Productivity Ratios, 1948-66
(1958=100)

Year	Output	Persons Engaged	Output per Person	Man-Hours	Output per Man-Hour	Net Capital Input	Output per Unit of Net Capital Input	Total Factor Input	Total Factor Productivity
1948	88.2	110.7	79.7	120.0	73.5	94.1	93.7	109.1	80.8
1949	87.3	106.1	82.3	112.9	77.3	100.8	86.6	107.6	81.1
1950	91.8	107.0	85.8	115.3	79.6	104.5	87.8	110.6	83.0
1951	91.8	108.9	84.3	112.6	81.5	111.2	82.6	111.7	82.2
1952	88.8	107.9	82.3	111.0	80.0	117.5	75.6	113.4	78.3
1953	91.3	107.0	85.3	111.0	82.3	114.7	79.6	112.2	81.4
1954	89.5	104.7	85.5	104.3	85.8	109.3	81.9	105.9	84.5
1955	94.2	104.7	90.0	103.8	90.8	104.7	90.0	104.1	90.5
1956	97.4	105.6	92.2	105.7	92.1	99.8	97.6	103.8	93.8
1957	97.9	104.2	94.0	104.3	93.9	96.5	101.5	101.9	96.1
1958	100.0	100.0	100.0	100.0	100.0	100.0	100.0	100.0	100.0
1959	105.4	100.9	104.5	103.1	102.2	105.3	100.1	103.8	101.5
1960	106.5	103.3	103.1	107.2	99.3	106.1	100.4	106.9	99.6
1961	109.7	101.4	108.2	106.0	103.5	108.9	100.7	106.9	102.6
1962	113.5	100.9	112.5	107.2	105.9	109.7	103.5	108.0	105.1
1963	120.1	101.4	118.4	104.3	115.1	108.3	110.9	105.6	113.7
1964	126.8	103.3	122.7	107.6	117.8	111.6	113.6	108.9	116.4
1965	133.1	106.1	125.4	110.3	120.7	118.0	112.8	112.7	118.1
1966	142.6	109.3	130.5	115.3	123.7	127.8	111.6	119.2	119.6

Note: Relates to *Productivity Trends*, Table D-IV.

TABLE A-38a

Manufacturing, Beverages: Gross
Capital Input and Gross Productivity Ratios,[a] 1948-66

(1958=100)

Year	Gross Capital Input	Output per Unit of Gross Capital Input	Gross Factor Input	Gross Factor Productivity
1948	85.8	102.8	103.9	84.9
1949	91.9	95.0	103.3	84.5
1950	93.9	97.8	105.5	87.0
1951	99.9	91.9	107.0	85.8
1952	106.4	83.5	109.4	81.2
1953	105.1	86.9	108.7	84.0
1954	101.7	88.0	103.3	86.6
1955	99.4	94.8	102.1	92.3
1956	97.3	100.1	102.4	95.1
1957	95.7	102.3	100.9	97.0
1958	100.0	100.0	100.0	100.0
1959	106.0	99.4	104.3	101.1
1960	108.2	98.4	107.4	99.2
1961	111.9	98.0	108.3	101.3
1962	113.7	99.8	109.8	103.4
1963	113.6	105.7	108.0	111.2
1964	117.1	108.3	111.4	113.8
1965	124.0	107.3	115.7	115.0
1966	133.5	106.8	122.5	116.4

[a] Index numbers of output are the same as those shown in Table A-38.

TABLE A-39

Manufacturing, Tobacco Products: Output, Inputs, and Productivity Ratios, 1948-66
(1958=100)

Year	Output	Persons Engaged	Output per Person	Man-Hours	Output per Man-Hour	Net Capital Input	Output per Unit of Net Capital Input	Total Factor Input	Total Factor Productivity
1948	85.6	107.5	79.6	106.1	80.7	90.7	94.4	97.4	87.9
1949	84.9	109.7	77.4	106.7	79.6	91.2	93.1	98.0	86.6
1950	86.1	105.4	81.7	103.4	83.3	90.5	95.1	96.1	89.6
1951	91.2	114.0	80.0	111.7	81.6	92.1	99.0	100.6	90.7
1952	94.2	114.0	82.6	112.8	83.5	95.2	98.9	102.9	91.5
1953	92.2	114.0	80.9	112.8	81.7	91.0	101.3	100.5	91.7
1954	88.3	111.8	79.0	108.9	81.1	92.7	95.3	99.8	88.5
1955	89.8	109.7	81.9	106.7	84.2	92.5	97.1	98.7	91.0
1956	91.5	106.5	85.9	101.7	90.0	93.5	97.9	97.1	94.2
1957	94.7	102.2	92.7	99.4	95.3	94.7	100.0	96.8	97.8
1958	100.0	100.0	100.0	100.0	100.0	100.0	100.0	100.0	100.0
1959	105.0	100.0	105.0	101.1	103.9	108.4	96.9	105.3	99.7
1960	107.1	100.0	107.1	101.1	105.9	112.8	94.9	107.7	99.4
1961	110.6	96.8	114.3	98.3	112.5	119.0	92.9	109.9	100.6
1962	111.8	96.8	115.5	100.0	111.8	123.8	90.3	113.4	98.6
1963	115.0	95.7	120.2	95.5	120.4	121.9	94.3	110.3	104.3
1964	120.6	97.8	123.3	100.0	120.6	118.4	101.9	110.3	109.3
1965	120.1	94.6	127.0	92.7	129.6	118.1	101.7	107.0	112.2
1966	119.8	91.4	131.1	91.6	130.8	128.4	93.3	112.3	106.7

Note: Relates to *Productivity Trends*, Table D-IV.

TABLE A-39a

Manufacturing, Tobacco Products: Gross Capital Input
and Gross Productivity Ratios,[a] 1948-66

(1958=100)

Year	Gross Capital Input	Output per Unit of Gross Capital Input	Gross Factor Input	Gross Factor Productivity
1948	90.6	94.5	97.2	88.1
1949	91.2	93.1	97.8	86.8
1950	89.8	95.9	95.6	90.1
1951	90.4	100.9	99.4	91.8
1952	93.8	100.4	101.8	92.5
1953	90.3	102.1	99.8	92.4
1954	92.2	95.8	99.3	88.9
1955	92.4	97.2	98.5	91.2
1956	93.7	97.7	97.1	94.2
1957	95.0	99.7	96.9	97.7
1958	100.0	100.0	100.0	100.0
1959	108.2	97.0	105.2	99.8
1960	113.0	94.8	108.0	99.2
1961	118.9	93.0	110.2	100.4
1962	123.6	90.5	113.6	98.4
1963	123.2	93.3	111.5	103.1
1964	120.7	99.9	111.9	107.8
1965	121.3	99.0	109.2	110.0
1966	132.5	90.4	115.2	104.0

[a] Index numbers of output are the same as those shown in Table A-39.

TABLE A-40

Manufacturing, Textile Mill Products: Output, Inputs, and Productivity Ratios, 1948-66
(1958=100)

Year	Output	Persons Engaged	Output per Person	Man-Hours	Output per Man-Hour	Net Capital Input	Output per Unit of Net Capital Input	Total Factor Input	Total Factor Productivity
1948	93.3	144.1	64.7	148.8	62.7	98.0	95.2	138.3	67.5
1949	86.3	129.3	66.7	129.9	66.4	104.4	82.7	126.1	68.4
1950	98.3	136.2	72.2	141.8	69.3	104.4	94.2	134.9	72.9
1951	97.2	134.3	72.4	136.2	71.4	107.7	90.3	131.7	73.8
1952	96.4	126.2	76.4	128.2	75.2	110.3	87.4	126.6	76.1
1953	98.4	125.5	78.4	127.6	77.1	104.4	94.3	124.4	79.1
1954	92.0	113.6	81.0	112.8	81.6	103.7	88.7	115.5	79.7
1955	102.5	114.8	89.3	117.9	86.9	105.6	97.1	116.2	88.2
1956	104.8	112.5	93.2	114.8	91.3	108.6	96.5	113.9	92.0
1957	101.5	106.8	95.0	107.3	94.6	104.4	97.2	106.9	94.9
1958	100.0	100.0	100.0	100.0	100.0	100.0	100.0	100.0	100.0
1959	116.2	102.9	112.9	107.8	107.8	91.3	127.3	105.5	110.1
1960	112.1	100.4	111.7	102.7	109.2	90.6	123.7	101.0	111.0
1961	114.7	97.3	117.9	99.8	114.9	88.0	130.3	98.2	116.8
1962	123.9	98.4	125.9	102.8	120.5	85.4	145.1	100.4	123.4
1963	126.1	97.0	130.0	101.4	124.4	86.2	146.3	99.3	127.0
1964	132.6	97.2	136.4	104.5	126.9	88.4	150.0	102.3	129.6
1965	145.5	100.8	144.3	109.1	133.4	91.6	158.8	106.7	136.4
1966	153.7	104.1	147.6	113.9	134.9	99.2	154.9	111.9	137.4

Note: Relates to *Productivity Trends*, Table D-IV.

TABLE A-40a

Manufacturing, Textile Mill Products: Gross
Capital Input and Gross Productivity Ratios,[a] 1948-66

(1958=100)

Year	Gross Capital Input	Output per Unit of Gross Capital Input	Gross Factor Input	Gross Factor Productivity
1948	106.7	87.4	137.6	67.8
1949	113.1	76.3	126.1	68.4
1950	113.6	86.5	134.8	72.9
1951	115.5	84.2	131.4	74.0
1952	119.1	80.9	126.7	76.1
1953	115.0	85.6	125.1	78.7
1954	115.9	79.4	113.4	81.1
1955	117.6	87.2	117.8	87.0
1956	119.9	87.4	115.8	90.5
1957	116.1	87.4	109.1	93.0
1958	100.0	100.0	100.0	100.0
1959	85.1	136.5	103.3	112.5
1960	84.8	132.2	99.1	113.1
1961	82.8	138.5	96.4	119.0
1962	81.0	153.0	98.5	125.8
1963	82.3	153.2	97.6	129.2
1964	85.0	156.0	100.6	131.8
1965	87.9	165.5	104.9	138.7
1966	93.3	164.7	109.8	140.0

[a] Index numbers of output are the same as those shown in Table A-40.

TABLE A-41

Manufacturing, Apparel and Related Products: Output, Inputs, and Productivity Ratios, 1948-66
(1958=100)

Year	Output	Persons Engaged	Output per Person	Man-Hours	Output per Man-Hour	Net Capital Input	Output per Unit of Net Capital Input	Total Factor Input	Total Factor Productivity
1948	85.2	104.2	81.8	107.7	79.1	89.2	95.5	105.6	80.7
1949	84.5	102.4	82.5	103.4	81.7	94.2	89.7	102.4	82.5
1950	90.9	104.5	87.0	106.1	85.7	105.5	86.2	106.1	85.7
1951	89.2	105.1	84.9	107.3	83.1	111.5	80.0	107.9	82.7
1952	93.8	106.4	88.2	110.1	85.2	110.3	85.0	110.2	85.1
1953	95.5	108.6	87.9	110.1	86.7	108.5	88.0	110.0	86.8
1954	92.3	103.5	89.2	103.2	89.4	106.3	86.8	103.5	89.2
1955	100.1	106.4	94.1	107.1	93.5	111.3	89.9	107.5	93.1
1956	102.9	106.7	96.4	107.4	95.8	113.1	91.0	107.9	95.4
1957	102.6	104.7	98.0	104.0	98.7	102.8	99.8	103.9	98.7
1958	100.0	100.0	100.0	100.0	100.0	100.0	100.0	100.0	100.0
1959	112.0	105.1	106.6	107.8	103.9	110.8	101.1	108.1	103.6
1960	114.2	106.2	107.5	105.7	108.0	115.3	99.0	106.6	107.1
1961	112.8	104.4	108.0	104.0	108.5	113.7	99.2	104.9	107.5
1962	117.9	108.6	108.6	109.8	107.4	123.3	95.6	111.0	106.2
1963	122.7	109.9	111.6	111.8	109.7	130.3	94.2	113.5	108.1
1964	131.0	111.6	117.4	115.1	113.8	138.2	94.8	117.2	111.8
1965	141.7	115.8	122.4	119.8	118.3	157.3	90.1	123.2	115.0
1966	146.6	120.2	122.0	124.5	117.8	180.9	81.0	129.6	113.1

Note: Relates to *Productivity Trends*, Table D-IV.

TABLE A-41a

Manufacturing, Apparel and Related Products:
Gross Capital Input and Gross Productivity Ratios,[a] 1948-66

(1958=100)

Year	Gross Capital Input	Output per Unit of Gross Capital Input	Gross Factor Input	Gross Factor Productivity
1948	81.0	105.2	104.2	81.8
1949	86.5	97.7	101.3	83.4
1950	96.2	94.5	105.0	86.6
1951	102.2	87.3	106.9	83.4
1952	102.5	91.5	109.3	85.8
1953	103.4	92.4	109.4	87.3
1954	103.8	88.9	103.3	89.4
1955	108.6	92.2	107.3	93.3
1956	110.3	93.3	107.7	95.5
1957	102.0	100.6	103.8	98.8
1958	100.0	100.0	100.0	100.0
1959	108.9	102.8	107.9	103.8
1960	111.9	102.1	106.4	107.3
1961	110.8	101.8	104.7	107.7
1962	120.0	98.2	110.9	106.3
1963	125.4	97.8	113.3	108.3
1964	132.6	98.8	117.0	112.0
1965	149.4	94.8	123.1	115.1
1966	169.9	86.3	129.5	113.2

[a] Index numbers of output are the same as those shown in Table A-41.

TABLE A-42

Manufacturing, Lumber and Wood Products except Furniture:
Output, Inputs, and Productivity Ratios, 1948-66
(1958=100)

Year	Output	Persons Engaged	Output per Person	Man-Hours	Output per Man-Hour	Net Capital Input	Output per Unit of Net Capital Input	Total Factor Input	Total Factor Productivity
1948	90.5	133.6	67.7	141.4	64.0	105.4	85.9	135.6	66.7
1949	79.9	117.7	67.9	111.7	71.5	106.4	75.1	111.2	71.9
1950	97.0	127.3	76.2	123.2	78.7	105.7	91.8	120.6	80.4
1951	96.8	136.4	71.0	131.8	73.4	113.3	85.4	129.0	75.0
1952	95.5	129.3	73.9	125.9	75.9	120.5	79.3	125.4	76.2
1953	101.0	125.0	80.8	123.6	81.7	118.7	85.1	123.2	82.0
1954	98.2	114.3	85.9	114.5	85.8	103.8	94.6	113.5	86.5
1955	109.6	119.7	91.6	120.7	90.8	93.1	117.7	118.2	92.7
1956	107.1	117.9	90.8	116.7	91.8	100.6	106.5	115.3	92.9
1957	98.9	106.6	92.8	104.0	95.1	103.0	96.0	103.9	95.2
1958	100.0	100.0	100.0	100.0	100.0	100.0	100.0	100.0	100.0
1959	115.4	105.5	109.4	107.7	107.1	99.5	116.0	107.0	107.9
1960	110.5	102.1	108.2	104.2	106.0	103.2	107.1	104.1	106.1
1961	111.4	95.4	116.8	97.6	114.1	106.5	104.6	98.4	113.2
1962	118.6	96.2	123.3	99.9	118.7	110.6	107.2	100.9	117.5
1963	123.7	95.9	129.0	99.4	124.4	112.9	109.6	100.6	123.0
1964	127.9	98.2	130.2	103.9	123.1	118.9	107.6	105.2	121.6
1965	133.4	99.4	134.2	104.9	127.2	136.4	97.8	107.7	123.9
1966	135.6	100.6	134.8	106.1	127.8	149.0	91.0	110.0	123.3

Note: Relates to *Productivity Trends*, Table D-IV.

TABLE A-42a

Manufacturing, Lumber and Wood Products except Furniture:
Gross Capital Input and Gross Productivity Ratios,[a] 1948-66

(1958=100)

Year	Gross Capital Input	Output per Unit of Gross Capital Input	Gross Factor Input	Gross Factor Productivity
1948	100.3	90.2	132.5	68.3
1949	101.4	78.8	110.0	72.6
1950	99.3	97.7	118.3	82.0
1951	105.9	91.4	126.5	76.5
1952	111.6	85.6	123.4	77.4
1953	108.9	92.7	121.0	83.5
1954	99.3	98.9	111.9	87.8
1955	92.5	118.5	115.8	94.6
1956	98.5	108.7	113.5	94.4
1957	100.9	98.0	103.5	95.6
1958	100.0	100.0	100.0	100.0
1959	101.2	114.0	106.6	108.3
1960	105.6	104.6	104.4	105.8
1961	109.5	101.7	99.7	111.7
1962	113.8	104.2	102.3	115.9
1963	116.4	106.3	102.4	120.8
1964	122.8	104.2	107.2	119.3
1965	139.4	95.7	110.9	120.3
1966	151.5	89.5	114.0	118.9

[a] Index numbers of output are the same as those shown in Table A-42.

TABLE A-43

Manufacturing, Furniture and Fixtures: Output, Inputs, and Productivity Ratios, 1948-66
(1958=100)

Year	Output	Persons Engaged	Output per Person	Man-Hours	Output per Man-Hour	Net Capital Input	Output per Unit of Net Capital Input	Total Factor Input	Total Factor Productivity
1948	75.0	96.4	77.8	102.0	73.5	102.6	73.1	102.5	73.2
1949	69.4	89.9	77.2	93.3	74.4	97.3	71.3	94.1	73.8
1950	84.7	102.3	82.8	108.6	78.0	98.8	85.7	108.1	78.4
1951	80.0	100.8	79.4	104.2	76.8	94.1	85.0	103.7	77.1
1952	82.2	101.6	80.9	106.9	76.9	100.4	81.9	106.7	77.0
1953	86.0	103.6	83.0	107.0	80.4	95.4	90.1	106.3	80.9
1954	89.6	96.4	92.9	97.6	91.8	95.3	94.0	97.5	91.9
1955	102.0	102.8	99.2	106.2	96.0	100.7	101.3	105.9	96.3
1956	105.5	105.4	100.1	108.4	97.3	105.8	99.7	108.2	97.5
1957	103.9	104.9	99.0	106.2	97.8	102.6	101.3	106.0	98.0
1958	100.0	100.0	100.0	100.0	100.0	100.0	100.0	100.0	100.0
1959	116.3	105.2	110.6	108.7	107.0	104.5	111.3	108.4	107.3
1960	117.8	104.9	112.3	108.8	108.3	109.2	107.9	108.8	108.3
1961	114.2	100.3	113.9	102.9	111.0	108.1	105.6	103.2	110.7
1962	121.8	105.2	115.8	110.0	110.7	107.3	113.5	109.8	110.9
1963	124.0	106.5	116.4	110.1	112.6	110.6	112.1	110.1	112.6
1964	133.6	110.9	120.5	115.4	115.8	112.2	119.1	115.2	116.0
1965	146.6	117.1	125.2	121.1	121.1	118.9	123.3	121.0	121.2
1966	160.1	125.4	127.7	129.4	123.7	134.8	118.8	129.7	123.4

Note: Relates to *Productivity Trends*, Table D-IV.

TABLE A-43a

Manufacturing, Furniture and Fixtures:
Gross Capital Input and Gross Productivity Ratios,[a] 1948-66

(1958=100)

Year	Gross Capital Input	Output per Unit of Gross Capital Input	Gross Factor Input	Gross Factor Productivity
1948	102.7	73.0	102.5	73.2
1949	98.4	70.5	94.3	73.6
1950	97.5	86.9	107.6	78.7
1951	98.8	81.0	103.9	77.0
1952	98.2	83.7	106.2	77.4
1953	93.5	92.0	105.7	81.4
1954	94.0	95.3	97.2	92.2
1955	98.3	103.8	105.4	96.8
1956	102.0	103.4	107.8	97.9
1957	100.8	103.1	105.7	98.3
1958	100.0	100.0	100.0	100.0
1959	104.7	111.1	108.3	107.4
1960	109.3	107.8	108.8	108.3
1961	109.2	104.6	103.5	110.3
1962	109.4	111.3	109.9	110.8
1963	112.7	110.0	110.4	112.3
1964	113.7	117.5	115.2	116.0
1965	119.6	122.6	121.0	121.2
1966	133.7	119.7	129.8	123.3

[a] Index numbers of output are the same as those shown in Table A-43.

TABLE A-44

Manufacturing, Paper and Allied Products: Output, Inputs, and Productivity Ratios, 1948-66
(1958=100)

Year	Output	Persons Engaged	Output per Person	Man-Hours	Output per Man-Hour	Net Capital Input	Output per Unit of Net Capital Input	Total Factor Input	Total Factor Productivity
1948	66.8	84.3	79.2	88.0	75.9	62.1	107.6	80.7	82.8
1949	63.8	81.2	78.6	82.9	77.0	65.5	97.4	78.8	81.0
1950	76.9	86.9	88.5	91.0	84.5	66.6	115.5	84.4	91.1
1951	81.4	91.4	89.1	95.0	85.7	70.6	115.3	88.5	92.0
1952	77.6	90.3	85.9	93.6	82.9	76.4	101.6	89.8	86.4
1953	84.5	95.5	88.5	98.6	85.7	78.2	108.1	93.8	90.1
1954	85.4	95.7	89.2	97.0	88.0	80.3	106.4	93.0	91.8
1955	96.0	98.7	97.3	101.6	94.5	83.1	115.5	97.2	98.8
1956	100.3	102.1	98.2	104.5	96.0	89.1	112.6	100.9	99.4
1957	99.3	101.6	97.7	101.8	97.5	95.9	103.5	100.3	99.0
1958	100.0	100.0	100.0	100.0	100.0	100.0	100.0	100.0	100.0
1959	110.2	104.3	105.7	106.7	103.3	99.7	110.5	105.0	105.0
1960	111.7	106.1	105.3	106.6	104.8	101.7	109.8	105.4	106.0
1961	118.5	107.3	110.4	108.3	109.4	105.3	112.5	107.6	110.1
1962	125.2	110.2	113.6	111.7	112.1	106.3	117.8	110.4	113.4
1963	131.4	111.4	118.0	113.1	116.2	107.1	122.7	111.7	117.6
1964	140.1	112.0	125.1	115.1	121.7	109.5	127.9	113.8	123.1
1965	149.5	114.7	130.3	116.8	128.0	114.0	131.1	116.1	128.8
1966	159.8	119.5	133.7	122.7	130.2	124.8	128.0	123.2	129.7

Note: Relates to *Productivity Trends*, Table D-IV.

TABLE A-44a

Manufacturing, Paper and Allied Products:
Gross Capital Input and Gross Productivity Ratios,[a] 1948-66

(1958=100)

Year	Gross Capital Input	Output per Unit of Gross Capital Input	Gross Factor Input	Gross Factor Productivity
1948	61.1	109.3	78.5	85.1
1949	63.8	100.0	76.6	83.3
1950	65.8	116.9	82.3	93.4
1951	68.1	119.5	85.7	95.0
1952	74.1	104.7	87.4	88.8
1953	76.4	110.6	91.4	92.5
1954	79.5	107.4	91.3	93.5
1955	82.9	115.8	95.5	100.5
1956	88.5	113.3	99.3	101.0
1957	95.0	104.5	99.6	99.7
1958	100.0	100.0	100.0	100.0
1959	101.7	108.4	105.1	104.9
1960	105.4	106.0	106.2	105.2
1961	110.7	107.0	109.1	108.6
1962	114.5	109.3	112.6	111.2
1963	116.7	112.6	114.3	115.0
1964	120.5	116.3	116.9	119.8
1965	125.6	119.0	119.7	124.9
1966	134.9	118.5	126.7	126.1

[a] Index numbers of output are the same as those shown in Table A-44.

TABLE A-45

Manufacturing, Printing and Publishing: Output, Inputs, and Productivity Ratios, 1948-66
(1958=100)

Year	Output	Persons Engaged	Output Per Person	Man-Hours	Output per Man-Hour	Net Capital Input	Output per Unit of Net Capital Input	Total Factor Input	Total Factor Productivity
1948	71.7	85.5	83.9	95.5	75.1	98.7	72.6	95.7	74.9
1949	73.6	85.5	86.1	97.9	75.2	101.2	72.7	98.1	75.0
1950	77.0	86.6	88.9	99.4	77.5	103.4	74.5	99.7	77.2
1951	78.5	89.3	87.9	99.3	79.1	104.4	75.2	99.7	78.7
1952	78.3	91.0	86.0	102.6	76.3	105.4	74.3	102.8	76.2
1953	81.9	93.7	87.4	97.1	84.3	103.9	78.8	97.7	83.8
1954	85.2	94.5	90.2	96.7	88.1	97.3	87.6	96.8	88.0
1955	91.7	96.8	94.7	100.0	91.7	92.4	99.2	99.4	92.3
1956	97.8	99.7	98.1	102.4	95.5	96.3	101.6	101.9	96.0
1957	100.8	101.1	99.7	102.8	98.1	98.7	102.1	102.5	98.3
1958	100.0	100.0	100.0	100.0	100.0	100.0	100.0	100.0	100.0
1959	107.9	101.6	106.2	103.0	104.8	102.1	105.7	102.9	104.9
1960	114.2	104.3	109.5	107.1	106.6	105.8	107.9	107.0	106.7
1961	116.1	105.1	110.5	107.5	108.0	108.3	107.2	107.6	108.0
1962	119.7	105.9	113.0	107.9	110.9	110.6	108.2	108.1	110.7
1963	121.9	106.3	114.7	109.4	111.4	117.2	104.0	110.1	110.7
1964	129.1	108.9	118.5	114.1	113.1	124.8	103.4	115.0	112.3
1965	136.5	111.7	122.2	116.3	117.4	135.3	100.9	117.9	115.8
1966	148.8	116.4	127.8	121.7	122.3	148.5	100.2	124.0	120.0

Note: Relates to *Productivity Trends*, Table D-IV.

TABLE A-45a

Manufacturing, Printing and Publishing:
Gross Capital Input and Gross Productivity Ratios,[a] 1948-66

(1958=100)

Year	Gross Capital Input	Output per Unit of Gross Capital Input	Gross Factor Input	Gross Factor Productivity
1948	88.7	80.8	94.6	75.8
1949	90.1	81.7	96.9	76.0
1950	91.5	84.2	98.3	78.3
1951	93.0	84.4	98.5	79.7
1952	94.3	83.0	101.5	77.1
1953	94.6	86.6	96.8	84.6
1954	92.7	91.9	96.2	88.6
1955	90.8	101.0	98.8	92.8
1956	94.7	103.3	101.4	96.4
1957	97.3	103.6	102.1	98.7
1958	100.0	100.0	100.0	100.0
1959	102.8	105.0	103.0	104.8
1960	106.5	107.2	107.0	106.7
1961	110.0	105.5	107.8	107.7
1962	113.8	105.2	108.7	110.1
1963	120.1	101.5	110.8	110.0
1964	129.5	99.7	116.1	111.2
1965	140.3	97.3	119.4	114.3
1966	152.9	97.3	125.8	118.3

[a] Index numbers of output are the same as those shown in Table A-45.

TABLE A-46

Manufacturing, Chemicals and Allied Products: Output, Inputs, and Productivity Ratios, 1948-66
(1958=100)

Year	Output	Persons Engaged	Output per Person	Man-Hours	Output per Man-Hour	Net Capital Input	Output per Unit of Net Capital Input	Total Factor Input	Total Factor Productivity
1948	48.5	81.6	59.4	85.3	56.9	58.2	83.3	74.6	65.0
1949	47.8	77.7	61.5	81.2	58.9	63.2	75.6	74.7	64.0
1950	59.8	80.3	74.5	83.8	71.4	66.1	90.5	77.4	77.3
1951	67.8	89.6	75.7	92.5	73.3	69.6	97.4	84.0	80.7
1952	70.8	92.5	76.5	95.6	74.1	77.9	90.9	89.5	79.1
1953	76.6	97.4	78.6	99.1	77.3	82.6	92.7	93.7	81.8
1954	76.4	95.9	79.7	97.0	78.8	83.7	91.3	92.6	82.5
1955	88.5	98.0	90.3	98.9	89.5	85.8	103.1	94.6	93.6
1956	94.6	102.0	92.7	102.8	92.0	90.9	104.1	98.9	95.7
1957	99.4	103.8	95.8	104.3	95.3	96.4	103.1	101.7	97.7
1958	100.0	100.0	100.0	100.0	100.0	100.0	100.0	100.0	100.0
1959	114.5	102.4	111.8	102.9	111.3	101.9	112.4	102.6	111.6
1960	121.4	104.5	116.2	104.8	115.8	105.2	115.4	104.9	115.7
1961	128.3	104.9	122.3	105.9	121.2	107.5	119.3	106.4	120.6
1962	141.4	106.9	132.3	108.1	130.8	110.5	128.0	108.9	129.8
1963	154.2	108.8	141.7	110.3	139.8	116.4	132.5	112.3	137.3
1964	165.6	110.3	150.1	113.1	146.4	121.1	136.7	115.7	143.1
1965	179.9	114.3	157.4	115.9	155.2	131.2	137.1	120.8	148.9
1966	200.5	121.2	165.4	123.6	162.2	146.7	136.7	131.2	152.8

Note: Relates to *Productivity Trends*, Table D-IV.

TABLE A-46a

Manufacturing, Chemicals and Allied Products:
Gross Capital Input and Gross Productivity Ratios,[a] 1948-66

(1958=100)

Year	Gross Capital Input	Output per Unit of Gross Capital Input	Gross Factor Input	Gross Factor Productivity
1948	55.3	87.7	71.4	67.9
1949	60.2	79.4	71.9	66.5
1950	63.8	93.7	75.0	79.7
1951	66.5	102.0	80.8	83.9
1952	73.6	96.2	86.1	82.2
1953	79.6	96.2	91.0	84.2
1954	82.1	93.1	90.8	84.1
1955	85.1	104.0	93.2	95.0
1956	90.7	104.3	97.8	96.7
1957	95.8	103.8	100.8	98.6
1958	100.0	100.0	100.0	100.0
1959	104.4	109.7	103.5	110.6
1960	109.1	111.3	106.6	113.9
1961	112.5	114.0	108.6	118.1
1962	116.8	121.1	111.7	126.6
1963	120.9	127.5	114.7	134.4
1964	126.0	131.4	118.4	139.9
1965	135.9	132.4	124.2	144.8
1966	150.3	133.4	134.6	149.0

[a] Index numbers of output are the same as those shown in Table A-46.

TABLE A-47

Manufacturing, Petroleum Refining and Related Industries: Output, Inputs,
and Productivity Ratios, 1948-66
(1958=100)

Year	Output	Persons Engaged	Output per Person	Man-Hours	Output per Man-Hour	Net Capital Input	Output per Unit of Net Capital Input	Total Factor Input	Total Factor Productivity
1948	67.1	98.2	68.3	105.0	63.9	71.5	93.8	86.1	77.9
1949	65.0	96.0	67.7	98.9	65.7	76.0	85.5	88.1	73.8
1950	71.6	96.9	73.9	101.1	70.8	72.4	98.9	85.8	83.4
1951	80.1	102.2	78.4	106.8	75.0	71.5	112.0	86.7	92.4
1952	82.1	104.4	78.6	106.1	77.4	75.8	108.3	89.9	91.3
1953	86.9	106.6	81.5	108.8	79.9	79.9	108.8	93.9	92.5
1954	86.2	105.3	81.9	106.8	80.7	83.8	102.9	94.9	90.8
1955	93.6	105.3	88.9	107.4	87.2	85.6	109.3	96.1	97.4
1956	99.3	104.8	94.8	106.5	93.2	92.6	107.2	99.3	100.0
1957	100.2	105.3	95.2	106.8	93.8	98.1	102.1	102.3	97.9
1958	100.0	100.0	100.0	100.0	100.0	100.0	100.0	100.0	100.0
1959	107.6	95.6	112.6	97.1	110.8	103.1	104.4	100.2	107.4
1960	111.3	92.5	120.3	95.0	117.2	102.8	108.3	99.0	112.4
1961	114.5	89.0	128.7	91.0	125.8	100.6	113.8	96.0	119.3
1962	120.0	86.3	139.0	88.7	135.3	102.2	117.4	95.7	125.4
1963	125.5	84.6	148.3	85.6	146.6	104.9	119.6	95.6	131.3
1964	129.7	82.4	157.4	85.4	151.9	109.2	118.8	97.7	132.8
1965	132.4	81.1	163.3	82.2	161.1	114.6	115.5	99.0	133.7
1966	137.5	81.1	169.5	82.7	166.3	123.2	111.6	103.6	132.7

Note: Relates to *Productivity Trends*, Table D-IV.

TABLE A-47a

Manufacturing, Petroleum Refining and Related Industries:
Gross Capital Input and Gross Productivity Ratios,[a] 1948-66

(1958=100)

Year	Gross Capital Input	Output per Unit of Gross Capital Input	Gross Factor Input	Gross Factor Productivity
1948	79.4	84.5	89.2	75.2
1949	83.3	78.0	90.4	71.9
1950	81.2	88.2	89.5	80.0
1951	79.5	100.8	89.8	89.2
1952	84.5	97.2	93.3	88.0
1953	89.6	97.0	98.0	88.7
1954	91.7	94.0	98.3	87.7
1955	89.7	104.3	97.4	96.1
1956	93.7	106.0	99.3	100.0
1957	97.7	102.6	101.7	98.5
1958	100.0	100.0	100.0	100.0
1959	104.1	103.4	101.1	106.4
1960	107.4	103.6	102.0	109.1
1961	108.3	105.7	100.8	113.6
1962	111.0	108.1	101.3	118.5
1963	116.8	107.4	103.2	121.6
1964	121.6	106.7	105.9	122.5
1965	127.8	103.6	108.0	122.6
1966	137.2	100.2	113.5	121.1

[a] Index numbers of output are the same as those shown in Table A-47.

TABLE A-48

Manufacturing, Rubber and Miscellaneous Plastics Products: Output,
Inputs, and Productivity Ratios, 1948-66
(1958=100)

Year	Output	Persons Engaged	Output per Person	Man-Hours	Output per Man-Hour	Net Capital Input	Output per Unit of Net Capital Input	Total Factor Input	Total Factor Productivity
1948	60.6	89.3	67.9	88.4	68.6	79.5	76.2	87.3	69.4
1949	57.2	82.1	69.7	79.4	72.0	77.4	73.9	79.9	71.6
1950	74.1	89.0	83.3	90.7	81.7	71.0	104.4	87.0	85.2
1951	75.7	96.3	78.6	98.4	76.9	72.0	105.1	93.1	81.3
1952	77.8	97.1	80.1	98.2	79.2	81.7	95.2	95.4	81.6
1953	83.4	103.7	80.4	104.4	79.9	84.6	98.6	100.8	82.7
1954	81.8	95.1	86.0	93.2	87.8	84.7	96.6	91.7	89.2
1955	101.9	104.3	97.7	109.0	93.5	88.4	115.3	105.3	96.8
1956	99.9	106.6	93.7	106.6	93.7	93.2	107.2	104.2	95.9
1957	104.8	106.9	98.0	106.9	98.0	97.1	107.9	105.1	99.7
1958	100.0	100.0	100.0	100.0	100.0	100.0	100.0	100.0	100.0
1959	120.6	108.9	110.7	111.0	108.6	103.1	117.0	109.6	110.0
1960	121.4	109.5	110.9	111.2	109.2	108.6	111.8	110.7	109.7
1961	122.8	107.2	114.6	109.4	112.2	112.8	108.9	110.0	111.6
1962	143.9	118.2	121.7	122.2	117.8	119.1	120.8	121.6	118.3
1963	154.9	120.7	128.3	123.2	125.7	125.2	123.7	123.6	125.3
1964	172.9	125.1	138.2	130.1	132.9	130.6	132.4	130.2	132.8
1965	190.1	135.2	140.6	139.6	136.2	139.7	136.1	139.6	136.2
1966	212.3	147.3	144.1	152.1	139.6	154.9	137.1	152.6	139.1

Note: Relates to *Productivity Trends*, Table D-IV.

TABLE A-48a

Manufacturing, Rubber and Miscellaneous Plastics Products:
Gross Capital Input and Gross Productivity Ratios,[a] 1948-66

(1958=100)

Year	Gross Capital Input	Output per Unit of Gross Capital Input	Gross Factor Input	Gross Factor Productivity
1948	68.9	88.0	83.6	72.5
1949	68.8	83.1	77.3	74.0
1950	65.6	113.0	84.1	88.1
1951	67.8	111.7	90.3	83.8
1952	75.7	102.8	92.5	84.1
1953	80.0	104.2	98.3	84.8
1954	81.2	100.7	90.2	90.7
1955	85.5	119.2	103.1	98.8
1956	90.6	110.3	102.6	97.4
1957	94.6	110.8	103.8	101.0
1958	100.0	100.0	100.0	100.0
1959	104.9	115.0	109.5	110.1
1960	109.1	111.3	110.7	109.7
1961	113.0	108.7	110.3	111.3
1962	119.0	120.9	121.4	118.5
1963	124.6	124.3	123.5	125.4
1964	129.8	133.2	130.0	133.0
1965	138.0	137.8	139.2	136.6
1966	150.9	140.7	151.8	139.9

[a] Index numbers of output are the same as those shown in Table A-48.

TABLE A-49

Manufacturing, Leather and Leather Products: Output, Inputs, and Productivity Ratios, 1948-66
(1958=100)

Year	Output	Persons Engaged	Output per Person	Man-Hours	Output per Man-Hour	Net Capital Input	Output per Unit of Net Capital Input	Total Factor Input	Total Factor Productivity
1948	91.9	114.2	80.5	115.6	79.5	112.3	81.8	115.4	79.6
1949	87.5	110.1	79.5	109.0	80.3	114.8	76.2	110.2	79.4
1950	94.6	111.5	84.8	112.6	84.0	113.9	83.1	113.1	83.6
1951	88.7	107.3	82.7	106.6	83.2	108.2	82.0	107.1	82.8
1952	94.4	108.1	87.3	110.7	85.3	112.3	84.1	111.2	84.9
1953	94.7	108.7	87.1	110.9	85.4	107.9	87.8	110.7	85.5
1954	93.8	104.2	90.0	104.3	89.9	105.0	89.3	104.4	89.8
1955	102.0	107.3	95.1	109.5	93.2	103.7	98.4	109.1	93.5
1956	103.9	106.4	97.7	107.7	96.5	104.5	99.4	107.5	96.7
1957	103.3	104.7	98.7	104.9	98.5	102.0	101.3	104.7	98.7
1958	100.0	100.0	100.0	100.0	100.0	100.0	100.0	100.0	100.0
1959	108.7	104.2	104.3	106.1	102.5	100.1	108.6	105.6	102.9
1960	103.1	101.1	102.0	101.7	101.4	100.5	102.6	101.6	101.5
1961	103.3	100.0	103.3	99.8	103.5	97.7	105.7	99.6	103.7
1962	105.3	100.3	105.0	101.8	103.4	91.4	115.2	101.0	104.3
1963	102.4	97.5	105.0	99.2	103.2	104.3	98.2	99.6	102.8
1964	105.3	97.5	108.0	101.4	103.8	114.3	92.1	102.4	102.8
1965	111.0	99.2	111.9	102.5	108.3	112.0	99.1	103.2	107.6
1966	114.6	101.7	112.7	106.1	108.0	118.1	97.0	107.0	107.1

Note: Relates to *Productivity Trends*, Table D-IV.

TABLE A-49a

Manufacturing, Leather and Leather Products:
Gross Capital Input and Gross Productivity Ratios,[a] 1948-66

(1958=100)

Year	Gross Capital Input	Output per Unit of Gross Capital Input	Gross Factor Input	Gross Factor Productivity
1948	107.5	85.5	114.4	80.3
1949	111.4	78.5	109.6	79.8
1950	111.0	85.2	112.5	84.1
1951	106.1	83.6	106.7	83.1
1952	109.9	85.9	110.8	85.2
1953	107.3	88.3	110.5	85.7
1954	105.1	89.2	104.4	89.8
1955	103.5	98.6	108.9	93.7
1956	103.7	100.2	107.3	96.8
1957	101.6	101.7	104.6	98.8
1958	100.0	100.0	100.0	100.0
1959	101.4	107.2	105.6	102.9
1960	102.8	100.3	101.8	101.3
1961	101.0	102.3	99.9	103.4
1962	94.3	111.7	101.0	104.3
1963	105.6	97.0	99.8	102.6
1964	114.8	91.7	102.7	102.5
1965	113.5	97.8	103.6	107.1
1966	120.1	95.4	107.5	106.6

[a] Index numbers of output are the same as those shown in Table A-49.

TABLE A-50

Manufacturing, Stone, Clay, and Glass Products: Output, Inputs, and Productivity Ratios, 1948-66
(1958=100)

Year	Output	Persons Engaged	Output per Person	Man-Hours	Output per Man-Hour	Net Capital Input	Output per Unit of Net Capital Input	Total Factor Input	Total Factor Productivity
1948	74.7	99.5	75.1	103.2	72.4	61.2	122.1	92.1	81.1
1949	69.7	92.6	75.3	93.8	74.3	61.3	113.7	85.6	81.4
1950	84.3	98.1	85.9	102.1	82.6	62.0	136.0	91.6	92.0
1951	93.1	104.8	88.8	109.8	84.8	66.8	139.4	98.6	94.4
1952	89.1	101.2	88.0	104.9	84.9	70.9	125.7	96.6	92.2
1953	91.3	103.1	88.6	105.4	86.6	73.7	123.9	97.8	93.4
1954	87.8	98.4	89.2	99.7	88.1	77.3	113.6	94.3	93.1
1955	100.8	104.1	96.8	106.8	94.4	79.6	126.6	100.3	100.5
1956	106.1	106.7	99.4	109.0	97.3	86.9	122.1	103.7	102.3
1957	105.0	105.0	100.0	105.3	99.7	94.0	111.7	102.6	102.3
1958	100.0	100.0	100.0	100.0	100.0	100.0	100.0	100.0	100.0
1959	116.2	106.4	109.2	107.9	107.7	103.8	111.9	106.9	108.7
1960	115.4	107.1	107.7	109.2	105.7	106.5	108.4	108.6	106.3
1961	113.7	102.9	110.5	104.9	108.4	108.0	105.3	105.6	107.7
1962	118.6	104.5	113.5	106.9	110.9	107.9	109.9	107.1	110.7
1963	125.3	106.4	117.8	109.3	114.6	110.0	113.9	109.5	114.4
1964	134.4	109.0	123.3	113.7	118.2	114.7	117.2	113.9	118.0
1965	142.4	111.9	127.3	114.9	123.9	118.8	119.9	115.8	123.0
1966	150.0	114.7	130.8	117.7	127.4	127.6	117.6	120.1	124.9

Note: Relates to *Productivity Trends*, Table D-IV.

TABLE A-50a

Manufacturing, Stone, Clay, and Glass Products:
Gross Capital Input and Gross Productivity Ratios,[a] 1948-66

(1958=100)

Year	Gross Capital Input	Output per Unit of Gross Capital Input	Gross Factor Input	Gross Factor Productivity
1948	63.6	117.5	90.1	82.9
1949	64.3	108.4	84.3	82.7
1950	63.8	132.1	89.5	94.2
1951	66.9	139.2	95.5	97.5
1952	70.5	126.4	93.8	95.0
1953	72.0	126.8	94.7	96.4
1954	76.1	115.4	92.2	95.2
1955	79.4	127.0	98.1	102.8
1956	86.2	123.1	101.7	104.3
1957	92.1	114.0	101.1	103.9
1958	100.0	100.0	100.0	100.0
1959	106.5	109.1	107.5	108.1
1960	110.3	104.6	106.4	108.5
1961	113.8	99.9	107.7	105.6
1962	116.2	102.1	109.9	107.9
1963	119.9	104.5	112.7	111.2
1964	125.7	106.9	117.5	114.4
1965	130.8	108.9	120.0	118.7
1966	139.2	107.8	124.6	120.4

[a] Index numbers of output are the same as those shown in Table A-50.

TABLE A-51

Manufacturing, Primary Metal Industries: Output, Inputs, and Productivity Ratios, 1948-66
(1958=100)

Year	Output	Persons Engaged	Output per Person	Man-Hours	Output per Man-Hour	Net Capital Input	Output per Unit of Net Capital Input	Total Factor Input	Total Factor Productivity
1948	106.9	110.4	96.8	119.3	89.6	70.8	151.0	107.8	99.2
1949	90.0	97.9	91.9	101.5	88.7	70.7	127.3	95.6	94.1
1950	113.2	107.1	105.7	116.4	97.3	70.0	161.7	105.4	107.4
1951	123.2	118.3	104.1	130.8	94.2	71.7	171.8	115.8	106.4
1952	112.6	112.7	99.9	115.9	97.2	80.4	140.0	109.1	103.2
1953	127.5	120.2	106.1	130.0	98.1	87.2	146.2	121.2	105.2
1954	103.5	105.9	97.7	108.2	95.7	88.5	116.9	104.1	99.4
1955	134.5	115.2	116.8	124.2	108.3	85.4	157.5	116.2	115.7
1956	132.5	118.3	112.0	123.8	107.0	86.4	153.4	116.1	114.1
1957	128.0	118.0	108.5	121.9	105.0	92.3	138.7	115.8	110.5
1958	100.0	100.0	100.0	100.0	100.0	100.0	100.0	100.0	100.0
1959	115.2	102.8	112.1	105.1	109.6	101.3	113.7	104.3	110.5
1960	116.7	105.9	110.2	107.5	108.6	101.8	114.6	106.3	109.8
1961	114.3	98.9	115.6	101.2	112.9	105.4	108.4	102.1	111.9
1962	121.4	101.2	120.0	104.9	115.7	104.3	116.4	104.8	115.8
1963	132.0	101.5	130.0	107.0	123.4	111.4	118.5	107.9	122.3
1964	150.4	106.4	141.4	115.3	130.4	113.3	132.7	114.9	130.9
1965	160.3	112.3	142.7	121.9	131.5	118.3	135.5	121.2	132.3
1966	166.2	116.5	142.7	126.5	131.4	125.8	132.1	126.3	131.6

Note: Relates to *Productivity Trends*, Table D-IV.

TABLE A-51a

Manufacturing, Primary Metal Industries:
Gross Capital Input and Gross Productivity Ratios,[a] 1948-66

(1958=100)

Year	Gross Capital Input	Output per Unit of Gross Capital Input	Gross Factor Input	Gross Factor Productivity
1948	74.6	143.3	105.1	101.7
1949	75.1	119.8	94.5	95.2
1950	74.8	151.3	103.4	109.5
1951	75.7	162.7	112.5	109.5
1952	82.0	137.3	106.2	106.0
1953	87.5	145.7	117.2	108.8
1954	89.1	116.2	102.5	101.0
1955	87.0	154.6	113.0	119.0
1956	88.5	149.7	113.2	117.0
1957	93.5	136.9	113.4	112.9
1958	100.0	100.0	100.0	100.0
1959	102.5	112.4	104.3	110.5
1960	105.0	111.1	106.7	109.4
1961	109.7	104.2	103.8	110.1
1962	111.3	109.1	106.8	113.7
1963	110.7	119.2	108.1	122.1
1964	114.9	130.9	115.2	130.6
1965	121.2	132.3	121.7	131.7
1966	128.1	129.7	127.0	130.9

[a] Index numbers of output are the same as those shown in Table A-51.

TABLE A-52

Manufacturing, Fabricated Metal Products except Machinery, Transportation Equipment,
and Ordnance: Output, Inputs, and Productivity Ratios, 1948-66
(1958=100)

Year	Output	Persons Engaged	Output per Person	Man-Hours	Output per Man-Hour	Net Capital Input	Output per Unit of Net Capital Input	Total Factor Input	Total Factor Productivity
1948	81.2	94.0	86.4	97.7	83.1	67.6	120.1	93.0	87.3
1949	73.4	84.7	86.7	86.3	85.1	67.2	109.2	83.8	87.6
1950	89.8	94.1	95.4	98.0	91.6	68.6	130.9	93.4	96.1
1951	96.0	100.8	95.2	105.9	90.7	76.8	125.0	101.6	94.5
1952	93.6	100.9	92.8	105.5	88.7	84.8	110.4	103.0	90.9
1953	105.5	108.9	96.9	113.6	92.9	88.1	119.8	110.3	95.6
1954	94.9	101.5	93.5	103.6	91.6	89.5	106.0	101.8	93.2
1955	104.0	107.1	97.1	109.6	94.9	89.9	115.7	107.0	97.2
1956	105.1	108.7	96.7	111.0	94.7	94.2	111.6	108.8	96.6
1957	108.6	109.6	99.1	110.6	98.2	97.7	111.2	108.9	99.7
1958	100.0	100.0	100.0	100.0	100.0	100.0	100.0	100.0	100.0
1959	111.8	104.6	106.9	107.8	103.7	102.1	109.5	107.1	104.4
1960	112.3	105.1	106.9	108.3	103.7	104.6	107.4	107.8	104.2
1961	109.4	100.3	109.1	103.2	106.0	105.3	103.9	103.5	105.7
1962	118.4	104.3	113.5	108.9	108.7	107.7	109.9	108.7	108.9
1963	122.8	106.0	115.8	109.6	112.0	111.3	110.3	109.8	111.8
1964	132.0	109.7	120.3	114.8	115.0	116.3	113.5	115.0	114.8
1965	147.1	116.7	126.0	123.0	119.6	126.4	116.4	123.4	119.2
1966	162.2	124.7	130.1	132.3	122.6	140.4	115.5	133.4	121.6

Note: Relates to *Productivity Trends*, Table D-IV.

TABLE A-52a

Manufacturing, Fabricated Metal Products except Machinery,
Transportation Equipment, and Ordnance:
Gross Capital Input and Gross Productivity Ratios,[a] 1948-66

(1958=100)

Year	Gross Capital Input	Output per Unit of Gross Capital Input	Gross Factor Input	Gross Factor Productivity
1948	68.6	118.4	92.1	88.2
1949	68.9	106.5	83.6	87.8
1950	70.5	127.4	92.8	96.8
1951	76.2	126.0	100.2	95.8
1952	83.1	112.6	101.9	91.9
1953	84.8	124.4	108.4	97.3
1954	87.2	108.8	100.6	94.3
1955	88.2	117.9	105.7	98.4
1956	92.2	114.0	107.6	97.7
1957	96.4	112.7	108.0	100.6
1958	100.0	100.0	100.0	100.0
1959	103.0	108.5	106.9	104.6
1960	106.5	105.4	108.0	104.0
1961	109.2	100.2	104.3	104.9
1962	113.5	104.3	109.7	107.9
1963	117.6	104.4	111.0	110.6
1964	122.3	107.9	116.2	113.6
1965	131.3	112.0	124.5	118.2
1966	143.9	112.7	134.4	120.7

[a] Index numbers of output are the same as those shown in Table
A-52.

TABLE A-53

Manufacturing, Machinery, except Electric: Output, Inputs, and Productivity Ratios, 1948-66
(1958=100)

Year	Output	Persons Engaged	Output per Person	Man-Hours	Output per Man-Hour	Net Capital Input	Output per Unit of Net Capital Input	Total Factor Input	Total Factor Productivity
1948	85.0	102.1	83.3	108.2	78.6	78.1	108.8	103.6	82.0
1949	72.5	88.0	82.4	90.3	80.3	77.4	93.7	89.3	81.2
1950	81.4	89.9	90.5	94.5	86.1	77.3	105.3	92.7	87.8
1951	103.4	108.5	95.3	118.8	87.0	85.1	121.5	113.6	91.0
1952	112.3	114.2	98.3	124.6	90.1	94.7	118.6	120.5	93.2
1953	115.8	116.1	99.7	124.8	92.8	96.5	120.0	121.0	95.7
1954	98.8	105.0	94.1	108.8	90.8	96.3	102.6	107.1	92.3
1955	107.6	106.8	100.7	112.5	95.6	96.9	111.0	110.4	97.5
1956	121.8	114.8	106.1	122.1	99.8	104.6	116.4	119.7	101.8
1957	119.4	115.4	103.5	120.1	99.4	108.5	110.0	118.5	100.8
1958	100.0	100.0	100.0	100.0	100.0	100.0	100.0	100.0	100.0
1959	118.9	107.1	111.0	110.7	107.4	94.6	125.7	108.5	109.6
1960	121.1	108.2	111.9	111.8	108.3	97.1	124.7	109.8	110.3
1961	117.2	104.3	112.4	107.1	109.4	95.9	122.2	105.6	111.0
1962	130.2	109.6	118.8	113.9	114.3	95.5	136.3	111.4	116.9
1963	136.5	112.4	121.4	118.6	115.1	97.3	140.3	115.7	118.0
1964	152.9	118.2	129.4	127.1	120.3	102.8	148.7	123.8	123.5
1965	172.5	127.8	135.0	138.0	125.0	113.9	151.4	134.7	128.1
1966	195.7	140.3	139.5	154.0	127.1	128.9	151.8	150.6	129.9

Note: Relates to *Productivity Trends*, Table D-IV.

TABLE A-53a

Manufacturing, Machinery except Electric:
Gross Capital Input and Gross Productivity Ratios,[a] 1948-66

(1958=100)

Year	Gross Capital Input	Output per Unit of Gross Capital Input	Gross Factor Input	Gross Factor Productivity
1948	72.1	117.9	100.4	84.7
1949	72.8	99.6	87.4	83.0
1950	73.7	110.4	90.8	89.6
1951	80.1	129.1	110.5	93.6
1952	88.5	126.9	117.4	95.7
1953	90.7	127.7	118.0	98.1
1954	92.1	107.3	105.5	93.6
1955	93.7	114.8	108.7	99.0
1956	100.8	120.8	117.8	103.4
1957	105.2	113.5	117.1	102.0
1958	100.0	100.0	100.0	100.0
1959	97.1	122.5	108.0	110.1
1960	101.0	119.9	109.6	110.5
1961	101.9	115.0	106.1	110.5
1962	103.5	125.8	111.8	116.5
1963	106.6	128.0	116.2	117.5
1964	112.9	135.4	124.3	123.0
1965	122.9	140.4	135.0	127.8
1966	136.5	143.4	150.5	130.0

[a] Index numbers of output are the same as those shown in Table A-53.

TABLE A-54

Manufacturing, Electric Machinery, Equipment, and Supplies: Output, Inputs, and Productivity Ratios, 1948-66
(1958=100)

Year	Output	Persons Engaged	Output per Person	Man-Hours	Output per Man-Hour	Net Capital Input	Output per Unit of Net Capital Input	Total Factor Input	Total Factor Productivity
1948	58.1	80.8	71.9	82.9	70.1	58.5	99.3	78.6	73.9
1949	54.5	69.7	78.2	71.8	75.9	57.1	95.4	69.6	78.3
1950	74.7	80.0	93.4	81.5	91.7	57.8	129.2	77.4	96.5
1951	75.1	89.6	83.8	92.0	81.6	65.6	114.5	87.5	85.8
1952	85.9	96.1	89.4	100.4	85.6	78.0	110.1	97.0	88.6
1953	99.7	107.6	92.7	109.5	91.1	84.7	117.7	105.6	94.4
1954	90.5	96.6	93.7	96.7	93.6	86.2	105.0	95.0	95.3
1955	103.1	100.9	102.2	102.9	100.2	88.5	116.5	100.6	102.5
1956	114.0	107.0	106.5	107.8	105.8	98.1	116.2	106.3	107.2
1957	112.0	108.6	103.1	108.8	102.9	100.9	111.0	107.5	104.2
1958	100.0	100.0	100.0	100.0	100.0	100.0	100.0	100.0	100.0
1959	123.9	112.5	110.1	114.5	108.2	103.9	119.2	102.8	120.5
1960	132.4	118.2	112.0	120.7	109.7	108.9	121.6	118.8	111.4
1961	138.1	119.2	115.9	121.6	113.6	113.8	121.4	120.4	114.7
1962	156.8	127.7	122.8	131.5	119.2	116.7	134.4	129.1	121.5
1963	165.1	126.5	130.5	128.2	128.8	132.6	124.5	128.9	128.1
1964	175.5	125.4	140.0	128.2	136.9	142.1	123.5	130.4	134.6
1965	200.4	134.4	149.1	139.2	144.0	153.5	130.6	141.5	141.6
1966	232.6	153.9	151.1	160.1	145.3	180.6	128.8	163.4	142.4

Note: Relates to *Productivity Trends*, Table D-IV.

318

Appendix: Sources and Methods

TABLE A-54a

Manufacturing, Electric Machinery, Equipment, and Supplies:
Gross Capital Input and Gross Productivity Ratios,[a] 1948-66

(1958=100)

Year	Gross Capital Input	Output per Unit of Gross Capital Input	Gross Factor Input	Gross Factor Productivity
1948	60.9	95.4	78.1	74.4
1949	60.9	89.5	69.7	78.2
1950	62.0	120.5	77.4	96.5
1951	69.3	108.4	87.1	86.2
1952	81.0	106.0	96.4	89.1
1953	88.4	112.8	105.2	94.8
1954	88.4	102.4	95.0	95.3
1955	87.8	117.4	99.9	103.2
1956	95.1	119.9	105.3	108.3
1957	98.0	114.3	106.6	105.1
1958	100.0	100.0	100.0	100.0
1959	105.6	117.3	112.7	109.9
1960	116.0	114.1	119.8	110.5
1961	127.7	108.1	122.8	112.5
1962	133.3	117.6	131.9	118.9
1963	143.4	115.1	131.2	125.8
1964	148.5	118.2	132.3	132.7
1965	160.4	124.9	143.4	139.7
1966	191.4	121.5	166.4	139.8

[a] Index numbers of output are the same as those shown in Table A-54.

TABLE A-55

Manufacturing, Transportation Equipment and Ordnance: Output, Inputs,
and Productivity Ratios, 1948-66
(1958=100)

Year	Output	Persons Engaged	Output per Person	Man-Hours	Output per Man-Hour	Net Capital Input	Output per Unit of Net Capital Input	Total Factor Input	Total Factor Productivity
1948	57.2	71.9	79.6	72.1	79.3	58.0	98.6	72.1	79.3
1949	57.5	69.8	82.4	69.7	82.5	55.8	103.0	69.5	82.7
1950	70.0	73.0	95.9	74.7	93.7	56.6	123.7	73.5	95.2
1951	85.0	91.1	93.3	93.0	91.4	66.3	128.2	90.3	94.1
1952	97.6	107.5	90.8	111.8	87.3	79.4	122.9	108.4	90.0
1953	123.0	123.8	99.4	127.3	96.6	87.8	140.1	122.6	100.3
1954	108.4	109.1	99.4	111.2	97.5	87.7	123.6	108.4	100.0
1955	125.6	112.9	111.2	117.4	107.0	89.2	140.8	114.1	110.1
1956	115.2	112.3	102.6	115.6	99.7	99.3	116.0	113.7	101.3
1957	121.1	116.0	104.4	117.6	103.0	104.9	115.4	116.1	104.3
1958	100.0	100.0	100.0	100.0	100.0	100.0	100.0	100.0	100.0
1959	115.5	104.4	110.6	108.9	106.1	98.6	117.1	107.7	107.2
1960	119.6	101.9	117.4	104.5	114.4	99.9	119.7	104.0	115.0
1961	115.5	96.6	119.6	98.1	117.7	98.0	117.9	98.1	117.7
1962	131.1	103.7	126.4	108.1	121.3	98.4	133.2	107.0	122.5
1963	139.8	106.5	131.3	112.3	124.5	103.7	134.8	111.3	125.6
1964	142.8	106.3	134.3	111.8	127.7	113.7	125.6	112.0	127.5
1965	162.1	112.3	144.3	119.2	136.0	126.3	128.3	120.0	135.1
1966	184.7	125.0	147.8	131.8	140.1	144.3	128.0	133.3	138.6

Note: Relates to *Productivity Trends*, Table D-IV.

TABLE A-55a

Manufacturing, Transportation Equipment and Ordnance:
Gross Capital Input and Gross Productivity Ratios,[a] 1948-66

(1958=100)

Year	Gross Capital Input	Output per Unit of Gross Capital Input	Gross Factor Input	Gross Factor Productivity
1948	56.8	100.7	71.0	80.6
1949	57.2	100.5	69.4	82.9
1950	58.1	120.5	73.2	95.6
1951	64.7	131.4	88.6	95.9
1952	75.6	129.1	105.7	92.3
1953	84.3	145.9	119.7	102.8
1954	84.9	127.7	106.6	101.7
1955	86.5	145.2	112.0	112.1
1956	95.0	121.3	112.0	102.9
1957	100.6	120.4	114.6	105.7
1958	100.0	100.0	100.0	100.0
1959	102.3	112.9	107.7	107.2
1960	106.5	112.3	104.9	114.0
1961	108.6	106.4	99.9	115.6
1962	112.3	116.7	108.8	120.5
1963	119.3	117.2	113.6	123.1
1964	129.9	109.9	115.0	124.2
1965	141.3	114.7	123.1	131.7
1966	157.2	117.5	136.3	135.5

[a] Index numbers of output are the same as those shown in Table A-55.

TABLE A-56

Manufacturing, Instruments, Photographic and Optical Goods, and Clocks:
Output, Inputs, and Productivity Ratios, 1948-66
(1958=100)

Year	Output	Persons Engaged	Output per Person	Man-Hours	Output per Man-Hour	Net Capital Input	Output per Unit of Net Capital Input	Total Factor Input	Total Factor Productivity
1948	56.3	76.9	73.2	78.2	72.0	40.4	139.4	69.6	80.9
1949	50.2	70.5	71.2	70.1	71.6	47.3	106.1	65.6	76.5
1950	58.5	76.9	76.1	78.7	74.3	53.0	110.4	73.6	79.5
1951	67.0	89.4	74.9	93.2	71.9	62.2	107.7	87.0	77.0
1952	79.7	96.0	83.0	99.7	79.9	70.7	112.7	94.3	84.5
1953	87.0	103.0	84.5	106.9	81.4	74.9	116.2	100.8	86.3
1954	84.6	98.8	85.6	100.3	84.3	75.7	111.8	95.6	88.5
1955	92.0	100.0	92.0	101.9	90.3	79.2	116.2	97.6	94.3
1956	100.5	105.8	95.0	108.5	92.6	90.7	110.8	105.1	95.6
1957	104.8	108.5	96.6	111.3	94.2	98.5	106.4	108.9	96.2
1958	100.0	100.0	100.0	100.0	100.0	100.0	100.0	100.0	100.0
1959	119.0	105.5	112.8	107.9	110.3	103.3	115.2	107.0	111.2
1960	125.8	107.6	116.9	109.6	114.8	109.2	115.2	109.5	114.9
1961	124.7	105.5	118.2	106.8	116.8	113.9	109.5	108.2	115.2
1962	132.1	108.8	121.4	111.6	118.4	123.6	106.9	113.9	116.0
1963	139.5	110.6	126.1	112.2	124.3	131.5	106.1	115.9	120.4
1964	146.1	111.2	131.4	113.6	128.6	126.9	115.1	116.1	125.8
1965	162.2	117.3	138.3	120.5	134.6	130.2	124.6	122.4	132.5
1966	189.1	130.7	144.7	136.1	138.9	153.1	123.5	139.3	135.8

Note: Relates to *Productivity Trends*, Table D-IV.

TABLE A-56a

Manufacturing, Instruments, Photographic and Optical Goods, and Clocks:
Gross Capital Input and Gross Productivity Ratios,[a] 1948-66

(1958=100)

Year	Gross Capital Input	Output per Unit of Gross Capital Input	Gross Factor Input	Gross Factor Productivity
1948	42.0	134.0	68.8	81.8
1949	48.6	103.3	65.1	77.1
1950	55.1	106.2	73.3	79.8
1951	62.9	106.5	86.1	77.8
1952	69.9	114.0	92.9	85.8
1953	72.3	120.3	98.8	88.1
1954	74.2	114.0	94.2	89.8
1955	78.9	116.6	96.5	95.3
1956	90.1	111.5	104.2	96.4
1957	97.4	107.6	108.1	96.9
1958	100.0	100.0	100.0	100.0
1959	104.1	114.3	107.0	111.2
1960	109.4	115.0	109.6	114.8
1961	115.4	108.1	108.8	114.6
1962	126.5	104.4	115.1	114.8
1963	135.4	103.0	117.6	118.6
1964	131.4	111.2	117.7	124.1
1965	133.9	121.1	123.6	131.2
1966	154.1	122.7	140.3	134.8

[a] Index numbers of output are the same as those shown in Table A-56.

TABLE A-57

Manufacturing, Miscellaneous Products: Output, Inputs, and Productivity Ratios, 1948-66
(1958=100)

Year	Output	Persons Engaged	Output per Person	Man-Hours	Output per Man-Hour	Net Capital Input	Output per Unit of Net Capital Input	Total Factor Input	Total Factor Productivity
1948	81.8	109.4	74.8	115.7	70.7	51.5	158.8	103.1	79.3
1949	75.8	101.7	74.5	102.8	73.7	61.5	123.3	96.0	79.0
1950	85.3	106.7	79.9	108.5	78.6	63.5	134.3	100.9	84.5
1951	82.6	107.2	77.1	108.9	75.8	69.7	118.5	103.0	80.2
1952	85.1	105.7	80.5	104.9	81.1	76.8	110.8	101.8	83.6
1953	95.9	113.1	84.8	115.8	82.8	78.9	121.5	110.8	86.6
1954	86.8	107.4	80.8	108.1	80.3	78.1	111.1	104.1	83.4
1955	99.6	108.4	91.9	108.9	91.5	80.2	124.2	105.0	94.9
1956	105.3	110.1	95.6	110.8	95.0	86.8	121.3	107.6	97.9
1957	102.5	105.2	97.4	104.2	98.4	90.1	113.8	102.3	100.2
1958	100.0	100.0	100.0	100.0	100.0	100.0	100.0	100.0	100.0
1959	113.8	103.5	110.0	104.2	109.2	97.7	116.5	103.3	110.2
1960	117.8	104.0	113.3	105.6	111.6	91.9	128.2	103.8	113.5
1961	119.2	101.2	117.8	101.9	117.0	86.8	137.3	99.9	119.3
1962	128.8	104.2	123.6	106.3	121.2	85.5	150.6	103.5	124.4
1963	131.5	103.5	127.1	104.7	125.6	84.4	155.8	102.0	128.9
1964	140.3	105.9	132.5	110.4	127.1	82.3	170.5	106.6	131.6
1965	153.6	110.6	138.9	112.8	136.2	83.3	184.4	108.8	141.2
1966	166.1	114.3	145.3	116.8	142.2	93.2	178.2	113.6	146.2

Note: Relates to *Productivity Trends*, Table D-IV.

TABLE A-57a

Manufacturing, Miscellaneous Products:
Gross Capital Input and Gross Productivity Ratios,[a] 1948-66

(1958=100)

Year	Gross Capital Input	Output per Unit of Gross Capital Input	Gross Factor Input	Gross Factor Productivity
1948	49.4	165.6	99.3	82.4
1949	59.5	127.4	93.6	81.0
1950	62.2	137.1	98.5	86.6
1951	67.2	122.9	100.5	82.2
1952	74.4	114.4	100.1	85.0
1953	76.5	125.4	108.5	88.4
1954	77.5	112.0	102.4	84.8
1955	80.9	123.1	103.7	96.0
1956	87.3	120.6	106.4	99.0
1957	92.0	111.4	101.9	100.6
1958	100.0	100.0	100.0	100.0
1959	100.9	112.8	103.6	109.8
1960	95.4	123.5	103.7	113.6
1961	90.6	131.6	99.8	119.4
1962	88.6	145.4	103.0	125.0
1963	86.2	152.6	101.3	129.8
1964	83.8	167.4	105.5	133.0
1965	85.2	180.3	107.7	142.6
1966	94.2	176.3	112.6	147.5

[a] Index numbers of output are the same as those shown in Table A-57.

TABLE A-58

Transportation and Warehousing: Real Product, Inputs, and Productivity Ratios, 1948-69

(1958=100)

Year	Real Gross Product	Persons Engaged	Real Product per Person	Man-Hours	Real Product per Man-Hour	Labor Input	Real Product per Unit of Labor Input	Net Capital Input	Real Product per Unit of Net Capital Input	Total Factor Input	Total Factor Productivity
1948	98.7	118.3	83.4	127.4	77.5	130.9	75.4	82.2	120.1	126.4	78.1
1949	87.1	110.5	78.8	115.4	75.5	117.9	73.9	84.6	103.0	115.4	75.5
1950	94.2	111.9	84.2	113.2	83.2	115.3	81.7	86.5	108.9	113.5	83.0
1951	103.6	117.7	88.0	119.8	86.5	122.0	84.9	88.8	116.7	119.7	86.5
1952	101.0	116.8	86.5	118.7	85.1	120.7	83.7	91.3	110.6	118.9	84.9
1953	101.2	116.5	86.9	117.1	86.4	119.0	85.0	93.4	108.4	117.8	85.9
1954	100.2	107.9	92.9	107.6	93.1	108.9	92.0	95.0	105.5	108.2	92.6
1955	105.0	109.1	96.2	110.0	95.5	111.4	94.3	96.2	109.1	110.7	94.9
1956	108.7	110.5	98.4	111.4	97.6	112.7	96.5	97.6	111.4	112.0	97.1
1957	107.5	109.0	98.6	109.9	97.8	110.8	97.0	99.1	108.5	110.3	97.5
1958	100.0	100.0	100.0	100.0	100.0	100.0	100.0	100.0	100.0	100.0	100.0
1959	106.1	100.4	105.7	101.5	104.5	101.1	104.9	100.6	105.5	101.1	104.9
1960	107.4	100.2	107.2	100.6	106.8	100.0	107.4	101.6	105.7	100.1	107.3
1961	107.4	96.6	111.2	97.5	110.2	96.6	111.2	102.3	105.0	96.9	110.8
1962	113.5	96.4	117.7	97.6	116.3	96.5	117.6	102.9	110.3	96.8	117.3
1963	120.2	95.9	125.3	97.9	122.8	96.8	124.2	103.8	115.8	97.1	123.8
1964	124.8	96.6	129.2	99.7	125.2	98.5	126.7	105.0	118.9	98.8	126.3
1965	136.6	97.8	139.7	101.9	134.1	100.3	136.2	107.2	127.4	100.6	135.8
1966	148.7	100.8	147.5	105.1	141.5	103.3	143.9	110.5	134.6	103.6	143.5
1967	149.9	102.1	146.8	104.6	143.3	102.8	145.8				
1968	158.3	103.5	153.0	106.7	148.4	104.9	150.9				
1969P	164.9	104.5	157.8	107.7	153.1	105.9	155.7				

P Preliminary (as of July 1971 *Survey of Current Business*).

TABLE A-59

Transportation and Warehousing:
Output and Productivity Ratios,[a] 1948-66
(1958=100)

Year	Output	Output per Person	Output per Man-Hour	Output per Unit of Labor Input	Output per Unit of Net Capital Input	Total Factor Productivity
1948	92.1	77.9	72.3	70.4	112.0	72.9
1949	86.5	78.3	75.0	73.4	102.2	75.0
1950	89.6	80.1	79.2	77.7	103.6	78.9
1951	100.1	85.0	83.6	82.0	112.7	83.6
1952	98.0	83.9	82.6	81.2	107.3	82.4
1953	98.4	84.5	84.0	82.7	105.4	83.5
1954	93.9	87.0	87.3	86.2	98.8	86.8
1955	103.2	94.6	93.8	92.6	107.3	93.2
1956	108.5	98.2	97.4	96.3	111.2	96.9
1957	103.4	94.9	94.1	93.3	104.3	93.7
1958	100.0	100.0	100.0	100.0	100.0	100.0
1959	106.4	106.0	104.8	105.2	105.8	105.2
1960	108.1	107.9	107.5	108.1	106.4	108.0
1961	107.7	111.5	110.5	111.5	105.3	111.1
1962	114.0	118.3	116.8	118.1	110.8	117.8
1963	119.9	125.0	122.5	123.9	115.5	123.5
1964	128.0	132.5	128.4	129.9	121.9	129.6
1965	139.4	142.5	136.8	139.0	130.0	138.6
1966	152.7	151.5	145.3	147.8	138.2	147.4

Note: Relates to *Productivity Trends,* Table G-I.

[a] Index numbers of the inputs are the same as those shown in Table A-58.

TABLE A-59a

Transportation and Warehousing: Gross Capital Input and Gross Productivity Ratios
in Terms of Real Product and Output,[a] 1948-66
(1958=100)

Year	Gross Capital Input	Real Product per Unit of Gross Capital Input	Gross Factor Input	Real Product per Unit of Gross Factor Input	Output per Unit of Gross Capital Input	Output per Unit of Gross Factor Input
1948	78.8	125.3	119.6	82.5	116.9	77.0
1949	80.9	107.7	110.4	78.9	106.9	78.4
1950	83.7	112.5	109.2	86.3	107.0	82.1
1951	86.8	119.4	115.1	90.0	115.3	87.0
1952	89.0	113.5	114.7	88.1	110.1	85.4
1953	90.8	111.5	113.9	88.8	108.4	86.4
1954	92.5	108.3	105.9	94.6	101.5	88.7
1955	94.9	110.6	108.4	96.9	108.7	95.2
1956	97.1	111.9	109.9	98.9	111.7	98.7
1957	98.7	108.9	108.6	99.0	104.8	95.2
1958	100.0	100.0	100.0	100.0	100.0	100.0
1959	100.3	105.8	101.0	105.0	106.1	105.4
1960	98.8	108.7	99.8	107.6	109.4	108.3
1961	97.5	110.2	96.8	111.0	110.5	111.3
1962	97.6	116.3	96.7	117.4	116.8	117.9
1963	98.4	122.2	97.1	123.8	121.8	123.5
1964	98.7	126.4	98.5	126.7	129.7	129.9
1965	98.9	138.1	100.0	136.6	141.0	139.4
1966	99.7	149.1	102.7	144.8	153.2	148.7

Note: Relates to *Productivity Trends*, Table G-I.

[a] Index numbers of real product and output are the same as those shown in Tables A-58 and A-59.

TABLE A-60

Railroads and Related Services: Real Product,
Inputs, and Productivity Ratios, 1948-66
(1958=100)

Year	Real Gross Product	Persons Engaged	Real Product per Person	Man-Hours	Real Product per Man-Hour	Net Capital Input	Real Product per Unit of Net Capital Input	Total Factor Input	Total Factor Productivity
1948	124.0	157.2	78.9	189.3	65.5	97.8	127.8	174.7	71.0
1949	103.4	141.1	73.3	159.7	64.7	98.1	105.4	151.7	68.2
1950	112.5	143.6	78.3	151.1	74.5	98.8	113.9	145.1	77.5
1951	125.6	149.9	83.8	156.3	80.4	99.5	126.2	149.4	84.1
1952	120.2	144.7	83.1	149.3	80.5	100.5	119.6	144.1	83.4
1953	117.6	142.3	82.6	145.4	80.9	101.1	116.3	141.2	83.3
1954	106.1	126.2	84.1	126.8	83.7	101.0	105.0	124.3	85.4
1955	117.1	125.2	93.5	128.0	91.5	100.5	116.5	125.4	93.4
1956	119.1	123.8	96.2	126.1	94.4	100.2	118.9	123.6	96.4
1957	112.3	116.8	96.1	117.7	95.4	100.3	112.0	116.0	96.8
1958	100.0	100.0	100.0	100.0	100.0	100.0	100.0	100.0	100.0
1959	105.2	96.7	108.8	97.1	108.3	99.2	106.0	97.3	108.1
1960	103.8	92.4	112.3	92.1	112.7	98.5	105.4	92.7	112.0
1961	102.9	85.0	121.1	84.8	121.3	97.6	105.4	86.0	119.7
1962	108.6	82.9	131.0	83.2	130.5	96.6	112.4	84.5	128.5
1963	114.9	80.5	142.7	81.4	141.2	96.0	119.7	82.8	138.8
1964	120.5	79.0	152.5	80.8	149.1	95.9	125.7	82.2	146.6
1965	130.0	76.9	169.1	77.9	166.9	96.4	134.9	79.7	163.1
1966	138.3	75.7	182.7	76.4	181.0	97.4	142.0	78.4	176.4

TABLE A-61

Railroads and Related Services: Output and
Productivity Ratios,[a] 1948-66

(1958=100)

Year	Output	Output per Person	Output per Man-Hour	Output per Unit of Net Capital Input	Total Factor Productivity
1948	122.2	77.7	64.6	126.0	69.9
1949	101.5	71.9	63.6	103.5	66.9
1950	108.8	75.8	72.0	110.1	75.0
1951	117.7	78.5	75.3	118.3	78.8
1952	111.7	77.2	74.8	111.1	77.5
1953	109.9	77.2	75.6	108.7	77.8
1954	100.0	79.2	78.9	99.0	80.5
1955	112.0	89.5	87.5	111.4	89.3
1956	117.7	95.1	93.3	117.5	95.2
1957	112.3	96.1	95.4	112.0	96.8
1958	100.0	100.0	100.0	100.0	100.0
1959	103.9	107.4	107.0	104.7	106.8
1960	103.1	111.6	111.9	104.7	111.2
1961	101.3	119.2	119.5	103.8	117.8
1962	106.0	127.9	127.4	109.7	125.4
1963	110.2	136.9	135.4	114.8	133.1
1964	116.1	147.0	143.7	121.1	141.2
1965	122.2	158.9	156.9	126.8	153.3
1966	128.8	170.1	168.6	132.2	164.3

Note: Relates to *Productivity Trends,* Table G-III.

[a] Index numbers of inputs are the same as those shown in Table A-60.

TABLE A-61a

Railroads and Related Services: Gross Capital Input and Gross
Productivity Ratios in Terms of Real Product and Output,[a] 1948-66

(1958=100)

Year	Gross Capital Input	Real Product per Unit of Gross Capital Input	Gross Factor Input	Real Product per Unit of Gross Factor Input	Output per Unit of Gross Capital Input	Output per Unit of Gross Factor Input
1948	89.6	138.4	162.7	76.2	136.4	75.1
1949	90.5	114.3	142.7	72.5	112.2	71.1
1950	91.8	122.5	137.3	81.9	118.5	79.2
1951	93.4	134.5	141.4	88.8	126.0	83.2
1952	94.5	127.2	137.1	87.7	118.2	81.5
1953	95.6	123.0	134.8	87.2	115.0	81.5
1954	97.1	109.3	120.5	88.0	103.0	83.0
1955	98.7	118.6	121.8	96.1	113.5	92.0
1956	99.6	119.6	120.5	98.8	118.2	97.7
1957	99.8	112.5	113.9	98.6	112.5	98.6
1958	100.0	100.0	100.0	100.0	100.0	100.0
1959	100.1	105.1	97.7	107.7	103.8	106.3
1960	98.9	105.0	93.5	111.0	104.2	110.3
1961	97.2	105.9	87.4	117.7	104.2	115.9
1962	96.3	112.8	86.0	126.3	110.1	123.3
1963	95.3	120.6	84.3	136.3	115.6	130.7
1964	94.0	128.2	83.6	144.1	123.5	138.9
1965	92.9	139.9	81.1	160.3	131.5	150.7
1966	92.1	150.2	79.7	173.5	139.8	161.6

a Index numbers of real product and output are shown in Tables A-60 and A-61.

TABLE A-62

Nonrail Transportation: Real Product, Inputs, and Productivity Ratios, 1948-66

(1958=100)

Year	Real Gross Product	Persons Engaged	Real Product per Person	Man-Hours	Real Product per Man-Hour	Labor Input	Real Product per Unit of Labor Input	Net Capital Input	Real Product per Unit of Net Capital Input	Total Factor Input	Total Factor Productivity
1948	81.0	95.0	85.3	96.2	84.2	95.2	85.1	47.7	169.8	92.1	87.9
1949	76.2	92.2	82.6	93.0	81.9	92.0	82.8	53.1	143.5	89.8	84.9
1950	81.0	92.9	87.2	94.1	86.1	92.9	87.2	57.8	140.1	91.1	88.9
1951	88.1	98.5	89.4	101.4	86.9	100.7	87.5	63.7	138.3	98.8	89.2
1952	88.1	100.1	88.0	103.2	85.4	102.5	86.0	69.8	126.2	101.1	87.1
1953	89.7	101.1	88.7	102.9	87.2	102.1	87.9	75.6	118.7	101.4	88.5
1954	96.0	97.1	98.9	97.9	98.1	97.4	98.6	81.1	118.4	97.0	99.0
1955	96.0	99.4	96.6	100.9	95.1	100.7	95.3	86.4	111.1	100.3	95.7
1956	101.6	102.4	99.2	104.0	97.7	104.1	97.6	91.4	111.2	103.8	97.9
1957	103.2	104.3	98.9	106.0	97.4	106.4	97.0	96.2	107.3	106.1	97.3
1958	100.0	100.0	100.0	100.0	100.0	100.0	100.0	100.0	100.0	100.0	100.0
1959	105.6	102.7	102.8	103.7	101.8	103.7	101.8	104.0	101.5	103.7	101.8
1960	109.5	104.9	104.4	104.8	104.5	105.1	104.2	108.8	100.6	105.2	104.1
1961	109.5	103.6	105.7	103.9	105.4	104.2	105.1	113.0	96.9	104.4	104.9
1962	115.9	104.4	111.0	104.8	110.6	105.0	110.4	117.5	98.6	105.3	110.1
1963	123.0	105.1	117.0	106.3	115.7	106.7	115.3	122.1	100.7	107.1	114.8
1964	127.0	107.2	118.5	109.2	116.3	109.9	115.6	126.4	100.5	110.3	115.1
1965	139.7	110.4	126.5	114.0	122.5	114.7	121.8	132.5	105.4	115.1	121.4
1966	154.8	115.8	133.7	119.5	129.5	120.5	128.5	141.0	109.8	121.0	127.9

TABLE A-63

Nonrail Transportation: Output and Productivity Ratios,[a] 1948-66
(1958=100)

Year	Output	Output per Person	Output per Man-Hour	Output per Unit of Labor Input	Output per Unit of Net Capital Input	Total Factor Productivity
1948	72.2	76.0	75.1	75.8	151.4	78.4
1949	76.5	83.0	82.3	83.2	144.1	85.2
1950	76.8	82.7	81.6	82.7	132.9	84.3
1951	88.4	89.7	87.2	87.8	138.8	89.5
1952	89.0	88.9	86.2	86.8	127.5	88.0
1953	90.7	89.7	88.1	88.8	120.0	89.4
1954	89.9	92.6	91.8	92.3	110.9	92.7
1955	97.4	98.0	96.5	96.7	112.7	97.1
1956	102.3	99.9	98.4	98.3	111.9	98.6
1957	97.4	93.4	91.9	91.5	101.2	91.8
1958	100.0	100.0	100.0	100.0	100.0	100.0
1959	108.0	105.2	104.1	104.1	103.8	104.1
1960	111.4	106.2	106.3	106.0	102.4	105.9
1961	111.9	108.0	107.7	107.4	99.0	107.2
1962	119.3	114.3	113.8	113.6	101.5	113.3
1963	126.4	120.3	118.9	118.5	103.5	118.0
1964	136.4	127.2	124.9	124.1	107.9	123.7
1965	150.8	136.6	132.3	131.5	113.8	131.0
1966	168.5	145.5	141.0	139.8	119.5	139.3

[a] Index numbers of inputs are the same as those shown in Table A-62.

TABLE A-63a

Nonrail Transportation: Gross Capital Input and Gross
Productivity Ratios in Terms of Real Product and Output,[a] 1948-66
(1958=100)

Year	Gross Capital Input	Real Product per Unit of Gross Capital Input	Gross Factor Input	Real Product per Unit of Gross Factor Input	Output per Unit of Gross Capital Input	Output per Unit of Gross Factor Input
1948	44.1	183.7	84.0	96.4	163.7	86.0
1949	49.8	153.0	83.0	91.8	153.6	92.2
1950	57.4	141.1	85.8	94.4	133.8	89.5
1951	65.8	133.9	94.0	93.7	134.3	94.0
1952	71.4	123.4	96.9	90.9	124.6	91.8
1953	75.2	119.3	97.6	91.9	120.6	92.9
1954	77.8	123.4	94.1	102.0	115.6	95.5
1955	82.9	115.8	97.7	98.3	117.5	99.7
1956	89.1	114.0	101.6	100.0	114.8	100.7
1957	95.2	108.4	104.5	98.8	102.3	93.2
1958	100.0	100.0	100.0	100.0	100.0	100.0
1959	101.0	104.6	103.2	102.3	106.9	104.7
1960	98.5	111.2	104.0	105.3	113.1	107.1
1961	98.3	111.4	103.2	106.1	113.8	108.4
1962	102.0	113.6	104.5	110.9	117.0	114.2
1963	108.5	113.4	107.0	115.0	116.5	118.1
1964	113.9	111.5	110.6	114.8	119.8	123.3
1965	118.1	118.3	115.3	121.2	127.7	130.8
1966	124.2	124.6	121.1	127.8	135.7	139.1

[a] Index numbers of real product and output are shown in Tables A-62 and A-63.

TABLE A-64

Local Transit: Output, Labor Inputs,
and Labor Productivity Ratios, 1948-66
(1958=100)

Year	Output	Persons Engaged	Output per Person	Man-Hours	Output per Man-Hour
1948	183.2	159.9	114.6	174.0	105.3
1949	168.3	155.2	108.4	165.0	102.0
1950	164.5	146.7	112.1	155.9	105.5
1951	152.8	141.1	108.3	153.0	99.9
1952	157.9	135.5	116.5	147.2	107.3
1953	148.8	131.8	112.9	139.2	106.9
1954	132.1	125.3	105.4	126.8	104.2
1955	130.5	115.9	112.6	116.9	111.6
1956	121.8	108.4	112.4	109.4	111.3
1957	119.4	104.7	114.0	106.0	112.6
1958	100.0	100.0	100.0	100.0	100.0
1959	91.2	96.3	94.7	97.2	93.8
1960	93.3	94.4	98.8	94.6	98.6
1961	90.8	91.6	99.1	91.4	99.3
1962	88.0	88.8	99.1	88.0	100.0
1963	81.8	87.9	93.1	86.1	95.0
1964	77.6	86.0	90.2	84.0	92.4
1965	75.6	87.7	86.2	85.9	88.0
1966	75.5	87.0	86.8	85.6	88.2

Intercity Bus Lines: Output, Labor Inputs,
and Labor Productivity Ratios, 1948-66
(1958=100)

Year	Output	Persons Engaged	Output per Person	Man-Hours	Output per Man-Hour
1948	118.5	138.0	85.9	149.5	79.3
1949	115.7	125.7	92.0	133.5	86.7
1950	109.3	125.4	87.2	133.5	81.9
1951	113.7	118.0	96.4	127.6	89.1
1952	119.0	118.2	100.7	127.9	93.0
1953	117.6	116.9	100.6	122.1	96.3
1954	106.0	115.3	91.9	117.0	90.6
1955	105.5	110.1	95.8	110.8	95.2
1956	104.5	102.8	101.7	102.9	101.6
1957	103.4	102.0	101.4	103.1	100.3
1958	100.0	100.0	100.0	100.0	100.0
1959	98.1	100.0	98.1	100.2	97.9
1960	95.9	96.0	99.9	96.5	99.4
1961	95.0	97.9	97.0	99.0	96.0
1962	102.5	99.5	103.0	101.2	101.3
1963	105.6	100.8	104.8	102.1	103.4
1964	109.4	103.8	105.4	104.9	104.3
1965	114.8	105.4	108.9	109.1	105.2
1966	118.6	108.2	109.6	113.4	104.6

TABLE A-66

Intercity Trucking: Output, Labor Inputs,
and Labor Productivity Ratios, 1948-66
(1958=100)

Year	Output	Persons Engaged	Output per Person	Man-Hours	Output per Man-Hour
1948	44.2	53.5	82.6	58.4	75.7
1949	45.8	54.1	84.7	57.5	79.7
1950	56.8	64.7	87.8	68.8	82.6
1951	68.4	71.3	95.9	77.2	88.6
1952	73.1	79.2	92.3	86.0	85.0
1953	79.9	87.7	91.1	92.7	86.2
1954	80.5	85.6	94.0	86.6	93.0
1955	90.8	93.5	97.1	94.4	96.2
1956	95.6	98.6	97.0	99.5	96.1
1957	98.2	102.0	96.3	103.1	95.2
1958	100.0	100.0	100.0	100.0	100.0
1959	116.9	110.2	106.1	110.3	106.0
1960	119.7	112.3	106.6	112.7	106.2
1961	122.1	112.7	108.3	113.6	107.5
1962	135.5	122.4	110.7	123.8	109.5
1963	144.6	125.0	115.7	127.4	113.5
1964	157.7	128.5	122.7	129.5	121.8
1965	173.5	133.9	129.6	137.7	126.0
1966	190.5	139.0	137.1	145.8	130.7

TABLE A-67

Water Transportation: Output, Inputs, and Productivity Ratios, 1948-66
(1958=100)

Year	Output	Persons Engaged	Output per Person	Man-Hours	Output per Man-Hour	Net Capital Input	Output per Unit of Net Capital Input	Total Factor Input	Total Factor Productivity
1948	107.5	121.1	88.8	124.4	86.4	99.2	108.4	123.0	87.4
1949	99.9	111.7	89.4	115.6	86.4	103.1	96.9	115.7	86.3
1950	103.7	107.0	96.9	111.3	93.2	98.5	105.3	111.2	93.3
1951	120.8	118.3	102.1	130.7	92.4	95.8	126.1	128.1	94.3
1952	111.8	115.0	97.2	128.2	87.2	96.9	115.4	126.1	88.7
1953	107.5	111.3	96.6	120.0	89.6	94.8	113.4	118.5	90.7
1954	104.7	102.3	102.3	109.1	96.0	94.2	111.1	108.3	96.7
1955	115.1	107.0	107.6	117.3	98.1	95.0	121.2	116.0	99.2
1956	120.3	110.3	109.1	119.8	100.4	95.9	125.4	118.4	101.6
1957	120.4	114.1	105.5	123.1	97.8	96.2	125.2	121.6	99.0
1958	100.0	100.0	100.0	100.0	100.0	100.0	100.0	100.0	100.0
1959	102.0	101.9	100.1	99.1	102.9	106.3	96.0	99.5	102.5
1960	105.9	101.9	103.9	98.7	107.3	113.7	93.1	99.6	106.3
1961	101.5	98.6	102.9	97.3	104.3	117.9	86.1	98.5	103.0
1962	106.7	96.7	110.3	95.1	112.2	120.6	88.5	96.5	110.6
1963	106.8	95.3	112.1	97.8	109.2	124.7	85.6	99.3	107.6
1964	111.1	99.1	112.1	104.9	105.9	129.2	86.0	106.3	104.5
1965	108.9	97.7	111.5	106.9	101.9	137.6	79.1	108.6	100.3
1966	111.0	103.3	107.5	113.3	98.0	150.1	74.0	115.4	96.2

Note: Relates to *Productivity Trends*, Table G-IX.

TABLE A-67a

Water Transportation: Gross Capital Input and Gross
Productivity Ratios,[a] 1948-66

(1958=100)

Year	Gross Capital Input	Output per Unit of Gross Capital Input	Gross Factor Input	Gross Factor Productivity
1948	93.2	115.3	121.8	88.3
1949	95.4	104.7	115.6	86.4
1950	93.1	111.4	111.6	92.9
1951	90.0	134.2	125.9	95.9
1952	87.6	127.6	123.4	90.6
1953	85.0	126.5	116.3	92.4
1954	85.2	122.9	106.6	98.2
1955	87.8	131.1	114.2	100.8
1956	91.0	132.2	116.8	103.0
1957	95.2	126.5	120.2	100.2
1958	100.0	100.0	100.0	100.0
1959	103.6	98.5	99.6	102.4
1960	104.3	101.5	99.3	106.6
1961	103.1	98.4	97.9	103.7
1962	104.5	102.1	96.1	111.0
1963	108.7	98.3	98.9	108.0
1964	114.4	97.1	105.9	104.9
1965	121.6	89.6	108.4	100.5
1966	131.2	84.6	115.2	96.4

[a] Index numbers of output are the same as those shown in Table
A-67.

TABLE A-68

Air Transportation: Output, Inputs, and Productivity Ratios, 1948-66

(1958=100)

Year	Output	Persons Engaged	Output per Person	Net Capital Input	Output per Unit of Net Capital Input	Total Factor Input	Total Factor Producti
1948	24.6	54.4	45.2	49.7	49.5	53.9	45.6
1949	27.6	53.3	51.8	50.2	55.0	53.0	52.1
1950	32.8	53.3	61.5	47.6	68.9	52.7	62.2
1951	41.6	58.6	71.0	45.3	91.8	57.1	72.9
1952	48.5	66.9	72.5	45.2	107.3	64.5	75.2
1953	56.0	71.1	78.8	48.4	115.7	68.6	81.6
1954	63.2	72.2	87.5	56.5	111.9	70.5	89.6
1955	75.2	78.1	96.3	62.2	120.9	76.3	98.6
1956	86.9	90.0	96.6	70.6	123.1	87.8	99.0
1957	98.4	100.0	98.4	88.1	111.7	98.7	99.7
1958	100.0	100.0	100.0	100.0	100.0	100.0	100.0
1959	115.4	105.3	109.6	111.8	103.2	106.0	108.9
1960	122.7	115.3	106.4	132.9	92.3	117.3	104.6
1961	129.8	117.2	110.8	150.5	86.2	120.9	107.4
1962	146.7	118.3	124.0	159.0	92.3	122.8	119.5
1963	166.1	121.9	136.3	155.4	106.9	125.6	132.2
1964	192.1	127.8	150.3	157.6	121.9	131.1	146.5
1965	234.0	137.2	170.6	173.3	135.0	141.2	165.7
1966	287.6	152.8	188.2	199.6	144.1	158.0	182.0

Note: Relates to *Productivity Trends,* Table G-X.

Hours used in computing total factor productivity were estimated at 41 hours per week 1948-66. This estimate was based on the *1960 Census of Population.*

TABLE A-68a

Air Transportation: Gross Capital Input and Gross
Productivity Ratios,[a] 1948-66

(1958=100)

Year	Gross Capital Input	Output per Unit of Gross Capital Input	Gross Factor Input	Gross Factor Productivity
1948	41.6	59.1	52.2	47.1
1949	46.6	59.2	53.7	51.4
1950	51.2	64.1	55.8	58.8
1951	55.9	74.4	62.1	67.0
1952	59.0	82.2	67.7	71.6
1953	58.1	96.4	69.9	80.1
1954	59.0	107.1	71.0	89.0
1955	62.7	119.9	76.7	98.0
1956	70.8	122.7	88.2	98.5
1957	86.8	113.4	98.8	99.6
1958	100.0	100.0	100.0	100.0
1959	108.3	106.6	105.6	109.3
1960	119.5	102.7	115.7	106.1
1961	131.5	98.7	118.5	109.5
1962	140.1	104.7	120.3	121.9
1963	142.5	116.6	123.8	134.2
1964	145.9	131.7	129.5	148.3
1965	157.3	148.8	139.1	168.2
1966	179.5	160.2	155.3	185.2

[a] Index numbers of output are the same as those shown in Table
A-68.

TABLE A-69

Pipeline Transportation: Output, Labor Inputs, and
Labor Productivity Ratios, 1948-66

(1958=100)

Year	Output	Persons Engaged	Output per Person	Man-Hours	Output per Man-Hour
1948	52.4	120.0	43.7	118.9	44.1
1949	51.1	116.0	44.1	115.1	44.4
1950	58.8	108.0	54.4	107.5	54.7
1951	70.4	112.0	62.9	111.3	63.3
1952	74.5	116.0	64.2	115.1	64.7
1953	80.1	112.0	71.5	111.3	72.0
1954	84.0	108.0	77.8	107.5	78.1
1955	90.1	104.0	86.6	103.8	86.8
1956	100.6	104.0	96.7	103.8	96.9
1957	102.4	104.0	98.5	103.8	98.7
1958	100.0	100.0	100.0	100.0	100.0
1959	107.3	96.0	111.8	96.2	111.5
1960	107.4	92.0	116.7	90.6	118.5
1961	109.8	88.0	124.8	86.8	126.5
1962	111.0	84.0	132.1	83.0	133.7
1963	116.8	80.0	146.0	79.2	147.5
1964	121.4	76.0	159.7	77.4	156.8
1965	139.0	72.0	193.1	73.6	188.9
1966	150.4	72.0	208.9	71.7	209.8

Note: Relates to *Productivity Trends,* Table G-XI.

TABLE A-70

Communication, Electric, Gas, and Sanitary Services: Real Product, Inputs, and Productivity Ratios, 1948-66

(1958=100)

Year	Real Gross Product	Persons Engaged	Real Product per Person	Man-Hours	Real Product per Man-Hour	Labor Input	Real Product per Unit of Labor Input	Net Capital Input	Real Product per Unit of Net Capital Input	Total Factor Input	Total Factor Productivity
1948	49.5	86.4	57.3	88.6	55.9	88.1	56.2	50.4	98.2	71.6	69.1
1949	53.1	87.3	60.8	88.2	60.2	87.9	60.4	55.3	96.0	73.7	72.0
1950	56.6	86.7	65.3	88.0	64.3	87.8	64.5	59.7	94.8	75.7	74.8
1951	64.3	89.5	71.8	91.5	70.3	91.3	70.4	64.1	100.3	79.6	80.8
1952	68.4	92.0	74.3	92.6	73.9	92.3	74.1	68.5	99.9	82.1	83.3
1953	74.0	95.0	77.9	95.7	77.3	95.4	77.6	73.6	100.5	86.1	85.9
1954	78.6	95.3	82.5	96.2	81.7	96.1	81.8	78.3	100.4	88.5	88.8
1955	84.7	96.8	87.5	98.4	86.1	98.2	86.3	82.7	102.4	91.6	92.5
1956	90.3	100.7	89.7	102.5	88.1	102.1	88.4	87.2	103.6	95.8	94.3
1957	95.9	102.4	93.7	103.2	92.9	102.8	93.3	93.0	103.1	98.6	97.3
1958	100.0	100.0	100.0	100.0	100.0	100.0	100.0	100.0	100.0	100.0	100.0
1959	107.7	98.1	109.8	99.2	108.6	99.3	108.5	104.0	103.6	101.3	106.3
1960	114.3	98.9	115.6	100.5	113.7	100.7	113.5	109.5	104.4	104.4	109.5
1961	119.9	98.0	122.3	99.3	120.7	99.5	120.5	113.6	105.5	105.5	113.6
1962	128.1	97.6	131.2	99.6	128.6	99.8	128.4	117.1	109.4	107.2	119.5
1963	136.2	97.7	139.4	100.2	135.9	100.5	135.5	120.9	112.7	109.2	124.7
1964	145.4	99.5	146.1	102.3	142.1	102.5	141.9	125.7	115.7	112.4	129.4
1965	156.1	102.2	152.7	105.7	147.7	105.9	147.4	131.0	119.2	116.6	133.9
1966	169.4	105.9	160.0	109.9	154.1	110.0	154.0	138.1	122.7	121.9	139.0

TABLE A-70a

Communication, Electric, Gas, and Sanitary Services: Gross Capital Input and
Gross Productivity Ratios,[a] in Terms of Real Product, 1948-66

(1958=100)

Year	Gross Capital Input	Real Product per Unit of Gross Capital Input	Gross Factor Input	Gross Factor Productivity
1948	58.7	84.3	72.9	67.9
1949	62.0	85.6	74.5	71.3
1950	65.2	86.8	76.1	74.4
1951	69.1	93.1	79.7	80.7
1952	73.0	93.7	82.2	83.2
1953	77.6	95.4	86.1	85.9
1954	81.7	96.2	88.6	88.7
1955	85.5	99.1	91.6	92.5
1956	89.3	101.1	95.4	94.7
1957	94.1	101.9	98.3	97.6
1958	100.0	100.0	100.0	100.0
1959	103.4	104.2	101.4	106.2
1960	108.1	105.7	104.6	109.3
1961	111.7	107.3	105.9	113.2
1962	114.8	111.6	107.6	119.1
1963	118.2	115.2	109.7	124.2
1964	122.6	118.6	113.0	128.7
1965	127.4	122.5	117.1	133.3
1966	133.5	126.9	122.2	138.6

[a] Index numbers of real product are the same as those shown in Table A-70.

TABLE A-71

Communication: Real Product, Inputs, and Productivity Ratios, 1948-69

(1958=100)

Year	Real Gross Product	Persons Engaged	Real Product per Person	Man-Hours	Real Product per Man-Hour	Labor Input	Real Product per Unit of Labor Input	Net Capital Input	Real Product per Unit of Net Capital Input	Total Factor Input	Total Factor Productivity
1948	53.1	87.0	61.0	89.0	59.7	88.3	60.1	53.9	98.5	76.5	69.4
1949	55.8	86.9	64.2	87.4	63.8	86.8	64.3	59.2	94.3	77.1	72.4
1950	58.6	85.1	68.9	86.4	67.8	85.9	68.2	62.0	94.5	77.3	75.8
1951	65.6	88.8	73.9	90.6	72.4	90.2	72.7	64.1	102.3	81.0	81.0
1952	69.1	92.2	74.9	92.5	74.7	92.0	75.1	67.7	102.1	83.3	83.0
1953	75.2	95.9	78.4	96.5	77.9	96.0	78.3	72.0	104.4	87.3	86.1
1954	76.8	95.9	80.1	97.1	79.1	96.9	79.3	75.7	101.5	89.2	86.1
1955	84.2	97.8	86.1	100.6	83.7	100.5	83.8	76.9	109.5	92.0	91.5
1956	89.9	103.6	86.8	106.4	84.5	106.1	84.7	85.1	105.6	98.5	91.3
1957	96.6	105.9	91.2	107.3	90.0	107.1	90.2	92.9	104.0	102.0	94.7
1958	100.0	100.0	100.0	100.0	100.0	100.0	100.0	100.0	100.0	100.0	100.0
1959	107.1	97.2	110.2	99.0	108.2	99.1	108.1	105.3	101.7	101.3	105.7
1960	113.4	97.9	115.8	100.6	112.7	100.9	112.4	111.3	101.9	104.7	108.3
1961	119.8	96.6	124.0	98.8	121.3	99.1	120.9	117.7	101.8	105.8	113.2
1962	129.5	96.1	134.8	99.5	130.2	99.9	129.6	124.2	104.3	108.7	119.1
1963	139.4	96.3	144.8	100.1	139.3	100.6	138.6	131.5	106.0	111.8	124.7
1964	149.3	98.8	151.1	103.1	144.8	103.6	144.1	139.9	106.7	116.8	127.8
1965	163.5	102.5	159.5	107.7	151.8	108.3	151.0	150.0	109.0	123.4	132.5
1966	179.8	108.1	166.3	114.1	157.6	114.7	156.8	160.7	111.9	131.3	136.9
1967	194.3	112.3	173.0	115.5	168.2						
1968	208.9	113.5	184.1	117.7	177.5						
1969P	228.5	121.6	187.9	128.2	178.2						

P Preliminary (as of July 1971 *Survey of Current Business*).

TABLE A-71a

Communication: Gross Capital Input and Gross Productivity Ratios,[a]
in Terms of Real Product, 1948-66

(1958=100)

Year	Gross Capital Input	Real Product per Unit of Gross Capital Input	Gross Factor Input	Gross Factor Productivity
1948	57.3	92.7	75.6	70.2
1949	60.9	91.6	76.1	73.3
1950	63.6	92.1	76.5	76.6
1951	66.6	98.5	80.3	81.7
1952	70.8	97.6	83.0	83.3
1953	75.4	99.7	87.2	86.2
1954	79.4	96.7	89.4	85.9
1955	83.3	101.1	93.2	90.3
1956	88.1	102.0	98.4	91.4
1957	94.3	102.4	101.6	95.1
1958	100.0	100.0	100.0	100.0
1959	104.6	102.4	101.4	105.6
1960	109.7	103.4	104.7	108.3
1961	115.6	103.6	106.1	112.9
1962	121.8	106.3	109.3	118.5
1963	128.2	108.7	112.4	124.0
1964	135.5	110.2	117.2	127.4
1965	144.4	113.2	123.7	132.2
1966	153.7	117.0	131.4	136.8

[a] Index numbers of real product are the same as those shown in Table A-71.

TABLE A-72

Telephone and Telegraph Communication: Real Product, Inputs, and Productivity Ratios, 1948-66

(1958=100)

Year	Real Gross Product	Persons Engaged	Real Product per Person	Man-Hours	Real Product per Man-Hour	Labor Input	Real Product per Unit of Labor Input	Net Capital Input	Real Product per Unit of Net Capital Input	Total Factor Input	Total Factor Productivity
1948	54.7	89.8	60.9	92.2	59.3	92.5	59.1	54.5	100.4	78.8	69.4
1949	57.6	89.3	64.5	90.1	63.9	90.3	63.8	59.5	96.8	79.0	72.9
1950	60.2	86.8	69.4	88.3	68.2	88.5	68.0	62.3	96.6	78.7	76.5
1951	66.7	90.3	73.9	92.3	72.3	92.4	72.2	64.4	103.6	82.0	81.3
1952	70.2	93.8	74.8	94.3	74.4	94.4	74.4	68.0	103.2	84.5	83.1
1953	75.9	97.3	78.0	98.0	77.4	98.0	77.4	72.3	105.0	88.2	86.1
1954	77.0	96.6	79.7	97.9	78.7	97.9	78.7	76.0	101.3	89.6	85.9
1955	83.9	98.3	85.4	101.3	82.8	101.3	82.8	79.8	105.1	93.1	90.1
1956	90.1	104.4	86.3	107.3	84.0	107.3	84.0	85.2	105.8	98.9	91.1
1957	96.4	106.5	90.5	108.1	89.2	108.1	89.2	92.9	103.8	102.3	94.2
1958	100.0	100.0	100.0	100.0	100.0	100.0	100.0	100.0	100.0	100.0	100.0
1959	107.9	96.6	111.7	98.6	109.4	98.5	109.5	105.4	102.4	101.1	106.7
1960	114.0	97.0	117.5	100.0	114.0	100.0	114.0	111.3	102.4	104.3	109.3
1961	121.2	95.3	127.2	97.7	124.1	97.8	123.9	117.7	103.0	105.4	115.0
1962	131.2	94.7	138.5	98.3	133.5	98.3	133.5	124.3	105.6	108.2	121.3
1963	141.7	94.6	149.8	98.3	144.2	98.3	144.2	131.6	107.7	111.0	127.7
1964	152.9	96.9	157.8	101.2	151.1	101.0	151.4	139.7	109.4	115.7	132.2
1965	167.9	100.4	167.2	105.5	159.1	105.4	159.3	149.4	112.4	122.1	137.5
1966	185.4	105.9	175.1	111.8	165.8	111.7	166.0	159.8	116.0	130.0	142.6

TABLE A-72a

Telephone and Telegraph Communication: Gross Capital Input and
Gross Productivity Ratios,[a] in Terms of Real Product, 1948-66

(1958=100)

Year	Gross Capital Input	Real Product per Unit of Gross Capital Input	Gross Factor Input	Gross Factor Productivity
1948	57.8	94.6	77.6	70.5
1949	61.4	93.8	77.8	74.0
1950	64.0	94.1	77.8	77.4
1951	66.9	99.7	81.3	82.0
1952	71.1	98.7	84.1	83.5
1953	75.7	100.3	88.1	86.2
1954	79.7	96.6	89.9	85.7
1955	83.4	100.6	93.4	89.8
1956	88.2	102.2	98.9	91.1
1957	94.3	102.2	102.0	94.5
1958	100.0	100.0	100.0	100.0
1959	104.5	103.3	101.2	106.6
1960	109.5	104.1	104.2	109.4
1961	115.4	105.0	105.6	114.8
1962	121.6	107.9	108.6	120.8
1963	128.0	110.7	111.4	127.2
1964	134.9	113.3	116.0	131.8
1965	143.4	117.1	122.2	137.4
1966	152.5	121.6	129.7	142.9

[a] Index numbers of real product are the same as those shown in Table A-72.

TABLE A-73

Electric, Gas, and Sanitary Services: Real Product, Inputs, and Productivity Ratios, 1948-69
(1958=100)

Year	Real Gross Product	Persons Engaged	Real Product per Person	Man-Hours	Real Product per Man-Hour	Net Capital Input	Real Product per Unit of Net Capital Input	Total Factor Input	Total Factor Productivity
1948	46.8	85.7	54.6	88.0	53.2	49.2	95.1	67.7	69.1
1949	51.4	87.9	58.5	89.2	57.6	53.9	95.4	70.9	72.5
1950	55.4	88.9	62.3	90.1	61.5	58.9	94.1	74.1	74.8
1951	63.5	90.6	70.1	92.6	68.6	64.2	98.9	78.2	81.2
1952	68.0	91.7	74.2	92.8	73.3	68.8	98.8	80.9	84.1
1953	72.8	93.8	77.6	94.7	76.9	74.2	98.1	84.8	85.8
1954	80.0	94.6	84.6	95.1	84.1	79.2	101.0	87.4	91.5
1955	84.9	95.4	89.0	95.6	88.8	83.8	101.3	89.9	94.4
1956	90.9	96.8	93.9	97.5	93.2	87.9	103.4	92.8	98.0
1957	96.0	97.6	98.4	97.8	98.2	93.1	103.1	95.5	100.5
1958	100.0	100.0	100.0	100.0	100.0	100.0	100.0	100.0	100.0
1959	108.0	99.4	108.7	99.6	108.4	103.5	104.3	101.5	106.4
1960	115.4	100.2	115.2	100.4	114.9	108.8	106.1	104.5	110.4
1961	120.6	100.0	120.6	100.0	120.6	112.1	107.6	105.9	113.9
1962	127.3	99.5	127.9	99.8	127.6	114.6	111.1	107.0	119.0
1963	134.5	99.7	134.9	100.4	134.0	117.1	114.9	108.5	124.0
1964	142.5	100.5	141.8	101.2	140.8	120.7	118.1	110.7	128.7
1965	150.8	101.9	148.0	103.1	146.3	124.3	121.3	113.4	133.0
1966	161.6	103.0	156.9	104.5	154.6	130.1	124.2	116.9	138.2
1967	166.7	104.6	159.4	105.9	157.4				
1968	179.2	106.3	168.6	107.6	166.5				
1969p	189.4	108.9	173.9	110.7	171.1				

p Preliminary (as of July 1971 *Survey of Current Business*).

TABLE A-73a

Electric, Gas, and Sanitary Services: Gross Capital Input
and Gross Productivity Ratios,[a] in Terms of Real Product, 1948-66

(1958=100)

Year	Gross Capital Input	Real Product per Unit of Gross Capital Input	Gross Factor Input	Gross Factor Productivity
1948	59.3	78.9	70.9	66.0
1949	62.3	82.5	73.2	70.2
1950	65.8	84.2	75.6	73.3
1951	70.0	90.7	79.2	80.2
1952	73.9	92.0	81.6	83.3
1953	78.4	92.9	85.0	85.6
1954	82.5	97.0	87.6	91.3
1955	86.3	98.4	90.0	94.3
1956	89.8	101.2	92.9	97.8
1957	94.0	102.1	95.5	100.5
1958	100.0	100.0	100.0	100.0
1959	103.0	104.9	101.6	106.3
1960	107.6	107.2	104.7	110.2
1961	110.2	109.4	106.1	113.7
1962	112.2	113.5	107.2	118.8
1963	114.5	117.5	108.9	123.5
1964	117.8	121.0	111.1	128.3
1965	121.1	124.5	113.9	132.4
1966	125.8	128.5	117.2	137.9

[a] Index numbers of real product are the same as those shown in Table A-73.

TABLE A-74

Electric and Gas Utilities: Output, Inputs, and Productivity Ratios, 1948-66
(1958=100)

Year	Output	Persons Engaged	Output per Person	Man-Hours	Output per Man-Hour	Net Capital Input	Output per Unit of Net Capital Input	Total Factor Input	Total Factor Productivity
1948	42.8	86.3	49.6	88.7	48.3	49.6	86.3	68.0	62.9
1949	44.9	88.7	50.6	90.0	49.9	54.3	82.7	71.2	63.1
1950	51.2	89.9	57.0	91.3	56.1	59.6	85.9	74.9	68.4
1951	58.0	91.5	63.4	93.5	62.0	64.7	89.6	78.8	73.6
1952	62.6	92.8	67.5	93.8	66.7	69.7	89.8	81.8	76.5
1953	68.0	94.7	71.8	95.7	71.1	74.9	90.8	85.6	79.4
1954	72.9	95.6	76.3	96.1	75.9	80.0	91.1	88.3	82.6
1955	82.1	96.2	85.3	96.5	85.1	84.5	97.2	90.7	90.5
1956	90.3	98.1	92.0	98.9	91.3	89.0	101.5	94.1	96.0
1957	95.8	99.0	96.8	99.3	96.5	94.4	101.5	96.9	98.9
1958	100.0	100.0	100.0	100.0	100.0	100.0	100.0	100.0	100.0
1959	109.7	100.3	109.4	100.6	109.0	104.5	105.0	102.5	107.0
1960	117.0	100.0	117.0	100.2	116.8	108.6	107.7	104.3	112.2
1961	122.9	100.0	122.9	100.0	122.9	112.1	109.6	105.9	116.1
1962	132.0	100.0	132.0	100.2	131.7	115.1	114.7	107.5	122.8
1963	140.4	100.3	140.0	101.0	139.0	117.9	119.1	109.2	128.6
1964	151.2	100.9	149.9	101.6	148.8	121.0	125.0	111.0	136.2
1965	160.9	102.4	157.1	103.7	155.2	124.8	128.9	114.0	141.1
1966	172.4	102.9	167.5	104.4	165.1	129.9	132.7	116.8	147.6

TABLE A-74a

Electric and Gas Utilities: Gross Capital Input and Gross
Productivity Ratios,[a] 1948-66

(1958=100)

Year	Gross Capital Input	Output per Unit of Gross Capital Input	Gross Factor Input	Output per Unit of Gross Factor Input
1948	59.7	71.7	70.6	60.6
1949	62.9	71.4	73.1	61.4
1950	66.6	76.9	75.8	67.5
1951	70.6	82.2	79.0	73.4
1952	74.7	83.8	81.6	76.7
1953	79.1	86.0	85.2	79.8
1954	83.3	87.5	88.5	82.4
1955	87.1	94.3	90.9	90.3
1956	90.9	99.3	94.1	96.0
1957	95.3	100.5	96.9	98.9
1958	100.0	100.0	100.0	100.0
1959	104.0	105.5	102.6	106.9
1960	107.3	109.0	104.4	112.1
1961	110.2	111.5	106.1	115.8
1962	112.7	117.1	107.7	122.6
1963	115.2	121.9	109.5	128.2
1964	118.1	128.0	111.5	135.6
1965	121.6	132.3	114.4	140.6
1966	125.8	137.0	117.2	147.1

[a] Index numbers of output are the same as those shown in Table A-74.

TABLE A-75

Trade: Real Product, Inputs, and Productivity Ratios, 1948-69

(1958=100)

Year	Real Gross Product	Persons Engaged	Real Product per Person	Man-Hours	Real Product per Man-Hour	Labor Input	Real Product per Unit of Labor Input	Net Capital Input	Real Product per Unit of Net Capital Input	Total Factor Input	Total Factor Productivity
1948	72.2	90.0	80.2	91.3	79.1	91.2	79.2	66.2	109.1	87.2	82.8
1949	73.5	89.3	82.3	91.0	80.8	90.6	81.1	72.3	101.7	88.0	83.5
1950	80.3	90.3	88.9	92.5	86.8	91.8	87.5	76.5	105.0	89.8	89.4
1951	81.7	94.1	86.8	96.3	84.8	95.9	85.2	83.6	97.7	94.6	86.4
1952	83.8	95.5	87.7	97.2	86.2	96.8	86.6	85.2	98.4	95.6	87.7
1953	86.4	96.1	89.9	96.8	89.3	96.6	89.4	85.7	100.8	95.6	90.4
1954	87.2	95.0	91.8	95.8	91.0	95.5	91.3	86.3	101.0	94.6	92.2
1955	95.4	97.4	97.9	98.5	96.9	98.3	97.0	88.9	107.3	97.4	97.9
1956	98.3	100.2	98.1	100.6	97.7	100.5	97.8	94.7	103.8	100.0	98.3
1957	100.0	101.0	99.0	100.7	99.3	100.7	99.3	98.6	101.4	100.5	99.5
1958	100.0	100.0	100.0	100.0	100.0	100.0	100.0	100.0	100.0	100.0	100.0
1959	107.6	101.5	106.0	102.1	105.4	102.3	105.2	102.0	105.5	102.3	105.2
1960	109.5	103.5	105.8	104.0	105.3	104.2	105.1	105.1	104.2	104.3	105.0
1961	111.2	102.6	108.4	102.7	108.3	103.1	107.9	108.6	102.4	103.6	107.3
1962	118.4	103.2	114.7	103.3	114.6	103.8	114.1	111.6	106.1	104.5	113.3
1963	123.6	103.8	119.1	104.0	118.8	104.7	118.1	117.1	105.6	105.9	116.7
1964	131.6	106.9	123.1	106.3	123.8	107.0	123.0	123.0	107.0	108.5	121.3
1965	139.6	110.7	126.1	109.3	127.7	110.1	126.8	129.7	107.6	111.9	124.8
1966	148.8	114.6	129.8	111.6	133.3	112.6	132.1	137.5	108.2	114.9	129.5
1967	151.6	117.1	129.5	112.1	135.2	113.1	134.0				
1968	160.8	120.8	133.1	113.9	141.2	114.9	139.9				
1969P	166.6	125.4	132.8	116.9	142.5	117.9	141.3				

P Preliminary (as of July 1971 *Survey of Current Business*).

TABLE A-75a

Trade: Gross Capital Input and Gross Productivity Ratios,[a]
in Terms of Real Product, 1948-66

(1958=100)

Year	Gross Capital Input	Real Product per Unit of Gross Capital Input	Gross Factor Input	Gross Factor Productivity
1948	63.0	114.6	83.5	86.5
1949	69.1	106.4	85.0	86.5
1950	73.0	110.0	87.0	92.3
1951	80.4	101.6	92.2	88.6
1952	83.3	100.6	93.7	89.4
1953	85.1	101.5	94.2	91.7
1954	86.2	101.2	93.6	93.2
1955	88.1	108.3	96.2	99.2
1956	93.3	105.4	99.0	99.3
1957	97.5	102.6	100.0	100.0
1958	100.0	100.0	100.0	100.0
1959	102.0	105.5	102.2	105.3
1960	103.9	105.4	104.1	105.2
1961	106.2	104.7	103.7	107.2
1962	108.0	109.6	104.7	113.1
1963	112.3	110.1	106.3	116.3
1964	116.6	112.9	109.0	120.7
1965	121.6	114.8	112.5	124.1
1966	127.3	116.9	115.6	128.7

[a] Index numbers of real product are the same as those shown in Table A-75.

TABLE A-76

Wholesale Trade: Real Product, Inputs, and Productivity Ratios, 1948-66
(1958=100)

Year	Real Gross Product	Persons Engaged	Real Product per Person	Man-Hours	Real Product per Man-Hour	Net Capital Input	Real Product per Unit of Net Capital Input	Total Factor Input	Total Factor Productivity
1948	69.1	89.5	77.2	89.6	77.1	58.8	117.5	83.2	83.1
1949	68.6	87.1	78.8	86.9	78.9	63.9	107.4	82.4	83.3
1950	74.7	87.6	85.3	87.3	85.6	70.0	106.7	84.2	88.7
1951	78.3	92.1	85.0	92.3	84.8	77.6	100.9	89.9	87.1
1952	80.0	93.9	85.2	94.0	85.1	80.2	99.8	91.8	87.1
1953	81.7	94.8	86.2	94.9	86.1	81.5	100.2	92.8	88.0
1954	82.4	94.0	87.7	94.0	87.7	82.3	100.1	92.2	89.4
1955	92.3	95.7	96.4	96.4	95.7	87.6	105.4	95.1	97.1
1956	96.9	99.5	97.4	99.9	97.0	94.9	102.1	99.1	97.8
1957	98.6	100.3	98.3	100.4	98.2	98.9	99.7	100.2	98.4
1958	100.0	100.0	100.0	100.0	100.0	100.0	100.0	100.0	100.0
1959	109.6	101.7	107.8	103.0	106.4	103.5	105.9	103.1	106.3
1960	112.7	104.2	108.2	105.3	107.0	108.1	104.3	105.7	106.6
1961	117.8	104.6	112.6	106.0	111.1	110.5	106.6	106.7	110.4
1962	125.2	105.9	118.2	107.7	116.2	113.9	109.9	108.6	115.3
1963	131.8	107.2	122.9	109.2	120.7	120.6	109.3	110.9	118.8
1964	141.2	109.6	128.8	111.6	126.5	128.6	109.8	114.2	123.6
1965	148.5	113.1	131.3	115.8	128.2	135.7	109.4	118.8	125.0
1966	159.6	117.2	136.2	119.7	133.3	145.2	109.9	123.6	129.1

TABLE A-76a

Wholesale Trade: Gross Capital Input and Gross Productivity Ratios,[a]
in Terms of Real Product, 1948-66

(1958=100)

Year	Gross Capital Input	Real Product per Unit of Gross Capital Input	Gross Factor Input	Gross Factor Productivity
1948	54.7	126.3	82.6	83.7
1949	59.9	114.5	81.8	83.9
1950	66.4	112.5	83.8	89.1
1951	74.4	105.2	89.5	87.5
1952	78.5	101.9	91.9	87.1
1953	81.1	100.7	93.2	87.7
1954	81.9	100.6	92.5	89.1
1955	86.9	106.2	95.2	97.0
1956	93.7	103.4	99.1	97.8
1957	97.8	100.8	100.0	98.6
1958	100.0	100.0	100.0	100.0
1959	104.0	105.4	103.1	106.3
1960	108.8	103.6	105.7	106.6
1961	111.4	105.7	106.7	110.4
1962	114.3	109.5	108.5	115.4
1963	120.4	109.5	110.6	119.2
1964	127.4	110.8	113.6	124.3
1965	133.9	110.9	118.1	125.7
1966	142.4	112.1	122.5	130.3

[a] Index numbers of real product are the same as those shown in Table A-76.

TABLE A-77

Retail Trade: Real Product, Inputs, and Productivity Ratios, 1948-66
(1958=100)

Year	Real Gross Product	Persons Engaged	Real Product per Person	Man-Hours	Real Product per Man-Hour	Net Capital Input	Real Product per Unit of Net Capital Input	Total Factor Input	Total Factor Productivity
1948	74.2	90.2	82.3	91.9	80.7	69.8	106.3	88.9	83.5
1949	76.7	90.0	85.2	92.3	83.1	76.4	100.4	90.5	84.8
1950	84.0	91.2	92.1	94.0	89.4	79.7	105.4	92.5	90.8
1951	83.9	94.8	88.5	97.6	86.0	86.6	96.9	96.8	86.7
1952	86.2	96.0	89.8	98.2	87.8	87.6	98.4	97.4	88.5
1953	89.4	96.5	92.6	97.4	91.8	87.8	101.8	96.8	92.4
1954	90.2	95.3	94.6	96.3	93.7	88.3	102.2	95.8	94.2
1955	97.3	98.0	99.3	99.2	98.1	89.6	108.6	98.6	98.7
1956	99.2	100.5	98.7	100.8	98.4	94.6	104.9	100.4	98.8
1957	100.9	101.2	99.7	100.8	100.1	98.4	102.5	100.7	100.2
1958	100.0	100.0	100.0	100.0	100.0	100.0	100.0	100.0	100.0
1959	106.3	101.5	104.7	101.9	104.3	101.3	104.9	101.9	104.3
1960	107.5	103.3	104.1	103.6	103.8	103.7	103.7	103.6	103.8
1961	107.0	102.0	104.9	101.6	105.3	107.7	99.4	102.0	104.9
1962	114.0	102.4	111.3	101.9	111.9	110.5	103.2	102.4	111.3
1963	118.3	102.7	115.2	102.4	115.5	115.4	102.5	103.2	114.6
1964	125.4	106.0	118.3	104.7	119.8	120.3	104.2	105.6	118.8
1965	133.8	109.9	121.7	107.3	124.7	126.8	105.5	108.5	123.3
1966	141.8	113.8	124.6	109.1	130.0	133.7	106.1	110.6	128.2

TABLE A-77a

Retail Trade: Gross Capital Input and Gross Productivity Ratios,[a]
in Terms of Real Product, 1948-66

(1958=100)

Year	Gross Capital Input	Real Product per Unit of Gross Capital Input	Gross Factor Input	Gross Factor Productivity
1948	66.6	111.4	87.6	84.7
1949	73.0	105.1	89.7	85.5
1950	75.8	110.8	91.8	91.5
1951	82.9	101.2	96.4	87.0
1952	85.4	100.9	97.5	88.4
1953	86.8	103.0	97.3	91.9
1954	88.0	102.5	95.0	94.9
1955	88.7	109.7	97.6	99.7
1956	93.2	106.4	99.6	99.6
1957	97.4	103.6	100.3	100.6
1958	100.0	100.0	100.0	100.0
1959	101.1	105.1	101.8	104.4
1960	101.8	105.6	103.3	104.1
1961	104.0	102.9	102.0	104.9
1962	105.3	108.3	102.4	111.3
1963	108.7	108.8	103.4	114.4
1964	112.0	112.0	105.8	118.5
1965	116.2	115.1	107.1	124.9
1966	120.8	117.4	110.9	127.9

[a] Index numbers of real product are the same as those shown in Table A-77.

TABLE A-78

Finance, Insurance, and Real Estate: Real Product, Labor Inputs,
and Labor Productivity Ratios, 1948-69

(1958=100)

ear	Real Gross Product	Persons Engaged	Real Product per Person	Man-Hours	Real Product per Man-Hour	Labor Input	Real Product per Unit of Labor Input
48	60.9	72.9	83.5	74.7	81.5	73.2	83.2
49	63.1	73.3	86.1	75.0	84.1	73.8	85.5
50	68.7	76.0	90.4	77.6	88.5	76.4	89.9
51	72.0	79.7	90.3	81.3	88.6	80.2	89.8
52	75.0	83.1	90.3	85.0	88.2	84.1	89.2
53	78.6	86.8	90.6	88.8	88.5	87.9	89.4
54	84.0	90.7	92.6	92.1	91.2	91.3	92.0
55	88.9	93.8	94.8	94.9	93.7	94.1	94.5
56	92.5	96.7	95.7	96.4	96.0	95.8	96.6
57	96.5	98.4	98.1	97.4	99.1	97.2	99.3
58	100.0	100.0	100.0	100.0	100.0	100.0	100.0
59	104.0	101.8	102.2	102.3	101.7	102.4	101.6
60	108.7	104.3	104.2	104.3	104.2	104.6	103.9
61	113.7	106.7	106.6	106.2	107.1	106.6	106.7
62	120.9	108.6	111.3	109.2	110.7	109.6	110.3
63	126.4	111.2	113.7	112.6	112.3	113.0	111.9
64	133.0	114.0	116.7	114.6	116.1	115.1	115.6
65	141.0	116.7	120.8	117.9	119.6	118.4	119.1
66	148.2	119.6	123.9	121.4	122.1	122.1	121.4
67	154.8	122.9	126.0	124.1	124.7	124.8	124.0
68	160.8	128.0	125.6	128.3	125.3	129.0	124.6
69P	163.0	134.6	121.1	135.2	120.6	136.0	119.8

P Preliminary (as of July 1971 *Survey of Current Business*).

TABLE A-79

Services, Excluding Households and Nonprofit Institutions and Including
Government Enterprises: Real Product, Labor Inputs, and
Labor Productivity Ratios, 1948-69

(1958=100)

Year	Real Gross Product	Persons Engaged	Real Product per Person	Man-Hours	Real Product per Man-Hour	Labor Input	Real Product per Unit Labor Input
1948	78.2	83.6	93.5	85.9	91.0	85.8	91.1
1949	77.9	83.3	93.5	85.3	91.3	85.5	91.1
1950	79.6	83.6	95.2	85.5	93.1	85.6	93.0
1951	82.7	86.5	95.6	86.3	95.8	86.5	95.6
1952	84.7	89.3	94.8	91.2	92.9	91.4	92.7
1953	86.4	90.3	95.7	92.4	93.5	92.6	93.3
1954	85.8	90.5	94.8	92.2	93.1	92.3	93.0
1955	91.2	92.6	98.5	94.3	96.7	94.4	96.6
1956	94.1	96.3	97.7	97.3	96.7	97.3	96.7
1957	97.7	99.4	98.3	99.8	97.9	99.7	98.0
1958	100.0	100.0	100.0	100.0	100.0	100.0	100.0
1959	105.7	102.8	102.8	102.9	102.7	102.9	102.7
1960	109.1	106.6	102.3	108.0	101.0	107.8	101.2
1961	113.6	109.4	103.8	109.9	103.4	109.8	103.5
1962	118.7	112.2	105.8	112.4	105.6	112.3	105.7
1963	122.7	115.5	106.2	115.8	106.0	115.7	106.1
1964	130.6	119.7	109.1	118.9	109.8	118.7	110.0
1965	138.5	124.4	111.3	124.3	111.4	124.0	111.7
1966	144.2	129.3	111.5	128.7	112.0	128.5	112.2
1967	149.4	134.3	111.2	135.1	110.6		
1968	156.9	139.8	112.2	140.1	112.0		
1969p	163.0	146.0	111.6	146.8	111.0		

p Preliminary (as of July 1971 *Survey of Current Business*).

TABLE A-80

Households and Nonprofit Institutions: Real Product, Inputs, and Productivity Ratios, 1948-69

(1958=100)

Year	Real Gross Product	Persons Engaged	Real Product per Person	Man-Hours	Real Product per Man-Hour	Labor Input	Real Product per Unit of Labor Input	Net Capital Input	Real Product per Unit of Net Capital Input	Total Factor Input	Total Factor Productivity
1948	69.4	75.3	92.2	82.4	84.2	81.5	85.2	71.3	97.3	80.3	86.4
1949	72.2	77.3	93.4	82.9	87.1	82.3	87.7	73.0	98.9	81.2	88.9
1950	76.4	82.4	92.7	88.0	86.8	87.3	87.5	75.3	101.5	85.9	88.9
1951	77.8	83.3	93.4	88.3	88.1	87.8	88.6	77.8	100.0	86.6	89.8
1952	78.5	81.4	96.4	86.9	90.3	86.9	90.3	80.1	98.0	86.1	91.2
1953	80.6	82.8	97.3	89.2	90.4	89.4	90.2	82.3	97.9	88.5	91.1
1954	81.2	81.9	99.1	85.2	95.3	85.2	95.3	85.1	95.4	85.2	95.3
1955	88.2	89.5	98.5	92.1	95.8	92.2	95.7	88.2	100.0	91.7	96.2
1956	93.1	93.8	99.3	95.2	97.8	95.3	97.7	91.6	101.6	94.8	98.2
1957	96.5	96.0	100.5	96.7	99.8	96.8	99.7	95.5	101.0	96.6	99.9
1958	100.0	100.0	100.0	100.0	100.0	100.0	100.0	100.0	100.0	100.0	100.0
1959	103.5	102.6	100.9	102.5	101.0	102.4	101.1	104.5	99.0	102.7	100.8
1960	107.6	106.1	101.4	108.0	99.6	107.9	99.7	109.6	98.2	108.1	99.5
1961	110.4	108.4	101.8	109.3	101.0	109.2	101.1	114.6	96.3	109.9	100.5
1962	115.3	112.0	102.9	111.7	103.2	111.5	103.4	119.9	96.2	112.6	102.4
1963	118.8	114.8	103.5	115.0	103.3	114.8	103.5	125.3	94.8	116.1	102.3
1964	123.6	117.6	105.1	116.7	105.9	116.5	106.1	131.5	94.0	118.4	104.4
1965	126.4	120.5	104.9	121.2	104.3	120.9	104.5	139.3	90.7	123.2	102.6
1966	133.3	125.2	106.5	126.2	105.6	125.8	106.0	147.8	90.2	128.6	103.7
1967	140.6	130.7	107.6	138.1	101.8						
1968	146.1	131.6	111.0	138.9	105.2						
1969P	150.6	129.4	116.4	137.8	109.3						

P Preliminary (as of July 1971 *Survey of Current Business*).

INDEX